BREAKING THE RULES

A VOLATILE SEASON WITH SPORT'S MOST COLORFUL TEAM: CHARLES BARKLEY'S PHOENIX SUNS

Mike Tulumello

Photography by Dave Cruz

LONGSTREET PRESS, INC.
Atlanta, GA

For Mom and Dad

Published by
LONGSTREET PRESS, INC.
A subsidiary of Cox Newspapers,
A division of Cox Enterprises, Inc.
2140 Newmarket Parkway
Suite 118
Marietta, Georgia 30067

Printed in the United States of America

1st printing 1996

Library of Congress Catalog Card Number: 95-77265

ISBN: 1-56352-269-1

Printed in the United States of America

Jacket design by Ken Graham
Book design and typesetting by Laura McDonald
Cover photo by Dave Cruz

Contents

1

The End?

CHARLES BARKLEY HAD DECIDED his future. Now he would tell his Phoenix Suns' teammates and—moments later—the world.

At age 32, he was retiring from the sport for which he'd become a worldwide marquee spokesman, known practically from outer Mongolia to inner Afghanistan as much for a "be his own man" persona as for his actual performances.

He carried himself in the swaggering manner associated in American sports with legends such as John L. Sullivan, Babe Ruth and Muhammad Ali. He played an important role in the growth of the National Basketball Association as a form of entertainment that had penetrated the world's consciousness far more than any other American sport.

In Arizona, the Suns had been the dominant focus of public interest for years. And Barkley was more than the focal point. He was the main attraction, the player whose presence ensured the team would be on national TV nearly as often as a syndicated sitcom rerun, whose influence was greater not only than his teammates but even his coaches. He was the player everyone, even opponents, came to see.

And now, it seemed, he would be gone.

His team sat in stunned silence in its locker room, having just experienced the most horrific loss imaginable to end its 1995 play-off run in the second round.

The Suns had blown a 3-1 lead in a best-of-7 series with the Houston Rockets. In so doing, they dropped, by one point (115-114), decisive Game 7 in Phoenix, breaking a streak of 20 series in the NBA (covering 13 years) in which the home team had come through when it counted most.

Barkley played a leading role in the fiasco. The Rockets, probably the toughest team to kill in sports, at long last were ready to be put out of their misery in Game 5 at Phoenix. Houston superstar Clyde Drexler showed up ill and played without effect; the Suns led throughout. But Barkley wasn't up to the task. He could have wrapped it up in the final two minutes, but he missed three of four free throws.

Instead, the Rockets tied it in the closing seconds, then won in overtime, 103-97. Later in the series, Barkley came up lame. His left knee was killing him. In decisive Game 7, his performance was both heroic (23 rebounds on one leg) and appalling (his seven turnovers was a key factor in the Suns blowing yet another lead).

Now, he could endure surgery and a second straight summer of time-consuming rehabilitation in an effort to halt, or at least slow, the decline of his once-awesome skills. Or he could slip quietly into the soft life of a celebrity, somebody who's famous for accomplishments fast fading from public memory.

Considering how Barkley felt about working out ("I admit it," he'd once said. "I hate it."), his decision seemed elementary.

He spoke with affection and conviction.

"More than likely, I've played my last game," he said to his teammates. He told them how much he'd appreciated playing with them, then he was off to meet reporters.

There, the qualification disappeared. He sounded more and more Sherman-esque in his finality.

"It's time. It's not debatable or discussible. There will be no soul-searching."

He said he'd been discussing the matter with his family for some time.

"I gave it one more shot. I don't see my skills getting any better. I'm tired of working, tired of traveling, tired of getting beat up every night. These young, up-and-coming guys are really tough. I don't know if I want to be playing against really good 25-, 26- and 27-year-olds every night. I don't need to do that anymore."

He also had immediate plans. "Tonight, I'm drinking."

All of this had a familiar ring.

In hauntingly similar circumstances the previous year, Barkley put his teammates on hold after the Suns lost Game 7 to the Rockets, 104-94, in the second round of the play-offs (despite winning the first two games on the road.)

Barkley promised the team a decision about his career plans before the

NBA's draft of college players. That way, the Suns could better prepare for the future.

He'd come through, but just barely. On the day before the draft, the superstar met Jerry Colangelo in the Suns president's posh office on the fourth floor of America West Arena in downtown Phoenix. Then Barkley took an elevator from the executive offices down to the arena floor. He stepped onto the team's practice court, one of the amenities to be found in its state-of-the-art playing facility, where he held a hastily arranged news conference. The affair started promptly, and no time was wasted once it began.

Already, the Suns were considering trades to move up from their No. 23 draft position. Decisions needed to be made.

Barkley stepped forward. But something didn't ring true.

His trademark swagger had taken a vacation. He seemed ill at ease. His hands were shaking.

Most uncharacteristic of all, he didn't speak with self-assurance. He conceded that if he retired, his legacy would at least partially be one of laziness, that he so abhorred working out as a requirement of earning his millions, that he simply had to quit. That said, he announced he would return, though he continued to moan about the rigors ahead.

But this time around, the words seemed to come from the heart. He spoke with emotion but not *so much* emotion that his message seemed impulsive.

Most observers believed, even more than they had the year before, that an American original had passed from the scene.

THE INTEREST IN BARKLEY'S decision was considerable. Even the most seasoned observers of big-time sport never had seen anyone quite like him.

He had become an international mega-star, one of those rare athletes whose persona crossed into the general culture.

The reason for this had much to do with a simple decision Barkley made early in his NBA career: He would not be just another highly paid servant on the pro-sports plantation. There would be no meek bows, with hands pointing to the supporting cast. There would be no bland observations like, "The other team was just too good for us today."

Barkley would speak his mind on whatever subject was raised, from racism and other inequalities in American society, to the perceived lack of desire to win in a team's management or even fellow players.

"Ask me a question, and I will give you an answer," Barkley said.

And so he did, often enough that a book and video of his observations was released.

Barkley could, and often did, swear like a sailor and—in the same breath—beseech the help of God. He managed to seem genuine going in either direction.

The persona didn't end with mere candor. Barkley could charm the socks off an Eskimo on a January night. Not only was he quick with a joke, he had a professional comic's sense of timing. Though he was a fine extemporaneous humorist, Barkley also took his clown's talent seriously enough to carry his best stock material to the appropriate high-profile occasions.

At first, playing on mostly non-contending teams in Philadelphia, he was more of a cult figure, appreciated by basketball fans for his extraordinary abilities, by blacks for his talk-back-to-the-man posture.

But many in the public at large were put off by his comments and even more so by his sometimes-erratic behavior. He once accidentally spat on a young girl sitting courtside (for which he apologized profusely). He once was arrested for carrying a gun in his car (for which he apologized not at all).

His career would reach new heights thanks to events that started to unfold at the opposite end of the country.

As the Phoenix Suns walked off the floor in May 1992 in Portland after another of their narrow play-off eliminations, Lionel Hollins, an assistant coach at the time, muttered, "We need to get us a Charles Barkley."

At the time, the Suns—as they had been throughout much of their history—were a beautiful team to watch, one that threw precision passes and looked to score at the earliest opportunity. Yet they were soft defensively and lacked a dominating presence down low where play-off games often are won.

In a matter of weeks, Jerry Colangelo, the Suns wily president, put together the deal that later would be hailed as the best of the 1990s by *The Sporting News*: The sharp-shooting guard Jeff Hornacek plus defensive-oriented big men Tim Perry and Andrew Lang were shipped to Philadelphia for Barkley.

The Suns had kept an eye on Barkley, off-and-on, for years. Cotton Fitzsimmons, the outgoing coach, had become friendly with Barkley through their work for Nike, the athletic shoe company. Fitzsimmons figured he knew him well enough to make the judgment that the mercurial superstar was not crazy, that—most of the time—he knew just how far to push his "I-don't-follow-rules" creed.

The Suns closed the deal moments after a Milwaukee jury found Barkley innocent in a battery case arising out of a scuffle with a weight lifter outside a bar. On that day, June 17, 1992, Barkley walked out of court and into his new life.

He heard of the impending trade from the 76ers to the Suns while waiting for a plane to take him from Milwaukee back to Philadelphia. "Phoenix is not a bad place," he said. "I could play golf every day." He even ordered a round of drinks for everyone on board the plane.

Paul Westphal, who had just taken over as Suns head coach, said, "Only one person gets to be Elvis. And only one person gets to be Charles Barkley. That's why we got him."

The Suns' vanilla image suddenly had become a swirl. It was as if the Mormon Tabernacle Choir had just added James Brown to the ensemble. Barkley enjoyed his dream season in his first year with Phoenix. He led the Suns to an NBA-best record of 62-20, the must successful regular season in franchise history. He won the league's most coveted award, that of Most Valuable Player. In the play-offs, he stumbled early but recovered to lead the Suns on a thrilling run to the NBA Finals.

The Suns lost to the Chicago Bulls, 4 games to 2, thanks largely to a last-second three-pointer by John Paxson in the final game. Even with the harrowing defeat, the city of Phoenix staged a Suns' parade that started from the arena. The festivities took place on a hot Saturday morning, when the downtown streets normally are so deserted that a flag football game could be staged and players would rarely have to stop for traffic.

If there ever were a doubt about the mania surrounding the team, it ended here. About 200,000 people turned out, no doubt the largest crowd ever to cheer a team that had just *lost* a pro basketball championship.

The crowd surging toward the car carrying Barkley became so raucous that police officers, fearing for his life, hustled him back to the safety of the arena.

Off the court, Barkley was everywhere. He sold shoes and hamburgers on TV. He battled Godzilla and won. His face could be seen on the sides of buses in Phoenix. His bald head filled TV screens in America and Europe, where he sold hamburgers and athletic shoes, and in Japan, where he sold noodles.

One commercial for his shoe company stood out.

In it, Barkley faces the camera squarely and says, "I am not a role model. I am not paid to be a role model. I am paid to wreak havoc on a basketball court. Parents should be role models. Just because I dunk a basketball doesn't mean I should raise your kids."

The commercial was one of the most popular—and widely reviewed—in history. The simple observation that celebrity shouldn't be confused with virtue struck many as profound.

E.J. Dionne, the *Washington Post*'s noted political writer, was moved to write: "Take Barkley's example of parenthood. Parents need to be patient and to take the long view. They need to take quiet pleasure in the ordinary achievements of day-to-day life.

"They often have to be self-denying. They need to believe in commitment. Celebrities, whether basketball players or actors or real estate tycoons, are rewarded—handsomely—for the opposite of most of these virtues. They need to be impatient; you have to win today.

"They're often punished for taking the long view: Make every endorsement ad you can now, because in two years, the fans might see you as a bum."

In Phoenix, the generally conservative public had gotten to know enough about Barkley to make a judgment.

Basketball fans saw a man who pined for the return to good health of his aching back, but who was reluctant to work on strengthening that back and to stay in better overall condition.

The general public saw a man who demanded his privacy not be invaded, all the while insisting on a nightlife that included frequent trips to noisy, low-common-denominator bars.

Then again, this childlike quality was part of Barkley's appeal. Most people found a measure of charm in most every situation. So when people took a look at the whole package, they gave him the benefit of the doubt. Barkley, according to the prevailing sentiment, was a man of refreshing, youthful innocence and honesty, not mere immaturity.

Of course, this wouldn't necessarily have been the case for a player of lesser skill. But Barkley's accomplishments by now had lifted him to an exalted platform.

Though he never quite carried a team in the dominating manner of a Michael Jordan, Kareem Abdul-Jabbar, Magic Johnson or Larry Bird, Barkley attained the status of a certain Hall of Famer.

He stands about 6-foot-5. That's below the NBA's average height. But he succeeded through a combination of quickness, strength and jumping ability that may have been unprecedented.

"I try to play physical and aggressive," Barkley once said. "I hit a guy and hit a guy, and sooner or later, if he doesn't hit you back, then you have an advantage."

He developed his game outside his home in Leeds, Ala., a small town east of Birmingham. Barkley would leap back and forth over a three-and-a-half-foot-high backyard fence while his mother and grandmother worried that he'd rip his testicles.

He played guard in high school, when he stood only 5-9 as a junior. That allowed him to develop his ball-handling skills.

Even though he battled a weight problem in college at Auburn, he led the Southeast Conference in rebounding three straight years.

In the NBA, he was the only player his size to consistently rank among the top rebounders. His accomplishments in this respect were staggering. He viewed each rebound as a personal challenge. It was the one aspect of his game where effort matched his ability. The result was that he consistently outbattled players several inches taller to get the ball. This was his greatest value, for the opponents couldn't win if they didn't get their hands on the ball.

At the same time, he was the only player considered a big forward who also had the ball-handling skill to dribble the length of the floor and finish with a dunk.

He was nearly impossible to guard one-on-one, particularly at his favorite spot on the baseline where his patented spin move usually led to a score or a foul.

Great players like Barkley almost always are compared to those who preceded them.

Among centers, Hakeem Olajuwon now is talked about in nearly the same category as Abdul-Jabbar and, before that, Wilt Chamberlain and Bill Russell and, before that, George Mikan.

Before Michael Jordan elevated the NBA with his acrobatic style, Julius Erving exhibited the same sort of flair (though not quite Jordan's overall dominance). And before Dr. J, there was Connie Hawkins. And before him, Elgin Baylor.

But when it came to Barkley, there was . . . nobody.

Paul Silas, an incoming Suns' assistant coach who'd been around the game nearly as long as anybody, would come to marvel at his ability.

"I've never seen anybody with the type of talent that he has: the strength, the agility, the grace. It's just awesome."

Despite all this, there were less appealing factors forever in the mix, aspects of Barkley's character that weren't nearly as well known publicly as his on-court heroics.

He set his own hours for arrival at games and practices. As for practices, he participated only on the margins. When the spirit moved him, he might use the time to exercise. Otherwise, he sat or laid down on the sidelines or in the trainer's room.

These habits tended to undercut Barkley's stated claim to the role of the team's unquestioned leader. Yet there was an undeniable humor in all of this. When Westphal, the head coach, once asked him, "Chuck, do you want in on this scrimmage?," Barkley replied in mock agony, "No, I can't! MY LITTLE FINGER'S GOT TENDINITIS!"

Such separate sets of rules exist in all sports (in all of life, actually) for the most accomplished. But there was a certain audacity about it that bothered some of the veteran players (the younger players tended to be awed by Barkley).

When a rookie embarrassed him by outplaying him at an early-season practice, Barkley told him, "Do whatever you want now. Just remember, I've got the club." Translation: Barkley had the most clout and wanted the young player to know it.

As long as the Suns were winning, any tension created by Barkley's idiosyncrasies was manageable. Yet the more the coaches, players and staff members got to know him, the more they realized Barkley's success was much more the result of natural talent than the will to be the best. He often kept late hours. He viewed exercise and overall physical maintenance as a low-priority chore. That his teams never had won a championship (save the Dream Team's Gold medal at the '92 Olympics) seemed to many to be the predictable consequence of these preferences.

Phil Jackson, the coach of the Chicago Bulls, once told the *Chicago Tribune* that he deemed Barkley "a great, great player. Maybe unstoppable. But he's got no discipline, none. You can't win with a player like that."

That seemed to be the case early in the Suns' '93 play-off run. Barkley all but disappeared and the Suns lost the first two games at home to the No. 8-seeded Lakers. They would have been swept had not James Worthy missed an open jumper at the end of Game 3 at the Forum, and they would have lost in Game 5 back in Phoenix had not Byron Scott missed a three-pointer at the buzzer. In the end, the Suns—thanks to the unlikely combination of rookies Oliver Miller, Richard Dumas plus playmaker Kevin Johnson—were able to nip the Lakers, 3-2, winning decisive Game 5 in overtime, 112-104.

Yet, Barkley went on to play the greatest games of his career in leading the Suns to narrow play-off series wins over the Spurs and SuperSonics. He continued to play well, despite an elbow injury, during the Finals against the Bulls. He'd come as close as possible, for one season at least, to proving Phil Jackson wrong.

Then, after the near-ultimate season, Barkley's physical condition deteriorated. His back ached and his legs sometimes didn't have the old spring that allowed him to dominate in the lane.

Other players his age faced similar problems. Their solution was to work harder than ever, fighting off retirement day as long as humanly possible.

Barkley, however reluctantly, pledged to join their ranks immediately after the Suns finished their dramatic run to the Finals.

"I have got to do a better job on my body. I haven't done a good job on that. But I'm getting old."

For the first time, he hit the weights and tried to lose 10 pounds.

"I want to get physically stronger and more defined. If I get on a weight-lifting program, my body will not be as sore or beat up. It'll hold up better. If I take care of myself and eat better, I'll have a different body."

This kind of talk is common among players, most of whom fail to follow through until, perhaps, the last few weeks before training camp. In Barkley's case, the weightiest object he lifted during this off-season turned out to be a three-iron. "I started lifting but I was so tired, mentally and physically, that I felt like it was better for me just to rest," he said.

Then, when he started to work himself into shape before training camp, he felt the same pain in his legs that had bothered him late in the title run, the same problem that led him to take several painkilling drug injections during the play-offs. Doctors examined him and found a slightly degenerative disc in his back, a problem related to a pinched nerve, which in turn seemed to be causing periodic numbness in his legs.

All of this, together with Barkley's poor conditioning, combined for one of the biggest scares of his career. While running a wind sprint at the close of one of the Suns' first practices at their training camp in the fall of '93, he collapsed. His legs felt like they'd fallen through the gymnasium floor. Instead of heading out for dinner and drinks, Barkley lay flat on his back for a half-hour as nervous teammates and team officials watched, then he hobbled from the gym.

He recovered and continued to play, though at less than his MVP form. At this point, Barkley said he was "99 percent sure" the '93-94 season would be his final go-round.

He hiked that figure by 1 percent in Chicago during November of '93.

Only this time, his reasoning had less to do with his back than with an alternative view of celebrity he had developed.

Twice earlier in the month, he was part of highly publicized altercations at one of his favored watering holes in Scottsdale, not far from his home in ultra-upscale Paradise Valley. No charges were filed in either case.

Despite this, much of the press and public automatically sided with Barkley. "Must be tough to go out and have to deal with over-wrought fans all the time . . ."

So, Barkley announced in Chicago, "I know when I'll retire: when this season is over. Championship or not, it's time to move on."

Then Barkley, a married man, explained why he insists on such a public nightlife.

"The prime years of your life are between 20 and 35. You don't want to spend them shacked up in some hotel room or sitting at home.

"But a guy goes after me and gets his 15 minutes of fame and makes my life miserable for two weeks. And then people read it in the newspaper and believe everything they read."

All the while, the Suns' medical staff pleaded with Barkley to work out. The team went so far as to import an $80,000 traction table from Canada in hopes Barkley would use it to strengthen his back. Mark West, the Suns' durable, stoic center, used the machine on his sore back. But not Barkley.

An exasperated Richard Emerson, the Suns' respected team doctor, said, "We keep trying to get him into it. Other players are finding it useful. Studies have shown it provides relief from pain."

Then, he said sarcastically, "It takes a time investment from a player. Charles is a busy guy, to put it very nicely."

Instead of working out, Barkley complained about his discomfort and thought out loud about immediate retirement.

After one game in December '93 against the Clippers, he said, "I felt like I was walking on glass. I don't have the strength and energy in my legs. I sat around in a whirlpool for hours getting ready for the game. I thought, 'This is crazy! This isn't how it's supposed to be. This takes the fun out of the game.' Right now, I'm just miserable."

He called former Celtics great Larry Bird, who had retired because of his own back problems. Bird suggested Barkley retire, if not immediately, then at the end of the season.

At times, he took painkilling injections.

Eventually, in helping to persuade Barkley to return for the '94-95 season, Emerson lined up several back specialists who put together a rehabilitation program. Barkley would work out two hours a days for six weeks. The rehab program involved stretching, isometric and resistance exercises, aerobics and weight lifting.

A couple of the doctors Barkley visited recommended he not play golf, his favorite leisure sport, while he followed his program. "I didn't like those doctors," Barkley said.

In the end, he was told he could tee it up during his rehab as long as he didn't make a full body turn during his swing.

After much stopping and starting (at one point, Colangelo dispatched Fitzsimmons to catch up with Barkley on his annual summer golf tour of North America to cajole him into taking the rehab program seriously), Barkley finally got with it. He exercised diligently enough to return to nearly his MVP form during much of the '94-95 season.

During Barkley's self-debates over retirement, one insider never quite believed the superstar would walk away from the game.

Colangelo, with his eye ever on the bottom line, thought a premature departure would be foolish. Indeed, the money Barkley never would see if he quit was staggering.

And as much as some fans and even sports media types prefer to pretend that such a matter is beyond the concerns of an athletic god, Barkley admitted the opposite.

Asked once what he liked most about being Charles Barkley, he didn't miss a beat: "The money," he said. He had been able to make life easier for his family, "And there's no price you can put on that."

His salary topped $4 million annually (which actually made him underpaid, by NBA standards, considering his marquee appeal). But then, there was all that endorsement money to consider. Barkley's annual income here has been estimated at $5 million and more. That would decline drastically if he retired.

"Do you realize how quickly people forget?" Colangelo once argued, in hopes Barkley would stay. "Not many people are going so good that they can give that all up.

"Retirement is permanent," Colangelo said. "Why not capitalize the next few years, then retire and live happily ever after?"

Barkley was moved to joke that if he retired, he'd become an owl, that people soon would say, "Charles Who?"

Then again, politics was said to be an option.

Barkley had opined that he'd like to run for governor in his home state of Alabama in the near future.

The idea was repeated in the press often enough that even experienced political figures started to talk up Barkley's political potential.

This was so even though Barkley was a loudly professed non-voter (he'd admitted *never* having voted), whose quote, "My one vote isn't going to mean much," was reprinted in *Newsweek* magazine.

In the one-in-a-million chance that a Barkley campaign actually started to gather steam, it surely would be derailed by the first opponent to shout, "Charles Barkley has spit on the graves of the millions of Americans who have died for this country's freedoms! . . ."

In fumbling for an explanation, Barkley suggested that politics didn't agree with him, that too many people are looking out for their own interests and not for the common good.

"It's Republicans against Democrats," Barkley said. "But we're all people. You're voting for who'll do the best for you, and I don't like that system. You should vote to help everybody."

For example, "If I just wanted a tax break, I'd vote Republican." He said he might consider voting for people who support Democratic-style, soak-the-rich taxes, "But I don't think they'll use the money to really help the lower class."

Of course, all this didn't prompt him to run out and join Common Cause.

Once, he appeared on the Maury Povich TV talk show. And when he started to give a similar rationale, the embarrassed host cut him off, shouting that his guest was not going to get away with telling people not to vote.

In the '94 off-year elections, Barkley continued this pattern, saying, "I don't think it's fair for me to vote in Arizona because I won't be here that long." Then too, "I don't have time to keep up with all the issues."

So, why not vote in Alabama, the state where Barkley sometimes suggests he'll run for office in the future?

"I don't vote in Alabama because I don't keep up with everything there," he said.

Moments after laying out this reasoning, he was asked by a broadcaster about the elections, and with a TV camera rolling, Barkley dutifully played the role of good citizen.

"There are some interesting races," he said. "I'm playing close attention. I hope everybody exercises their right to vote."

Of course, there were even more obvious problems with the idea of Barkley for Governor.

While married to a white woman, Barkley talked of running in the Republican primary in a state where the GOP is at least partially a white-flight party.

He had the image of a conservative, in part because of this anecdote in his autobiography, *Outrageous*:

"In 1988, my mother and I were discussing the upcoming election when I told her that I was going to vote for George Bush, the Republican, rather than Democrat Michael Dukakis.

"She was stunned. As a longtime Democrat, like most blacks, she thought I would naturally pull the lever for Dukakis.

"But Charles," she said. "Bush only will work for rich people."

"But Mom," I responded. "I am rich."

What wasn't generally known was that the punch line was just that: a joke that worked well for the book. (In fact, though Barkley sometimes complained about high taxes in country-club fashion, he generally pulled for life's underdogs.)

In fact, in 1992, he said he might have voted for Bill Clinton. If he ever voted.

And then there was his shoot-from-the-lip candor, precisely the opposite of the prerequisite for success in politics.

Opponents could choose from a host of Barkley-isms, including the time after a bad game in Philadelphia when he said he felt like "beating his wife." (After seeing this in print, he immediately recognized it was one poor joke, indeed.)

Or how would this succinct view of American society, as revealed to *Playboy* magazine, go over with Southern conservatives marching to the polls?

"I feel white people are treated better than blacks. I think the rich are treated better than the poor. And I think men are treated better than women."

(For the sake of balance, Barkley also said in the same interview that blacks sometimes are too quick to use racism as a rationale for their problems.)

But Barkley's pronouncements generally are repackaged by broadcasters and written and published by sportswriters and sports editors, many of whom have political instincts somewhere below that of the average *New York Times* White House reporter.

So, while Barkley continued to have fun with the subject of his burgeoning political "career," stories on his prospects were written in a funeral-parlor serious vein. And the story grew.

Then, while Barkley debated retirement in the summer of '94, news surfaced of a raucous, season-ending party orchestrated the previous month, in part by Barkley. It was a gala affair, complete with porno videos and women recruited from nearby bars, and drew police attention.

According to a police report, as the party started to kick into gear, Barkley made an announcement: "I just want everybody to know one thing before this party starts. Anything that goes on in this house doesn't leave this house."

Barkley then pounded his fist into his hand for emphasis and said, "If you can't handle that, leave now." (Barkley later said he spent the party listening to music and playing video games.)

The party attracted official attention when a woman called police later in the morning. The woman expressed concern that a friend had been sexually assaulted by the Suns' Oliver Miller, who—along with Barkley— had helped organize the affair.

The party was another of a series of embarrassments for Miller. He admitted having sex with the woman but denied the assault allegations.

The woman agreed to allow the officers to take her to a nearby hospital for an exam. But she decided not to cooperate in prosecution. According to the police report, "All she wanted to do was to go home, be with her kids, pray to God she did not wind up with AIDS, and put everything behind her."

The story didn't become public until a few weeks after the party, during the NBA Finals won by the Houston Rockets and at about the same time Dan Quayle spoke approvingly of Barkley at a charity golf tournament. Among the reasons Quayle gave for his comments was that Barkley believed strongly in family values.

No, politics would not be an option any time in the foreseeable future.

Then too, Colangelo was right: Retirement was permanent. And, despite the carping about his physical ailments, Barkley appeared to enjoy himself as much as anybody in sports.

He claimed to "hate" the press, while playing reporters like a Steinway, pandering to their need for verbal gems and his own desire to make himself heard. Reporters consistently voted him the best interview in the NBA.

A typical routine would include Barkley emerging from his post-game shower, towel wrapped around his waist, then just an instant before the usual horde of reporters realized he was approaching, he'd shout, "WAKE UP WHITE PEOPLE!"

He'd act like the host of a party, making sure everyone felt at home. Sure, he'd throw insults; the softball-team attire of sportswriters was a favorite target. He knew the regular beat writers could handle it. For those he thought couldn't, he later made sure they understood he was joking.

Generally, he answered questions for 10 to 15 minutes after every game and practice. On the road, where reporters only got to see him once or twice a year, he also held court at length before games, as well.

"Charles, how are you feeling?" a reporter once asked him before a game in Chicago.

Replied Barkley, "I'm a black multimillionaire. Why wouldn't I feel good?"

Then Barkley began waving his hands, like a politician responding to a cheering crowd. He shouted, "I'm rich! I'm rich!"

Taking this all in was Dan Schayes, a Suns newcomer, who was stretching on the locker-room floor. "This is like a live floor show every night," Schayes said.

In the PR-conscious NBA, players are all but forced to answer questions. So, Barkley once said, just before explaining in intricate detail to reporters the differences in the various shoes made for him, "I really don't like doing this, but as long as you HAVE to, you might as well have fun."

And so he did, becoming the master at dealing with the media. So popular was he among beat reporters that upon his selection as the league's Most Valuable Player, one writer asked him, "Charles, when you retire, will you have a 1-900-number we can call to get quotes from you?"

FOUR DAYS AFTER BARKLEY issued his 1995 retirement declaration, the Suns met in their locker room in Phoenix, divided the play-off shares, and broke for the summer. As they did, Barkley took his position at center stage. And what had been "not debatable or discussable " suddenly was back on the table.

The latest of his incantations: His mind was willing, maybe even eager, to keep playing. He just wasn't sure about the rest of him.

"Of course I want to play," he said.

"I've just got to ask myself, 'Can my body take it?' It's a hard answer to a simple question."

Indeed, now he was an old 32.

To continue playing, he would have to undergo arthroscopic surgery on his left knee the next day to remove loose cartilage from his Game 6 injury. (Because of the injury, Barkley almost certainly could not have played against the San Antonio Spurs even if Phoenix had beaten Houston in Game 7). Then he would spend several weeks working on both his knee and his back.

"I'm not into this 'working out in the summer' stuff," he said. "I never worked out in the summer until last year, and now I've got to go through the same crap again. My summer is supposed to be vacation. Play 36 holes of golf a day and relax."

The Suns wanted an early commitment from Barkley so they could make plans for the next season. But he wasn't going to be hurried. "I'm going to take my time. I'm in no rush."

It seemed clear enough that he would be back, though. For the second straight year, he'd fooled even most seasoned observers on his plans.

One by one, his teammates filed out of the arena.

That's when Kevin Johnson, the team's longtime leader at point guard, learned that Barkley likely would return.

He was asked if it was a positive development for the team.

To outsiders, the question probably would have seemed preposterous. After all, Barkley still was one of the top players in the NBA. But Johnson was becoming increasingly disillusioned with the team's direction.

Three years earlier, Johnson had dutifully turned the Suns' leadership over to Barkley. During their near-championship season, this was no problem. Yet during the ensuing two play-off seasons, the team hadn't fared any better with Barkley at the helm than in the old days when Johnson was the leader. During both stretch runs, Johnson valiantly carried the team on his back, playing the best basketball of his life, while Barkley didn't come through. Johnson's career was winding down, too, though the annual talk about Barkley's possible retirement overshadowed Johnson's future.

Barkley deemed Johnson too serious. Johnson deemed Barkley not nearly serious enough. Considering their respective performances, opinion was starting to swing Johnson's way.

With the question posed, Johnson demurred. He'd played the role of good soldier in the past. No reason to do an abrupt about-face now. He shrugged his shoulders and said nothing.

2

Of expectations, preparation and God's gift to women

THE BUS LEAVING THE ARENA for Flagstaff, the Northern Arizona city where the Suns stage their annual training camp, would be much lighter this year. The vehicle wouldn't be hauling, along with players, coaches and equipment, the heaviest baggage of all: NBA title expectations for the 1995-96 season.

This was a notable change. For the previous three years, the Suns had been the pro game's winningest team. Before the 1994-95 season, about half of the basketball writers surveyed by one publication picked the Suns to win it all, far more than favored any other team.

Now, the strong sense was that they would be swimming upstream to equal their recent feats. The team's management had seen what happened to powerhouses in Detroit and Boston, where teams got old all at once and hit bottom with surprising suddenness. To prevent this, the Suns added five rookies, hoping they could reload and keep winning simultaneously. Perhaps they might win a more-than-respectable 50 games in the NBA's grueling 82-game schedule, enough to give them a decent seeding in the play-offs. And then, if no clear favorite emerged, perhaps they would have as good a shot as anybody.

In a sense, the change was good for them. There was much less pressure bearing down now on a team that didn't seem particularly well suited to handling it. The past two years, they'd distinguished themselves by battling through injuries to finish with fine regular season records, only to suffer spectacular come-from-ahead play-off losses to the Houston Rockets.

Both times, the Rockets won in the seventh and deciding games of second-round series. And both times, they went on to win the NBA title. Both times, the series against Phoenix was the Rockets' most harrowing. But Houston had two world championships to show for their struggles. The Suns had nothing.

Even though their losses to the Rockets had been by a razor-thin margins, the Suns' serious weaknesses had been exposed, particularly in the previous season's collapse. Their once deadly three-point game had gone south, in part because of the sudden and mysterious decline of Dan Majerle, their wildly popular off-guard. In addition, Barkley had played erratically, then ended up dragging around a sore knee late in the series.

Then, too, the Suns were dead last among the 16 play-off teams in forcing turnovers. And they blocked shots about as frequently as Barkley shouted "No comment!" to TV crews. This was caused in large part because of their perennial problems in finding someone who could battle the big-time centers on even terms. If last year's team had a notable statistic, it was that—combining the regular season and play-offs—they were 8-11 against the teams with the most dominant centers (the Rockets, Magic, Spurs and Knicks). Against everyone else, their record was 57-16.

Additionally, in an attempt to inject the franchise with younger players, management had declined to re-sign two key players, Danny Ainge and Dan Schayes.

In Ainge, the Suns had enjoyed the services of one of the greatest clutch perimeter shooters in history. He'd been a key figure on two world championship teams in Boston. He was an emotional player, not above taking occasional cheap shots, and he had a well-deserved reputation as a whiner. His image was so deeply engrained in the public's consciousness from a pileup early in his career that many people later recalled Ainge as the guilty party in the incident from which he received bite marks from the 7-footer Wayne "Tree" Rollins (some called it the "Tree Bites Man" story).

In fact, Ainge might have been the NBA's chief villain, a role he both cherished and encouraged. Once, when he sensed his black-hat role was fading into that of a benevolent elder statesman, he encouraged Los Angeles writers to explain to Laker fans that he considered them front-runners. This, he reasoned, would ensure the fans would continue to boo him.

He was the classic example of a player who opponents couldn't stand but teammates loved. That the Celtics' decline began almost immediately after they traded him didn't seem a coincidence. Ainge was perhaps even more valuable in the Suns' locker room, where he got along well with Johnson and Barkley. He possessed both a mature sense of leadership and Barkley's knack for comic relief. On the eve of a big play-off game, he would take a stethoscope and place it on the chests of various players, pretending to listen for a heartbeat. As he performed the routine on him, Barkley roared, "You don't have to worry about me, baby!" Then, he would approach a hapless and disappointing rookie, listen intently, then—as if he'd just diagnosed a terminal illness—shake his head gravely.

The Suns had hoped to sign him as an assistant coach, then bring him back as a replacement player on an as-needed basis. But Ainge wanted a regular playing role. When he couldn't reach an agreement, he decided to take an offer for a TV analyst's role.

In Schayes, the Suns at least had had a center crafty enough to battle the superstar big men (albeit for only 15 or 20 minutes a game before he used his foul allotment). He also had the sense of perspective that allowed him to laugh at his role. When he won the starting job for a stretch the previous season, he'd said, "Now is the time for my 15 minutes of fame: eight in the first half, seven in the second." More tangibly, Schayes could shoot the ball from the top of the lane. And in so doing, he would draw the opposing center out to cover him, thus giving Barkley more room to maneuver down low. Then, too, Ainge and Schayes had the sort of veteran leadership and knowledge associated with champions. Now, they were gone, exacerbating the team's major weaknesses on the floor and removing welcome personalities from the locker room.

Because of all these matters, both tangible and otherwise, "I don't see anybody picking us to win 70 games this season," Westphal acknowledged. "There seems to be less unrealistic pressure. That stuff can smother you."

He knew the Suns had to improve at center. Joe Kleine, a respected backup but a backup nonetheless, was the only returning natural center. The Suns had tried to play Wayman Tisdale, a wide-bodied, 6-foot-9 forward, in the middle. But Tisdale, even though he had played 10 years in the NBA, somehow was only learning to play defense. Worse, he was a reluctant warrior at center. "I'd rather play more at forward, if that helps you," he said. Westphal conceded, "We keep finding all these 6-5 guys. But we need a center."

Barkley's doubts ran even deeper. He knew well the game's nuances, even if he sometimes damned the consequences of them in his own game (which focused almost exclusively on rebounding and scoring to the detriment of defense). The likelihood of erratic outside shooting combined with porous interior defense wasn't the conventional formula for contending for a title. Only Barkley and Johnson were explosive enough to create their own shots (one of the prime definitions of a superstar). If either went down with an injury at any time, the Suns would be in trouble, Barkley judged.

Through all the acerbic barbs he'd thrown out over the years on topics such as the imperfect judgment of certain referees, the lack of effort by some young players, the eagerness of many sports franchises to make money over actually trying to win, Barkley had had little negative to say about the Suns' management. Besides, how much criticism could be offered? The Suns had been touted by independent observers as a model franchise, perhaps the best in the NBA or even in all of big-time sport. When a newcomer to the field looked for advice, he sometimes was steered by others to Colangelo's office, the one so close to Phoenix's financial and government complexes that the team president joked he could pull out a small telescope and spy on the city's other movers and shakers.

Colangelo had ripped up the team before, and with astounding results. He'd done so in 1988, and the Suns shot from 28 wins to 55 and fell one play-off round short of the NBA Finals. When the team started to run out of steam in '92, he made the deal for Barkley himself. This time, the Suns made the Finals, and—in one of the most dramatic series ever (the all-important TV ratings broke records) nearly beat Michael Jordan and the Chicago Bulls. But this year's changes seemed cosmetic. Five rookies? Seldom did first-year players have an impact, except to run up stats on losing teams. Rookies seldom even cracked the regular playing rotations on perennial winners like the Suns.

Colangelo wasn't in the habit of solicting opinions on personnel matters from players, no matter their smarts or stature. In his view, they simply were too close to matters to make the properly detached judgments. So, as the players gathered to have their pictures taken on the team's annual media day, Barkley spoke out.

"Every team is doing stuff but us," he said. "It's very frustrating. Even teams that have won championships have added something." Most notably, the Rockets had traded for Clyde Drexler the previous season, a move that was a key in the successful defense of their title. Now, they were adding Mark Bryant, a solid backup big man. "Even when you're on top, you have to keep trying to get better," Barkley said. "We need to make sure other teams aren't passing us by."

To describe the Suns as "longshots" is "legitimate," Barkley said. "We have not gotten better."

If they had any hope of winning the title, "We need to play better defense and stay healthy," Barkley said. Most importantly, they needed an interior defender and shot blocker to make up for their defensive liabilities.

The Suns still had enough talent to be successful in the regular season. "But you have to compare yourself to teams you'll have to compete against in the play-offs," Barkley pointed out. Among the players who had been available in the off-season was Dennis Rodman, the eccentric rebounding specialist who changed his hair color as frequently as Barkley shaved his head. The Bulls landed him for what seemed a modest price. The Suns should have gone after him too, Barkley said.

"I don't care what color hair he has. He can wear a wig if he gets 20 rebounds. Dennis Rodman would have been terrific with this team."

THE CITY OF FLAGSTAFF is a living postcard, surrounded by forests, lakes and the highest mountains in Arizona. Within a short drive are the Navajo and Hopi Indian reservations and some of America's best known scenic wonders, including the Painted Desert, the Petrified Forest, the remnants of old volcanic eruptions and meteor crashes, and, of course, the Grand Canyon. It's also the home of Northern Arizona University where the Suns stage their annual, weeklong training camp.

For millions, Flagstaff has served as a resting place on old Route 66 and, now, Interstate 40. Perhaps half the living population of North America has passed through at one point, but nobody else with quite the impact of Barkley, who is, if nothing else, a master at making any place a little livelier.

During his first Flagstaff camp, Barkley sightings abounded everywhere. There he was meeting a waitress, asking to borrow her car. "If I wreck it, I'll buy you a new one." She handed over the keys. There he is at a pool hall. An Indian gentleman rubs his head for good luck. A media member encourages Barkley's congeniality with women fans, some of whom hand Barkley the number of their dorm rooms. Just as Barkley and the journalist prepare to hop into the borrowed car with one young woman for adventures unknown, a friend of the woman shows up, a college kid who could pass for a 20-year-old Beaver Cleaver. The woman decides they should take Beaver home. Barkley and the media member return to the hotel. And the car is returned without a scratch.

As far as basketball was concerned, Barkley preferred to take it easy at camp. There was the memory of his collapsing in the fall of '93; he had problems with his back and legs for much of the next season, in which he played erratically. So, at the next year's camp, Westphal allowed Barkley to take it easy, exercising off to the side while the Suns scrimmaged, a routine that included back rubs from a spinal expert who also happened to be a stunningly attractive young woman. "This is a great idea," Barkley said. "Paul is getting to be a better and better coach."

Now, he was coming off minor knee surgery. He didn't figure to do much scrimmaging with his teammates. Now was the time to start working himself back into playing shape (true to his career form, he hadn't done much over the summer). With so many new players, Westphal would effectively divide the operation into two camps. He would try to teach the younger players the nuances of the NBA game while allowing the veterans to ease their way back into their regular routines. All in all, the camp seemed sure to be as smooth and serene as a walk in the Northern Arizona woods.

It was, at least until the players started unpacking their bags. Rumors out of Cleveland reached Flagstaff that the Suns and Cavaliers were talking about a deal that would send Dan Majerle to Ohio. In return, the Suns would get John "Hot Rod" Williams, a 6-11 forward who could fill in reasonably well as a center. Williams could block shots, thus filling the Suns' sorest need, yet was still able to play at the Suns' preferred up-tempo pace.

Majerle had become hardened to trade rumors. He'd been hearing them for nearly 18 months. In fact, he'd become hardened to just about everything. Few athletes had ever experienced such wild swings of adulation and vilification. And the pendulum never seemed to stop swinging.

He rose from obscurity at Central Michigan; his selection by the Suns in the 1988 draft was roundly booed by about 2,500 fans gathered in Phoenix to watch the proceedings. Here, they judged, was another white hope, the kind the Suns seemed to favor but who often didn't work out.

How did you even pronounce the name of this bust-to-be? It was MAR-lee, said Cotton Fitzsimmons, the coach and player personnel director at the time. Anybody who had just booed would regret it, he promised.

Indeed, Majerle, changed local opinion almost immediately by making the 1988 Olympic team. That team was the worst in American Olympic history, but the experience was a boon to Majerle, the least-known player who proved his game was at least as good as most of his famous teammates. On the floor, the 6-foot-6 guard/forward developed into an all-star. His authoritative charges to the hoop defined the rise of the Suns in the late '80s. He became the team's fair-haired star. Kevin Johnson had long been the favorite of kids, but the passion of the average fan seemed to burn brightest for Majerle. This was so for a while, at least, even after the arrival of Barkley, the international superstar.

At Majerle's peak, it would have been easier to find someone bobsledding down Apache Boulevard than to get someone to admit booing the decision to draft him.

Majerle had the rugged good looks and sculpted body to go with his hard-charging game. And he was a man of action rather than words. A Gary Cooper in shorts. All of it combined for the Thunder Dan persona. Male fans saw in him a regular guy, the type who might be found eating at Denny's.

Women saw much more. The tales of Majerle's appeal by now had grown legendary.

Whether at home or on the road at some fancy hotel, just about every NBA player is accustomed to receiving phone numbers and photos from women (and sometimes from men). In Majerle's case, the affection was off the scale.

From his side, Majerle had the ability to mingle; he could party hard while wearing his fame easily. He had to chuckle over the media story line about the rigors of celebrity that came out after the sudden retirement of Michael Jordan in 1993. It went something like: "Fame. A cruel fate that amounts to a living hell for those so burdened."

"Adulation? Oh the pain!"

"Flattery from the opposite sex? A ghastly plight to which nobody should be subjected."

Yet the theme died with Majerle, who seemed to handle being mobbed wherever he went. "It's not something that will always be the situation for me. I feel I'm extremely lucky. I'm going to enjoy it while I can. Why not? Most people would love to have that. I do, too. You just can't let the fame run your life. If you want to go out and do things, then go out and handle stuff as it comes. Be as nice as you can to people, and most of the time, they'll be nice to you."

So Majerle autographed not only basketball programs and trading cards, but bras, breasts, thighs, even a pregnant woman's belly. Then there was the schoolteacher who drove 100 miles across Northern Arizona to meet him at training camp in Flagstaff. She learned where the Suns liked to hang out after hours, spotted Majerle, and talked with him, saying she now would be able to tell her class she'd met the great Dan Majerle. Once, a woman saw Majerle about to enter a movie theater. She ditched her date, then called a few friends, and together they breathlessly watched Majerle watch a movie. On the darker side, there was the time a strange woman somehow walked into his bedroom at 3 a.m. Majerle was so frightened he almost hit her.

Much like Barkley, Majerle enjoying toasting the town at night. On occasion, that brought him into contact with fans fortified with alcoholic bravery. Once, during a stopover in the college-dominated suburb of Tempe, Majerle had a pitcher of beer poured over his head and got into a fracas. The police blamed Majerle's antagonists. But for the most part, Majerle led the life of a male fantasy, tooling around town in his black Mercedes with license plates reading "NINE." After a game, he'd enter his downtown bar-and-grill, which had become THE place to be seen during the basketball season. As soon as he settled into the booth reserved for him, the mob scene began. "Dan, can I have an autograph?"

"Dan, can you sign this?"

"You're the greatest, Dan."

Women of all shapes, sizes and hair colors would converge. Some just wanted their pictures taken with him. Others wanted more. The ones that didn't approach would linger on the periphery, hoping that Majerle would notice. "I feel like such an idiot," said one. "Dan Majerle's known for liking the ladies. But I wanted to meet him. He's got such a nice body. He's Dan Majerle."

These tales were backed by the enormous volume of mail he received. The story of his marriage to his pregnant girlfriend on Christmas Eve in 1994 was played in the local papers on a par with the fall of the Berlin Wall.

On the floor, he never was a pure scorer. But he scored nonetheless, thanks to his drives, his knack for grabbing clutch offensive rebounds, and his ability to hit three-pointers. He might have been the only NBA player whose 25-footer was more reliable than his 18-footer. But his hard charges directly to the basket best captured his game. His typical stat line: 16 points, six rebounds, five assists.

On defense, he was strong enough to guard forwards, quick enough to take on off-guards. He generally guarded the opponent's top offensive threat.

He attained all-star status in 1992 and '93. Yet even with what was now international fame, fans sensed he hadn't changed much.

A remarkable game late in the '92-93 season captured this relationship. Majerle had just hit a 35-footer to beat the Lakers at the final buzzer. Majerle leaped over the press table and into the crowd. With Colangelo and Fitzsimmons, now spectators, applauding in the background, Majerle—with the boyish joy of a kid who'd just hit a home run to win a Little League game—began slapping hands with everyone from little old ladies to well-dressed businessmen. Westphal admired Majerle's game so much he frequently played him the entire 48 minutes. (This tactic probably earned the Suns coach more criticism than any other issue.)

At times, Majerle led the NBA in minutes played, a point that was brought to Westphal's attention when Majerle's game started to decline. At other times, Westphal would start Majerle on the bench. That way, he couldn't use him the entire game, no matter how much he was tempted. Said Westphal, "It's sort of like a gambler who gives his money to his wife and says, 'Don't give it to me, no matter how much I beg for it.'"

Then Majerle's game started to show signs of wear. Inevitably, his exotic level of popularity started to slip at about the same pace. He'd lost a step, which hurt his defense and his trademark drives to the hoop. With the arrival of Barkley, he played more at off-guard and shot more from the perimeter. During the '93-94 season, he even set what was then an NBA record for making three-pointers with 192 and nearly set the mark for attempts with 503.

But in the play-offs in '94 and again in '95, those shots were off the mark, sometimes wildly, and the perception of him began to slide. Worshipful fans now wondered whether he was slipping, whether the nightlife had gotten to him or whether he'd just had an off-season.

Majerle heard rumors about his personal life that he believed coincided with his purchase of the bar-and-grill. Fans would see him drinking Coke and believe he was tasting a heavy dose of rum as well. He heard that he was drinking too much, that he had been forced to stop drinking. Majerle, a pinup of male virility, even heard rumors he was gay. He grew more cautious with fans, who he used to believe liked him for his low-key, oh-shucks demeanor. Now, he realized that what counted most was his shooting percentage. "I've grown up a lot," he said wistfully.

Yet after the '93-94 season, trading him was unthinkable to management.

Colangelo was emotionally committed to him. From his seat in the mid-arena press level, Colangelo would pound his fists in appreciation of one of Majerle's clutch plays. In fact, Majerle was such a highly regarded part of the Suns that Colangelo once hired an actor to play the role of an Arab potentate eager to invest in Majerle's bar-and-grill. The actor joined Colangelo and Majerle for lunch. Majerle had all but agreed to add "Mediterranean" to the name of his place before the actor let down his guard.

So, in that off-season, Colangelo traded Cedric Ceballos, the Suns' rising small forward, instead of Majerle.

Back on the floor, Majerle revived his reputation in the summer of '94 during his stint for the United States team at the World Championships in Toronto. Then, during the regular season, his shots started dropping. His overall game came together nearly as well as ever. He was named to the All-Star team again, with the game this time being played on the Suns' home floor. And then . . . nothing. The shots started clanking off the rim; opponents were tougher to guard. And this wasn't the sort of to-be-expected slump that happens to everyone. It continued into the play-offs, where he again couldn't find the range against the Rockets and he had trouble trying to chase Clyde Drexler around the floor (a player he used to fare well against).

For this, many fans dared to criticize him and suggested that he should be traded.

Now, on the night of the team's very first practice in Flagstaff, reporters approached him and told him about the emerging rumors. "Cleveland?" he shrugged. "What can I say?"

Then, he started thinking. This time, the trade rumors made sense. In the off-season, Westphal had told him he couldn't guarantee that a trade wouldn't be made. "I don't think Paul thought I had it any more. I figure he was pushing for it."

Actually, talks had been going on for a few days before Barkley made his "We need a shot-blocker" proclamation. Members of each team's front office had high regard for the other. In addition, there was a family connection: Cavs executive Gary Fitzsimmons was the son of Cotton Fitzsimmons, the Suns' ex-coach turned broadcaster and executive. Sometimes, the various front-office members of the teams would check with each other on detailed matters.

In this case, Bryan Colangelo, the Suns' general manager and son of the team president, was finishing the deals for the Suns' rookies. He called the Cavs' Wayne Embry to check on how they were working contracts for their own recently drafted players.

Embry then asked Colangelo's opinion of one of the Cavaliers veteran big men. "What do you think of Hot Rod Williams?" A surprised Colangelo replied, "Our people like him."

The Suns coaches greeted the idea enthusiastically. "There wasn't much resistance at all," Jerry Colangelo said.

After the morning practice on the second day of camp, Majerle was directed to a classroom on the floor above the gym used by the Suns. He was greeted by Jerry Colangelo and Cotton Fitzsimmons. As soon as Majerle sat down, he knew. A teary-eyed Colangelo told Majerle that a trade was about to go through. Majerle then thanked Colangelo for his years in Phoenix and said, "I have no complaints."

Majerle went out and played a round of golf with Kleine, his closest buddy on the team. He met Westphal, who praised him and then said, "Things happen." Majerle replied: "You're right. It's a business."

Then he met reporters. He started out laughing and boasting about how he'd just shot a 78. But by the time he finished, his eyes were glistening. He praised everyone and everything about the Suns, then he embraced Johnson, his teammate of seven years. Majerle thought the deal probably would be good for his basketball career. "This is my first trade," he said. "I've grown up in one place. It's kind of tough."

Though he never protested too loudly, he felt he'd been made a scapegoat for the Suns' play-off failings. He reminded everyone who would listen that he'd been made more of a complimentary player with the arrival of Barkley, that his role had never been to carry the team. He also pointed out, "I've always been the guy who plays when Kevin and Charles were hurt. Never missed a game. Never missed a practice. Never was late. Never caused a problem. "I hope people realize that."

And then he was gone.

Barkley, the same man who had called for a deal, was upset when the news came. He and Majerle had gotten along extremely well. "It's frustrating to lose such a good friend as a teammate," he said. Some shook their heads at Barkley, wondering, "How can he try to have things both ways?" What many didn't consider was that this really was the norm.

Yet in fairness, Barkley had a nobler motive. Though Majerle—like all Barkley's teammates at one time or another—occasionally questioned Barkley's focus, he generally had taken the most indulgent view of his idiosyncrasies. Barkley had made the team, the game itself, fun for him. Majerle felt the team needed a more single-minded approach, but he knew this never would come from Barkley. In his mind, the only solution was for everyone else to make up for what Charles lacked and then try to enjoy the humorous, if eccentric ride through the NBA.

Now it was Barkley's time to repay the sentiments. In speaking out, he simply wanted to defend a friend who'd just been told his services—so recently deemed crucial—no longer were needed at all.

IN TRAINING CAMP, the younger players tried to learn the game. The veterans knew all the Xs and Os, so Westphal decided they needed something else entirely. He knew this season could not be like the last one, when internal squabbling threatened to tear apart the team's usually close-knit makeup. Coaches often are reluctant to call team meetings except when absolutely necessary; the widely held belief is that teams that have frequent meetings on their problems are teams where the coach is about to be fired. But the consequences of not talking to each other were worse, he decided. So the veteran players, Barkley, Johnson, Danny Manning, A.C. Green, Joe Kleine and Wayman Tisdale, gathered on a racquetball court adjacent to the gym in which the Suns practiced.

Westphal directed the proceedings. The topic: communication. "I don't want anybody holding grudges. If something is bothering you, speak up." The team's key players had spoken up the previous season, all right. The trouble was they didn't speak to each other. Still didn't.

Barkley and Johnson had never been close. But until the previous season, they'd always managed to get along. When the Suns made the big trade for Barkley, Johnson didn't protest Barkley's assumption of leadership. But in recent seasons, Johnson had asserted himself more.

Barkley thought Johnson was uptight at times. Johnson didn't think Barkley took his responsibilities to heart. Both had evidence to support their theories.

Johnson was tight early in the '93 Finals vs. the Bulls. Barkley worked to loosen him up. And when Johnson came around, the Suns came within an eyelash of coming back from a 3-1 deficit to win the title. But in the next two seasons, it was Barkley who came up short at clutch time. Johnson's belief that Barkley and the Suns in general needed a more severe, rear-end kicking attitude was starting to win converts.

The team, he thought, at least needed someone or something to counter Barkley's perpetual comedy routine and the leadership of Westphal, who generally assumed his players would take a professional, hardworking approach.

So a year earlier, Johnson arranged to have himself appointed team captain. Westphal, who'd never attached much importance to the title, went along with the idea. "Paul expects everybody to be a professional," Johnson said. "So, I need to be more assertive. I'm ready to be the bad cop."

A player's stature, of course, largely is determined by performance. Johnson came up big in the '94 play-off series vs. the Rockets. Thus, his reputation had been enhanced. Barkley, conversely, struggled then came up lame. But players usually are considered only as good as their last game. Only modest allowances are made for superstars.

So when Johnson struggled through a series of minor injuries during the '94-95 season, doubts about him emerged. He started to hear whispers inside the organization from people wondering just how much his injuries were affecting him.

Whenever a player misses games repeatedly, no matter what the reason, there are questions about his diligence and resilience from fans and sometimes even from coaches and teammates. In Johnson's case, this was minimized by his past performance. He'd taken as much of a pounding as any NBA player over the years with his persistent drives into the heart of opposing defenses. And off the floor, everyone knew he wasn't a party animal. Yet the trend was disturbing. He'd been relatively durable in his first five years in the NBA. But in the previous three seasons, he'd missed about one-third of the games.

The injuries frustrated everyone around the team. Johnson didn't confide in the coaches or many of his teammates in great detail. The subject of his health was a question most every day. He might rest for a few days and say, "I feel great." Then he'd go out and test himself in practice and later experience soreness in a hamstring or some other leg muscle. He'd then report, "I feel good, but I'm not sure I'm 100 percent." To some, the statements didn't add up.

What bothered him most was that nothing was said in his defense. Even Westphal, in the past an animated supporter of everything about Johnson, seemed frustrated. Westphal still defended Johnson as a superstar, as integral to the team, but not in quite the fist-pounding tones of the past. He wasn't sure whether Johnson sometimes was playing the role of a dying gunfighter suffering in silence. If he was playing hurt and— with only limited effectiveness—the Suns were better off going with reserve Elliot Perry. Considering he'd carried the Suns in the years before Barkley arrived and carried them to pretty much the same success AFTER

Barkley came on board; considering all the times he'd been knocked down driving to the hoop; considering he'd never been accused of shirking his rehab and conditioning, Johnson was incensed.

"People were questioning my character. There's no compromise there. There's no middle ground."

The problem arose, in part, because of the normal frustrations that come with injuries and a team's unfulfilled expectations. Then too, Johnson was, as Barkley pointed out, pretty much a loner. His closest friend on the team, Mark West, had been traded, so Johnson seemed more and more a mysterious figure. At the same time, the team had been struggling right along with Johnson. Because of his leg problems, he wasn't able to put defensive pressure on the opposing team's playmaker. And without a shot-blocker to cover up for defensive weaknesses, Phoenix found that opponents often got what they wanted.

The Suns had been playing poorly for weeks late in the '94-95 season when they ran into a team even more troubled and even more injury prone: the Golden State Warriors. The Warriors were missing four of their top players: Tim Hardaway, Latrell Sprewell, Chris Gatling and Rony Seikaly. They were left with nine bodies; only one belonged to an established starter (Chris Mullin). Surely, this would be the Suns' chance to get a breather.

Instead, Barkley and Johnson came out sluggish, to the point of appearing disinterested. (One partial explanation: Barkley had been spotted out late the previous night). A rookie named Carlos Rogers outplayed Barkley. The 5-foot-7 Keith Jennings played circles around Johnson. The result: rock bottom. Hades. Or any other term for "lowest point imaginable." The Suns were blown out by the NBA's biggest flops. The postmortem was as ugly as the game.

The veteran Ainge lamented the team's "defensive chaos."

Barkley, struggling to control his temper, said, "It's a disgrace and an embarrassment. I don't want to say anything more because I'll lose it." But he did say more.

"Go talk to Kevin," Barkley said. "He says the right things. It may not mean anything, but he always says the right things."

In conveying his thoughts publicly, Johnson—unlike Barkley—could manage a rare combination of abilities. He could be both candid and thoughtful while still being diplomatic. Barkley, by contrast, was candid. Nothing more, nothing less.

Everyone searched for the answers. What happened? What's wrong?

Said Johnson, "One of the toughest things about basketball is to analyze what's just happened. But I don't have an answer. In the seven or eight years I've been in Phoenix, we've never played this poorly for this long a stretch. I have to find a way to give the team more. But beyond that, I don't have an answer. I'd just be making something up. I need time to reflect. I don't have a profound response."

When he learned of Barkley's comments, Johnson was stunned. He was doubly jolted when Westphal promptly benched him. He was particularly disturbed that Westphal informed him of the demotion in a team meeting in a Washington D.C. area hotel, rather than one-on-one. For all he'd done for the team over the years, he thought he deserved better treatment.

Yet Westphal, for all his progressive "players-coach" methodology, would seldom do anything he deemed "touchy-feely." His approach, and general demeanor, seemed to follow that of his old TV hero: the irreverent but agreeably macho Bart Maverick.

Johnson now felt himself in the most improbable situation of all: peering out of a foxhole dug to avoid fire from both his coach and his fellow superstar. Said Johnson, "I've learned that you can't have both eyes on your enemies. You always have to keep one eye on your enemies and the other on those who are supposed to be your allies. You've got people who are your allies, people who you can go to the well with and never have to watch your back. Then you see something thrown at you from behind, and you're shocked." Eventually, Westphal and Johnson met.

Said Johnson, "We talked about communication. We both got a chance to speak our minds. We reestablished a relationship. That's important." At the same time, "That doesn't mean everything has been resolved."

Barkley, too, went into a damage-control mode. Of his outburst following the loss to the Warriors, he said, "I was just frustrated. "Sometimes, I would like him (Johnson) to not say the perfect P.R. thing. I'd like to hear him say, 'This was embarrassing' and 'This was a disgrace.' I would like to see him get mad more instead of trying to rationalize things."

Almost as soon as he'd spoken, the Suns suddenly came around, finishing the regular season with an 8-1 run. Then, Johnson absolutely dominated his competition in the '95 play-off series vs. the Rockets. While Barkley clowned off the court and faded on it, Johnson nearly pulled the Suns over the top.

So, Johnson used his reemerging stature to critique the Suns in a meeting with Colangelo in June, a month after the Suns' latest play-off demise.

He sought assurances that Colangelo had no doubts about his commitment to doing everything possible to overcome his injuries. If Colangelo had any doubts, then they could revisit Colangelo's no-trade promise to him when he signed his contract extension the year before. Colangelo supported him completely.

Then Johnson turned his attention toward the Barkley-led nature of the Suns. He raised such topics as: "Are we really the team we can be? Are any one or two individuals more important than the team? Can we reach our potential? Why have we lost the past two years? Can you really tell me they (the Rockets) are a better team?" Then Johnson told Colangelo, "There's something about the character of our team. It's something you need to look at."

Continued Johnson, "Did everyone do what is necessary to put ourselves in the best position to win, regardless of the outcome? "I'd like to feel at the end of the season, that, even if we lose, we did everything we could. That's beautiful. That's what sports is all about. Play the game the way it's supposed to be played."

Later, he suggested the shortcomings wouldn't be solved by tearing the team apart and rebuilding every couple of years. Championship teams, after all, almost always grow together for a few years. "Adding players all the time? Time out. Houston subtracts players and still wins," he said. The Suns' much-maligned centers had gotten too much blame for the team's demise, he thought. "David Robinson, the MVP, gives up 40 points to Hakeem Olajuwon (in the ensuing Spurs-Rockets series) FOUR TIMES. We didn't give up that much."

In contrast, he pointed to the struggles of the lowly Sacramento Kings. They once again failed to make the play-offs. But they had their best season in years, ending their home schedule with a rousing win over the Seattle SuperSonics, a game that put them in position to play for the No. 8 play-off spot on the season's final day. Though the Kings lost that game, Johnson asked, "Who feels worse, us or them?" Then he answered his own question: "Us, because we underachieved."

Johnson tried to arrange a powwow over the summer with Barkley. But during the off-season, "Sir Charles" prefers to wander the country as much as Charles Kuralt ever did. Johnson never could pin him down for a heart-to-heart.

(Among Barkley's wanderings that summer: He visited his home state of Alabama, presenting himself once again as potential gubernatorial material. Jittery GOP officials, apparently taking him seriously, tried to talk him into running for a congressional seat held by a Democrat. Barkley also arranged to sail on a round-trip cruise from New York to the Bahamas. Passengers would pay an extra $1,000 to be with their hero. For this, Barkley would be paid $100,000. But at the last minute, he pulled out in a dispute over whether the organizer made the proper insurance arrangements. The passengers were incensed.)

So now, Westphal advised, when problems arise, don't speak up to the media. "Talk to each other and handle things like adults. We don't want petty things to turn into great big things." Barkley and Johnson gave their assent, with Johnson saying they needed to watch out for each other's interests. "We've got to protect each other's backsides." Joe Kleine added, "We've got to communicate with everybody about everything."

Johnson judged the meeting to be a success.

"Charles has a strong personality, Paul has a strong personality, and I have a strong personality. It's no secret we haven't gotten along great.

"But I hope we can put our differences aside for the betterment of the team," he said. "Nobody really dislikes each other."

The meeting served as Westphal's attempt to put behind the problems between Johnson and himself and between Barkley and Johnson. But the tension ran too deep to wipe the slate clean in one training camp get-together Three days later, when somebody asked him about his "feud" with Barkley, Johnson replied, "Why are people coming to me and asking about the feud. Why aren't people going to him?" Referring to Barkley's outburst in Oakland, he said, "I didn't start the feud. He started the feud."

At some point, Johnson believed there would come a "defining moment" involving the two of them and Westphal that would determine the season's fortunes. The key question: Which direction would things go?

"I think it will be a great year, or totally the opposite," Johnson said.

Barkley summarized the standoff to *The Arizona Republic*, "He likes to go to church. I like to go to strip joints. So, we can't do a whole lot together.

"We've got to compromise. I don't mind going to church with him. But we'll have to be different until he comes to my joints."

IN FLAGSTAFF, MUCH TIME had to be devoted to integrating all the new faces. They had picked up a big man from Europe: Stefano Rusconi, a 6-9 center from Italy who would need time to learn how to play forward in the NBA.

In the draft, they'd scooped up a shooter named Chris Carr late in the second round from Southern Illinois. Normally, a player taken this late had only a prayer of making a team, particularly a top-level team. But with the departure of Majerle and Antonio Lang, a guard thrown into the Majerle-Williams deal, Carr had a chance.

There was John Coker, a 7-foot rookie with a history of foot problems. He was the latest experiment in the Suns' eternal search for a center.

Then there was Mario Bennett, who'd played locally at Arizona State. Bennett was an outstanding shot-blocker who had inside scoring instincts. But questions over his maturity abounded. He was a terrible free-throw shooter, and he'd had knee problems to boot.

The biggest prize was Michael Finley, a midsized player who—like Majerle—had a rugged physique. He'd been a college superstar as a junior at Wisconsin. But he shot poorly as a senior. His stock slipped on draft day, and the Suns were fairly shocked to be able to land him with their first pick, at No. 21.

In the NBA, many old hands believe that a player's future can be determined in the first few practices. Either you can play or you can't. So, Westphal watched Finley carefully. Like Majerle, he wasn't a natural shooter. But he had scoring instincts and, more importantly, an overall command of the game. He knew how to defend. He could play.

THE EXHIBITION SEASON didn't do much more than training camp to jump-start Barkley. For years, he'd called the exhibition season a sort of scam, a way for the owners to separate the customers from their money without giving them anything in return. He had a point.

The owners generally charged full price for exhibition games, making them a mandatory part of season ticket packages. The starters played maybe half their usual minutes—sometimes even less during the earliest games—and seldom were terribly concerned over the game's outcome.

In the old days, teams at least would take the NBA game to the hinterlands, giving people in midsized cities their only chance to see the world's best players. But with teams increasingly able to sell out their pricey tickets at home, there was less incentive to play in unfamiliar neutral courts.

This year, the Suns would play three of their four designated home exhibition games in their own arena. The fourth would be a mere 120 miles south in Tucson, Arizona's other major metropolitan area. The only game in the hinterlands would be against the Miami Heat in Albany N.Y., near where the Heat's coach, Pat Riley, grew up. (Far from getting a hero's welcome, Riley was booed by a crowd of mostly Knicks fans for leaving New York for the greener—as in cash-laden—pastures of Miami.)

"I always felt the pre-season was a waste of time," Barkley said. At most, cut the exhibition schedule from eight games to three or four, he advised.

On top of this, because he was easing back from knee surgery, Barkley pronounced he would only play in the final three exhibitions. Almost predictably, he abandoned this plan, opting to play in the second game at home vs. the New Jersey Nets. The game was notable for a scuffle between Rusconi and Jayson Williams, an old Barkley teammate from his Philadelphia days. Barkley then began jawing with Williams, who threatened to come find Barkley later in the Suns' locker room. So, Barkley drew a map, showing how to get from one locker room to the other in the bowels of the arena and had a ball boy deliver it to Williams on the Nets bench.

"I just wanted to make sure he didn't get lost," Barkley said.

Westphal, encouraged that Barkley at least took part in the game, said he expected to see him on the three-game trip that started in Albany. But almost at the same moment, Barkley said he'd stiffened sufficiently that he thought he could better spend the time working out in Phoenix. And so he did. By the time Barkley returned to action, the Suns were finishing their exhibition schedule in less than ideal conditions. Because of a series of minor injuries, Westphal had to sew patchwork lineups comprised mostly of younger players. Even when the veterans were able to play, they weren't sharp.

In Tucson, Westphal hoped to close the exhibition season with one strong game vs. the Clippers. Instead, the Suns unraveled with horrendous ball-handling; Barkley, who'd played 18 holes of golf earlier in the day, scored 25 but had six of the team's 21 turnovers. The Clippers pulled away at the end.

The Suns were 4-4 in the exhibitions. Much worse, the NBA's best ball-handling team the previous season had committed 20 turnovers or more in all eight games! "Pathetic," Westphal judged.

He barked at his team, "We've got a lot of work to do." The season opener, on the road against those same Clippers, was five days away. "I'm concerned," he told reporters. "We're far from ready. We'll have to play a lot better or we'll lose the first game."

Barkley professed to be unconcerned, saying, "I don't care about the pre-season. Everyone is bored and ready for the real season to start." As always, he maintained that talent, not precision or that elusive team "chemistry" determined success and failure. "Practice is the most over-rated thing in the world. If you're good enough to win, you'll win. This is not brain surgery."

Johnson, almost predictably, took the opposing view. Practice, he said, is "highly desirable. I'd like to be together for at least a week. This way, we won't be as precise. But that's what we have. We'll have to make the best of it."

N·O·T·E·W·O·R·T·H·Y

OCT. 6, PHOENIX

There's no question where Barkley stands in the matter of O.J. Simpson. "I understand somebody in the media thinks O.J. didn't do it. That confirms my opinion of the media." The previous season, he'd said, "Some of the rookies don't think he did it. That's why they're rookies."

Later, he would say, on the possibility of Simpson answering questions on the murder case, "He's not going to say anything that will change my mind. I know what I'd ask him: If you're innocent, why were you driving around (instead of surrendering to authorities) with all that money?"

OCT. 8, FLAGSTAFF

As Hot Rod Williams talks to Arizona reporters at length for the first time, Barkley pokes his head in the middle of the proceedings, shakes Williams' hand, then tells him, "Remember, they'll turn on you."

OCT. 16, PHOENIX

Reacting to the Louis Farrakhan-organized Million Man March in Washington D.C., Kevin Johnson says he didn't like the notion of de-emphasizing women, but otherwise, "I support the spirit of the march, certainly."

Says Barkley, "I think it's a good concept. But I think it would have been better to march in your own community. To meet in Washington D.C., a place that's against poor people and black people, is counterproductive."

Westphal has his opinions on the march but is reluctant to elaborate. He indicates he is opposed to the concept if the intent is to support a racial separatist movement. "I like what Martin Luther King had to say about every man being judged on the content of his character, not the color of his skin," Westphal says.

The giant TV in the Suns' locker room is tuned to the march. Barkley hears someone talking and asks the identity of the speaker. Informed that Al Sharpton, the flamboyant preacher, is talking, Barkley says, "Oh God, not him! I don't want to hear all black people talking. I'd rather hear Jesse Jackson than him."

OCT. 19, NEW YORK

Shock jock Howard Stern and a couple of his talk show cohorts are given a list of celebrities, including A.C. Green, then are asked, "Which one is still a virgin?" The panel was stumped. Told the answer was Green, Stern says, "I never heard of her."

3

Enjoy the moment

PAUL WESTPHAL SAT ALONE on the Suns bench, long before fans would be allowed to enter the Los Angeles Memorial Sport Arena on Opening Night of the NBA's 1995-96 season. He thought long and hard about what to say to his players.

His teams had won more games than anybody else in the entire NBA the past three seasons. Had a shot or two gone differently in the play-offs vs. the Bulls or the Rockets, he might have been a championship coach a time or two. But they didn't, and so he wasn't. Who knew how many more chances, if any, he'd get to lead a team that close to the NBA title?

Now for the first time since he'd taken over from Cotton Fitzsimmons, there were real doubts about the Suns' status as a title contender. There had long been carping about the team's inconsistent defense. Fashioning a better one with a group of mostly offensive-oriented players had Westphal running uphill the past two years. He'd made the team practice more often than in that nearly dream-like first season of 1992-93 and placed more emphasis on watching videotape. Still, the defense came and went; critics wondered if he shouldn't be doing more.

Now, because of the relatively poor exhibition season marked by all the turnovers and poor shooting—characteristics that hadn't been associated much with his teams—the Suns didn't open the schedule with the swagger of the past three years. "There's a sense of being unsettled," Westphal conceded.

Then, too, there were the usual concerns about injuries. With the Suns, more than most teams, there always were injuries and potential injuries to think about. Eddie Johnson, a shooting specialist who spent his best years playing for the Suns, had a theory about the team. He believed the Suns would forever be injury prone because of their fast pace and attacking style. Some evidence existed for this: Slower teams such as the New

York Knicks and—even more remarkably—the Utah Jazz seldom had runs of debilitating injuries. (Jazz superstars Karl Malone and John Stockton had missed only a handful of games between them over the course of a decade). Then again, those infernal Houston Rockets were somewhat fast-paced yet didn't have much of an injury history. But it certainly was true that the Suns had more problems than other elite teams over the past few seasons.

The pattern held, even as the season was getting started. For this team was led by three players who were as great as they were fragile. Barkley, who'd come up lame at the end of each of the last two play-offs, was coming off arthroscopic surgery on his left knee.

Danny Manning, one of the game's most versatile players, wasn't even expected back until around New Year's. He'd blown out a knee for the second time in his career in the previous season; at the time, the Suns were battling for the NBA's best record. After the injury, they faded.

Then there was Johnson. The team doctor, Richard Emerson, once described Johnson as akin to an expensive sports car. When he was in top shape, he was a sight to behold. Otherwise, he was in the shop, with technicians trying to figure what was wrong. His game depended on explosiveness and speed. If he played with leg muscles pulled or hurting, he pulled his punches for fear of making things worse. And when he held back, particularly on defense, the team suffered greatly. Though he was known around the basketball world as an offensive player, he had blossomed—when healthy—into a fine defender.

Increasingly, his legs were giving out. Though he'd generally been healthy late in seasons (he'd been available in most every play-off game), he'd missed 83 games combined—almost exactly a full season—over the past three years.

The same problems were evident even before the exhibition season started. Johnson felt a calf muscle tighten during a practice in Flagstaff, an injury that was aggravated when he was kicked during the team's intra-squad scrimmage at Northern Arizona's indoor football stadium. He missed the first few exhibition games. A.C. Green, Wesley Person and Wayman Tisdale also suffered minor injuries. The Suns were so depleted that they took off on a three-game exhibition tour of the East with their top seven players missing: Johnson, Barkley, Manning, Tisdale, Green, Person and Williams. They were reduced to playing backups Elliot Perry and Joe Kleine plus six rookies. Somehow, they won one of the three.

They were all together for only one exhibition, a game in Anaheim against the Clippers. Then Johnson went up for a slam and injured a thigh muscle. He didn't play again until Opening Night.

In addition to all this, Westphal was coming off his worst season. For the first time as a player or coach, he hadn't really enjoyed himself. The Suns not only had been expected to win, but win big. That they frequently were unable to do so became the source of criticism he found wearying. The heat was turned up to the point that for the first time, he endured a feeding frenzy about whether he should—and more importantly WOULD—be fired.

This would have been a harsh sentence indeed for a coach who had won 150 games faster than anybody in history not named Pat Riley.

But the Suns were the pride and joy of Arizona, a state that had endured so many political and business scandals that some thought of the Grand Canyon State as the new Louisiana. The Suns were the one institution that was supposed to radiate excellence. High expectations now were a permanent part of the coach's job.

It certainly didn't help Westphal that during the fiasco against the Warriors late in the season the cameras caught him smiling as the Suns were being routed. What fans didn't know was that Westphal was trying to do a little coaching for the future by engaging in some public relations work with the officials. He had just joked to them, "I wish I could blame this all on you." It was a case where a picture didn't tell the true story, and it damaged Westphal, seeming to confirm the suspicion that losses didn't eat at him as they did with most athletic types.

"It's hard to know what will be picked up on television and how it will be interpreted," he said. "It's hard to coach for perception. But perception can get you fired."

It also didn't help him that he declined to disclose that club president Jerry Colangelo had already given him a contract extension several weeks earlier. Westphal deeply believed that this was a players' game, and while the season was ongoing, the players should be in the limelight. News of the coach's contract could come later. Colangelo had hinted that a new contract was in the works, but Westphal wouldn't confirm it. Had he done so, the speculation over his job might have been short-circuited.

Yet when the Suns went into a tailspin, who knew just what the new contract meant, other than guaranteeing him a healthy salary over the next few years? Colangelo was known to be as disappointed with the team's slide as the most ornery fan, and his quick temper was legendary.

Westphal never sensed he was in danger. He figured that if Colangelo really believed he fit the fans' image of being too "laid back" that the team president would come to him and order specific changes instead of pulling the trigger on him. Yet, after thinking about the whole period, he wasn't completely sure how safe he'd been. Maybe he really was walking under a cliff with a huge boulder dangling above him.

During the time of greatest turmoil, he left himself one choice. If he didn't defend himself publicly, in the strongest terms, who would? "This team is as disciplined as it needs to be to function at its best," he said. The critics, he countered, weren't at practice, "They don't know the idio-syncrasies (hint: Barkley) the coaches have to deal with. I have a feel for the situation. And I don't think discipline is the problem."

That said, he wasn't going to spend a lot of time and energy trying to give a perception of "toughness" just to please the public. The way to do that was to lambaste the players publicly. That went against his beliefs. But if he didn't do so, he admitted, "I'm an easy target."

Indeed, he was.

That Westphal didn't fit the traditional mold of a coach, where images evoked are that of a gruff drill sergeant, a guy who eats nails for break-fast and then runs 10 miles to blow off steam, didn't help him in times of crisis. Instead, he was the model of civility. He could be—and sometimes was—the traditional barking-dog coach in practice and in other private settings. But most of the time, he actually was downright polite, even when his team was playing poorly. In addition, he used humor almost as much in the bad times as the good. Maybe, fans wondered, he didn't real-ly hurt as much as they did when the team fared poorly.

In all of this, he believed, could be found the source of his image problem.

"My philosophy is to treat triumph and disaster just the same. I try to live up to that. Some people don't understand that. They think it's weak-ness, softness or lack of discipline.

"It's true that I don't walk around puffing out my chest to show how tough I am. I do what I need to do behind closed doors. If that makes me appear soft, then that's the way it will appear." Then he joked, "Maybe I should get a tattoo and start cussing."

Westphal believed plenty of coaches could succeed with the Suns—but not many who were perceived publicly as tough disciplinarians. "It would be a riot to sit back and watch it," he said. Westphal used his insti-tutional memory to point out that through much of the late 1970s and the 1980s, the Suns had the reputation of being a bunch of "6-5 white guys who ran all these beautiful plays. But the critics said they needed a few characters. "Well, now we have a few characters.

"Everybody would like to have a team where the guys all wear flat-tops, tuck in their shirts, and say, 'YESSIR!' But then, they'd better be able to play, too."

Westphal made another local analogy, pointing to how Buddy Ryan, coach of the NFL team, sometimes would attack his Arizona Cardinals players. (Once, after Luis Sharpe—the lineman who played for the Cardinals longer than anybody else—went out with a season-ending injury, Ryan said the team hadn't lost anybody who counted.) "Some people thought he was one tough son of a gun," Westphal said. "Other people thought he was a jerk. The bottom line is: How do the players respond to that?"

As far as the Suns are concerned, "The last thing in the world they would respond to is embarrassing them in public. They'd jump ship so fast that I wouldn't blame them. So, what we're stuck with is that when we lose, I'll take a lot of heat.

"We're a very high-profile team. When things go right, some people think they should go even better. When things go rough, they think they have the answers. That's the nature of the business. That's why we all get paid a lot of money. I'm sure people have good intentions. But they just can't know."

Westphal's take on the heat: "Criticism goes with the job. To take it personally would be a mistake. To overreact would be a huge mistake."

Thus, Westphal would change neither his coaching style nor his principles to suit the troubled times. When the Suns went into the tank against the Warriors the previous season, the popular theory was that he needed to "crack the whip" and blast his players for not giving the proper effort. He indeed made lineup changes and reminded his team that they were operating on the merit system. But that was about the extent of it. After their flop in Oakland, they had to fly across country to Washington D.C. to play the Bullets in a makeup game. (The regularly scheduled game early in the season had to be postponed because of condensation on the Bullets' home floor.)

Surely, their slide couldn't get any steeper. But it did. The woeful Bullets, who—like the Warriors—had injury problems themselves, scored 77 points in the first half. Maybe the critics were correct. Maybe a change was in order. As Colangelo (unbeknownst to Westphal) ruminated over the coaching situation back in Phoenix, even Westphal had begun to doubt his methods. But he decided he couldn't be somebody he was not. He entered the locker room, as tense as ever on a team that normally was as loose as any in sports, and . . . he lightened up.

He told his team, "I can come in here and rip you. But they were on fire. We have the better team. Let's go out and have fun and win the game." The players were relieved. They came back to beat the Bullets, then proceeded to start hustling effectively on defense, closed the season on a winning streak, swept the Trail Blazers in the play-offs' opening round, then suffered the heartbreaking, 1-point loss in Game 7 against the Rockets.

In the end, it was hard to see what all the fuss was about. They'd gone 59-23 in the regular season even though Barkley, Johnson and Manning, their three most accomplished players, missed 85 games between them. All in all, it probably was Westphal's finest coaching job.

Westphal realized that he'd almost certainly be fired one day. Then again, it seemed a dream that he ever made it to this position in the first place. The notion that Paul Westphal ever would be handed the coaching reins of the Phoenix Suns once seemed about as likely as the chewing tobacco industry hiring figure skater Nancy Kerrigan as a spokesperson, or maybe Westphal's buddy, Rush Limbaugh, pitching Jenny Craig memberships.

Not that there ever was a question about the depth of his understanding of the game. In his day, Westphal was a genuine superstar, though his day—in the late 1970s—was not the NBA's heyday. So, his exploits, then and now, never were fully appreciated. He was a deft, ambidextrous shooter and ball handler. His lob passes to teammate Alvan Adams epitomized the best of finesse basketball. He led the Suns, generally considered a last-place prospect, on their shocking run to the NBA Finals in 1976.

He attained first-team, all-NBA status three times. No one else in Suns history had accomplished this feat more than once. Next to George Gervin, an athletic scoring machine who played in San Antonio, he was considered the game's greatest guard in the mid-to-late 1970s.

Westphal always believed the game should be much less a coaching chess match than a battle of the players' creative talents. The author/journalist David Halberstam, in his definitive study of the NBA during that period when the game had just become a predominantly black sport, noted that Westphal had become restless with coach John MacLeod's structured system. "He was a white player that the blacks greatly admired. In their view, he *played* black, that is, he could free-lance, he could drive and he could dunk. . . ."

He also seemed a step ahead of the competition. His famous illegal time-out call in the historic triple-overtime game of the '76 Finals against

the Celtics stamped him as a sharp student of the game. The move resulted in a technical foul and cost the Suns a point. But it allowed them to
advance the ball to half-court (instead of taking it out under their own
basket) with one second left. Then the Suns miraculously tied the game at
the buzzer.

He learned the trick watching the Southern Cal football team as a kid.
When the Trojans were down in the waning moments of a game, coach
John McKay would call a time-out when the team had none, thus picking up a five-yard penalty but still stopping the clock. "The punishment
wasn't worse than the crime," Westphal explained.

But at the same time, Westphal had been the most rebellious player in
Suns history. He left the team twice in the midst of stormy disputes with
management, an odd legacy for this conservative, religious-minded man
with the angelic good looks of a well-scrubbed Boy Scout.

He grew up in the comfortable beach life of the South Bay area of Los
Angeles, listening to the tunes of the Kingston Trio and Bob Dylan. He
learned the ways and means of sports from his father and older brother.
He was a prep contemporary of the baseball Bretts (George and Ken). He
absorbed knowledge at the feet of the most famous basketball coach in
history, UCLA's John Wooden, at the guru's camps.

He could have played for the Wizard of Westwood, but he disliked the
liberal atmosphere at UCLA at the time. Instead, he went downtown to
Southern Cal. Though he disdained campus activism, he liked the non-
conformist message of Dylan. His idea of a good time was to take a
friend's challenge and wolf down as many Der Weinerschnitzel hot dogs
as he could stomach. He quit after 15.

On the basketball floor, Westphal led a Trojans team that sometimes
challenged Wooden's Bruins for supremacy, both locally and nationally.

The Boston Celtics drafted him in 1972. Westphal played a bit role on
the Celtics' championship team of 1974. At the time, he was just starting
to come of age as a player. The Suns liked him enough to trade Charlie
Scott, their leading scorer, to acquire him before the '75-76 season. The
Suns struggled, as expected, through much of the season. But with Westphal leading the way, Phoenix put together a season-ending run that carried into the play-offs. The Suns shocked the Golden State Warriors, the
NBA's defending champs, in the Western Conference Finals before falling
to the Celtics in a thrilling Finals.

Though the Suns wouldn't make another serious run at the title, they
enjoyed solid winning seasons in four of Westphal's five seasons. Yet

through it all, Westphal was growing increasingly frustrated with what he saw as an overly structured system. The coach was John MacLeod, a knowledgeable, by-the-book sort.

Westphal considered MacLeod's practices long and dreary, particularly for the veterans whom Westphal thought should save their best for games. And Westphal didn't like MacLeod's rigid substitution pattern, the one criticism that found sympathetic ears among fans who wondered why a team with a strong starting unit but weak bench so often played its reserves.

As Westphal saw it, MacLeod didn't merely want to win. He wanted to win in a fashion that was as symmetrical and balanced as a Mozart composition. Nobody should stand out.

This was an approach Westphal never would follow as a coach. He didn't care if the melody was as off key as the national anthem when sung by Roseanne Barr. He would only care who won. Westphal felt so strongly that he went public with some of his criticisms.

Years later, MacLeod replied. In an interview with the weekly *New Times*—a discussion that took place after he and Westphal supposedly made up—MacLeod let off some steam and blasted his former star guard: "It was Paul's philosophy that he could take his man out of the game by his scoring ability. But how many times did you have to give Paul Westphal the ball while the other four guys stood there watching him? Paul didn't like our passing game, he didn't like our defense. Let's see. He didn't like our practice sessions on the days of games. He didn't like our substitution patterns. When he was here, there were very few things Paul Westphal liked. "Who would he like? A guy who played him 48 minutes and let him do exactly what he wanted and go off on his own and never say anything to him?"

Westphal was surprised by the attack. He acknowledged differing philosophies, "But I didn't think I was disruptive. The only thing I bucked him on was weight training. I didn't make a fuss. I just didn't do it. John felt that was poor leadership on my part."

The Suns had brought in a weight-training expert, a fellow Westphal deemed a "moron" about basketball for telling him to build up his wrists to shoot long jump shots. "On a long jumper, the power comes from your legs," Westphal said. "The touch comes from your fingers and wrists. I knew more about it than he did. I wasn't going to put my future in his hands."

With all of the bickering, it was time for Westphal to depart. Colangelo sent him to Seattle in 1980 for another guard, the rising Dennis Johnson.

Like Westphal, Johnson was considered a malcontent, but he was young and talented and a great defender. On paper, it seemed an even trade.

But Westphal started to break down. Foot injuries contributed to two wasted years in Seattle. Johnson, meanwhile, established himself as one of the game's best guards in Phoenix and Boston. (The Suns, in the worst trade in franchise history, later sent him and a less favorable draft position to the Celtics for journeyman Rick Robey. One of the main reasons for the deal was MacLeod thought Johnson, like Westphal, didn't fully believe in his program.)

In 1982, Westphal considered returning to the Suns. He apologized, not for his difference of opinion, but for his public airing of his gripes. "Trying to explain things, sometimes you can talk too much," he said later.

But the Suns were loaded with guards, so he signed with New York. He had a solid year and was named the league's comeback player of the year. The Knicks, however, considered him a defensive liability and released him at the end of the '83 season.

All the while, Colangelo continued to stay loyal to Westphal, who he viewed as the team's identity. He met with his former star at New York's Waldorf-Astoria Hotel and, feeling that the Westphal-MacLeod feud had been settled, signed him to a two-year contract. But the Westphal magic now could be found only in scrapbooks. Injuries limited him to just 59 games. That number was most significant because he had to play in, or be available for, 60 games to qualify for the guarantee on the contract's second year. There was much disagreement on whether he was available for a game just before he went on the injured list.

At the end of that '83-84 season, Colangelo met with Westphal and MacLeod.

Nine years earlier, MacLeod had pounded his fist on the table when he learned the Charlie Scott-for-Westphal trade with Boston had been approved. Said MacLeod at the time, "Now we have a chance!" On this day, Colangelo delivered a different message: "Paul, we think it's time." If Westphal would retire, he would get a job in the organization. Westphal resisted. He filed a grievance asking that his second year be guaranteed. At the same time, he persisted in trying out for the team in the fall of '84. But the Suns cut him. He filed another grievance charging that the Suns let him go for financial reasons.

While the first dispute was a close call, the second one really wasn't. Had the Suns been so concerned about money in deciding whether to keep him, they would have waited to cut him until after an arbitrator ruled they won on the first issue (that way, they wouldn't give Westphal any more potential ammunition).

Even though the Suns eventually won on both counts, Colangelo called the whole process "the worst experience of my life." He felt he didn't have enough clout to settle the dispute. Though he continued to carry the title of general manager, his status had been reduced when the triumvirate of Donald Pitt, Richard Bloch and Don Diamond increased their ownership from 20 to 80 percent in October 1983. Instead of acting instinctively and quickly, as he preferred, Colangelo found himself in the middle of decisions by committee.

So, Westphal and the Suns went their separate ways, though the Prodigal Sun continued to live in Phoenix.

And when a tiny Bible school called Southwestern College needed a coach, Westphal offered his services for free. The team won 21 games and, because of Westphal's presence, for the first time a few people at least knew the school existed.

"I never had a year that was more fun," said Westphal. "I was very proud of the guys on that team. We had all these 5-foot-10 white guys, but they were pretty good."

Next he took over as the basketball coach at Grand Canyon College, an NAIA school in Phoenix with a solid basketball tradition. He twice enjoyed winning seasons. In his second year, his team emerged as a strong national title candidate.

Then, just three weeks before the team was to enter the 1988 national tournament, his two leading scorers violated team rules, indiscretions he described as "more serious than missing the team bus." Worse, the players crossed Westphal's strong sense of propriety. So, he suspended them, knowing full well that his action almost certainly would prohibit his team from winning the NAIA title. But to Westphal, none of this made any difference.

"One of the problems today with college coaching," he would say later, "is that everybody is trying to get a better job. It used to be that coaches were there to help kids. Now, you're there to win and help the organization make money.

"But if I had stayed at Grand Canyon for 20 years, that would have been fine. I wasn't there to try to get a better job. And because I wasn't, I was able to make decisions for what I felt were the right reasons."

Then, miraculously, Grand Canyon won and won some more in the tournament. All of a sudden, the Antelopes found themselves in the final minute of a tense championship game. A Grand Canyon player went to the line for two free throws that almost certainly would decide the game. In a move that isn't often seen with a championship on the line, the coach leaned back in his seat and . . . began to laugh.

Westphal was chuckling over what little control he had over his team's fate.

"I think I said, 'What a crazy way to make a living! A guy is shooting a free throw, and if he makes it, you're doing a great job.'"

The player, Rodney Johns, hit the free throws. Grand Canyon won the title.

Colangelo saw this develop and was impressed.

Could this be the same antiestablishment Paul Westphal whose disputes with management seemed to ensure that his uniform never would hang from the rafters alongside those of Connie Hawkins, Alvan Adams and Dick Van Arsdale?

Yet Westphal never used to see himself as rebellious any more than he later saw himself as a disciplinarian. He merely rejected the flexible sense of right and wrong than that generally found in big-time sports.

At this time, Colangelo was thinking of ousting his head coach, John Wetzel, after one disappointing season. Colangelo had decided that Wetzel, a fine assistant coach, was too low key to run the team.

In addition, Colangelo had been taken aback by Wetzel's reaction to the decision he and Fitzsimmons made to trade Larry Nance, the team's cornerstone. In February 1988, the Suns sent Nance and fellow forward Mike Sanders to Cleveland. The key to the deal was a promising Cavaliers rookie point guard with exceptional explosiveness. But he was only 21 years old and hadn't played much behind the Cavs' Mark Price. His name: Kevin Johnson.

Wetzel reacted with deep emotion to the trade, a response that raised Colangelo's eyebrows to the roof. This was, after all, a business in which bodies are moved constantly, usually with as much sentiment as trading pork futures.

So, Colangelo decided he would install Cotton Fitzsimmons, the team's player personnel director, as head coach. Colangelo first spotted Fitzsimmons as a college coach in the 1960s. He was a driven personality who also had the carnival barker's talent for salesmanship, a valuable asset when the NBA in general and the Suns in particular were struggling to gain popularity. So Colangelo—who had just coached the team himself for a half-season and guided it to its first play-off appearance—named

Fitzsimmons to coach the two-year old Suns in 1970.

Under Fitzsimmons, the team enjoyed two winning seasons. Then he left and became an NBA vagabond, building a successful career and a reputation as somebody who could take over broken-down teams with mediocre talent and make them competitive.

In this second go-round as the Suns coach, the idea was to find a capable assistant for the 56-year-old Fitzsimmons. That way he could stabilize the team, then turn over the reins to a well-prepared successor.

Colangelo had always looked past the financial disputes with Westphal. He continued to view him as embodying the Suns' identity as a brainy, flexible, aesthetically pleasing team.

Why not hire Westphal as the assistant? He approached Fitzsimmons, who was thinking the same thing.

Fitzsimmons once attended a Grand Canyon game and came away shaking his head in amazement at Westphal's coolness under fire. He recalled the time Westphal's young son Michael, about 7 at the time, interrupted the team's huddle by asking his dad for a dollar to buy a soda. Fitzsimmons figured that if his own son, Gary (who later became an executive with a couple of NBA clubs), had done the same thing, "I would have strangled him." In Westphal's case, Dad calmly pulled a dollar out of his wallet, then resumed instructing his team.

Westphal agreed to be the Suns' lead assistant and learned the art of playing second banana to Fitzsimmons. Then, whenever the time seemed appropriate, the Prodigal Sun would run the team. As player personnel director, Fitzsimmons had masterfully rebuilt the team, thanks to the deal for Johnson and the free-agent signing of Tom Chambers, an agile 6-foot-10 forward who could both shoot and drive to the basket with authority. As head coach, Fitzsimmons transformed the Suns into a running-gunning team of nearly overwhelming offensive firepower. They advanced to the Western Conference Finals—the NBA's Final Four—in his first two seasons. But they didn't quite have the defensive or rebounding prowess to make it all the way.

Then when Chambers' skills declined dramatically, so did the Suns' fortunes the next two seasons. They still won their standard 50-plus games. But most every game was more of a struggle.

Then too, Fitzsimmons' constant courtside chatter ("See the ball! WAKE UP TIM PERRY!") had begun to wear on a host of players. Chambers and Fitzsimmons argued on occasion. Young players Jerrod Mustaf and Negele Knight blamed their lack of playing time on Fitzsimmons (a complaint that was not borne out by their performances later in their careers). Westphal had become the good cop, Fitzsimmons the bad one.

Fitzsimmons and Colangelo realized after the fourth season of the rebuilt Suns that Westphal should get the chance to run the team. Said Fitzsimmons, with unusual succinctness, "It's time."

The contrasts between Fitzsimmons and Westphal couldn't have been more obvious.

The 5-foot-7 Fitzsimmons was emotional. He tossed out the normal set playing rotation and coached on instincts, often on a spur-of-the-moment basis. Then there was his constant ravings on the sideline. If Fitzsimmons was the Energizer Bunny, Westphal was Garfield the Cat, a cool, hip, seemingly serene observer of the events unfolding before him. He brought to the head coaching table about as much preparation as anyone ever had: 12 years as an NBA player, four as a lead assistant coach. And along the way, he'd been able to pick up tips from the two most noted basketball minds in history.

From Wooden, who both taught him as a youngster and coached against him while he was a college player, he learned to prepare as thoroughly as possible but—on game day—to relax and let the players do their thing.

From Red Auerbach, the Celtics' guru who Westphal observed for three years in Boston, he learned to focus only on matters of importance. From both, he learned that honest mistakes should be tolerated.

Yet his most important influence may have been a man named Ken Brown, who coached Westphal at Aviation High School in Redondo Beach. Brown stressed flexibility, a quality that became the key to Westphal's approach. Centers should be able to catch and pass the ball, as well as block shots and rebound. Hence, Westphal pushed to draft Oliver Miller. Guards should be able to rebound. Forwards should be able to defend centers or guards. Just about everyone should be able to play more than one position.

If your five best players are short or medium-sized, don't hesitate to play them all at once. Sure, your team may miss a few rebounds or blocks, but at least you're playing to your strengths. Let the other team worry about matching up to you, not the other way around.

Less tangibly, he learned the sort of perspective about sports that was more common then than now. Opponents were to be respected, and the world didn't end with a loss as long as you tried your best.

With this in mind, it's not surprising that as Westphal took over as head coach in 1992, he had no particular career highlight that he drew on more than any other. He considered winning the small-college title at Grand Canyon as significant as playing for the world champion 1974 Boston Celtics.

And with this perspective, it was no surprise that he didn't surround himself with a circle of friends from the jock world. His post-game guests, other than his wife and kids, sometimes included longhaired artists. Or, in the '93 NBA Finals, sitting in the coaches' office between assistants Scotty Robertson and Lionel Hollins was a heavyset fellow whose wrinkled shirt looked like it had come directly from the clothes hamper. His name: Rush Limbaugh.

Westphal's main assignment with the Suns, other than trying to fine-tune a team that had more offensive than defensive prowess and was too short along the front line, was to manage one Charles Wade Barkley.

The stay-at-home, religious-minded Westphal would have to figure a way to deal with his rules-be-dammed, night-prowling superstar. West-phal let Barkley know early that he wouldn't haggle over missteps of no consequence. This wasn't a departure for him. As a player, he was quick to detect dictatorial tendencies. He wouldn't follow them as a coach, as long as his players worked hard and didn't violate his senses of propriety and seniority. Veterans could stretch the limits, but not young players.

In one of this first games with the Suns, Barkley missed the team bus for a game in Utah. The arena was just a few blocks away, so Barkley caught a cab and got to the locker room at the same time as his new teammates. Instead of fining Barkley, Westphal laughed.

Later that season, also in Utah, Westphal coached and Barkley played for the NBA Western All-Star team. With a straight face, he intoned that he would install a strict curfew for the players and put Barkley in charge of enforcement.

When Barkley got into one of his inevitable bar scuffles, Westphal would give him the gentlest of jabs: He'd point to A.C. Green, who ran up and down the court every time as if operating on batteries that never wore down, and say, "A.C. gets his rest at night."

Westphal challenged his superstar only rarely. In the middle of Barkley's second season in Phoenix, with Sir Charles playing lethargically, Westphal benched him at the start of a second half. Barkley grumbled about the move after the game, then let it drop. Westphal knew enough not to try to fool his players with out-of-character Knute Rockne speeches. This was a veteran team that should know the effort required to win.

Along the way, he'd play the role of a pioneer of the unorthodox. At half-time of a home rout over the Clippers, Westphal pronounced, "I don't really have anything to say. You're playing well." He left the locker room. The Suns then turned on their giant TV screen and watched Oprah interview Michael Jackson about his lightening skin pigmentation and other weighty matters.

In the 1993 NBA Finals vs. the Chicago Bulls, the Suns found themselves down, 3-1, in games. They had to win Game 5 in Chicago to send the series back to Phoenix or else watch the Bulls' party begin. Police expected the celebrations to include rioting and looting, so much so that posters were plastered around town urging fans to keep cool. In the Suns locker room before Game 5, Westphal responded by scrawling on a portable blackboard propped up on two folding chairs: "Save the City!" The Suns won the game.

The downside to all this was that Westphal came to be perceived as a less-than-fiery coach. The phrase "laid-back" became attached to him as much as the term "controversial slugger" had once preceded the name Reggie Jackson or "immaculately dressed" now wrapped itself around Pat Riley.

The perception gnawed at him. He knew the public saw a serene figure in interviews and while coaching games. They didn't see him run a more standard ship at practice (with the notable exception of Barkley). Besides, one didn't get to be a three-time, first-team All-NBA performer without competitive fire.

"I think I'm an intense competitor," he said. "But I don't think I'm a madman. I've ripped the team behind closed doors. But I don't like to publicly criticize the team. I think that's the best way of dealing with them. And I think jumping up and down, yelling and screaming at them during the game, is another way of criticizing them publicly.

"I prefer to concentrate on winning the game. That doesn't make me any less a competitor. I think controlling yourself makes you even more effective."

Yet, at least in relation to many other head coaches, it was true. Westphal didn't exactly sit on his hands during games. Indeed, bench coaching—recognizing the subtle shifts in the course of a game, responding with the correct substitutions, devising impromptu plays—was considered by some to be his greatest strength. But the practices were the coach's forum. The games were for the players to decide. This was good enough for Wooden. It would be good enough for him.

His pre-game speech on opening night of the '95-96 season reflected these beliefs. "This league is an unreal existence," he said. "People are international celebrities." Referring to the broken-down contract negotiations between the Charlotte Hornets and Alonzo Mourning, the star center they'd just traded, he said, "Players turn down $10 million-a-year contracts. It's easy to take that stuff too seriously.

"The reason we're here is that at some point we loved playing this game. We loved the competition. Let's not have that taken away from us. The game is the thing. The other stuff is not that important."

In Westphal's mind, the previous season had been unnecessarily sour because too often they'd bow to the community pressure to "win every game by 40 points or else explain what happened," that no matter what they did, they should have done more. This needed to change, he said. Each game should be attacked with enthusiasm. "Embrace the ups and learn from the downs. The bad games should be kept in perspective."

Though the public would be dissatisfied with inartistic wins or anything less than a blowout over an inferior team, he counseled, "This is the NBA. It's tough to get a win. Respect the league. Respect the competition. Every win is a good win."

With this rejoinder ringing in their ears, the Suns came out sharp, passing and shooting the ball crisply, and took a matter-of-fact 32-19 lead.

This much was expected. The Clippers had long been one of the laughingstocks of the NBA, all of sports really. Their owner, Donald Sterling, had spent the better part of a decade trying to make up his mind on plans for a new arena. The Clippers played in south-central Los Angeles; their parking lots were used as a staging area for troops trying to shut down the Rodney King-trial riots. They'd started to play a few regular season games in Anaheim at The Pond. One of them the previous season was against the Suns. Westphal took one look and said, "It's a beautiful building. It's sold out. No wonder they don't move here."

The previous season, the Clippers fielded one of the worst rosters in NBA history, one that many thought would challenge the record for the fewest wins (nine) in history. The veteran coach Bill Fitch was hailed as a genius for somehow coaxing 17 wins out of his woeful team.

Now, the wise guys around the NBA were chuckling at the Clippers' latest major move: trading the No. 2 pick in the entire college draft the past summer to Denver. But, what the "experts" failed to consider was the package the Clippers got in return. Brian Williams and Rodney Rogers were solid inside players who could give solid minutes at two positions. They also got a tall point guard in Brent Barry, a fine passer and a possible future star.

Thus, the Clippers at least had decent talent and depth. But from a perception standpoint, it didn't matter much. The Clippers' reputation was such that losing to them carried one of the worst stigmas in major-league sports.

Depth had been one of the Suns' longtime strong points. So, Westphal was distraught that every time he reached into his bench, the Suns' lead began shrinking immediately. The ball-handling problems of the exhibition season continued. During a key stretch when the Clippers started to take control of the game, the Suns threw it away six times in five minutes (including two turnovers each by Barkley and Johnson).

Then there were a couple of longer-standing troubles. Wayman Tisdale played erratically, forcing Westphal to use Barkley for 40 minutes. And when this happened, Barkley faded down the stretch, failing to score in the fourth quarter.

The small and sleepy crowd came alive. Johnson did everything he could to try to counter, pouring in 39 points. But with Barkley struggling late and nobody else able to do much, the Clippers took advantage, pulling away to a 112-106 win.

Though the Suns reacted stoically to the loss, the pre-season doubts had been confirmed.

"I played terrible; everybody played terrible," Barkley said. "I thought we'd play with more poise down the stretch. But I think we'll be fine. I didn't expect us to go 82-0."

After the Suns' fast start, "We gave them hope," Johnson said. "Then they started getting emotional. Then we weren't playing an average Clipper team. We were playing a good Clipper team."

Westphal chided Barkley for his practice-is-for-mere-mortals theory. "Charles says training camp doesn't mean anything," Westphal said. "But it does. That's how you build up your conditioning. We're so far from being in mid-season form, it's a joke."

The schedule makers had opted to tease, or even torment, the Suns by having them open their home season against the Houston Rockets. Long before those harrowing play-off losses the previous two years (and Houston's two subsequent NBA titles), Westphal had considered them to be the Suns' most dangerous opponent.

They boasted the game's most dominant player (at least during the time Michael Jordan was trying baseball as a career), which is always a nice place to start.

Hakeem Olajuwon had long been one of the game's greats. The NBA's better interior players are able to guard their opponents effectively, one-on-one, or at least be quick enough to slide away from their man to plug the lane and stop a guard's penetration, or else be a shot-blocker who could minimize teammates' mistakes. Olajuwon could do all three.

On offense, he had a shooting range any forward, and even some guards, would envy. Nobody could defend him alone. And when he got the ball in his favored spot, along the left baseline, all anybody could do was simply hope he'd miss his jumper.

In recent years, he had improved his passing and his overall recognition of the game's nuances. Now, he was one of the few players in NBA history (maybe the ONLY player) to be referred to simultaneously as the best offensive and defensive player in the game. At the very least, most everyone was starting to add his name to the traditional Big Three centers in NBA history: Wilt Chamberlain, Bill Russell and Kareem Abdul-Jabbar.

Off the floor, Olajuwon projected a dignified and eloquent spokesman for the game. He spoke several languages, and he often talked of the positive influence of a spiritual reawakening he'd experienced during the middle of his NBA career.

In addition to the game's ultimate weapon, the Rockets also had about a half-dozen players who could knock down a healthy percentage of three-point shots. (The rule change the previous season that shortened the three-point line from 23 feet, 9 inches to 22 feet helped them all the more.) Combined, Houston had the game's best inside-outside balance. They also had the quickness and the fundamental soundness to play defense effectively.

The Rockets seemed so spectacularly well-balanced that Westphal and the Suns were surprised to see them trade Otis Thorpe, their power forward, near the end of the previous season. Thorpe, with his rebounding and defense, had taken the pressure off Olajuwon. (He'd always played Barkley particularly well.) In return, the Rockets got Clyde Drexler, Olajuwon's old college teammate at the University of Houston.

Drexler was a slashing off-guard who'd been a superstar in his prime. Clearly, the Rockets got the better end of the deal in terms of pure talent. But Drexler had been slowed by injuries the past few seasons. Besides, the Rockets had enough scoring punch to win their first title without Drexler. Why lose Thorpe's rebounding, already a team weakness? And why mess with the team's terrific internal balance, the so-called "chemistry" that every coach and general manager seeks?

Yet the trade proved to be a case of tangibles outweighing the intangible. Drexler gave the Rockets a second player, along with Olajuwon, who couldn't be guarded effectively one-on-one. And they still had enough defense, if not rebounding, to get by. They went on to win another title.

Most of all, the Rockets had heart. In the playoffs, they won an astounding eight straight games over two seasons in which a loss would have eliminated them. The Suns could only try to put behind all those blown chances against Houston.

They'd finally seemed to exorcise the Rockets in the second round of the play-offs just six months before. The Suns routed Houston twice in Phoenix, meaning they merely had to win two of the next five games to eliminate the defending NBA champions.

But doubts started surfacing as soon as the players boarded their plane to Houston. Accompanying Barkley was one of his golfing and partying pals. Barkley, knowing the Suns were to play a game on Saturday morning (at 10 a.m. Arizona time) and knowing that all eyes would be on him if he stayed out late, was thought to have gone to his room early the previous night. But he played as if sleepwalking, shooting 0-for-10 (the worst offensive performance of his career). The Suns lost, 118-85.

Then with Barkley playing well early but fading late in Game 4, Kevin Johnson put on a tremendous show. He scored 43 and, with some late defensive work by Schayes, the Suns won in the final minute, 114-110.

Returning to Phoenix for Game 5, the Suns figured to put away the Rockets, especially when Drexler showed up ill and played without effect.

The Suns were convinced this was their time. The certainty of victory was propounded by, of all people, the ever-cautiously speaking A.C. Green. Of the chance for a Rockets' comeback, he said, "It won't happen. We will wind up getting the job done."

Countering this was Olajuwon: "When you think like a loser, even when you are ahead, you are always wondering, looking at the clock, worried about when the other team is going to come back."

Neither team played well, but the Rockets hit just enough of their three-pointers to hang close. They trailed, 77-74, after three quarters. Then the Suns learned from watching TV monitors that the Lakers had beaten the Spurs, extending that series to at least six games. That meant the Suns would have plenty of rest until the Western Conference Finals if they simply could put away the Rockets.

"At this point, I just thought we'd run away with it," Johnson said.

All the while, Barkley continued to miss shots so badly as to suggest his confidence was fading.

The Suns went from cold to freezing. The Rockets plodded ahead, 90-86. Schayes came into the game and hit a layup, then the teams continued to trade misses; Barkley's shots were particularly brutal. The Rockets' Chucky Brown heard this exchange between Barkley and Johnson.

Barkley: "Give me the (expletive) ball!"

Johnson: "The play is so-and-so."

Barkley: "Forget the play. Give me the ball."

Johnson did. Barkley missed.

Once again, Barkley called for the ball.

Johnson: "Are you going to score?"

The ball went to Barkley, who missed again.

Majerle, hitting 29 percent for the series, finally nailed a three-pointer to give the Suns a 91-90 lead. Then the teams exchanged more misses, included two free throws by Barkley that weren't close.

Now, it was down to the final minute, and it was still 91-90 Suns.

Johnson drove the baseline from the right. He might have had a clear path, but he left the ball behind him for Barkley, who wasn't expecting it. The ball sailed out of bounds.

Still, the Suns were in good shape when the Rockets' Mario Elie missed a driving shot and Barkley was fouled on the rebound with 18 seconds left.

Barkley, 0-for-4 from the line at this point, strolled over to the bench and joked with Westphal, "If I miss 'em both, we'll still be up by one." He missed the first. Westphal smiled.

Chirped broadcaster Fitzsimmons, "Paul's a better man than I am. I wouldn't smile. I'd kill him."

Barkley finally hit one. Suns 92, Rockets 90.

The Rockets worked the ball to Olajuwon in the paint. He turned and fired a 12-footer that swished with eight seconds left. Tie game. After a timeout, the Suns elected to inbound the ball under their own basket. Johnson raced up the court and down into the paint. Olajuwon retreated, trying to get himself in position to defend the hoop. Instead of challenging Olajuwon, he spotted Wesley Person open for a three-pointer, angle right. Person got the ball but his shot spun out. Overtime.

The Rockets went on to win, 103-97.

The Suns brain trust came to believe Barkley had been at less than his best because he'd been keeping late hours after the Suns took their commanding series lead. In any case, Barkley had let down his team. He missed

12 of his last 13 shots, and he hit just 1-of-6 from the free-throw line.

"It's my job to make something happen," Barkley said. "I started pressing, and I screwed up."

"The next game can't come soon enough," Johnson said.

Said Olajuwon, "The pressure is on them. They are afraid to lose. We have a winning attitude."

Said Ainge, "We choked."

After the Rockets won in a blowout at home in Game 6 (116-103) to even the series, Barkley talked loudly about how the outcome would take some of the fun out of his trip to a topless bar later on. This was the kind of joke that might wear well during the dreary regular season. But it didn't draw many laughs during the year's most stretch.

Then upon returning to Arizona, where the Suns would prepare for one of the biggest games in franchise history, Barkley announced that, "Basketball isn't all-important to me."

(Because basketball paid the freight for a salary and benefits that allowed him to live in the most-elite circumstances imaginable—Barkley himself estimated he was worth about $20 million—some thought basketball should be all-important, at least during the season.)

At the time, Westphal had a ready response to all this.

"When you shoot from the hip, you don't always hit 100 percent," he said.

On the eve of decisive Game 7, Westphal recalled a story involving Bill Russell and Red Auerbach, the old Boston Celtics' legends.

It seems that Russell, the superstar center, had been given a number of special privileges by the Celtics. Auerbach, the longtime coach, reminded Russell of those benefits when the Celtics visited St. Louis for a big game with the Hawks.

The Hawks were putting on a special promotion in which they mocked Auerbach's habit of lighting a cigar when a Celtics' win was imminent. So, the Hawks prepared to pass out cigars to male fans to celebrate a win.

"Red hated to be embarrassed," said Westphal, himself a former Celtic. "So he told Russell, 'This is the time to pay for all those special privileges. Don't let them light the cigars.'"

And so the Celtics won. The moral of the story: "People don't mind special privileges for players who get the job done."

Barkley entered the locker room only about an hour before tip-off (about 40 minutes past the assigned 11 a.m. arrival time) then walked to the blackboard and erased the ritualistic instructions. He looked around and saw there weren't many players in the room; a few of them were in the pre-game prayer meeting.

Then he wrote, "God only helps those who help themselves. We've got to do it."

In practicing for the game, Westphal stressed the need for the complimentary players to contribute. They couldn't merely wait for Barkley and Johnson to carry them. They had to take the open shots when they had them.

They all knew they had to force the pace. In theory, this strategy would favor the team with more firepower. But the Suns' complimentary players had been disappointing. The only thing that was certain was that Barkley and Johnson would play virtually the entire game. The others would be fighting for minutes.

By contrast, the Rockets knew their roles inside-out, literally and figuratively. Let Olajuwon score on the inside or the left baseline and let everyone else score outside (with an occasional slashing drive by Drexler, Sam Cassell or Robert Horry). They knew seven players would get virtually all the minutes. (Depth isn't as much of a factor in the playoffs when games are seldom played on back-to-back days and timeouts are both longer and more frequent.)

And as long as their own complimentary players were throwing up bricks, the Suns expected the Rockets to continue double-teaming Barkley.

In these cases, "The guys have to make the shots," Barkley said. "They WILL make the shots."

At the same time, the Suns had a tangible disadvantage: Barkley had felt pain in his left knee while running down court in Game 6. He would have to take an anti-inflammatory shot in the posterior before Game 7.

The Suns started the game with the sort of energy they'd displayed in the first two games. Johnson controlled the floor, Barkley the boards. As for the Rockets, they simply couldn't find the range. The Suns led, 51-41, at halftime. But Barkley pulled up lame and took another anti-inflammatory shot at the break.

Then, with nearly 6:00 left in the third quarter, Olajuwon was whistled for his fourth foul. He had to leave with his team trailing, 68-59. The Suns finally were on an even playing field at center. And at long last, the nearly hysterical crowd sensed the Suns finally could put away this longtime nemesis.

But Barkley proceded to throw away the ball, and the Suns' complimentary players struggled.

The Rockets hit a stunning number of shots, 70 percent in the third quarter, many from the most distant locations. They actually pulled into a five-point lead until Johnson and Ainge rescued the Suns.

The game was tied at 110 in the closing seconds, and the Rockets had the ball. Mario Elie, Houston's cagey veteran, sneaked into the left corner. He leaped to prevent a pass to him from going out of bounds. He'd been told not to shoot until three seconds were left. But he was wide open, and with a more-than-respectable 40 percent marksmanship rate from three-point range for the season, who could argue with his thought?

He set his feet and lined up the shot with about 10 seconds left. From his spot under the hoop, Schayes saw what was happening and ran at Elie, hoping to distract him.

Swish!

Elie then blew a kiss to the stunned and disbelieving crowd. It came to be known as "The Kiss of Death." Elie's "biggest shot in my career" would live in infamy among Suns fans, ranking only behind the three-pointer by Chicago's John Paxson that sealed the NBA title two years earlier at nearly the opposite corner of the floor.

The Suns had lost. The privileges hadn't been repaid.

Said Olajuwon, the winner on the floor and in the war of psychology, "Game 5 was the championship game. We knew if we won that game, we would win the series."

The Suns retreated to their silent locker room. Westphal thanked and congratulated his players for their effort. And, true to his never-criticize-the-players-publicly principle, he went on to say he thought the Suns had a "sensational" year.

Sensational?

Kevin Johnson wasn't buying a feel-good cure. He had done his part. He scored a career-high 46 points in Game 7 and passed for 10 assists. Incredibly, despite handling the ball most of the time in a high-speed game, he had just one turnover. But it didn't matter.

"This burns in my belly. This is a scar that will be around for another year," he said. "All the people who predicted we would fold were right. I wouldn't define us as chokers, but the only way you disprove that is to win and advance. We didn't do that.

"I can't take anything away from them. But look at their personnel! There is no way they should beat us, and they beat us four times. Obviously, we think a little more highly of ourselves than we should."

Johnson expected the local press to go easy on the Suns. But he argued,

"How can you let us off the hook after losing this series? There are no excuses." No, there were just regrets.

"We were in control of the series this year and last year," Johnson said. "Something is not right. I thought we learned our lesson last year, but obviously we didn't. I think we underachieved, period."

The Rockets went on to win their second straight NBA title. But despite all their achievements, they weren't recognized by many people for just how good they really were. The Rockets kept the same basic cast for the '95-96 season.

Coach Rudy Tomjanovich had seen "no sign of slippage" from Olajuwon and Drexler. They also boasted two players, forward Horry and playmaker Cassell, who were blossoming into stars. All of this prompted Tomjanovich, the Rockets' gravel-voiced spiritual leader and a playing comtemporary of Westphal, to suggest, "We feel we have a very good chance to be a contender again."

Yes, and Barkley had a very good chance of issuing an opinion any day now.

Even when the Rockets made changes, the job got done. With the trade of Thorpe, Tomjanovich threw into the previous play-off wars a journeyman and CBA refugee named Chucky Brown.

"Who the hell is Chucky Brown?" Barkley had taunted.

Brown, almost predictably, came back to embarrass Barkley at times.

Now, as the Rockets prepared for the Suns' home opener, Brown was doing all he could to instill the impression that Barkley's foot had yet to be removed from his mouth.

"I got a ring and he doesn't," Brown said. "He can say anything he wants. I don't have to listen to that clown."

Brown would have nodded approvingly had he been in the Suns' locker room beforehand to note that Barkley, as usual, was the last to arrive. Players watched videotape of the Rockets on the locker room's giant-screen TV. At the same time, Westphal entertained an old friend, the New York sportswriter Mike Lupica, around the corner in his office. As Barkley passed on his way to his locker, he poked his head into Westphal's office and noticed the TV was tuned to an NFL game. Barkley immediately wanted to know who won a few games played earlier that day and, more importantly, the score. He pulled out a couple of slips of paper and was pleased to know the teams he bet on covered the spread.

As the scores were discussed, Lupica noted the relative success of the NFL's expansion teams, the Carolina Panthers and the Jacksonville Jaguars.

The days of expansion teams taking years just to reach mediocrity were gone, he figured. Talent chases money, and shiny new expansion franchises have plenty of money. "But basketball is different," Barkley pointed out.

He was correct.

Though an NBA team's fortunes could be changed dramatically by the addition of as few as two great players, the demand for them far exceeded the supply. In addition, the NBA had far less free agent movement than the NFL or major league baseball. And the infusion of rookie talent usually meant little, at least in the short run.

Unlike football, where the difference between the top college players and the professionals was more a matter of experience than ability, the top NBA players far exceeded anyone but the most dominant of college players. Quick fixes through the draft were rare. Building a solid team, much less a title contender, took both skill and luck.

Barkley then disappeared to the dressing area of the locker room, where he regularly entertained reporters. He teased the Rockets about their garish new pinstriped uniforms. "They're the two-time defending world champs and they dress them like this!" Barkley said.

Reporters cleared the locker room and coaches' office 45 minutes before tipoff, according to NBA rules. A short time later, Westphal addressed the team.

The idea was that the Suns had a good chance to win as long as they took much better care of the basketball and beat the Rockets in the one area in which they were vulnerable: on the boards.

Of course, the Rockets might have been the first team in basketball history that could be outrebounded consistently . . . and win just as consistently.

On the way to the playing floor, the Suns would pass a few large blue rectangular signs with white lettering, bearing world-wise advice that could be applied to sports. These bromides were commonplace in locker rooms. A football team might daily look at such cheery reinforcement as "The only thing worse than death is losing!"

The advice favored by Westphal generally had a more intellectual flavor. Sometimes the quotations came from the Bible. A new sign this season was a Proverbs/Philippians combo: "A man's pride will bring him low. But a humble spirit will obtain honor. Let each regard one another as more important than himself."

But the sign under the double-door main exit was as secular as they come. The author: Bill Russell, the legendary Celtics center, who said,

"The game is scheduled. We have to play it. We might as well win."

For three quarters, the Suns followed their plan.

They led, 52-51, at the half and, 83-82, after three quarters despite a huge Rockets advantage in shooting percentage.

The teams were tied at 97 with a little more than 2:00 left when Houston's Robert Horry, who'd been struggling, nailed a three-pointer from the right corner. That was enough to seal the outcome.

It was the classic Rockets' characteristic. No matter who happened to be hot or cold, everyone had a role, and everyone had the confidence to take a big shot. And, to a remarkable degree, they made them.

Johnson would marvel at this later. "People don't understand how important chemistry is," he said. "It makes the games so much easier. Everyone knows their roles. You don't have guys trying to do things they can't do. You don't have guys complaining. You can tell they've got it." Tomjanovich agreed: "Because we've been in a lot of tight games . . . and elimination games . . . you learn to believe in your teammates and you really rely on them. I think that's what helped us win."

Overall, the Suns played much better than in their Opening Night flop. They had indeed outrebounded the Rockets by 15. But the Rockets outshot the Suns, 53-44 percent, and won, 106-104.

"We've still got to make shots," Westphal said.

The Suns had started the season 0-2 for the first time since 1988-89 when they'd just added a 22-year-old point guard named Kevin Johnson to direct the attack.

This startling development prompted Barkley to try to dissuade any panic attacks by Suns fans, lest any mobs come looking for them or their coach: "I know everyone is ready to burn down the arena, but . . . I don't think we'll kill ourselves. Nothing in life is easy. It's a long season. You can go from sugar to (expletive) in a hurry, and you can go from (expletive) to sugar in a hurry. We've got a great coach, probably the best in the league. And we've got a great team."

Then, he backed down from his practice-is-meaningless theory, saying, "You can't throw a team together for one week and set the world on fire. I wish people wouldn't panic. We'll be fine in the long run. Give us some time."

On to New York. Immediately after arriving in the Big Apple, Westphal was set to dine with a pal who does a talk-radio show out of the city. Hint: He's a heavy-set fellow, has got an unusual first name, and his politics lean heavily right of center.

The bombastic Rush Limbaugh didn't—on the surface—seem to have much in common with the mild-mannered Westphal. The Suns coach wasn't even a Republican. He registered independent because, "I'm not big on joining groups."

The Westphal-Limbaugh relationship started in 1991 when Westphal was in his last year as a Suns assistant coach. "A friend of mine told me that there was a guy on the radio I'd really get a kick out of," Westphal said. "And I did. I thought he was hilarious."

Then Lupica, Westphal's sportswriter pal, learned of his fondness for Limbaugh. When Lupica spotted Limbaugh in the press box at a Giants' football game, he called Westphal and put the Big Dittohead on the line. They hit it off and kept in contact. The relationship carried inherent dangers. Westphal had become identified with someone who talks constantly to a huge audience. If Limbaugh said something Jesse Helms-ish in its outrageousness, his coach-friend might pay a public-relations price.

"He speaks for himself," Westphal argued. "I don't agree with him on everything or feel that I'm accountable for what he says. I'm not that political. I happen to think the guy is very, very funny. People in general need to lighten up and laugh a little."

Then too, there was the possibility of the Suns being perceived as a partisan political team, that Democrats need not feel welcome. Westphal hadn't considered the possibility.

"We don't have a Young Republicans Club on our team. I don't think about the politics of our team. We're just here to play basketball." (Maybe so, but when visiting Phoenix for the Finals in '93, Limbaugh didn't miss a chance to give the Suns some advice. He suggested—jokingly?—the Suns run their entire offense from the right side of the basket.)

Barkley prepared for the Knicks game in his unique way. Recognizing New York remained the nation's most influential media market, he brought his "A" comic material to the game. (The next night in Boston, he would don a subdued "senior statesman" role, repeating a portion of Westphal's Opening Night theme of denouncing the big-business aspect of sports and emphasizing that "The Game" was more important than money or any individual.)

Barkley got off the bus, took the elevator in Madison Square Garden up to the playing-floor level, and found his way to the locker room. There, about a dozen reporters awaited him. He walked in, looked around and shouted, approvingly, "Oh (expletive), they finally cleaned up this pigsty!" A dramatic pause followed, then, "Now all they need here is a team." (This was just a joke, he later told reporters who—looking for a story and perhaps a World War III-sized tabloid headline—wanted him to expand on this point.)

"I couldn't live here," he told the assembled group. "I can't drive fast enough."

Asked about salaries now escalating to seven figures per season, he said, "I'm mad at my mother for having sex so soon. If she had held out for a few years, I could be making big money."

Q: What about the Suns' chances once Manning comes back?

A: Once we get healthy, some people will have hell to pay. There are six or seven legitimate contenders. We're one of them.

Q: What about the Knicks? What about the idea that their time has come and gone, that if they were going to win it, they would have done it by now?

A: I don't buy anything you guys say. I'm not like the general public. I got a brain.

Q: You talk to Patrick? Is he happy?

A: Patrick's always happy. He's making $18 million. How can he not be happy?

Q: Money doesn't buy happiness.

A: That would buy my happiness.

Q: You still thinking about running for governor?

A: That's always in the plans. I'll think about that when I stop running up and down the floor.

Even after the scribes had put down their pens, Barkley continued to talk.

NORMALLY ABOUT AN HOUR before each game, a staff member of the home team will inform the coaches of the other team's starting lineups and the identify of the referees.

Coaches generally know their opponent's starting lineup. But the names of the refs are a mystery; their revelation constitutes food for thought. The better officials could be counted on for consistency; the weaker ones not only lacked this crucial trait, but they could be intimidated by the crowd.

But this ritual was of no interest to Westphal early this season; he would waive away the person about to tell him the refs' names. They meant nothing to him. Because of a labor dispute between the NBA and the union representing the referees, the regular refs had been locked out.

In their place, the league employed officials who mostly had worked in the Continental Basketball Association, the NBA's developmental league. At best, their judgments often mystified players and coaches, many of whom continually questioned the new refs' credibility. At worst, their decisions reflected an ignorance of the rules themselves. Said Barkley, referring to his oldest antagonist among the regular refs (who also happened to be their union leader), "I want Mike Mathis back." Worst of all, the replacement referees were working games only in pairs because the NBA deemed there weren't enough trained to field the standard three-man crews. In the Suns-Knicks game, one of the replacement refs called goaltending when Michael Finley leaped to grab an air ball that was about two feet short. The Suns went wild and eventually the official walked over to the Phoenix bench and said, "I blew it."

The same ref waived off a three-pointer by Wesley Person, judging that the shot clock had expired. Trouble was, there was clearly a full second left when Person shot it. The buzzer sounded when the ball nearly was swishing through the net. This time, however, the ref gave no admission of guilt.

Another time, Barkley scored on a driving layup and was fouled. The refs gave Barkley two shots, even though they disallowed the basket and the Suns weren't in the bonus. (In this situation, the basket should count with Barkley getting one free throw, or else the shot doesn't count and the Suns get the ball without taking a free throw.) Barkley pointed this out, "But I never got an explanation."

While this was going on, Westphal walked toward the end of the bench and wondered aloud, "Where is Rod Serling?"

(But as the labor dispute wore on, the replacement officials gained more knowledge and confidence. In a close win by the Suns over the Hawks, the new refs whistled five traveling calls on Barkley. He was outraged, figuring his superstar status and the fact that fans don't pay $40 a ticket to watch refs call traveling should eliminate such pedestrian offenses. A couple of times, however, Barkley spun his wheels enough for ANYBODY to be whistled. "I've been doing this for 12 years!" he told one ref. "What makes you think you can call traveling?" But he did, just the same.)

At that point, Barkley wished more than ever for the regular refs' return. He scratched his head at their rejection of the NBA's offer of a contract that would have salaries range from about $75,000 for starting refs to more than $200,000 for the most experienced, plus an annual raise of about 10 percent. "That looked pretty good to me," he said.

(Eventually, the refs—by a one-vote margin—agreed with him.)

The Suns-Knicks game was a marquee matchup, one that would be seen on national cable TV. The flamboyant, high-scoring Suns were, if nothing else, a made-for-TV production. They would appear this season on NBC eight times and on TNT and TBS a combined 11 times.

As for the Knicks, they'd won 172 regular-season games over the previous three seasons, second only to the Suns themselves with 177. Yet heading into the season, the media spin was that the Knicks—far more so than the Suns—were tired, old and declining while trying to get used to a new coach to boot.

Don Nelson, who had played and coached in the NBA for more than 30 years, was trying to diversify the plodding offense the Knicks used under Pat Riley while maintaining the tight defense. But Knick-bashing had become so in vogue during the off-season that even the Knicks were bashing the Knicks. Superstar center Patrick Ewing openly questioned whether they had enough outside shooting to compete for the title. But which team had gotten off to a better start? The Knicks, who were 2-0.

Said Barkley, "I think they're more dangerous this year than any year because people are counting them out."

Said Westphal, "Riley's a great coach but so is Don Nelson. He's not going to wreck a team that wins 60 games a season. They had good players. They still have good players."

This view was borne out in the first three quarters when the Suns futilely chased the Knicks. By the time the fourth quarter started, the Knicks enjoyed an 80-70 lead. But Anthony Mason, probably the Knicks' best all-round player outside of Ewing, was tossed out for challenging the referees. ("He can't put himself in that situation," Barkley would say later. "He's too valuable. I've done it sometimes. It's stupid.")

In part because of Mason's absence, the Knicks had to shuffle their players around. Instead of going with Charles Smith, one of their regulars, to relive Ewing, they turned to Herb Williams, a veteran in the waning days of his career.

The Suns were struggling at center, as they had been for much of the franchise's 27-year history. Williams was expected to at least minimize the problems, but he had been playing tentatively at both ends of the floor.

Williams' back, injured in an August car accident in Cleveland, was coming around ever so slowly even with daily exercise and therapy. All of this was messing with his mind. Against the Knicks, he was missing so badly that they left him wide open. He still couldn't convert his shots, leaving the Suns in a four-on-five posture when he was in the game.

So, the Suns turned to Tisdale, the reluctant warrior, when defending centers. The Knicks were double-teamming other players, leaving Tisdale open, and suddenly Tisdale started scoring. As the Knicks continued this tactic, apparently against the wishes of Nelson who appeared to be pulling out his hair on the sideline, Tisdale continued to connect. He played well—even on defense and when Ewing was in the game!

The Knicks also hurt themselves by missing 15 of 31 free throws and failing to solve a trapping Suns defense.

Phoenix finally took the lead on a three-pointer by Perry. Then A.C. Green hit a wild, running layup to cap a 20-6 Suns' run and give them a 90-86 lead.

The Knicks managed to tie it at 90, but Barkley hit a reverse layup, then Finley leaped high to slam home an offensive rebound. After a driving shot by John Starks made it 94-92, Barkley converted a three-point play on another reverse. The Suns had their first win of the season in hand. They outscored the Knicks 32-14 in the fourth quarter for a 102-94 win.

The fans at Madison Square Garden were stunned at the quick turnaround. The pressure, for one night at least, was off.

"We expect to be good," Westphal said. "It would take more than three losses to change that. But it's always nice to validate your opinions with a win, especially against a good team like the Knicks."

"This was huge," Barkley pronounced. And seeming to have reversed course on his beliefs about practice, he noted the Suns had only three hard practices and three games when they'd all been together. "People ought to watch out for us by the end of the month. I think it's scary how good we can be."

The next night in Boston, they faced the Celtics, a team with such dim prospects that their owner had just pronounced, "I think we all know we stink." The Suns spurted to a quick lead, but their defense couldn't hold up. Neither could Johnson, who twisted a knee dribbling all by himself and had to come out (he missed the next four games). The Suns lost. With their record at 1-3, the only resemblence to their recent great teams was the uniform.

N·O·T·E·W·O·R·T·H·Y

NOV. 3, LOS ANGELES

Wayman Tisdale, who released a highly regarded jazz album over the summer, notes in the locker room that the TV program "Lifestyles of the Rich and Famous" is putting together a segment on him.

Replies Barkley, "Even I haven't been on 'Lifestyles.'"

Yet it's not for lack of credentials. He reveals his standard requirement for appearing in a TV commercial: All shooting should be done in one day, with Barkley pulling down a $1-million fee.

Barkley also picks Riddick Bowe to win the next night's big fight vs. Evander Holyfield in Las Vegas. He isn't flying to Las Vegas to attend, however, because the Suns host Houston the night after the fight and he doesn't want to be questioned about his priorities.

Westphal is neutral. "I hate boxing," he says.

His reasoning: "First of all, it's pretty corrupt. And I don't like any sport where the idea is to really hurt somebody. We should be too civilized for it, I'd like to think."

NOV. 8, BOSTON

Talking to a young fan in the locker room, Sir Charles says, "How are you doing in school? The world has enough dumb people. You ever been to Arkansas? There's a whole state of them there."

NOV. 10, TORONTO

On a night with NHL competition, attendance was announced at 25,207. Thousands of fans were seated in the cheap seats hundreds of feet away in the upper deck of the SkyDome.

"If there is a way to make an assembly of 25,000 people invisible, the SkyDome's basketball venue has achieved it," writes the Toronto Sun's Ken Fidlin. "From the floor, the people seated on the 500 level are like wolves circling the campfire, a vague presence just beyond the perimeter of light."

Says Barkley, "I'm glad people came to see me play. I like Toronto. It's unfortunate we only play here once a year."

Just WHY Barkley likes Toronto becomes clear a moment later when he mentions the bar he'll visit afterward. He's going to meet several members of the Buffalo Bills who made the 100-mile trip to Toronto. "But that's a strip joint!" says an incredulous TV reporter. Barkley seems surprised by this response.

"Hey, I'm old enough to go," he says.

Nov. 15, Phoenix

Before the Suns hosted the Nuggets, Barkley greeted his buddy and ex-teammate Danny Ainge, now a broadcaster for TNT and TBS.

"How could you sell out and become one of 'them'?" Barkley asked.

"Huh?" says Ainge.

"You're a reporter," Barkley says. "You now serve no useful purpose except to try to (expletive) successful people."

"I love it," replies Ainge.

4

Party time, troubled times

BARKLEY HAD NOT BEEN ABLE to carry the Suns through difficult times because he'd played erratically himself. He'd been slow to work into shape after knee surgery and still was trying to find his legs.

So, in a home game against the Lakers, Westphal devised a way to get him going. The idea was to run their "elbow" play, with Barkley getting the ball near the free-throw line, then attacking the hoop with one or two dribbles.

Barkley, normally a solid ball handler (that he could both start and finish a fast break made him unique among power players), was leading the team in turnovers by a wide margin. Then too, he was feeling sluggish. Players who do not feel in top form tend to take the easy approach, casting perimeter shots rather than taking the grittier route to the basket.

This wouldn't have been a problem had not Barkley been such a poor perimeter shooter. His three-point shooting was particularly disastrous; his 23-percent accuracy against the Rockets was one of the biggest factors in the Suns blowing their 3-1 series lead the past spring. This pattern had been long established. Though his marksmanship seldom was detailed—a practical benefit of his skilled media relations—Barkley actually had the poorest percentage among all players with at least 1,000 attempts since the NBA adopted the three-point shot in 1979.

Making matters worse, when he threw up one of his errant shots, Barkley—one of the greatest rebounders ever to play the game—wasn't in position to hit the boards. Sometimes the result not only was a zero for the Suns, but a long rebound that triggered a fast break for the opponent. All in all, this was a self-defeating strategy.

Some of the veteran players had objected to Barkley getting away with it for some time. On occasion Danny Ainge, seeing Barkley about to hoist a three-pointer, would turn to teammates on the bench and say, "Here comes another turnover." (Indeed, the effect was the same).

But Westphal figured Barkley would ignore any coaching edicts. So he had to figure out another approach. The elbow play would maximize Barkley's strengths and minimize his weaknesses. So seconds into the game, Barkley got the ball in the desired spot, drove to the hoop, and got two free throws. And then. . . .

. . . Nothing.

Barkley had no energy. He didn't take the ball to the hoop, he didn't rebound. He simply disappeared. In a rare move indeed, Westphal made him the subject of the night's first substitution. It was as if he knew Barkley wouldn't have it this night.

And, in fact, he did know.

Barkley, accompanied by the same pal he'd brought to Houston the past spring, had spent the previous evening gambling in Las Vegas. He flew home in time to make the shoot-around for the Lakers' game, then tried to catch some sleep before the game. Barkley played as poorly as he ever had for the Suns. Until the closing minute, he had more turnovers than rebounds. And the rest of the Suns, as they so often did, took their cue from Barkley, playing with little energy or effectiveness. They appeared to be one of those lottery teams that Barkley and the Suns so often struggled to take seriously, a team that needed a hot streak just to have a chance to win at home.

The Lakers had this one wrapped up. They led by nine with 57 seconds to go. If the Suns didn't score on the next possession, Westphal might as well clear the bench. To win in these circumstances required a team to play extremely well and to get extremely lucky.

Then Johnson hit a three-pointer.

So did Finley.

And, as the Lakers misfired, Barkley defied the odds by hitting a three-pointer of his own. Still, the Lakers had the ball and a one-point lead in the closing 15 seconds. As the Lakers broke their huddle, play-maker Nick Van Exel forgot to check how many time-outs his team had left.

So Van Exel, trapped on the right side about 35 feet out, tried to cover the ball instead of calling for time. Barkley tied him up with 6.7 seconds left. The tip went to A.C. Green, who whipped it to Finley, who drove to the free-throw line.

Finley HAD checked the clock, giving him an idea of how much time he had left. He pulled up calmly and nailed a jumper at the final buzzer to win it.

The Suns celebrated as if they'd won the NBA title.

"The most amazing final minute I've ever seen," said Westphal, who'd played or coached in the NBA for 20 years. For a few moments at least, Barkley's wandering attention to his duties could be smoothed over.

Sitting in the locker room, Barkley apologized to his teammates for his poor performance (though not for the Vegas trip itself). Then after reporters, who didn't know about the all-night adventure yet, cleared out, Barkley sipped a beer and made light of it all: "The moral of the story is don't go to Vegas and gamble the night before a big game. I would have felt bad spending all the money I'd won if we'd lost."

Yes, it WAS a big game.

Certainly, there never was any question of the importance of a game with the Lakers from a Suns' perspective. Until the Rockets' emergence the past couple of seasons, the Lakers seemed to be at the root of every circumstance in which the Suns came up short. The Lakers won championships. The Suns always seemed to finish second to them. The Lakers always seemed to have a great center. The Suns never did.

In the mid-1970s, the Suns even successfully arranged to move out of the Midwest Division, where the Milwaukee Bucks' Kareem Abdul-Jabbar ruled, to the Pacific. Alas, Abdul-Jabbar followed them there when the Lakers picked him up in one of the biggest trades in NBA history. There, joined by Magic Johnson, he terrorized the Suns for more than a decade.

There was more than enough tradition here for the rivalry to hold.

Now, Westphal was in a tough spot. He'd given Barkley as much rope as he needed or wanted over the past three-plus seasons. In return, he now seemed like he would be hanged by it. His credibility in the way he handled Barkley was in a crisis. He had to address the situation.

When the team next gathered, in preparation for a game against the Utah Jazz, Westphal finally let Barkley have it, saying, "If you don't think you can do what's right, you should go ahead and retire." Barkley responded with a show of halfhearted defiance, saying, "If things were going great, you wouldn't be saying anything."

The issue of whether the team was undisciplined was a long-running one. But like politely avoiding talk about the emperor's choice of clothes, it was easier for fans and media members to debate whether Westphal was enforcing discipline than to talk about whether Barkley possessed it.

This wasn't the usual coach-player relationship. Or the usual coach-superstar relationship. Or even a merely unusual one.

Everyone knew that Barkley's voice was the loudest. He was the mar-quee attraction. As Barkley himself said, "They've got my picture here everywhere." The value of the franchise had been pegged as the fastest growing in all of sports, roughly doubling to $190 million in the Barkley years. (Most all of this would have happened anyway. The arena was built and sold out before Barkley's arrival. Yet it was also true that the presence of "Sir Charles" helped ensure the good times, in terms of tick-et sales, ad revenues, pay-per-view revenue, etc., would continue to roll.)

Westphal knew the coach had to get along with Barkley. He'd once said that the head coach and marquee player needed to be allies; or at least they couldn't be enemies. "Otherwise, one of them probably has to leave," he said. And he knew which one that would be. If he needed direct evidence, he merely had to look at what happened the previous sea-son with the Golden State Warriors. Don Nelson, one of the winningest coaches in NBA history, was deemed too negative in his approach by Chris Webber, supposedly the franchise player. The differences weren't completely patched. Then the Warriors traded Webber in one of a series of ruinous moves, and Nelson himself soon was dispatched.

For Westphal, giving freedom to Barkley didn't equate to a cave-in, based on his own history. He had, after all, been quick to detect dictato-rial tendencies in his own coaches. But he was paying a price with others who wanted to at least hear Westphal TRY to pull the reins on Barkley for the good of the team, even if the practical effect was minimal.

The one person who had the best chance to keep Barkley in check was Colangelo, the club president. But Fitzsimmons, because he'd known Barkley longer and better than anyone else in the Suns organization, vol-unteered early for the role of front-office conduit. Indeed, he sometimes acted effectively as a sort of rodeo cowboy, roping in the wild steer. In 1994, when Barkley bolted from his physical rehabilitation program, the one designed to save his career, it was Fitzsimmons who was sent across country to track him down and persuade him to get with the program. In the end, the program got with Barkley. The Suns' physical conditioning expert, Robin Pound, followed him around the country that summer, making sure he did his exercises.

But Fitzsimmons, by design, wasn't around the team a great deal. Because he had been Westphal's predecessor, he didn't want to seem to be intruding. Besides, he genuinely enjoyed his role of broadcaster and dab-bling in anything else Colangelo needed.

Colangelo was reticent to get involved. In his view, the coach was paid to work out these matters. There had been a few exceptions. The most notable came after the season-ending party in '94. Barkley's relaxed standards for his life had been a source of worry for Colangelo and others who were concerned about the franchise's good name. So, Colangelo addressed the issue of staining the organization. This was one rule Barkley couldn't break. "I want you to be a leader on and off the floor," Colangelo told him.

Barkley's Vegas gambit brought the issue back into focus for the team. Johnson had seen the act before.

"I don't even want to know about it," he said after reports of Barkley's trip began to surface.

If Charles Barkley was the class clown, Kevin Johnson was the student body president. He was an earnest man who forever pondered doing the right thing and—when things went wrong—wondered what could have been done differently. Johnson also was nearly as strong-willed as Barkley and wasn't afraid to express himself.

The Suns were immediately transformed into Barkley's team after the big trade. Thus, the relationship between Barkley and Johnson always had the potential for sparks. Initially, Johnson accepted the fact that Barkley, when healthy, was the greater player. And he genuinely admired the way Barkley rode his celebrity with good humor.

But the more he got to know Barkley, the harder time he had understanding Barkley's jack-in-the-box-like focus on the task at hand, especially with the Suns so close to winning a title. In addition to his reluctance to work enough to stay in top shape, Barkley had a maddening tendency to turn his jets on and off (particularly against the lesser teams). The rest of the team—Johnson included—followed, brilliant and focused one night and lethargic the next. Barkley's attempt to place the game in "perspective" by saying, "Win or lose, I'll be playing golf," didn't go over with Johnson. He knew he didn't have many more chances to win a title. Now it was an all-consuming goal.

Johnson accepted Barkley as a teammate. Yet Johnson went his own way, keeping both a private world and a high-profile public one. In fact, he didn't seem close to any of the other Suns except for A.C. Green, with whom he shared common interests. For along with Green, Johnson was one of the sports world's best-known Christians.

He helped stage prayer meetings before games in every NBA arena, no matter the accommodations. In Chicago during the NBA Finals, he once gathered to pray with longtime teammate Mark West in a filthy space used as a locker room by janitors and as a bathroom by journalists wandering the bowels of old Chicago Stadium. (Their prayers came minutes after one janitor asked another, "You ever killed someone?" "Well, er, no," said the other.)

He carried the social Gospel to his old inner-city neighborhood in Sacramento where he set up St. Hope Academy as a learning and recreational center for disadvantaged kids. He won the NBA's citizenship award. He was one of the few sports figures to be named one of President Bush's "1,000 points of light," a program to honor voluntarism.

He had an optimistic view of the world, perhaps because of his unusual upbringing. Johnson was raised mostly by his grandparents, one white, one black. He learned to mingle easily in both worlds. He tried to see the bright side in everyone, from controversial political figures such as Clarence Thomas, to reclusive teammates such as Jerrod Mustaf. (He was one of the few players to try to get to know Mustaf.)

Unlike Barkley, Johnson followed politics closely. When a Democratic U.S. senator, though conservative, switched parties, he said, "What do you mean it's no big deal? There are only 100 seats!" Johnson also had more of a consistent political philosophy. He believed the principle of "good works" applied to secular matters.

That he kept his head in the Bible—and in the newspapers—didn't mean he couldn't keep an eye on Hollywood. The limelight appealed to him almost as much as to Barkley. He felt at home in Tinseltown and became a regular guest on such shows as Arsenio Hall.

Like Barkley, he entertained reporters at length. His answers generally were less entertaining, but often more thoughtful than Barkley's. Notably, while he would talk for as long as needed after games, he shunned interviews before games, lest he be distracted.

Around Phoenix, Johnson became as much a part of the landscape as Camelback Mountain. There he is at a hospital, visiting a kid mauled by a pit bull.

There he is hosting a fund-raising reception for the United Negro College Fund.

There he is at the Urban League's big annual fund-raising dinner, mingling with politicians, business executives and high-society types while serving as master of ceremonies. He trades jokes with the youthful mayor, who, like Johnson, doesn't look old enough to vote. He refers to a recent bout with chicken pox, then tells the mayor, "You don't look old enough to have had it either."

The line gets the desired laugh. He sends the crowd home content and lighter in the wallet.

For all this, the public—though appreciating his skills and his good works—never completely embraced him. His superstar status never got the Suns a title. And he was injury prone. He was viewed as the key player on a very good, but not great, basketball team.

Johnson's real constituency was the kids. Perhaps because he resembled a 20-something Beaver Cleaver, the "KJ" persona was kid-friendly. As soon as he first became prominent in Phoenix, children began bombarding the Suns' office, asking to have their messages passed to Johnson. After a while, Johnson hired a full-time secretary to handle his correspondence.

His public appearances at shopping malls took on the trappings of a touring president or pope, with parents holding their children on their shoulders to get a glimpse. For one such outing, the crowd started lining up at 10 a.m. for KJ's appearance at 4 p.m. By the time he arrived, the crowd had swelled to about 2,000, mostly teenagers and young kids, inside and outside a department store. He arrived in a limo to squeals of "HE'S HERE!"

One father, who had shown up to shop, was bewildered by the commotion. He turned to mom, and said, "Must be some sort of rock star."

"Nope," she replied, "it's just KJ."

As Johnson furiously signed autographs, the crowd had to be restrained by store security guards, city police officers, county sheriff's deputies, and even a dog from the sheriff's canine unit.

But even with all the affection, adulation, awards and honors, Johnson had grown bored with the "St. Kevin " image. The result was he began developing a much harder edge on the floor.

The roots of this evolution could be traced to the Barkley trade when the team's leadership passed away from Johnson. The change was all the more evident because Johnson sat out the start of Barkley's first season in Phoenix with injuries. Despite Johnson's absence, the Suns were winning. This in turn led to talk by some casual fans that he—not Jeff Hornacek—should have been traded to acquire Barkley. Johnson even was beaten out by Hornacek (who Johnson liked and admired) in a newspaper-sponsored fans' vote for the Suns' all-time team. Notably, all the players favored by the fans were white, except Barkley, who had just joined the team.

In addition, Johnson became increasingly incensed over his omission from American teams that competed in international play. He was beaten out by Utah's John Stockton for a spot on the 1992 Dream Team that competed in the Barcelona Olympics. Johnson privately considered himself the superior point guard; he usually outplayed Stockton head to head. But the opposite was true in '91 when the Jazz whipped the Suns in the play-offs. So, he didn't protest his omission too loudly.

But in the next go-round, the selection for Dream Team II, Johnson couldn't understand the selections of Mark Price and Tim Hardaway, fine talents but still players he regularly outplayed and outpolled in the all-NBA balloting. And when basketball officials named Isiah Thomas, whose superstar skills had long since faded, as a replacement for the injured Hardaway, he was outraged. "It's a joke," he said.

Johnson began having occasional nasty exchanges with opponents. Once, he scuffled in practice with a teammate, journeyman Tim Kempton. Another time at a home game, he actually gave the one-fingered salute to a fan who merely advised him to "Get with it!"

"I don't believe in winning by any means necessary," he said. "But there was a time when guys fell, I would pick them up." Indeed, there was a time when he even confessed to a ref that he, not the opponent, knocked the ball out of bounds. "But not any more."

This edginess helped the Suns, who had long needed all the toughness they could muster. But it came at a steep public-image cost for Johnson. Talk could be heard around the league, though rarely expressed in public, that he was a whiner and a phony.

He got to the point of toying with his image. He once appeared in a spoof video for a charity event in which he created his alter ego. This character wore shades and baggy clothes. He talked in slang, the kind of guy who might hang around on the streets waiting for his beeper to go off. This was his evil twin, Mevin Johnson.

It was all for laughs, but it got him thinking. Maybe having a split-personality could have practical applications. So, sometimes when he was out in public and people greeted him as KJ, he replied, "No, I'm Mevin. But people say we look a lot alike." Mevin wouldn't help his image, but maybe if he dragged him out on the floor every now and then, the Suns would win more games.

All this came to a head during the week before the Knicks visited the Suns in March 1993. The game matched the teams with the NBA's best records. The Suns were thought to have more talented players, but could they withstand the punishing, physical play of the Knicks, who reveled in their "tough town, tough team" image?

The Knicks yapped their jaws early in a display of the distasteful practice of taunting known as "trash talking." Johnson responded by throwing a blind-side body block on the Knicks' Doc Rivers. "A pick," Johnson called it. The trouble with this explanation was that a pick, or a screen, is an offensive maneuver. The Knicks had the ball at the time.

Rivers chased Johnson down the floor and a predictable melee ensued. Just as things started to calm, a man in street clothes leaped off the Knicks' bench and slugged an unsuspecting Johnson. Only a few observers knew the assailant was the Knicks' Greg Anthony, sitting out the game with an injury. Had the crowd not been better mannered than the players, the worst scenario imaginable could have unfolded: an all-out riot.

A dozen players piled up at midcourt. Fists flew as Barkley tried unsuccessfully to act as peacemaker. Pat Riley risked damage to one of his impeccable suits as he pulled players off the pile. Ejections, fines and suspensions set NBA records.

Johnson took a fair share of the heat. A substantial number of people enjoyed seeing his public image swimming upstream for the first time.

Making matters worse, he flamed out in the first two games in the NBA Finals that same season, both losses at home against the Bulls. In Game 2, fans booed him off the floor. Then, as the series moved to Chicago, Westphal made a strategic switch. He assigned Johnson, instead of Dan Majerle, to guard Michael Jordan. Jordan chuckled at the move, not realizing Johnson had transformed himself into the team's most consistent defender. Thus Jordan's points came with a bit more difficulty, and the Suns broke through for a 129-121 win in an historic triple-overtime thriller.

When the Suns, improbably, won two of three games in the old Chicago Stadium to force the series back to Phoenix (the only loss came when Westphal switched back to Majerle on Jordan and His Airness scored 55), the apologetic Suns crowd greeted Johnson with an emotional standing ovation.

Then, for two straight years against the Rockets, he established himself as the team's most productive player during the play-offs' most crucial time. His shortcomings, real or imagined, were forgiven. Once again, he was the athlete-humanitarian. In some people's minds, he once again was the team's key player, even more than Barkley.

Finally, Johnson had the clout to try to iron out the team's flaws. He shared the consensus view among fans that the team was too soft, that it lacked a killer instinct. In addition to Barkley's on-and-off intensity (and the coaches' and management's toleration of it), he believed the problems he perceived were caused in part by all the adoration the Suns received locally, including from the media. In fact, he might have been one of the first athletes in history to scold the press for writing flattering things about his own team.

"I get tired of reading all the flowery, nice stuff you guys write about us.

"I can read. I've been here six years, and I travel all around the country. I have something to compare it to. In other cities, like Chicago, Boston and Philadelphia, their writers are hard. That doesn't mean you have to beat a dead horse. But if we play bad, you guys ought to rip us. I'd like an honest perspective. If I'm not playing well, you should write it."

He also was prepared to reassert himself on the floor whenever necessary. That was clear enough in the '95-96 season-opener when—with his teammates misfiring—he took the ball to the hoop like in the old days and poured in 39 points. Then he suffered the tendon injury to his left knee the next week in Boston and, once again, his chance to take charge had slipped away.

Back in Phoenix, he sat in front of his locker, fired a towel into the carpet and said, "I need to set the tone!"

In his first game back, at home against the Portland Trail Blazers, he did. Emerson, the Suns' chief doctor, advised Johnson to play only six minutes per quarter. Then the Suns began throwing the ball away. Johnson entered with the Trail Blazers leading, 23-17, and the Suns having six turnovers. He dominated the floor and pulled the Suns to a lead, causing Westphal to tell him, "Go talk to the doctor." Emerson gave his OK, Johnson continued to play, and the Suns had a hard-earned win.

He had a similarly dominant game at home against Minnesota, leading the Suns to a narrow win. The next night in San Antonio, Johnson felt tightness in his hamstring and groin before the game. He struggled to stay with the Spurs' Avery Johnson, shot 0-for-6, had four turnovers, then suggested to Westphal that he turn to Perry and reserve Tony Smith.

Games on two straight nights ("back-to-backs" in NBA jargon) were always a dangerous adventure for him. The Suns' doctors discussed with Johnson the prospect of only playing in one game when the Suns played on consecutive nights. "But my theory is to play in the first one," he said, and then hope for the best.

In a mid-December game, he leaped at midcourt to steal a pass just seconds before the halftime horn, badly hurting the ever-fragile muscles in his upper left leg. He limped through the rest of the game, then disappeared from the playing scene for more than a month.

At 29 years old, he seemed to be going on 49.

THE SUNS HOPED TO USE the miracle against the Lakers to jump-start their sagging fortunes. The first chance to do so came at home against another Western rival, the Utah Jazz. Every year, the pundits came with their shovels and Bibles, pronouncing the Jazz deceased and wishing their spirits well. Yet every year, the Jazz persevered, showing little sign of fading from the contenders' list. The Jazz featured the Suns' superstar counterparts, Karl Malone opposite Barkley and John Stockton going against Johnson. The Suns' leaders usually got the better of the head-to-head competition. More importantly, the Suns in the past usually had fared better in the play-offs when the Jazz' opponents could concentrate mostly on Stockton and Malone without much fear of getting beaten by their so-so complimentary cast.

Still, Malone and Stockton, unlike Barkley and Johnson, were superstars who could be counted on every single game. They'd missed only four games apiece over a combined 1,750 games spanning more than a decade. Said Jazz coach Jerry Sloan, "I know some day it will be tough for them to carry the load. But that day hasn't come yet.

"Those two guys work harder off the floor than anyone in the league. And every year, they come into camp in better shape than the rookies we bring in.

"They do what they get paid for. They don't think people should spend $200 for courtside seats to watch them work themselves into shape."

The teams played on even terms through the first half, but after the break, the Jazz pulled away to a victory. The Suns now were 6-6.

At center, Williams was outplayed by Utah journeyman Greg Foster and relic Antoine Carr, who shoved his ample gut into the lane and made four easy baskets as the Jazz spurted ahead for good. The Jazz were so superior in every area that a mini-debate ensued. Which was worse: the Suns' offense or their defense?

"I think our offense is struggling now," Barkley said. "It's hard to shoot 40 percent and win." Johnson took the opposing view, arguing that the team's poor defense was the heart of the matter, that it affected confidence at the other end. "Defense is hard," he said. "You have to play with your heart and your feet. Our defense always left something to be desired. But in the past, we shot better and won more games."

Nobody doubted the Suns' center spot was awful. Foster and Carr outscored Williams and Kleine, 17-6, a bigger gap than the final 114-105 spread.

Williams, still struggling with his sore back, looked like a guy in a YMCA seniors' league trying to match up with the world's best players.

Westphal was perplexed: "He obviously set a standard in Cleveland he hasn't been able to achieve here. How long it will last, I don't know. I'm not a doctor."

As for the Jazz, they appeared to be a team heading for a different level altogether than their familiar rivals. Stockton had a near-perfect game, shooting 8-for-9 with 14 assists to boot. Malone was almost as good with 25 points and 12 rebounds.

Afterward, Malone credited Stockton for his continuing success, gushing, "Stockton is the best point guard ever, and I wouldn't want to play a game without him. I'm spoiled and I love it. When he's finished, I'm finished." (Could anyone imagine Barkley and Johnson saying the same things about each other?) At the time, Malone and Stockton were working on contracts that would ensure this goal.

THAT THE SUNS WERE struggling at center and with their shooting wasn't surprising. Their mix of players had started to show deterioration the previous season. What was most disturbing was Barkley's play. Against the Jazz, he was nearly invisible, preferring to cast up perimeter shots. He earned only three free throws (missing all of them), a reliable gauge of a player's willingness to do battle inside. Just as telling, his bravado had disappeared, as well.

Maybe he should have retired after the last season. Maybe he should retire now. Quit right in mid-season. "It's crossed my mind, no question," he said.

With all their other problems, the Suns didn't need the distraction of another self-debate about retirement. But they got one just the same.

An uncharacteristically downcast Barkley moaned, "I've got to do a better job of leading. Seriously, I'm struggling.

"I'm just terrible right now. I'll never lose my confidence, but I'm struggling with it right now. There are five or six players in the league who are great, and their job is to lead their team and take it to the next level. I'm supposed to be one of those guys. But I'm not playing like it now.

"In my heart, I knew last season was probably the last season I could play really, really well consistently. I know I can't jump as high and I feel like I've lost a couple of steps, but my ability to make plays always has been there for me. I knew it was going to be tough, but I felt in my heart, I could push it one more year." Instead, he felt like "just another 6-4 guy out there.

"I've got to play with more energy. Even if I'm screwing up, I think it's important I play with a lot of energy because the team feeds off me.

"I'm the most important part of the puzzle, and if the engine's not working, the car is not going to run. Right now, the engine is terrible. It's sputtering. There's a lot of hesitation.

"I've got to do something. Right now, everybody is doing their part except me." He would not accept becoming a secondary player because, "If I do that, we're not going to win. If I don't lead, we're not going to win."

Westphal thought Barkley was too self-absorbed.

"He's analyzing himself so much he's lost some of his aggressiveness. I don't think he's slipped as much as he thinks he's slipped. I think he's in the process of learning what he's capable of and not capable of doing. He will work that out, but obviously he hasn't worked it out yet.

"The problem is a guy like Charles has had no limits. It's hard to play with some enthusiasm when you're not sure what's going to work." He advised Barkley, "Just go out and play."

There was another factor at work, one that wasn't generally known. Westphal believed Barkley still hadn't made the commitment to work himself back into top form after the minor knee surgery. In effect, he was playing himself into shape. While doing so, he was taking the easier road of taking perimeter shots.

Westphal was starting to wonder whether the Suns would see a repeat of their problems in getting Barkley to follow through on his physical therapy, just like the time they needed Fitzsimmons' intervention in 1994. Now it was up to Westphal to try to make sure Barkley followed through.

"From a time commitment and (personal) organization standpoint, it's easy to let it slide," Westphal said. "He's acknowledged he needs to do it. But getting him to follow through isn't as easy as the theory behind it all."

On the floor, the operating "theory" was that Barkley needed to work inside to score, draw fouls and rebound.

"We're trying to run plays that keep him inside and emphasize the offensive boards. The only way to do that is to be near the basket. We're telling him that's what we really want from him. He's got to do that to help us."

Though Westphal spoke out of Barkley's earshot, the tension between the two was evident moments later when the Suns took the floor for a game against the Timberwolves. When Barkley passed him, Westphal stuck out his hand to shake. Barkley glanced at his coach's extended hand, then started to walk away. Westphal grabbed him weakly around the wrist.

Then Barkley went out and proved Westphal's points. He shot 6-for-9 inside, including two clutch follow shots to help put the Suns over the top. He also nailed 3-for-6 from mid-range (about eight to 15 feet). But he was 0-for-4 from farther out.

Informed of Westphal's comments, Barkley steered clear of a direct answer. "I'm struggling a little physically. But struggling makes you a stronger person. I can handle anything. I'm not a shrinking violet."

Slowly, Barkley came around, agreeing to lift weights with emphasis on strengthening his legs. The results were immediate. The Suns visited another rival at the top of the Western Conference. In San Antonio, Barkley bounced around the court like the dynamo of old, 34 points and 18 rebounds. Maybe a little exercise wasn't such a bad idea.

"I never believed athletes should lift weights," he said. "But as you get older, I think you have to." The result: Surprise! He no longer wanted to retire. "I'm feeling quick. I'm getting to balls I couldn't get to last week. A week ago, if it didn't come to me, I couldn't get it."

He even made the sort of joking analogy that only he would verbalize: "I'm comparing myself to Jesus. He came back. He resurrected."

The early retirement talk died a quick death—not that many insiders believed it. Barkley said he'd never play well past his prime and risk putting himself in the class of such undignified spectacles as Willie Mays, Muhammad Ali and Kareem Abdul-Jabbar, athletes who continued to perform until they were ugly shells of themselves at their best. But some thought Barkley would play into his late 30s. Nobody loved the limelight more.

THOUGH BARKLEY WAS SHOWING new life, his comments about his teammates were overly generous. Several others hadn't been doing their part. Indeed, the slump-fest had spread throughout the team. Every player but Perry and Johnson was shooting significantly less than his career percentage.

Management's off-season deals had left the team with only one natural perimeter shooter. The Suns had high expectations for Wesley Person, coming off a rookie season where he filled in splendidly. Normally, those who can play with impact in the NBA improve noticeably between their first and second seasons. Instead, Person played erratically.

He seemed taken aback by the immediate impact of Finley, who started to eat into his playing time. He wasn't one to compete enthusiastically in such matters. He seemed equally shy when games reached the do-or-die stage. He seemed to view the game as an artist would a landscape, taking his time to size up the scene before making the emotional commitment to paint the picture.

The easiest explanation was the most troubling. The soft-spoken Person (he seemed a polar opposite of his brash brother Chuck, a longtime NBA mainstay) perhaps was too timid to play a leading role. Could a backup's responsibility be his limit?

Westphal rapidly was losing confidence in him. Yet he was young, far too young to be declared a washout, and the Suns needed him desperately. To discard him, in the sense of letting him know his ability to contribute now was in doubt, might rob them of a player who could someday bail them out.

Then there was Wayman Tisdale.

Nobody ever pronounced him a resident of the Suns' doghouse. But it looked like a doghouse, and it smelled like a doghouse. What else could it be?

With Manning out, Williams struggling, and Barkley playing inconsistently, the Suns badly needed help from Tisdale. He wasn't providing much. Tisdale's problems comprised an example of how personal character isn't always transferable to the sports world. Tisdale, the son of a minister, was universally viewed as a prince of a person. A bright, charming man with other talents—he was a well-regarded bass player who composed jazz tunes—he was considered as devoted a family man as could be found in the sports world.

But on the floor, his considerable ability was perceived internally as far exceeding his desire to excel. His recent saga was the sort that makes sports fans throw up their hands in despair. He had just signed a two-year contract for $7 million (he unsuccessfully campaigned for a third year), then came into camp in mediocre shape and pulled a muscle almost immediately. He struggled with his weight; at one point he ballooned into the 280s. Westphal, who preferred to see him in the 260s, scorched him behind closed doors.

The Suns had long been concerned about Tisdale's fitness and conditioning. That's why his summer routine was viewed somewhat comically. Because of the NBA's labor problems, the players had been locked out of the team's training facilities during labor-management talks and the Suns weren't allowed to supervise off-season activities. So, Tisdale went out and, with the help of a personal trainer, lifted weights and "bulked up," the opposite of what they needed from him.

Said Westphal, "A lot of guys have stories for their troubles. That's why they're underachievers."

In addition to all this, because Tisdale had always been slow to react on defense (Westphal often directed him at the defensive end like an over-worked air-traffic controller), he needed to be around his career shooting average of 51 percent to have a positive impact.

Tisdale, like most struggling players, blamed a lack of consistent play-ing time. "For me to be effective, I need at least 20 minutes per game," he said.

Replied Westphal, "He's got to earn it."

The result was that the Suns' four most vital players either were out (Manning) or were struggling with physical problems (Barkley, Johnson and Williams), while two others (Tisdale and Person) were underachieving.

"We have players performing at less than their historic abilities," West-phal said. "But we're going to hang with them and hope we come togeth-er."

He really had no other choice. The Suns had few trade options, having dealt a first-round pick to the Cavaliers in the Williams-Majerle exchange. Making matters worse, the Cavs had the option of picking the year to use the pick. In effect, the Suns couldn't trade any first-round choices in the near future.

They could only hope all of this wasn't terminal. Perhaps they could return to their contending form. After all, this was the basic cast that won 59 games the year before and came within one point of defeating the Rock-ets, who were on their way to repeating as world champs. But to have a chance, the Suns needed to come close to shooting their career percentages.

Barkley, a career 56-percent shooter, had sunk into the mid-40s, in part because he continued to hoist so many errant three-point shots. In an effort to get him to stop the long-range firing, while not publicly singling him out, Westphal ordered his entire team to refrain from shooting any three-pointers before a home game against the expansion Vancouver Grizzlies. They shot well and won the game, barely.

The Suns next had a gift handed to them. The visiting Miami Heat saw their two dominant inside players, Alonzo Mourning and Kevin Willis, leave the game with injuries. (At the time, the Heat had one of the NBA's hottest teams. But after the injury to Mourning—in trying to block a slam dunk by Finley, he was corkscrewed into the court and hurt his foot—the Heat went into a nosedive.)

But the Suns once again couldn't shoot. In contrast, Miami's European import Sasha Danilovic put on a shooting display for the ages. In the closing moments, he hit two three-pointers, a driving layup and two free throws to tie it. Then rookie Kurt Thomas got a follow shot to drop with nine seconds left. Johnson tried to tie it, but got caught in traffic and had his shot blocked.

It was another loss, this time at home to an average team. The sagging fortunes—they were now 8-10— prompted Barkley to reverse everything he'd ever said about what it takes to win, namely talent over chemistry. "Talent is the most overrated thing," he said. "You can have too much talent. You've got to have chemistry. Right now, our chemistry is just not there."

"Surely, the Suns would defeat the sub-.500 Charlotte Hornets at home. But there were signs of trouble from the start. Instead of attacking the basket aggressively, Barkley waited for double-teams to attack him. Then he passed to an open teammate.

Newcomers to the scene often wondered why Barkley just didn't make his move quickly. After a while, they realized this was a pattern that wouldn't change, that Barkley simply liked to hold the ball and dribble a few times. With this approach, the problem was twofold: The Suns didn't shoot well enough to take advantage of any openings Barkley spotted when he delivered his teammates the ball. That is, *when* he delivered them the ball, for his ball-handling problems were continuing.

In the past, Barkley knew from his years of playing with Ainge and Majerle where they would be on the floor most any time. Now, Person and Green were most often out on the wings. Neither was as adept at finding the open spaces on the floor or—once receiving the ball—making the instant decision of whether to pass, shoot or drive. In the Charlotte game, Barkley stumbled at making his own decisions and turned the ball over six times. Williams still was a step slow. He got in early foul trouble and disappeared from view. The Suns couldn't turn to Tisdale or Kleine for inside help with much confidence since neither had been playing well. Green, usually a stalwart in times of crisis, also had been struggling in a reserve role.

Despite all this, the teams played on even terms throughout the first half.

With seconds remaining before halftime, Johnson leaped to steal a pass at midcourt. In doing so, he injured his groin and thigh and hobbled through the second half. This ruined the Suns' chance for a wide-open game and hurt the half-court approach, too, since Johnson was much more effective exploding to the hoop than in running a slow-down game.

The Suns collapsed completely and the Hornets won going away.

The locker room had one of those funeral-parlor atmospheres usually seen only after a season's final play-off loss.

A downcast Barkley emerged from the shower, quietly took his seat in front of his locker, and said, "Obviously, this is the low point of my Phoenix career. It might be the low point of my basketball career."

In Philadelphia, he pointed out, the 76ers didn't have the talent to compete at the elite level. "But we do here. If somebody had told me a mediocre Charlotte team could beat us by 20 . . ." His voice trailed off. He couldn't finish the sentence. "I have to laugh just to keep from crying."

Said Johnson, "This is the low-water mark of my career. We're playing terrible in every facet of the game." Then he addressed the issue that nobody else would: Maybe this was the death of a title-contending team, one that had three legitimate chances to be the world's best but would have no more.

"We're all on the same ship," Johnson said. "If it sinks, we all go down together. If it sails, we'll all enjoy the good times together."

Colangelo had become alarmed by all these developments. Had Westphal suddenly lost his touch? Or had Colangelo and his underlings fouled up the team by making too many changes after their razor-thin play-off losses? Certainly, the wisdom of spending wheelbarrows full of money to attract free agents and lock up players for long-term contracts now was in question. He had commitments of $100 million on players who were injury-prone, declining or just plain ineffective.

Until now, Colangelo's judgment seldom had been questioned on making money or running a basketball team. He was recognized as one of the sports world's leading operators. He was finishing a year in which he'd organized a group that landed a Major League Baseball franchise (one that would sell 40,000 tickets in three months) and now was in the process of wooing the NHL's Winnipeg Jets to the Suns' arena.

In addition, his influence had grown way beyond life's toy department. Here's what a big wheel Colangelo had become in Arizona. Politicians came courting for his blessing, rather than the other way around. He ran his office like that of a governor, hosting government officials, big business types, and community leaders. Political leaders called him the most influential person in the state.

Astounding! He was, after all, a sports entrepreneur, an occupation whose occupants normally range from modest in stature to outright laughingstocks. Colangelo came to all this while rocketing up the social and economic ladders in a way that seems so peculiarly American. He grew up in a troubled family on the wrong side of the tracks near Chicago. He chose to move to the right place at the right time. Then he simply endured in a state that seems to breed embarrassment and scandal.

The public in Arizona, even by the nation's embarrassingly low standards, had a history of below-average voter turnouts. The Census Bureau has called Arizona the fourth-most transient state; many people are still more concerned with the goings-on back "home" in Indiana or Minnesota. And over the years, the media and public regulators had shown only sporadic interest in probing the activities of suspicious characters.

The soil was fertile for the likes of such swindlers as Charlie Keating, who roamed uncontested for years before federal and California authorities sent him to prison. The same for the likes of numerous political figures, many of whom eventually went to jail. A governor was impeached. Business tycoons saw their empires crumble. The two U.S. senators comprised 40 percent of Congress' notorious "Keating 5."

Just before this very basketball season started, the sitting governor declared bankruptcy. (Just after the season ended, that same governor— Fife Symington—would be the subject of criminal indictment by federal prosecutors. He was hit with 23 counts, a list of charges that read like a glossary of white-collar crime jargon.)

Even the other sports institutions floundered. The NFL's Cardinals had struggled since moving from St. Louis to Arizona in 1988. At Arizona State University, the athletic department, at times, had been a virtual factory for bad news.

While all this was going on, Colangelo kept his personal reputation intact. He was active in civic and charitable affairs. He stuck his neck out much farther than was necessary in pushing for a full state holiday honoring the Rev. Martin Luther King Jr. by becoming the fund-raising leader for the pro-holiday group. (He didn't run into many politicians or other bigwigs out of the campaign trail).

He took the lead in bailing out the financially troubled local orchestra. He pushed to integrate one of the last of the city's old-line, all-white country clubs. He even took over as the leader of a group of power brokers that sought to push elected leaders into action on various issues.

He did his homework and had a way of anticipating questions, enabling him to dominate the topic at hand, whether it be sports and entertainment or issues closer to the hearts of bottom-line businessmen or wine-and-cheese arts supporters.

In a booming, sun-drenched state where mere payment of taxes and avoidance of prison can lead to a bountiful life, Colangelo had more than passed the test.

Then too, it helped that he was in the right place at a time when professional sports, more so than Hollywood's products, was becoming society's cultural bond.

This seemed particularly true for the Suns in Arizona. Here, all the embarrassing problems both benefited Colangelo personally, in the sense that he stood out in contrast, and helped create the mania that began to surround the Suns in the late 1980s. This was one institution that seemed to stand out among the best in its field, that could be counted on to bring good news and good cheer and unify a disjointed community.

The franchise's early high point came in 1976 when Westphal led them to the NBA Finals. Colangelo, watching the legendary Red Auerbach being interviewed at one corner of Boston Garden while he answered questions at the opposite corner, thought, "We've arrived."

The franchise went through an extreme downturn in the mid-1980s. The coach at the time, John MacLeod, tired of Dennis Johnson, a gritty defender the Suns had acquired from Seattle for Westphal. Johnson had blossomed into an all-NBA performer and the team's best player. But he could be moody and he wasn't much of a practice player. MacLeod complained frequently about him to Colangelo. The Suns perennially needed another big man, and the Boston Celtics had one available in Rick Robey, a journeyman MacLeod and Colangelo believed could help the Suns. So they sent Johnson to the Celtics for Robey in a deal that also included a swap of draft picks that actually favored Boston. Auerbach could light another victory cigar.

Colangelo recognized the mistake almost as soon as it was made. The team's downturn then began apace. But the sagging won-loss record represented a seaside vacation compared to a police investigation that became public in 1987.

Evidence of drug use surfaced among players and people who hung around them. In all, 13 men were indicted, including five current and former players. Several other current or former players were mentioned in the indictments but not charged.

The case centered on Walter Davis, the team's highest-scoring and most popular player. Davis entered a drug rehabilitation program for the second time. He was given immunity from prosecution in return for his testimony.

In the end, Davis and another key witness began developing foggy memories about the case's details. A third witness died in a car crash. The case unraveled and most charges were dropped or reduced. But the franchise had been tarred. Colangelo backed up the truck and moved players tainted by the scandal. Davis was allowed to sign with Denver. (Years later, Colangelo opted to turn the other cheek and permit Davis' number to be retired.)

The scandal convinced the team's majority owners to sell what had become an embarrassing property. Colangelo quickly seized the moment by putting together a large group of limited partners. He weathered a brief storm when two corporations backed out at the last minute by arranging for the old owners to retain a share of the team. The deal put Colangelo completely in charge. He would own about 17 percent of the team (which would come to make up the bulk of his estimated $25 million net worth). He would serve as team president and control every aspect of the operation. He would no longer have to report to the committee of owners. Instead, he would operate the way he felt most comfortable, by instinct and impulse.

With Fitzsimmons' help, he immediately made the trade for Johnson, drafted the little-known Majerle, and signed a high-scoring free agent named Tom Chambers.

The Chambers-Johnson combination worked better than planned. Instead of squeezing into the play-offs with a break-even record, the Suns were transformed almost immediately into an offensive powerhouse. They won 55 games and reached the Western Conference Finals before they were eliminated in four close games by the Los Angeles Lakers.

The success dramatically changed the temperature for a Colangelo plan that critics deemed nearly loony: a new 19,000 seat downtown arena. The cost would be split by the Suns and the city. The building would be placed in one of the state's few truly urban neighborhoods, sandwiched between a grimy warehouse area and downtown office buildings.

The idea seemed perfectly sensible to Colangelo, a city fellow by nature and background. But the concept sailed directly into the wind of a cherished Arizona-ism: that urban projects in general, and those involving downtown Phoenix in particular, were a waste of time and money. And Colangelo wasn't helped by the fact that some sports franchises, notably the Detroit Pistons, had found success in the suburbs.

Early public hearings in which Colangelo predicted the arena would draw a host of events downtown drew snickers. But Colangelo pushed ahead relentlessly, formed a partnership with a former political foe, Mayor Terry Goddard, and—thanks to the team's success—won approval. The building, named America West Arena after the Tempe-based airline agreed to kick in about $500,000 a year, had all the bells and whistles, everything from New Age video art, a broadcast studio and lavish locker rooms to a posh bar and restaurant. In a league-wide vote in 1994, the arena was named the NBA's finest by an overwhelming margin.

Because of the Suns, Colangelo had grown to be such a tower of influence that politicians, eager to attract a major league baseball franchise but reluctant to lead the charge for a tax-supported stadium, asked Colangelo to cover their flanks.

So, he plunged into the issue full-speed, yet as analytical as ever, calling baseball just another sport, albeit with "a downsized ball." He organized a group of investors, then took most of the heat for a quarter-cent sales tax to build the stadium.

The criticism ate at him to the point where he threatened to bail out entirely. Though almost every public official and leading citizen continued to back him, the stadium tax only increased public suspicion that Colangelo forever was scheming to fatten his wallet.

The caricature of Colangelo as a fat cat was, in part, self-created. He carried himself in a regal manner, wearing expensive clothes and driving cars that were as exotic as they were expensive. Much worse, he chose to implement a pay-per-view system for Suns' games at about the same time he began his push for the baseball franchise and stadium tax. The combined moves became a first-order fiasco, the kind that his well-oiled public-relations antennae normally would detect on the drawing board. But he was such a luminous figure within the Suns organization and the community that telling him "bad idea" wasn't as simple as it sounded.

The franchise over which he presided was known as thoroughly strait-laced. Colangelo himself underwent a spritual awakening in middle age. Now, thanks to his bold trade in 1992, his major business alliance was with Charles Barkley. It wasn't necessarily inconsistent. In the old days, when he ran the team but had little final authority in matters, he always wanted to rock 'n' roll with the club, to trust his instincts and take more chances, to take the franchise down less-traveled, paths. Barkley's presence was the result.

Those who knew Colangelo in his rough-and-tumble days in Chicago are stupefied that he one day would be mingling with the social butterflies, that he would be acclaimed—or derided by conspiracy theorists—as the most influential person in a growing state. For if everything seemed to come to Westphal with casual ease, everything for Colangelo came the hard way.

"He certainly didn't excel as a gentleman," said Michael Ratner, a downtown Phoenix bar owner and a college buddy of Colangelo's at the University of Illinois. "To see him develop into a person with finesse and charisma is almost revolutionary."

Colangelo grew up in a working-class Italian neighborhood called Hungry Hill in Chicago Heights, south of the city. Today, in his marble-floored office that overlooks downtown Phoenix, he reserves a corner dedicated to his Italian heritage: a photo of his family's old two-story flat; a container used to store olive oil; and an accordion sent to him by an old friend.

He used to dream of making a few hundred dollars a week and living like a king while pitching in the major leagues. He'd walk to the nearby playground to play basketball with a saltshaker in his back pocket. The salt came in handy when the boys plucked tomatoes ("everybody in the neighborhood grew them," he said) and snacked on them.

Even so, he knew little of the idyllic 1950s, *Father Knows Best* family life. The source of his turmoil was Colangelo's father. When Colangelo was about 17, in coming to the defense of his mother, he acted impulsively and boldly rather than with carefully crafted caution. He threw his father out of the house (literally). In this early, but definitive moment, he displayed a defining characteristic.

In sports, he was such a widely recruited basketball player that he chose to attend the University of Kansas, where he hoped to join Wilt Chamberlain and play on championship teams. But when he got there, Chamberlain told him he was about to leave school to join the Harlem Globetrotters. So Colangelo transferred closer to home, to the University of Illinois.

In between, he took a semester off and landed a job in the Chicago sanitation department. There, he worked in the sewers and rode a garbage truck to earn money to go to school since he didn't get financial aid for a year.

At Illinois, he met his wife, Joan, and became a star guard and captain of the team during his senior year.

After graduation, he and a friend went into the tuxedo rental-and-sales business. But after three years, with his second child on the way, Colangelo had virtually nothing to show for his labor. He pulled out his wallet and found a card that had been there for more than a year. It bore the name and phone number of a man introduced to him by his father-in-law. The man's name was Dick Klein, who bought and sold high-dollar merchandise throughout the Midwest. Colangelo called Klein and told him he was in the area.

"I remember you," Klein said. "You used to play at Illinois." Klein also had an interest in basketball and already had been thinking about trying to land an NBA franchise for Chicago. So Klein hired Colangelo to help him. His starting pay: $800 a month. Driving around the country's heartland during their first major sales trip, Klein detailed his dream to Colangelo. The idea of working in pro basketball intrigued Colangelo, who had kept his hand in the sport by playing for $50 a game on an otherwise all-black, semipro team based in Chicago.

In fact, Colangelo was set to play a game on the day he got the dramatic call in early 1966 from Klein in New York. "We're in!" Klein told Colangelo. So, Colangelo distributed a news release informing the press of a news conference the next day at the Water Tower building. It was signed, "The Chicago Bulls."

Colangelo then drove through a snowstorm to Grand Rapids, Mich., where he scored 37 points, including the game-winning shot in overtime. The only downside to this night was that he locked himself out of his car. So he broke in, grabbed a second key in his glove compartment, and drove back to Chicago by morning. At home, he showered and drove to the birth announcement of the Bulls.

Colangelo started out as the team's sales manager but quickly elbowed his way into player-personnel matters. He proved himself a solid judge of talent. He recommended the Bulls draft a guard named Walt Frazier. But Klein, who had overspent his budget, opted for Clem Haskins, a guard who would come cheaper.

Colangelo's reputation grew, boosted by the Bulls' feat of winning 33 games and making the play-offs in their first year.

A couple of years after Colangelo hooked up with Klein, two young businessmen out West were starting to hatch their own off-the-wall plans. A Los Angeles entertainment executive named Dick Bloch and a lawyer/developer from Tucson named Donald Pitt, old college buddies at the University of Arizona, began talking about investing in the pro sports world. They considered buying a share of the San Diego Chargers. But they wanted a majority interest, so they thought they might get in on the ground floor of an expansion team.

Sometime in 1967, Bloch suggested to Pitt: "We should get a basketball team. We'll go for Phoenix."

Said Pitt: "Is there a place to play?"

Bloch, "How should I know?"

They soon found Phoenix indeed had a suitable arena. Bloch and Pitt later realized that had they done an intelligent marketing survey, they'd likely have gone to Dallas or Houston. But they didn't. And Phoenix was convenient and familiar and certain to grow.

They began making contacts. They had a leg up in this process because each knew an important NBA figure. Bloch was pals with Sam Schulman, the owner of the new Seattle SuperSonics. And Pitt, as a youngster in Tucson, had known a businessman in town who turned out to be an NBA executive in the East. So, they both worked their connections, then Bloch set up a meeting in New York with Walter Kennedy, the NBA commissioner, to promote Phoenix as an NBA city.

Kennedy wasn't even sure in what state Phoenix was located. "He knew it was out West, but he wasn't sure if it was in Texas, New Mexico or Arizona," Bloch said.

On Jan. 22, 1968, officials from each of the 12 existing NBA franchises met at the St. Regis Hotel in New York. They listened to Bloch and Pitt and representatives of a group pushing for a franchise in Milwaukee. The Knicks' Ned Irish, viewing Phoenix as a backwater burg, was opposed.

"We walked out of the room, then we came back and were told that we'd been awarded the franchise," Pitt recalled. "The reality of all the hard work ahead hadn't set in, but the fact that we had the OPPORTUNITY had set in."

The public read the announcement the next day in the papers. It was the first people had heard of the team. There had been no public campaign, no talk about the dire need for major-league sports to boost the economy and serve as a linchpin for boosting the area's status. Not a peep about it at all in the sleepy local press. One day, the team wasn't there. The next day it was.

In retrospect, in this era of hundred-million-dollar sports franchises, the ease with which they financed their bid also seems breathtaking. In 1968, the NBA entry fee was $2 million. But Bloch and Pitt needed only to put up $100,000 of their own money (a third partner, businessman Don Diamond from Tucson, later picked up his share of this bill). The NBA carried half the fee, with the Suns repaying the $1 million over the next several years.

The other $900,000, plus about $150,000 in working capital, mostly was raised through a Los Angeles law firm that represented show biz folks. Singer Andy Williams, who put up about $300,000, was the largest investor. Other celebrities who joined included Henry Mancini, Ed Ames and Bobbie Gentry. During a trip to Los Angeles, Colangelo had gotten wind of the expansion bids by Phoenix and Milwaukee a few days before the New York meeting. With the practiced air of sophistication, the 28-year-old scout laughed at the insider gossip. "Phoenix?" said Colangelo, who had never seen the city. "How could they give a franchise to Phoenix? There's nothing there."

But the gossip proved true, and soon both Phoenix and Milwaukee were courting Colangelo to run their new franchises. Colangelo probably could have stayed and taken over as general manager of the Bulls eventually. But Klein had to deal with an unwieldy board of directors, some of whom wanted to get their relatives involved in the franchise. Klein knew Colangelo would be better off leaving. Colangelo nearly committed to Milwaukee. Then the Phoenix group made one final pitch.

When Colangelo left Chicago, it was 20 degrees. In Phoenix, it was 70. Before he had a chance to start admiring the palm trees, Bloch surprised him by meeting him at the airport. Colangelo figured Bloch was serious, thinking he met him to make sure things went right. The partners huddled with their young applicant.

Asked Pitt: "What makes you think you can run this team?"

Replied Colangelo, without missing a beat: "Unless I have it backward, I'm here because you think I can."

This moxie made its mark on the Suns' investors. They'd already checked him out and deemed him reliable and principled. They considered his age. But then, the investors themselves were only in their 30s. They were more concerned about his experience level. In the end, they figured his characteristics were more important than a heavy resume.

The group next met with some local bankers, then Colangelo was given a quick tour of the town, including a look at the Coliseum, where the team would play. Pitt asked Colangelo what kind of deal he wanted. Colangelo had done his homework, so numbers were tossed back and forth.

The idea was that Colangelo merely would carry the title "administrative manager." But he knew he could run his own show and soon would be named general manager.

Colangelo said he'd have to weigh his options and talk it over with Joan. The homefront "discussion" then took place. Colangelo called home and said, "Pack the bags. It's Phoenix!"

His first major decision was to name the team. The choice of "Suns" wasn't made just for chamber-of-commerce types. Publicity was precious and editors preferred short names, the better for flexibility in writing headlines. "They like team names with four or five letters," Colangelo said.

Considering the reception the exhibition season received, the team's organizers would have to have been clairvoyant to sense the interest that would surround the Suns a generation later.

A game against the Lakers at Fort Huachuca, a major military installation in the southeast corner of Arizona, drew a handful of fans.

Pitt remembered the time he and Diamond drove from Tucson to the mining town of Globe for another exhibition and saw "about 500 snakes" on or about the highway.

After all this, on Oct. 18, 1968, two days after the fists-in-the-air protest at the Olympic Games and two days after the news broke that Jackie would marry Ari, the Suns played their first game. The opponent was the Seattle SuperSonics.

In front of a half-full arena (or half-empty, as it must have looked to Colangelo), the Suns won, 116-107. The concept of Phoenix as a major-league sports town now had a visible form. But whether this impulsive gamble ever would pay off was anybody's guess.

AFTER THE CHARLOTTE LOSS, Colangelo flew in from from the East Coast for an "evaluation" session. Though these meetings don't necessarily lead to a coach's firing, it's usually a sign that the coach should start thinking about his career options.

Trying to fight his way out of an ever-shrinking corner was distasteful to Westphal. Even in good times, he didn't think the coach should be the focus of the day's events. And he didn't think he was to blame for these bad times.

Yet he had made the mistake late in the previous season of not strongly defending himself strongly enough when the heat was on. He wouldn't make it again.

Westphal believed Colangelo was in his corner. After all, weren't the problems obvious enough?

Of his three best players, one (Barkley) was coming off knee surgery and hadn't been able to play to form consistently. Another (Johnson) was hobbled by his usual assortment of ailments. The third (Manning) hadn't played at all.

Westphal's three most consistently effective players were Green, a reserve (Perry) who was two years removed from the minor-league CBA, and a rookie (Finley).

Before facing Colangelo, Westphal was peppered by reporters with questions about his job security. Yes, it's true Colangelo has been disappointed. "But it's uncomfortable to be sitting here answering questions on whether I should be fired. How can you answer that? This is not an ideal place for the focus to be. But it's my turn under the microscope. I'm the story today; somebody else will be the story tomorrow."

Westphal knew he was still—and likely would always be—fighting the perception that he was "too laid back," an image that was indelibly stamped during his first season as head coach. At the time, the Suns started flying high from the start, racing to the NBA's best record and maintaining it throughout the season. Westphal was smart enough to get out of the way. (One of his slogans hanging on the locker room walls came from baseball manager Sparky Anderson: "If you got a group that wants to win, you gotta let 'em.") He'd been much more animated in the years since. But the initial image had remained, one that more and more exasperated him.

"You get a label and you spend the rest of your career trying to live down that label. I'm not here to wage a PR campaign to show everybody how tough I am or how laid-back I am or whatever else they may want me to be.

"I've never rated the job I'm doing as a coach. I do the best I can. Players win and lose games."

Not all of these players supported him. Though Barkley spoke in Westphal's defense, the silence on the matter from Kevin Johnson was notable. He knew that if Westphal was fired, the likely replacement would be Fitzsimmons, the man who had arranged for his trade to the Suns and had coached him when he blossomed into an impact player.

Fitzsimmons' relationship with Johnson was summed up early in their coach-player relationship. Johnson asked him a question in practice, and Fitzsimmons responded by throwing him the ball and shouting, "You figure it out!" The two had their spats but came to trust each other. Johnson became close to both Fitzsimmons and his wife, JoAnn. Indeed, some teased him by referring to him as "Kevin Fitzsimmons."

ON A CLEAR AND PLEASANT Thursday afternoon in December, Westphal would give his report on the team's problems to Colangelo in the president's office. Fitzsimmons noticed Westphal waiting to meet with Colangelo. The ex-coach knew Colangelo had his doubts about Westphal. Fitzsimmons and Colangelo had talked about the coaching situation the previous spring, with Fitzsimmons helping Westphal to step off the plank and back on ship's side. Now he sensed Westphal was in his most serious danger yet. "If you want this job, you gotta fight for it," he advised. "Be firm with your ideas."

(Westphal presumed Fitzsimmons was in his corner. He became less certain of this belief later, when stories circulated that the ex-coach hadn't always been so supportive. He learned that during one of the times Colangelo was debating the coach's fate, Fitzsimmons walked up to one of the players after a game and said he was pleased the Suns won because he didn't want to have to take over as coach. Though the words sounded pro-Westphal, saying such a thing had the opposite effect, undercutting his clout with the team by suggesting his position was extremely tenuous.)

So, Westphal gave his report on the Suns' problems.

Barkley had been playing his way back into shape. If he continued to come around, and if Johnson ever could play at peak form, as he had in the play-offs vs. the Rockets the previous two years, the Suns could compete with anybody.

But with Johnson hobbled, the Suns struggled badly. He was not only their offensive spark plug (he ranked in the top 20 in NBA history in assists even though he was a natural scorer to boot), but also their best defender on the perimeter. With Perry at the helm, the Suns were somewhere in the middle, able to beat the NBA's weaker sisters and even have a shot at the stronger ones (at least at home). Until Johnson was reasonably healthy, they were better off going with Perry.

"That's one of the things we learned last year," Westphal would say later.

In addition to the obvious manpower problems, they sometimes had a disorganized presence on offense, as if they really didn't know each other's tendencies. There was good reason for this. Barkley and Johnson rarely practiced with the team. So in scrimmages, other players would dominate the ball. Then in games, they'd have to play to their two leaders' strengths.

Barkley was coming off knee surgery, but even when health wasn't a concern, he often simply chose not to practice. Johnson didn't practice to minimize the chance of injuries. The benefits of these privileges required the biggest adjustments for the most important complimentary players. In the past, that often meant Majerle. He always thought the change-ups between practice and games hurt them. But the Suns won enough that it hadn't been a major issue. Now, they weren't winning.

Before their debacle against the Hornets was even complete, Westphal had decided their routine had to change. "We're strangers out there," he said after the embarrassing loss to the Hornets. "The only time we're all together is in front of 19,000 people."

At the end of the game, he summoned Barkley and Johnson into his office. They would have to practice with the team to start. Both went along, Barkley more reluctantly.

"It's something I didn't need for three years," he said testily. But when you lose, people are full of (expletive). I don't agree with anything that people change when you lose that you don't change when you win." (Just why Barkley would want to stick with a losing pattern wasn't clear, other than the new routine didn't place his convenience as the top priority.)

Johnson, as usual, was more circumspect. He deemed the change more a matter of "making noise than anything. Things aren't going well, so you try to do something. But some of our problems are bigger than that. We've lost something. Either our confidence, or what's expected of us, or our enthusiasm. We have to find it."

Colangelo listened patiently. For the past couple of years, his doubts about Westphal's approach had been ongoing. Shortly after the Suns' trip to the NBA Finals, Colangelo congratulated Westphal. Giving Barkley a free reign, considering he was extremely motivated to show what he could do to lead an outstanding team, turned out to be the correct move. But this was history. Colangelo thought the team needed more structure, more control from the head coach or else it could deteriorate.

In Colangelo's mind, the coach's job was a 24-hours-a-day, 365-days-a-year mission, one that included making sure players were doing everything possible to stay in shape and develop their skills in the off-season. He deemed Westphal's approach too low key, more in line with the way Westphal himself wanted to be coached in his playing days.

The problem, he believed, was that Westphal and his playing contemporaries grew up in the 1950s and early '60s, a time when life (in retrospect) seemed as simple as the Norman Rockwell paintings it spawned. Those players didn't as often have to deal with the staggering problems of fatherless homes, drugs, lack of discipline, etc. (This particular team, however, didn't have players with tendencies to end up on police blotters; only Barkley had a history of getting in public scrapes that ended up in police scrutiny, and even he'd avoided major embarrassments the past couple of years.)

Today's players, Colangelo felt, needed more guidance than those of past generations. It was, as much as anything, Westphal's style that made him uncomfortable.

Moreover, even though Colangelo had other meetings along similar lines over the years, he hadn't noticed much of a change in his coach. In addition to all this, Colangelo had a more basic and general theory, that coaches generally were most effective for three to four years before starting to lose their hold on players. This was Westphal's fourth season. Then too, there were Colangelo's lifelong instincts on the matter of action vs. caution. In rocky times, he found this to be an easy call.

Still, the team was limping along at far less than full power. Westphal carried the distinction of having led them to the Finals as both a player and a coach, making him—next to Colangelo himself—the most durable and important figure in the franchise's history.

And there never was a question of Westphal's loyalty. When he coached under Fitzsimmons, his contract called for him to start receiving the head coach's salary after three seasons even though it didn't specify when he would take over as head coach. When he reached this point, however, he recognized Fitzsimmons wasn't ready to give up his job quite yet.

So, not wanting Fitzsimmons to feel any pressure, he gave up his greatly increased paychecks in the fourth season. This kind of gesture was almost unheard of in big-time sport.

Westphal did so on his own, without consulting his wife, Cindy. When she heard that her husband's move was greeted with emotion by Colangelo, she joked to a Suns official, "It almost brought tears to my eyes, too!"

So, if Westphal didn't hear a ringing endorsement when he left Colangelo's office, he didn't seem to be terribly bothered. He didn't think he needed one. He left the meeting feeling reasonably secure.

Moments after walking out the door, he ran into an acquaintance in the arena parking garage. Of his immediate status, he said, "Everything is fine. He doesn't like what's been happening, and I don't like what's been happening. I could sense his concern, but I didn't sense he thinks I'm doing a terrible job. He knows what the problems are."

Then he got into his gold Infiniti and made the twists and turns down from the garage's fourth floor to the exit on the south side of the arena. Waiting there were about a dozen reporters, photographers and cameramen.

This is known in the trade as a death watch. The absurd result: TV cameras recording Westphal driving onto a two-lane city street. His car recorded for posterity in case he'd just been fired.

He hadn't been, of course. When Colangelo learned of the Westphal watch, he quickly released a statement, saying, "No one is happy with the current state of affairs. It begins with me, down through the coaching staff and players. This is a time when people have to come together, support one another, and look in the mirror, carry your own weight and get the job done. Over a period of time, I hope this ship will right itself. I think everyone is committed to making that happen.

"I don't think it's appropriate for everyone to camp out and wait for some ax to fall. We will concentrate on getting our team healthy and ready to get the job done. We've got a tough, tough season ahead of us. This season is far from over."

He could have quieted the speculation by simply saying, "Westphal is the coach. He has my support." But he didn't.

And so, as the Suns boarded their bus to the airport the next day and took off for Dallas to play the Mavericks the next night, Westphal was—for the first time—concerned about his job.

The buzz in the air just wouldn't go away. He started to figure that maybe nobody understood anything except the won-loss record. The Suns were said to have overwhelming talent, but where was it? He decided he needed to have another meeting with Colangelo to find out where he stood, to say he didn't feel there was any justification for having his name dragged publicly through the finger-pointing process.

But first, the Suns had to get past the Mavericks.

To compete as effectively as possible, Westphal narrowed the team's rotation to the most experienced players plus Finley. With Johnson out of the picture, Westphal would go with Perry and Person at guard, Williams at center, and Green and Barkley at forward. In reserve would be Finley, Tisdale and Tony Smith, a veteran who could back up at either guard spot.

With a few minutes gone, Williams jumped to try a simple blocked shot. He ended up on the floor, holding his right knee, writhing in the sort of pain that conjured up images of a war wound treated without anesthesia. For Williams, it felt similar to the pain he first experienced after he was in a car accident that summer in Cleveland.

A few days after the wreck, his back had started hurting. He told the Cavs' doctors about the back, but not about the knee. "I had so much pain in my back that I forgot about the pain in my leg," he explained. When the Suns made the trade for him, they checked his back, found it to be structurally sound, and the deal went through. Sure enough, eventually, the back pains went away. But now his right leg was the problem.

Richard Emerson, the Suns's chief doctor, determined Williams experienced occasional episodes of abnormal movement of a leg joint below his right knee. This, in turn, appeared to cause a nerve irritation on the outside of the joint that intermittently caused numbness up and down his leg. The Suns' doctors weren't convinced the problem was caused by the accident, but that was the appearance.

Williams missed much of the next several weeks, 14 of 19 games. When he returned, the Suns' doctors devised a specially designed knee brace to minimize the motion in the joint. But the end result was that Williams looked like he was dragging a ball-and-chain. For practical purposes, he was useless.

Williams didn't know much of this at the time he went down in Dallas. His leg didn't feel that terrible afterward. He figured he might be able to start playing again the next game. His loss didn't seem as though it would matter against the Mavericks, who seemed to be overrated as an up-and-coming play-off team.

The Suns moved the ball sharply and, behind Barkley and Green, quickly assumed a 22-11 lead. The Mavericks made a couple of charges, but they couldn't take control.

The Suns started to pull away at the end of the first half. On the half's final play, Finley stole an inbound pass and got the ball to Person for a three-pointer at the buzzer. That made it 58-40 Suns, their biggest lead of the season.

For once, they could cruise.

Then, all of a sudden, their boat started to rock wildly. Without Williams, the Suns' interior defense—often a perilous line of resistance even in the best of times—wilted badly. Jason Kidd, Dallas' touted superstar-in-the-making, and the other Mavericks began to attack the hoop with great results.

Then, in trying to cover their deficiencies inside, they began to leave shooters open on the three-point line. This had been an ongoing problem; between their own collective Mr. Magoo shooting eye from the perimeter and opposing teams' success from outside, they had the NBA's worst overall three-point game.

Green tried to cover down low while chasing shooter George McCloud up top. McCloud had once been so highly regarded that he was the No. 7 pick in the entire 1989 draft by the Indiana Pacers. But he had been deeply distressed by the deaths of his parents, his play suffered, and he ended up in the the minor-league CBA. Now, he was getting another shot.

McCloud began to let them fly, with results few players get practicing alone in a gym.

In they went, one three-pointer after another. McCloud, often guarded by Green, ended up tying an NBA record by hitting 10 three-pointers (in just 12 attempts), prompting Barkley later to joke, "We need some ice for A.C.'s rear end. He was lit up." Westphal shouted instructions. But whatever the Suns did, the Mavericks countered. Trying to clamp down out on the perimeter, leaks opened once again inside.

Westphal often preferred center-less lineups, the better to employ a quick, versatile attack (though it often didn't work so well at the other end). At this desperate point, he would have given anything for a center. Yet the appearance was that he was being nailed to the cross of the center-less philosophy.

The Mavericks' lead reached five points as the teams came down the stretch. Westphal's shoulders sagged. This was the kind of collapse that gets coaches fired, particularly those who already are in trouble. His planned meeting with Colangelo now might be his last act.

In the closing seconds, the Suns had the ball, trailing by three points.

They might have time for two possessions, so they looked for a quick two points. Barkley had the ball up top, 25 feet out. The Mavericks backed off, virtually inviting Barkley to try a three-pointer. Considering he was one of the NBA's worst at this range, it made sense. God only knew how many close games the Suns had lost by taking too many three-pointers, with Barkley's shots being the most prayerful of all.

With the game, and perhaps Westphal's job on the line, Barkley launched it.

"You know me," he would say later. "I'm never scared to take the big shot."

This time, the basketball gods smiled on the Suns. Swish! The shot created in Reunion Arena the kind of silence known only by deep-sea divers and astronauts.

In overtime, both teams mostly misfired until the final minute. Then

Perry, Westphal's biggest booster on the team, nailed two jumpers. It was enough. They'd survived McCloud's amazing shooting and won, 111-108.

A relieved Westphal praised his team's effort. "We've been playing hard. We'll get it right."

THEIR NEXT GAME WAS Tuesday in Houston. But instead of hanging out in Texas, Westphal had them return to Arizona for the two full days in between. This served a dual purpose: Not only could they practice and rest in their more comfortable home surroundings, but it would minimize Barkley's time in Houston.

Every city has its notable features. The Phoenix area is perhaps most distinctive for its impressive surrounding mountains, some of which are inside the city limits and make a most unique setting for urban parks. In an infinitely less aesthetic sense, the Valley of the Sun almost certainly has more quick-stop convenience markets than any place on Earth. In an automobile-driven city that boomed with astonishing speed and power in the 1960s through the '80s (often with little regard for planning), the quick-stop markets appeared at seemingly every major intersection.

Houston has its own peculiarities, one of which is favored by Barkley: The city appears to be the nation's leader in "men's clubs," the high-falutin' term for stripper joints. A couple of them are within walking distance of the Suns' hotel, allowing you-know-who easy access to one of his favorite forms of entertainment.

Just what caused Barkley's collapse in the previous spring's play-offs wasn't completely clear. But there was no reason to encourage his extracurricular activities. Thus, the Suns made a Texas-Arizona round-trip.

Before leaving, Westphal once again visited Colangelo, this time vigorously making his case that the team's problems were not his doing, that he was the right man for the job, that he didn't feel he deserved to have his name dragged so nakedly through the public process of analyzing the team's miseries.

In Colangelo's view, the notion that their problems (outside of injuries) weren't anchored in coaching, but were related to his rapid (and, so far, unsuccessful) makeover of the team, plus the age and deterioration of the veterans, wasn't an issue. As with most any supremely successful person, he had trusted his instincts before and they seldom failed him. This certainly had been the case in the past several years during his rise to national prominence in the sports world and locally to his lofty perch in the business and political communities. He wouldn't doubt them now.

In making his suggestions and critiques to Westphal over the years, Colangelo mostly had spoken in general tones. "I never told a coach to do 'A, B, C,'" he would say later. "Coaches have to sink or swim on their own."

Westphal seemed to take this as at least a tacit endorsement of his approach. After all, they had been successful, more so than any other team that hadn't won a title. More than once, dating back to the troubled times of the last season, he wondered what all the speculation was about, that if Colangelo wanted him to change his procedures, he certainly would tell him before pulling the trigger.

All in all, none of this would get a student an "A" in Theory of Communications 101. But Westphal had more to lose. He finished making his case by telling Colangelo that if there'd been a loss of confidence in his coaching, the time to fire him was now. There was a practical consideration. He was about to break ground on a new house. If there was a chance he was about to explore his career opportunities in other cities, he wanted to know.

Colangelo sympathized with the injury dilemma and reassured him to the point that Westphal left feeling comfortable he had the necessary support. At least he still had his seat on the Suns' plane as the team flew back to Texas.

WITH THE SUNS STRUGGLING, the Rockets could reflect on their own good fortune, on how they managed to use all their prodigious talent and heart, not to mention all available luck, to slip to the desirable side of that narrow line that separates heroes from goats in big-time sport.

Their champions' persona was borne at the time they should have been killed, back in the '94 play-offs when the Suns won the first two games of their second-round play-off series. Both games were played in Houston; in the second, the Suns were down by 18 after three quarters. Nobody had ever blown such a lead in the play-offs. But as the fourth quarter progressed, the Suns began to right themselves. At the same time, the Rockets got a deer-in-the-headlights look about them. They hesitated and their shots stopped falling. The crowd began an audible buzz. The Suns managed to force the game into overtime, where they won.

The winner of this series would have homecourt advantage the rest of the way and be the title favorite. And because both Suns' wins came in Houston, the Rockets surely had blown their chance. Rudy Tomjanovich, the Rockets' coach, could remember the next day's headlines vividly.

He'd never seen letters so big in a newspaper. "CHOKE CITY!" was the cry in the city's papers.

"Six inches tall!" he said, exaggerating by, oh, say, five inches.

Seldom had such a seemingly safe judgment turned out so premature. With Barkley playing sluggishly, the Rockets came back to win the next two games in Phoenix, prompting Tomjanovich, in between puffs on a cigarette, to exclaim, "These guys are not chokers. They are men!"

They not only went on to win the series, 4-3, but went on to become known as the anti-chokers, the toughest team in sports to kill. The result: the first of two world titles.

The "Choke City" series (quickly recast as "Clutch City") changed everything. Until then, the Rockets had enjoyed only modest support in Houston. Their first few play-off games in '94 hadn't even sold out. The opener against the Suns featured about 3,000 empty seats, prompting Colangelo to buy hundreds of tickets for game No. 2 and fly in hundreds of fans at the Suns' expense.

Yet now, the Rockets not only were the champs, but also international celebrities and near deities in Houston. Looking back, Tomjanovich talked about those "big" headlines passionately, even bitterly. To him, the words had a cruel, almost gleeful tone that went beyond the normal disappointments of sports.

He knew they would have reflected the conventional judgment had the Rockets not eked out the series. And he likely would have lost his job somewhere between then and now.

"If we don't win that first series with Phoenix, you probably are not talking to me and some of the players," he said.

"The label 'Choke City' was put on us. If we don't win that series, the label might stay with us for years . . . My career would have been linked with the chokers.

"People wanted us to fail," he said. "You don't see headlines six inches tall. Things happen and you put labels on people, and it's not true. I don't see that label put on them (the Suns).

"That's how myths are made, how labels are made. But the label was a bunch of bull."

Tomjanovich had been a '70s playing contemporary of Westphal's. He didn't have Westphal's superstar pedigree, but he was tough and dependable. He'd survived one of the most vicious attacks in NBA history, a roundhouse punch by a player who had otherwise been well-regarded, a muscular forward named Kermit Washington. The punch connected so solidly some feared Tomjanovich could have been killed. As it was, his face was severely rearranged. Yet he eventually resumed a successful playing career.

Now, thanks to those two pivotal series with the Suns and the ensuing championships, he was regarded as one of the game's great coaches. Reflecting on those two series, Tomjanovich said, "It's amazing what happened. You never think lightning would strike twice."

Conversely, had the Suns played just a shade better, had Barkley not played erratically in both series before coming up lame, had Barkley not missed crucial free throws in Game 5 in the '95 series, the situation would have been vastly different in Arizona, too. Most obviously, Westphal wouldn't be having to justify his existence in seemingly every game.

Houston's Robert Horry sounded sympathetic.

"If you lose big games at crucial times . . . they think something is wrong with the team's chemistry. Then they try to change things even if they don't need to be changed.

"You can't dismantle a team because you lose a big game."

For Horry, the Suns were "the team that could have dismantled the Rockets." But they didn't.

In this game, despite the absence of Johnson and Williams, the Suns put up a furious battle, losing only in the closing moments. The game was their finest performance of the season. It was still another loss, sliding their record to 9-12, but Westphal's immediate crisis had passed.

N·O·T·E·W·O·R·T·H·Y

NOV. 21, PHOENIX
What's wrong with the Suns? Barkley has this analysis: "We can't score and we can't stop anyone else from scoring. Those are the two little things stopping us from being the best team in the league."

NOV. 21, PHOENIX
Barkley, talking about how his physical condition affects his up-and-down play, says, "My knee is getting better. As long as I don't have back-to-back games, I feel pretty good." In any case, "Seventy percent of me is better than 98 percent of other guys in the league."

DEC. 2, SAN ANTONIO
Barkley writes on the blackboard in the visitors' locker room: "7-8"

(the Suns' record after losing) and "67" the number of games left. "They don't give trophies in December, just Christmas presents. Y'all have your fun. Vultures like to see successful people struggle. They're looking for a funeral. But it's a long way from being over. Don't write us off yet."

DEC. 5, PHOENIX

Before a game with the Grizzlies, the normally mild-mannered A.C. Green is positively manic. The reason: He's watching a videotape of the previous night's pro wrestling action at the arena. Green attended the event and sat in the first row. But that wasn't enough. Not nearly enough.

He whoops and hollers while watching a replay of the action on the giant screen in the Suns' locker room. He shouts, "These are the greatest athletes in the world!"

Asked if he's bothered that the matches are "scripted," he replies, "Scripted? Are you crazy. Us knowledgable fans will almost punch you for that. It's real. You can tell."

His favorite moves include "the flailing kick, the gouge, and smashing the head into the turnbuckle." Says Green, "After the Bible, it's wrestling for me."

Jokes Westphal, "That's the dirty little secret of this team. A.C. is the craziest guy we have."

DEC. 9, PHOENIX

Westphal speaks at the funeral of Rodney Johns, the hero of Westphal's NAIA national championship team at Grand Canyon University in 1988. A few days earlier, Johns drove his car at over 80 miles per hour straight into a concrete freeway embankment in south Phoenix, killing himself and his sister. Westphal had tried to help Johns, who had been troubled for years.

At the services, attended by an overflow crowd in a church in probably the most troubled urban neighborhood in Arizona, Westphal turns to Johns' children and tells them not to repeat the mistakes of their father. "Drugs rob you of your soul," he says.

DEC. 9, PHOENIX

Before the game with the Miami Heat, Westphal critiques Pat Riley's ban on his players helping up a fallen opponent, a "rule" supposedly enforced by a $1,500 fine:

"If that's the case, it's abhorrent to me. It's classless and ridiculous and childish. It's not in the interests of good sportsmanship, which I still think is important. If that's the rule he put down, he should be ashamed of himself."

DEC. 24, PHOENIX

An observer of Charles Barkley once said that the world of big-time sport is full of bad guys who spend their time trying to make themselves look good. Barkley, this fellow said, is the reverse: a basically good guy who often tries to convince people he's bad.

Evidence for this theory surfaces in Barkley's Christmas Eve routine. As he does every year, he loads about 20 homeless youngsters aboard a bus that takes them to a Phoenix toy store. There, Barkley buys thousands of dollars worth of presents. Barkley also brings the youngsters' mothers and fathers, most of whom live in shelters, because he doesn't want the kids to think he's upstaging the parents.

Barkley has engaged in this practice for several years, say those who are familiar with his Santa Claus efforts. But he loathes publicity about the ritual, not wanting people to think he's trying to polish his image. His affection for children is genuine. Columnist Joe Gilmartin once noticed Barkley sitting transfixed in front of his locker about an hour after a game. He was listening reverentially to a seriously ill young girl singing "Jesus Makes Everything Better."

5

Up, down, a bad bounce, and out

IF THE NOOSE HAD BEEN PUT away, one didn't have to search the attic to find it. Instead, it had been placed in a more easy-to-reach spot. Like, say, the kitchen pantry.

There didn't seem to be much hope for Westphal surviving the holiday season, not when the Suns hosted the Washington Bullets just before Christmas.

The Bullets, who were missing their powerful young forward Chris Webber, raced through and shot over the Suns' porous defenses.

Barkley, as he had done so often through the early portion of the season, bogged down the offense by throwing the ball away. And in this game, he didn't score nearly enough to compensate.

At the other end, a journeyman named Tim Legler lit up the Suns with a trio of three-pointers, helping the Bullets stretch their early lead to 21 points. Legler had once played for the Suns, among several other teams. He had shuttled back and forth between the minor league CBA, where players earned perhaps $20,000, to the NBA on short-term, make-good deals. Once, he was cut minutes before the deadline that would have guaranteed his contract. He'd finally shown enough to earn a two-year guaranteed deal with the Bullets worth $250,000 a season, a pittance for most, an extravagance for Legler.

Westphal called time-out. He screamed at his players, reminding them Legler used to play for the Suns, that he'd been let go because management and coaches thought his chances to make it weren't as good as some of the players now on hand. "Maybe we were wrong!"

In particular, he challenged Finley to guard Legler. Legler didn't score again in the first half and beyond. Westphal's opinion of Finley was reconfirmed. "He's got a hole card," Westphal figured. "He can dig deeper."

The Suns gradually started to chop down the lead before halftime. Then Tisdale, who had done little since his big game at Madison Square Garden in early November, found his shooting range. He'd told Barkley earlier, "I'm going to help you out, big fella. Nobody's going to stop me." And sure enough, nobody did. He poured in shots from all over the floor.

He hit a 19-footer with 1:05 left to give the Suns a 95-94 lead. The fans, who had become accustomed to Suns' wins and often made for a sleepy audience, came alive. They howled as Bullets' rookie Rasheed Wallace stepped to the line. He missed both free throws. At the other end, Barkley grabbed his own miss and drew a foul. He hit one of two free throws to give the Suns a two-point lead with 17 seconds left.

The Bullets' speedy Robert Pack then drove to the hoop. Barkley blocked his shot but was called for body contact with 10 seconds left. Pack hit both free throws to tie it. Perry missed an open 17-footer with five seconds to go, and Pack missed a running 30-footer at the buzzer. The teams headed to overtime.

Perry hit a three-pointer and then a 15-footer; the Bullets responded with two turnovers. The Suns were cruising. But nothing came easily for them, and this would be no exception.

By the time Barkley missed a driving layup and Perry misfired on one of two free throws, the Bullets were down by three points in the closing seconds. The automatic play in such situations is to foul immediately, forcing the trailing team to shoot two free throws. But the Suns failed to put down a foul, and the Bullets' Juwan Howard nailed a three-pointer to tie it with 8.5 seconds left.

Barkley got the ball far out on the right baseline and threw up a prayer. It was answered when the Bullets' Calbert Cheaney was whistled for a foul with 1.8 seconds left. Barkley hit both shots, and the Suns had the win, pulling their record to 10-12.

Barkley threw himself to the floor. He probably was too tired to celebrate any other way. He'd just played 47 of the 48 minutes, even though the Suns also had played the previous night. He'd come up with one of his strangest stat lines ever, one reflecting effort over excellence. On one hand, he'd hit just 2-of-16 shots, and he'd committed five turnovers. But he'd also hauled down 14 rebounds, and he'd attacked the hoop enough to be awarded an astounding 27 free throws (he hit 22).

Tisdale poured in 30 points. He didn't come through with big games often, but when he did, the Suns usually won.

Westphal had dodged the Bullets, but the Suns had merely beaten their mirror image, a struggling, undermanned team.

Westphal was losing the battle of attrition. There was no hope in sight of an early return by Johnson. Then there was Manning. The hoped-for holiday return had been pushed back, perhaps by a month. The Suns had invested more than just hopes and dreams in Manning, they'd put $40 million in him. He wouldn't come back until he was absolutely sure he was ready to go.

Williams continued to try to play, but he couldn't jump with any explosiveness, and leaping was part of his rebounding and shot-blocking skills. Even as he improved physically, he played as if debating with himself whether he could function effectively. If the Suns had gotten anything from their centers in the first several games, they at least would have a winning record. Now, the position seemed worse than ever.

Of the players on hand, only Barkley had shown signs of playing like his old explosive self while the others had tailed off from their career norms.

This left an opportunity to take a look at the Italian experiment, the 6-foot-9 forward Stefano Rusconi. He was a project of Colangelo, who was friendly with the owner of the Italian team for whom Rusconi had played. There was some thought to taking Kleine's minutes and giving them to Rusconi. Perhaps he could learn the game quickly enough to play against second-level centers.

But Westphal resisted. Most every game was a cliff-hanger. A mistake at the wrong time, even by a player asked to perform a limited task, could cost them. The Suns departed the previous year's play-offs with a severe shortage of both perimeter shooting and defense at the center spot (sort of an inverse equation to the Rockets' title-winning inside-outside balance). That management would give a guaranteed contract to someone who could offer neither, at least immediately, was surprising.

But for the Suns' inner circle, Rusconi gave them a chance to reenter a field they had pioneered. Everyone had forgotten the Suns were the first team to sign a player directly out of Europe: Bulgaria's rebounding forward Georgi Glouchkov (YOR-gee GLOOCH-kov).

Colangelo traveled to Bulgaria in 1985 and traversed the red tape inherent in a country then still firmly locked behind the Iron Curtain. He emerged with a player who showed inside strength, but who had little knowledge of the NBA game.

John MacLeod, the Suns' coach at the time, worked with Glouchkov after practices. He'd point to various spots on the floor; his instruction would be repeated by an interpreter, then Glouchkov would say, "Da!" But midway through the season, the interpreter had to return to Bulgaria.

At the same time, Glouchkov's strength seemed to dissipate. Given Bulgaria's notorious reputation for steroid use in international athletic competition, Colangelo had to wonder whether his past strength had been a by-product of chemical wizardry. In the end, Glouchkov, homesick and unable to adjust to the NBA game, returned to Bulgaria after one season.

When Glouchkov didn't work out, the Suns shunned foreigners, even passing up Vlade Divac, later a stalwart for the Lakers, in the draft. Rusconi seemed to be a low-risk way to get back in the act.

The problem was that at the NBA level, Rusconi was just another backup big forward, already the Suns' most crowded roster spot.

Rusconi hailed from the north of Italy, near the edge of the Alps. In appearance, he seems far more Scandinavian than Mediterranean. He is a playful sort who entertained the Suns as he polished his English. "Are you having fun?" Barkley asked him. "Fun?" Rusconi repeated. "Oh, you mean happy?"

In studying the schedule, Rusconi's eyes brightened when he saw the Suns opened with the Clippers. "I think, 'Good, I get to play.' " But when the Suns struggled, he sat on the bench. The pattern would be repeated.

Rusconi looked around him. He could count as well as the next guy, in more than one language.

"I didn't know how many big guys there are here," he said. The Suns, of course, had to know, he pointed out. "They wanted me. They signed me. They know what position I play."

The prospect of an intractable position on the bench half a world from home left him one sad Italian. He thought about working out a deal to leave, saying, "I want to stay here. But if I don't play, it's no good."

Rusconi finally got a chance in the Suns' first trip to the shiny Canadian city of Vancouver, British Columbia. They finished a spectacularly clear, mild day by playing nearly flawlessly at night. They ran up leads of as many as 36 points over the expansion Grizzlies before coasting home. Barkley looked sharp, as did A.C. Green.

Rusconi got to play 13 minutes (he'd played a season total of only 12 minutes entering the game) and looked like a real NBA player, at least as effective as any of the Grizzlies. He scored seven points and blocked two shots. Speaking of his European experience, he said, "For 10 years, I play 40 minutes a game. Tonight, I am happy."

His "big" game turned out to be an aberration. He would make two more token appearances. Then he took a buyout offer from Bryan Colangelo, Jerry's son, who—as the team's general manager—had been taking over more and more of the team's operations. Rusconi headed back to Italy. The Suns needed immediate help, and he wasn't in a position to do much. He just didn't fit.

BACK AT HOME, THE SUNS prepared to host the San Antonio Spurs on network TV on Christmas Day. The Suns always seem to play on Christmas and Super Bowl Sunday, dates that draw big numbers on TV but are among the least favorite for players and coaches (and reporters, for that matter).

The matchups were impossible. Green would get the bulk of the time defending the much taller, stronger, faster David Robinson. Finley would try to cover Sean Elliott, now one of the game's best small forwards. Elliott had scorched Finley earlier in the month in San Antonio.

The Suns' best matchups were Williams on Robinson and Manning on Elliott. But Williams and Manning, of course, were out, as was Johnson. Green used all his wily, shirt-pulling tricks and battled heroically. Tony Smith, dropped off Avery Johnson and helped Green with "The Admiral." Barkley put together a terrific game (in every aspect except three-point shooting, where he was 1-for-5).

Somehow, the Suns led 97-93 with 3:10 to play. At this point, Person had a wide-open jumper on the left from about 8 feet away. He threw up an air ball.

Then Elliott tore into Finley at the other end. The Spurs won going away.

The Suns now were 7-5 in games they led after three quarters. They were 45-2 in the same circumstance the previous season.

"That's a matter of depth and not being used to each other," Westphal said. "We get a little tired and we don't make plays we're used to making."

Still, the overall trend was up. Barkley was taking his physical maintenance program more seriously, and the results were encouraging for him and the team. The Suns had now at least reached the point where they could be expected to beat the poor teams and battle (though usually lose) to the best.

The point was reinforced when they blew out the woeful Philadelphia 76ers and then the Denver Nuggets, who were—unlike the Grizzlies and

76ers—a real NBA team, one that now figured to be battling the Suns for one of the final play-off spots.

The Suns were 13-13. This was an embarrassing record judged by their recent standards. Yet based on their earlier erratic play and the fact they'd gotten little from Johnson and Williams and nothing from Manning and up-and-down play from Barkley, the .500 level seemed nearly exotic.

Surely, they were ready to take off, if they could only get the biggest engines out of the repair shop.

Said Barkley, "It's been a great feeling. We're playing with confidence."

Said Westphal, "If we keep playing this way and keep getting healthier, we'll win our share." Maybe, someone suggested, the terrible start was simply a way to lower expectations that now would be met and surpassed. Westphal laughed. "Now, we've got to leave .500 behind," he said.

ALONG THE WAY, THE SUNS had remade themselves. No longer were they a racehorse, shoot-first, ask-questions-later team. They were bigger up front and slower-moving on offense, yet trying to speed up on defense through increased use of double-teams.

On defense, Westphal would have a bigger man trap out front. This would both pressure the start of the other team's attack and minimize foul trouble underneath for the big man. On offense, they would patiently work for a good shot and—with a front line of Barkley, Green and Williams—expect to outrebound every opponent.

The key was Williams at center. He needed to start producing. "Hod Rod is our best player at knowing how to rotate," Westphal said. "He lets us play different than when we have a short small forward and a slow center."

By moving Green back in as a starter, the Suns now had a tall "small" forward (the "three" spot on a coaching diagram) and a quick center. This meant the Suns could switch assignments on the front line and not worry so much about mismatches.

Said Barkley approvingly, "You just have to adapt. A good team has to know its limitations. Do what you do best."

The major change would be to reemphasize the role of Green, who was steady early but lately had slid along with the rest of the team. He had a history of playing best in troubled times. And these times were the most urgent since the team was rebuilt after the drug scandal.

Starting Green gave the Suns a sense of certainty: Above all else, he would play. He *always* managed to play. Green's consecutive-games streak was at 750, third-longest in NBA history. As long as he could walk, it would continue.

Sometimes, this was a close call. An hour after one distressing, early-season loss, Green was the last to leave the locker room. The Suns had just lost in triple overtime to the Denver Nuggets, a defeat caused, in part, by a missed free throw by Perry in the closing seconds of regulation. (Perry was inconsolable for days.)

Green noticed a non-playing acquaintance at the far end of the locker room, near where Barkley dressed, and said, "How are you feeling?" The visitor was taken back: "How are *you* feeling?"

The question was a good one. Green's left ankle had a huge wrap around it. He walked with all the dexterity of Dennis Weaver as "Chester" the peg-legged sidekick to Marshall Dillon on the old "Gunsmoke" TV series. Even more troublesome was a sore back. He'd just received therapy from trainer Joe Proski, and he was carrying a prescription form to obtain medicine. Yet he continued to play.

The signing of Green in 1994 was one of the most trumpeted transactions in franchise history. At the time, because of his role on the Lakers' late-1980s title teams, he was the most high-profile of that summer's free agents. That they'd signed him away from the Lakers, for $15 million over five years (about $2.5 million less than the Lakers' offer) made it doubly delicious.

It helped that Johnson encouraged Green to join the team. So, too, did Green's visit to Phoenix when the Suns brought him into a darkened locker room, then turned on a spotlight over a space—next to Barkley's—bearing Green's name and uniform.

It helped even more that the Suns now had title aspirations and the Lakers did not. The torch, it seemed then, had been passed.

In obtaining Green, the Suns also acquired a philosopher, preacher and—like Johnson—a one-man social welfare agency. He was probably the game's best-known promoter of Christianity and, as the leader of a group called Athletes for Abstinence, had been called "the only virgin in pro sports."

On the floor, he was a gritty defender and hardworking rebounder who also could run fast breaks all night and never seem to run out of steam. He'd also been around long enough to know such tricks as how to grab an opponent's jersey when the referee wasn't looking. He was willing enough to mix it up under the hoop that the concept of Green as a dirty player, though not often mentioned publicly, had passed the lips of opponents.

In some people's minds, Green's longshoreman-tough stature supposedly demonstrated the irony of life for a Christian athlete: The fact that Green refused to turn the other cheek showed that occupational necessity differed with and outweighed personal values.

The way Green saw it, he was perfectly consistent, that he was a tough guy on and off the floor. "I have to be a tough, solid, focused person or I won't be able to sustain my way of life. There are a lot of people or things who will distract you and pull you down."

Indeed, some would say he had to be as tough as a collection agent for the mob during the eight years he played for the Los Angeles Lakers. This was a team with players known almost as much for their ability to dance all night on tabletops as for their basketball prowess.

"Obviously, I've had friends and teammates who are not Christians," Green said. "But I still respect them and hang around them because I'm a people person. But at the same time, I don't compromise.

"I don't preach to everyone. But neither do I have to listen to how they took advantage of somebody at a party the night before." In a personal sense, Green was more concerned with shaping the views of young people, not other pro athletes. He once told the Los Angeles Times: "I don't want to scare kids. I don't tell them, 'You're going to get a disease if you have sex.' I'm more concerned with what kids have to go through in terms of emotional scars.

"And they hear those stories about entertainers and athletes being promiscuous. They don't know what commitment is. They think you're a piece of property. And I'm concerned with young people not having a chance to grow up happily. There's enough problems trying to survive economically. You see a lot of single-family homes, and that's enough of a burden in itself."

In fact, at the same time Green joined the Suns, his abstinence group released a rap video titled "It Ain't Worth It."

"We focus on self-control instead of birth control," he said. "The point is to show young people that should you abstain from sexual involvement until you decide to get married, you're not strange or weird." He acknowledged that candidacy for sainthood was not a membership requirement. "Not everyone in Athletes for Abstinence—nor everyone who will be in the group—is a virgin. Almost nobody will be, I'm guessing. Everybody in there will have at least chosen an abstinent lifestyle from a certain point. It's not about beating somebody down for past mistakes."

He continued in his role as spokesman for abstinence after joining the Suns. The producers of the Phil Donahue show apparently considered him such an oddity that, during a stopover in New York, they allowed him to elbow aside the usual collection of transvestites and spouse-swappers to talk about his status as a celibate celebrity.

The only problem was that when flashing the phone number for Green's youth-services company, the TV screen showed 800-AC-Green instead of the correct 800-AC-Youth. The result was that befuddled workers for an Oregon trucking company began receiving hundreds of calls about sexual abstinence.

Though he got along well enough on the surface with his Lakers teammates, Green had become an irritant with his saintly image, according to some reports. The same concern seemed obvious with the Suns, now that he would be half of the oddest forward couple of all time with the Suns' No.-1 night owl, Charles Barkley.

The contrast was apparent enough just a couple of weeks after Green joined the Suns. The team was about to embark on a weeklong trip to Europe, where they would play a couple of exhibition games. It became clear that Green and Barkley wouldn't bump into each other much off the floor. Green's plans for the trip: To shop for a particular brand of German perfume. "My mom and my sister love it."

Barkley's plans for the trip: "I'll visit the German strip bars. I want to see if they're as good as the ones we have here."

Green kept his distance from Barkley. Even his locker was at the extreme end of the room from Barkley's. At the same time, he was the most inscrutable of all the Suns. He seldom expressed an opinion on the team's operations, though those who knew him said he came to be extremely dismayed at its Barkley-oriented looseness.

In his book, *Victory*, he emphasized the discipline and structure enforced by coach Pat Riley during the Lakers' dominance of the NBA. Yet he knew, or should have known, full well what he was getting into when he joined the Suns. He was acquired with the hope he would act as a defensive counterweight to Barkley's deficiencies. Intangibly, he would help balance Barkley's clown-at-heart nature with a fair dose of seriousness. He tended to play best in times of injury-filled crisis. But when the Suns were at full strength, he sometimes faded into the background.

The Suns and their fans were intimately familiar with Green because of his role with the hated Lakers. Thus, expectations for him were oversized, especially for a guy who was essentially a role player. Yet Green somehow succeeded in surpassing them his first season.

In part because of injuries to Barkley and Cedric Ceballos, the Suns counted more heavily on Green than they'd planned. And he responded by not only carrying out the dirty trenchwork, but displaying a scoring touch he only occasionally flashed for the Lakers. He finished with a career-high 14.7 scoring average. Westphal called him the team's unofficial MVP.

Afterward, Green exercised a clause in his contract allowing him to "escape" after one year and negotiate around the league for a better deal (a device owners and players agreed to drop in their next Collective Bargaining Agreement). The Suns rewarded him with a stunning package: $26 million over five years.

Colangelo proclaimed that losing him would have been a "disaster" both on and off the court, so he decided to take no chances. Indeed, this was true, as much for perception purposes as anything else.

Along with news of the season-ending party in 1994 (which had surfaced by the time of Green's re-signing) and various bar fights involving Suns players, Colangelo had another matter on his hands, one that made the other PR problems seem like a rainy day at a company picnic.

Among the players on the '93-94 Suns was a mysterious figure, a guy who often buried his head in books about the music industry while others talked basketball.

Jerrod Mustaf might have been the first athlete to spend a full season on the roster of a big-league sports team as a potential suspect in a capital crime.

Mustaf was known in Suns' circles as one who talked a good game. On the day of Magic Johnson's initial retirement because he'd contracted the virus that eventually causes AIDS, Mustaf vowed that off-court problems never would wreck his career. He said he'd taken seriously the NBA's orientation program for rookies, which warns of the dangers of life in the fast lane. The temptations of drugs and casual sex were discussed in detail. Then, he said with pride, "Nobody in our rookie class has gotten into trouble."

His work ethic on the basketball floor and off-court judgment constantly were in question. Once, he suffered a mysterious injury to his hand. He said he'd caught it in a car door. Joe Proski, the trainer, never was quite sure what happened.

In his final season, he played 196 minutes. He shot 36 percent and had eight assists. For this, he earned $1.1 million.

Westphal privately chafed at all the money Mustaf earned in return for little production: "Sometimes you have to pay somebody on potential, not accomplishment. When you do that, you bet on the wrong horse sometimes. That's what's wrong with the system."

In July 1993, Mustaf opted against joining the Suns' summer activities for young players. Learning this, Colangelo faced Mustaf down in the locker room: "I don't understand. You haven't done a thing as a professional. When do you think you earned this contract? In college? In high school?" Mustaf replied that he felt he'd earned his money.

A couple of days after this blowup, on the afternoon of July 22, 1993, a police officer in the west side suburb of Glendale was on his way to the west-side's police station. He was in a hurry, trying to take care of details so that he would be free to start his California vacation.

But he couldn't help but take notice of a red Mercedes convertible. He was sure he saw one of the Phoenix Suns. He was an "avid fan," so he'd seen the player "on numerous occasions on television as well as in person at a game" that season. Not that he needed to be such a fan. Coming off their run to the Finals, the members of the Phoenix Suns at that moment probably were the 12 most well-known citizens in the entire state.

In any case, the officer was sure this was Jerrod Mustaf. So, he thought quizzically, what is he doing way out here, driving into this nondescript Glendale apartment complex? A fair question, as it turned out, considering Mustaf lived an hour's drive away at the opposite end of the Valley of the Sun. According to officer Brent Coombs, "The Mercedes was being driven very slowly, and the top was down. Directly behind the Mercedes was a black Porsche hardtop, either a 928 or 944 model. . . .

"I was very curious about what he would be doing at this apartment complex and who might be in the Porsche. I almost turned around and went back to the complex to watch what they were going to do or where they were going to go within the complex. However, I was very pressed for time with personal business, so I did not."

At the time, Mustaf owned a black Porsche and had been loaned a red Mercedes. That night, Mustaf staged a dinner party for friends at his suburban Chandler home.

That same night at the Glendale apartment complex, a 28-year-old woman named Althea Hayes made what seemed to be a harried phone call to a friend. Hayes said, in a low voice, that Mustaf's cousin was present.

The cousin, LeVonnie Wooten, had served time in a North Carolina prison for a drug conviction. Both Wooten and Hayes had worked at an African-American-oriented store run by Mustaf. Wooten had been flown from Maryland to Phoenix the previous day by Mustaf.

Shortly after making the call, Hayes was shot to death, execution style. Genetic tests indicated she was carrying Mustaf's unborn baby at the time she died. Surviving family members said in court records that the two quarreled over the pregnancy and that Mustaf offered her $5,000 to have an abortion.

Mustaf denied involvement in the murder and said he believed Wooten was innocent.

During a grand jury probe into the case in April 1994, Mustaf told the judge overseeing the jury that he planned to invoke his Fifth Amendment rights against self-incrimination if called to testify. So, he was not called to testify.

The Suns put him on the injured list for good near the end of the '93-94 season. That move came after a Mustaf companion allegedly waived a gun at some of Mustaf's neighbors.

Management's thinking in keeping Mustaf that final season was purely practical. If he ever had been convicted of a crime serious enough to put him in prison, the Suns likely could have avoided paying him because of the standard "citizenship clause" in NBA contracts.

But the case proceeded slowly. Finally, as the '94-95 season approached, the Suns relegated Mustaf to their scrapbooks at a steep price, paying about $2.8 million to buy out the $3.8 million he had coming in the final two years of his contract.

In early 1996, Wooten was convicted of murder. Prosecutors alleged Mustaf had arranged the killing, but he had not been charged with a crime.

Colangelo was correct. At the time, the Suns REALLY needed Green to stay, lest the public continue to associate their players' lifestyles with the fall of Rome.

ALL OF WESTPHAL'S ADJUSTMENTS sounded swell. Yet there remained serious deficiencies, as recorded in cold and heartless detail by the stat sheets.

The Suns were the NBA's worst team in forcing turnovers. This was attributable in part to the absence of Johnson, their most effective player at disrupting the starting point of the opposing offense, plus the overall age and sluggishness of the frontline players.

Their three-point game, measured by the combination of their shooting and their defense on opponents' three-point gunners, also was the NBA's worst.

At the defensive end, they had to be so concerned about their interior shortcomings that they often left three-point shooters wide open. Opponents knew this coming in, and the NBA's three-point specialists fired away with the sort of elevated confidence players generally possess when facing expansion teams. Opponents hit more than 40 percent (the NBA average was 36 percent); during one three-game stretch, the figure was a phenomenal 55 percent.

That they would be a team with shooting woes seemed foreordained. They'd shot poorly ever since late the previous season; management hadn't re-signed their only proven clutch shooter (Ainge); yet they continued to fire three-pointers at a rate one would expect from a group of sharp-shooters.

Other than his one-game ban on three-pointers, at home against the Grizzlies, Westphal had done little to crack down on the low-percentage shots. His task was made more difficult by Barkley's fondness for hoisting them despite having one of the NBA's worst three-point percentages. Barkley's argument, "If I never shoot them, I won't have confidence," didn't have many backers.

Beyond this, Westphal didn't like to get into full-blown confrontations over such matters. He didn't like dictators overseeing him as a player; he wouldn't act like one as a coach. Yet in this case, a touch of Mussolini might not have been such a bad idea.

THE SUNS SURELY WOULDN'T have to worry about these matters against the lowly Minnesota Timberwolves. This was the kind of game where scalpers across the street from the arena normally are satisfied to peddle for face value.

NBA tickets, beyond the price range of most mere mortal working people, largely are purchased by corporations. The boss gets to see the Bulls, Magic and SuperSonics. The secretary sees teams like the Timberwolves, who had lost *all 25 games* in franchise history to the Suns.

As for the Suns, they'd followed their two best weeks of the season by enjoying two solid days of practice, part of a most unusual and welcome five-day schedule break.

Then, as the game unfolded, the results seemed to beg for a quick current events quiz: Who had reason to take the keenest interest in the ongoing debate over the future of Medicare?

A) The American Association of Retired Persons.

B) Large portions of the citizenry in Palm Beach, Fla. and Sun City, Ariz. or

C) Certain members of the Suns' front line.

The 32-year old Barkley had a great opening four minutes as he powered home four inside hoops. Then he faded from view completely. He scored only two points in the second half, and he pulled down just six rebounds for the game.

He moved so sluggishly that Westphal thought he must have been ill. He also knew that Barkley had a history of not putting forth energetic performances against lightweight opponents. And with a game the next night in Los Angeles against the Clippers, he rested Barkley "as long as we could afford it" in the second half. But when Barkley returned, he just didn't have it.

"I felt fine," Barkley insisted later. "No sense resting me. We're desperate."

Green, also 32, had trouble finishing layups, a routine matter for most every NBA player, but an increasingly difficult proposition for him. He'd never had much jumping ability, and playing with frequent back and leg pains, he seemed to doubt his ability to score in the paint surrounded by more powerful, athletic inside players.

The 31-year-old Tisdale, the player who most often appeared sluggish, had five fouls and three turnovers but only four rebounds in 20 minutes.

The 33-year-old Williams, who briefly seemed to have shaken his season-long slump, played tentatively, failing to plug the lane on opposing drives to the hoop.

And Kleine, who was celebrating his 34th birthday, didn't get a rebound or a point in a brief appearance.

It all helped add up to an epic 98-93 loss to the Timberwolves, big enough for Minnesota's Sean Rooks to display a multicultural sense of appreciation: "A huge, huge muy grande win."

For the Suns, it was a new low, a pratfall that caught them by surprise. Westphal's wife, Cindy, had a worried look when she greeted her husband after the post-game news conference. And for good reason. All the old problems had resurfaced. Said Westphal, "It's never a good time to lose to a team for the first time, and this was a terrible time."

A fan summed up the game nicely, shouting, "Paul, we're not only bad, we're boring!"

What fans were thinking, management types were thinking, too. Bryan Colangelo noted a "lack of enthusiasm and a lethargic style that ultimately seemed responsible for the loss."

The next night in L.A., there were bad signs from the start against the Clippers. Williams came out appearing confused. He picked up two quick fouls, but not before he threw the ball away, missed two free throws and a field goal. He made one more brief appearance, when he again felt numbness in his leg. With Kleine out with the flu, the Suns were down to seven players in the second half.

The teams plodded along; it was an evenly matched game between two teams that appeared headed for the draft lottery (where all the league's weak teams get a chance at the No.-1 college player), not the play-offs.

As Barkley waited to reenter the game for the final time, he pounded the press table and shouted, "THIS IS A BORING-ASS GAME!"

Somehow, the Suns managed to lead, 88-87, in the closing minutes. Then the Clippers' Pooh Richardson hit a running shot in the lane, and Person missed an open three-pointer. The game's key play came with 1:10 left, when Barkley threw it right to Richardson for his fifth turnover of the game and his 100th of the season. The Clippers' playmaker fed Loy Vaught, who hit a 20-footer. Barkley and Perry missed three-pointers, and the Suns were done.

Phoenix once again displayed the shooting of an eyesight-challenged group, hitting 2-for-16 from three-point range.

Barkley, asked if the Suns needed to trade for a shooter, laughed quietly and said, "All you can do is your best." Then, when the subject turned to the overall state of the team, he said, "Are we good enough to win right now? No. We can't win anything big right now." In losing to the Timberwolves and the Clippers, "We've played two bottom-of-the-barrel teams and kept it close. But we can't beat a really good team now."

Told the Suns had beaten only three winning teams this season, he said, "I wish we could find those teams right now."

The Suns would face the Clippers again at home. Surely, they couldn't drop two straight to this most woeful of sports franchises. But they would have to do it without Barkley, who had aggravated a sore toe in Los Angeles. He had his entire left big toenail removed, a procedure that was projected to sideline him for about a week, meaning he would miss three or four games.

Instead, he missed six.

This left the Suns to head into battle with eight players, forwards Green and Tisdale, Kleine at center, guards Person, Perry, Carr and Smith, and Finley, who could play the off-guard or small forward.

Their situation was so dire that Westphal seemed to be out of danger for the moment. Certainly, he wouldn't be fired while leading the NBA's minimum number of players required to avoid a forfeit. Indeed, Colangelo said as much.

All eight either were backups or complimentary players, a mere popgun against the NBA's heavy artillery. Only Green, Finley and Perry could be counted on to contribute regularly at a high level. All three had to have great games for the Suns to have a chance.

Among the others, Carr was just learning the game, and Kleine and Smith were deep reserves. Person and Tisdale had continued their inconsistent play. Yet if one of them found the shooting range, they might have a chance to steal a win here and there.

"In a way, I like this better," Westphal said. "If somebody is hurt, I'd rather have him out than play at less than his capabilities, so our team isn't judged that way." All in all, "It's bleak right now," he said. "All we can do is the best we can and hang on until reinforcements arrive." He made the case that unlike the previous season, when the Suns lost Manning for good, "None of the guys is out for the year. If they can come back and play to their form, they'll have a chance to be really good."

Until then, the experience would be "invigorating," Westphal said. "It's a challenge, an opportunity to work together, leave it all out there and play basketball, which is why we're all here in the first place." The fact that fans were writing them off "will make it that much more fun to turn it around."

Westphal was preaching a sermon that had the sound of artificial bravery. He'd had doubts about the makeup of the team for some time. But he would try to convince those around him, and himself, that there was no predetermined destiny, that the Suns could be like the Rockets, who struggled badly early the previous season before successfully defending their world title.

He recalled his season with the Knicks, in '82-83, when the team played through injuries and a losing run. Crowds of only a few thousand appeared at Madison Square Garden. "They booed us the whole time," Westphal recalled. "And not coming out to watch us was worse than booing."

Then the Knicks turned it around, enjoyed one of the NBA's best records in the second half, and gave the eventual champion 76ers their toughest play-off series.

"We were the darlings of the city," getting ovations on the court and praise in the press. Of course, by that time, "We didn't believe any of it," he laughed.

ALL ALONG, JOHNSON, with the blessing of the team's doctors, worked to strengthen his upper left leg to the point where once he came back, he stood a good chance of remaining in the lineup for the duration. No matter what exercises he'd performed in the off-season, he'd established a pattern of falling to injuries early in recent seasons, then staying reasonably healthy late. Perhaps the most favorable part of the pattern would hold.

There were those who wondered whether he was stalling, waiting for the ax to fall on Westphal before returning. Barkley shared his own doubts about Johnson (which were not shared by the medical staff) with friends on this point. But he wasn't in a position to talk much; his own injury was taking longer to overcome than had been announced. In the end, Johnson's plan worked well enough. After he came back to the lineup, he missed only five of the final 49 regular-season games because of injuries.

In the absence of his most prominent weapons, Westphal figured his best option was to start Finley and Green at forward, Kleine at center, and Carr and Perry at guard. Coming off the bench would be Tisdale, Person and Tony Smith, who could fill in at both guard spots.

This would put the Suns in the unenviable position of starting two rookies, usually a formula for a decisive loss. But if Westphal started all veterans and they got off to a poor start, he would be left with the option of going with inexperienced players to rescue them or staying with the same players who got them in trouble in the first place.

This way, he could have experience in reserve, players such as Tisdale and Person who (theoretically, at least) had considerable scoring punch.

In the rematch against the Clippers, Green, playing the more comfortable power forward spot in place of Barkley, had a terrific game. He scored 29 points and tied a career high with 20 rebounds. Perry ran the offense sharply, and—despite great shooting games from the Clippers' Richardson and Rodney Rogers —the Suns trailed just 101-100 with 48 seconds left.

Then Green was whistled for a foul on Charles "Bo" Outlaw with 27 seconds remaining. Outlaw was one of the game's worst shooters. He missed his first 12 free throws of the season and his average was a pathetic 39 percent. Later, he would be asked if he wanted to have the game in his hands at his least favorite spot. "What do YOU think?" he replied. (His clear meaning: NO!)

Outlaw wound up a little like a baseball pitcher and calmly hoisted the decisive shots. He hit them both. Green then fumbled away an inbound pass, and the Suns once again were done.

BARKLEY WAS STARTING to make noises as though on the whole he'd rather be, if not in Philadelphia, then somewhere other than Arizona.

The trade deadline was about a month away; it was time for the sports-talk shows that increasingly populate the radio band to toss out trade rumors. In L.A., the talk was of a deal that would send Barkley to the Clippers for Brent Barry, their promising rookie playmaker. The rumor was typical of such trade musings: It made little sense.

Barkley never would agree to finish his career on a perennial loser. "I'm not going to a bad team," he confirmed. If the Suns tried to make such a trade, he could simply declare his intention to retire. "I'm in control, no matter what happens."

And referring to a just-started ad campaign in which Barkley fumbles to remember the correct wording of an old hamburger jingle, he said, "The last time I checked, I had $20 million. And that was before the latest McDonald's deal."

At the same time, he hinted there WERE places he might agree to go. "Things are in disarray here. If we get healthy, we'll be very formidable. But that's a big 'if,' considering the last two years."

As it turned out, Barkley later said he talked directly to two teams that inquired about his services. He didn't identify them directly, but he said the Rockets and Knicks were the most interested in him. Then too, there were the Bulls, who could offer Barkley the dream-like scenario of playing with his pal, Michael Jordan.

Colangelo, with his basketball world crashing around him, became enraged that Barkley would engage in such talk.

"I don't want to be in the position of responding to what the hell he has to say," he snapped. "He should be worrying about getting healthy. Everyone should get heathy, start playing and doing their jobs. That's all they have to do."

Yet Barkley continued on the same lines the next day when he effectively laid down his terms for a deal. The place would have to be "ideal," meaning a contender who could use his rebounding and scoring prowess.

Moreover, his musings took on the tone of a campaign for a trade, similar to how he escaped Philadelphia three-and-a-half years earlier. In effect, Barkley said the Suns were done as contenders.

"I've got some bad news for you. This is as good as it gets," he said. And when somebody asked if a trade of Barkley would be a concession the team no longer has what it takes, he replied, "I can concede that right now, without making a trade."

Of the Suns' most recent personnel moves, he said, "Obviously, we've made some mistakes." He suggested it might be the time to make the biggest move of all. "I'm the only tradable player they've got," he said. The Suns had huge commitments to several, older (or injury-prone) players, he pointed out. "They're locked into these other guys for two or three years. They've got to make decisions on their future now."

Barkley could have minimized the speculation by flatly stating he wanted no part of a trade. But that, he said, would be a form of groveling, something he would never do. "I would never kiss management's rear end like that."

ON THESE CHEERY NOTES, the Suns took their dwindling band of players to the Bay Area, a metropolis with a competitive media curious about the Suns' woes.

The Suns were of considerable interest here. Johnson, who grew up in nearby Sacramento, had been a star at the University of California, just a few miles from the Warriors' arena. When Johnson's college coach, Lou Campanelli, was involved in a controversial firing, a host of Bay Area reporters hung on Johnson's every word for 15 minutes, trying to decipher subtle nuances in his studiously neutral stance. (Campanelli never used Johnson's explosiveness to anywhere near full advantage.)

Barkley, of course, was of considerable interest everywhere.

Beyond this, the Suns generally had crushed the Warriors over the years (the debacle the previous spring, notwithstanding). That they could come crashing down so quickly, for reasons other than the obvious injuries, seemed inconceivable. Westphal conducted a freewheeling session with reporters. To this point, he had tried to maintain his humor, but in trying to respond to questions about his job status, he started to alternate between defensiveness and an icy nervousness. Now he appeared to be laughing in the face of danger. The truth be told, Westphal didn't know how much danger awaited him.

Referring to the just-concluded blizzard in the East, Westphal talked about the Suns' upcoming two-week road trip. "With our luck, by the time we get there, the snow will melt. We could use a few snowouts there."

A reporter told him that his pal, Rush Limbaugh, now had his radio show aired twice daily in the Bay Area. "There's hope for this town," Westphal joked.

Asked about his relationship with the rotund right-winger, he said, "I don't tell him how to run America, and he doesn't tell me how to run the Suns."

Then he talked about how the Suns' problems were being dissected by such distant figures as the New York-based Regis Philbin, who recently talked up the possibility of Barkley being traded to the Big Apple.

"We're holding out for a trade for Kathie Lee and Regis," Westphal said. "The morning talk shows are weak in Phoenix."

Said a Bay Area scribe upon leaving, "Best locker room stuff I've ever heard."

ON THIS NIGHT, GREEN, Finley and Perry, the three players the Suns needed to come through to even have a chance, all played well. Person hit a couple of three-pointers in the fourth quarter, the time he usually couldn't be found. Tisdale struggled again, but even he hit a clutch shot that put the Suns up by 10 in the closing minutes. Kleine battled the Warriors' Rony Seikaly effectively. Carr avoided silly turnovers. (The previous day in practice, after Smith knocked the ball away from Carr a couple of dozen times, Westphal said, "Did it ever occur to you why you're losing the ball?" He instructed the rookie to dribble off to one side, protecting it with the other arm instead of dribbling it straight in front, which has the same effect as carrying a neon sign exclaiming, "Steal it from me.")

The Suns won the game.

The next night, they put on a frenzied rally to push past the Dallas Mavericks by 10 early in the final quarter. Conventional opinion would be changed. No longer would the Suns be considered lethargic underachievers. They would be overachieving upstarts. Two straight wins with eight players! Without Barkley, Johnson, Williams and, of course, Manning. Westphal would be hailed a genius, if only for a day or two.

Except that they ran out of steam. As usual.

Still, they had a one-point lead in the closing seconds, and they had the ball. The game was theirs.

Except that Finley missed a free throw with 12 seconds left.

Still, they had the win. They were up by two, and the Mavs' Jason Kidd dribbled it off his knee.

Except the ball didn't do what it usually does in such situations. It didn't sail out of bounds. Didn't roll to one of the Suns. Didn't end up on the floor as the subject of a pileup and a jump ball.

Instead, it rolled to the Mavericks' Popeye Jones as efficiently as any of Kidd's crisp passes. Jones missed, then took a whack at it on a tip. So did Kidd, who finally grabbed it and tossed it in with two seconds left.

The game went to overtime, where the Suns completely ran out of gas. Mavs win.

WESTPHAL WAS EMOTIONALLY drained, his voice barely more than a whisper. With his eyes glistening, he said, "I have a hard time describing that one."

He implored his team to keep working hard. "This snake-bit stuff is going to stop!"

Next up was a game with the Cleveland Cavaliers, the team that had been doing the most with the least. Their top players over the past decade, Larry Nance, Mark Price, Brad Daugherty and Williams, either had retired, been traded, or were hurt. They'd started the season 0-7, yet—using a team of little-known players "a glorified CBA roster" some said—they'd already scrambled back to above .500.

They did so with a butt-ugly style that slowed games to a wagon-train pace. They used an aggressive, in-your-face defense that was perhaps the best in the entire NBA. On offense, they took high-percentage shots and had players with the skill to make them.

The game served as a welcome home for Majerle. Upon entering the game, he got a thunderous standing ovation, one that lingered for more than a minute when ref Dick Bavetta conveniently discovered a wet spot that he deemed needed mopping.

Unlike the Cavs, the Suns neither were adept at shooting or ball-handling. In this game, all their negative characteristics shot forth like a desert plant after a spring rain.

Perry would dribble the ball, look one way and pass just as the intended recipient broke the other way. They appeared to have been introduced to each other minutes before tipoff. On and on it went, disorganized, chaotic, through 24 brutal minutes. The Suns were everything the Cavs were not.

By halftime, they'd recorded 30 points, a record low for the building. Incredibly, they had 13 turnovers while making only 11 shots from the floor.

The Cavs led, 45-30, at the break. The Suns made a run, drawing to within 62-57 early in the final quarter. Then Majerle drove to the hoop, converted a three-point play, and the Suns never challenged again.

Coming into the game, despite the massive personnel losses, the Suns had battled gamely; they'd only been blown out twice all season. For Westphal, this was the worst time for the third. The final was 89-74, the fewest points a Suns' team had scored in more than a decade. They now were 14-19, and with Johnson and Barkley not expected back for a game or two, at least, more losses seemed assured.

Majerle was the game's dominant player. He charged to the hole and filled in wherever the Cavs needed him. Just like in his (and the Suns') heyday. He was the game's high scorer with 20.

In these situations, where a trade has worked out better for one team than another, there are many "I told you sos" among the affected parties, almost always in private. Before the game, Majerle would just smile when the subject was raised, admitting only that he was surprised the Suns would deal him for an injured player. Afterward, he acknowledged feeling vindicated. As far as the Suns' woes, he said, "I have no answers. I'm a Cavalier now."

Then he headed to his bar-and-grill where he was treated as the conquering hero. One sign proclaimed, "Our Suns don't shine without our No. 9."

The operators of the bar had received permission to block part of Second Street in downtown Phoenix outside the bar, where a huge party was staged. Bands played, beer flowed. Inside, fans used any story they could think of to get close to their hero.

With the music throbbing, Majerle stood on a table, autographing memorabilia for breathless teenagers, more "well-developed" young women, season-ticket holders, chubby bar regulars, the works.

"My wife and I made a sign for you. It got on TV. Could you sign it? We're you're biggest fans."

"Dan, could I get a picture taken with you?"

Majerle's buddy, Joe Kleine, was on hand, and Barkley made a brief appearance. But for the most part, the Suns went home to brood over another loss.

In the Suns' postmortem, Westphal was less distraught than in the improbable loss to the Mavericks. Instead, he seemed numb, almost zombie-like. He recited the Suns' problems in an emotionless monotone and pronounced, "That's the worst it's been."

Jerry Colangelo agreed.

After the first-half bomb, he caught glimpses of the second half from the runway under the baseline stands leading to the locker room, as if unable to take in the whole ugly spectacle.

Two days earlier, he'd told a national NBA reporter that Westphal was in charge "for now" while remarking that the coach had a fine severance package should his tenure end.

Now, he stood grim-faced, his arms folded at his chest as rigidly as a cigar-store Indian. To act or not to act? The body language fairly shouted that he'd made up his mind.

By the next day, Colangelo had placed calls to Westphal's house, leaving messages that he needed to speak to him. He went on radio early in the evening to blast the Suns' clumsy performance, saying injuries couldn't excuse it.

Westphal was finishing a Bible study session with his teenage son Michael and several of his high-school friends when the two finally connected about 9:30 p.m. Colangelo said he was in the area of Westphal's Paradise Valley home and needed to speak with him.

"Why not drop by the house?" Westphal suggested.

"No, I'd rather do it at a hotel."

Do it?

Westphal now saw the score as clearly as if he were reading inning-by-inning updates on an electronic billboard in Times Square.

As he drove to the Hyatt Gainey Ranch hotel in adjacent Scottsdale, Westphal was amazed at what was about to happen. The decision hit him like a body blow from Mike Tyson. He'd always been realistic about the business, often saying, "I'm sure Jerry will fire me some day." But this day? With eight players, none of whom were named Barkley, Johnson, Manning or Williams, the four most vital to the Suns' chances?

They met in a sitting area near the lobby and, sitting on an L-shaped sofa, Colangelo delivered the verdict: "I've been in this business a long time. I think it's time to make the change."

Said Westphal, "There's nothing I can say?"

"No, I've considered it really seriously. This is what I have to do." Colangelo said he hoped they could still be friends.

Westphal said he disagreed with the decision but respected Colangelo's prerogative to make it and that he appreciated the opportunity to coach the team.

He then called his wife, Cindy, who was out of town. They both grew up in Southern California. Cindy's younger brother played basketball for Paul's older brother at an L.A.-area high school. The brothers combined to arrange a blind date for Paul and Cindy when the two were on a break from their respective colleges. They were married in 1972.

On this night, Cindy was in San Diego, checking out a potential college for their daughter. Cindy had been reluctant to leave town in the midst of all the losing, but the two of them felt reassured enough by Westphal's second meeting with Colangelo that she could go.

She picked up the phone and heard her husband say, "Hi, sweetie. You're talking to the ex-coach of the Phoenix Suns." After a sleepless night, she drove back to Arizona the next morning.

The messages of condolences came pouring in the next afternoon and evening after the decision had been announced.

The Lakers' Del Harris told him, "Sometimes, they can't pay you enough for all the aggravation. Other times, you'd do it for free." This got Westphal thinking of a quote he remembered from the veteran coach Abe Lemons. "In the old days, we didn't make much money, but we sure did have fun. Now, we get a lot of money but we don't have much fun. I like it better now!"

Though Westphal couldn't fully appreciate this line at the moment— friends said he was extremely low the next few weeks—Colangelo had taken care of him. He would get more than $1 million through the end of the next season.

Westphal, fully mindful of his two stormy departures as a player, had only one brief public comment. "I'm thankful for the opportunity to have coached the team. I'm sorry it ended."

He continued to bite his tongue, telling one friend, "The high road is the best road." Yet he had to admit, "Sometimes the high road sucks."

COLANGELO CALLED FITZSIMMONS, who knew his boss had been considering the move. He agreed to return as coach. There was no discussion of money at this point, for Fitzsimmons had no contract.

In one of the most extraordinary of sports relationships, he'd operated for the past nine years on a handshake agreement with Colangelo. The handshake would cover this move as it did everything. Fitzsimmons was surprised to find that his next paycheck after taking over as coach included a substantial pay hike.

The odd result of this relationship was that the lack of a contract seemed to give him more security, rather than less. If ever he or Colangelo decided Fitzsimmons would better serve the Suns by changing roles, either could make the decision to go at any time and it wouldn't be a big deal. And because he also had Colangelo's ear, meaning he could steer players out of town, he could command their respect even if wasn't planning to coach over the long haul.

After midnight, a news conference was scheduled for late morning. TV and radio stations figured out the purpose, so the players knew what had happened by the time they arrived at the arena that morning.

No matter their personal feelings on the change, they were respectfully somber when Fitzsimmons first addressed them. They would start to get familiar with his gravel voice with the country accent as flat as a Kansas plain.

He told them not to get discouraged, that better days were ahead, but that improvement would take time. He urged them to know that they merely needed to "Play hard, have fun, and stay together."

By the time he'd finished, they were more upbeat. Fitzsimmons was a better speechmaker, more up tempo, than Westphal. While Westphal used words judiciously, Fitzsimmons continually tossed them around as though he'd just been granted the power of speech.

Then, Colangelo and Fitzsimmons took Barkley aside and assured him they wouldn't trade him unless they got a "blockbuster" offer.

Barkley poked fun at this posture, saying this was like telling his wife, "I love you. I'm with you . . . as long as I don't get any blockbuster offers."

At the news conference announcing the change, Colangelo did what he could to make the proper bows to Westphal as a coach who had a "good run," who could only be praised as a fine man, an exemplary spokesman for the franchise, that injuries certainly were a factor.

Still, any coach firing is inherently the time when blame is officially handed out. And in the sports business, the people who put the teams together also assess and assign the blame. Colangelo lamented the team's lack of "togetherness" in the short run and its looseness over the longer term. "Do you ride a ship into the depths? You don't do that. In this business, if you hit bottom, there's no guarantee you'll come up."

Pressed on the team's personnel decisions, he expressed pride in the way the team had been put together, even saying he "couldn't understand" why so many questions had been raised.

Fitzsimmons, who had a sense that there were indeed problems with the team's makeup, figured this was the time to remind people that their decisions had been made by committee and that Westphal's voice had been important. To make the point effectively, he stuck the knife in his old protege. "Everybody on the roster, he wanted on the roster. Everybody that's gone, he basically wanted to be gone. We never got in the way of what he wanted to do."

His point wasn't true on every count. Westphal opposed the addition of Rusconi, which worsened an already lopsided imbalance of too many big forwards, not enough shooters, not enough centers capable of offering resistance to the superstar big men. Yet in a general sense, Fitzsimmons was right. Westphal, along with Colangelo and Fitzsimmons, had played a leading role in the moves that remade the team since their run to the Finals. If Fitzsimmons' barb didn't hit a bull's-eye, it at least managed to land in one of the nearby circles.

As far as the team was concerned, Fitzsimmons put on his best sales job: "I DO see a light at the end of the tunnel. I DO think we can play winning basketball. We will get back in the play-off picture. We will be a force once we get there."

TISDALE AND PERSON, the two players whose confidence Westphal had lost, endorsed the change. So did Green, who the previous month had called the talk of firing Westphal "stupid." All of this stung Westphal, according to friends. He expected that even those at odds with him would at least take the perfunctory "This-is-the-tough-part-of-the-business" route.

The biggest wound was inflicted by Johnson; Westphal thought their differences had been patched to a greater extent than really was the case. When a couple of dozen reporters and cameramen converged on the hushed locker room after the change had been announced, he at first spoke in respectful tones. Then, as the media started to drift away, he felt emboldened, needling Barkley over a phrase Barkley had coined to describe himself the previous season.

He pointed to himself and said, "This is Franchise Senior." Then he pointed to Barkley, whose locker was on the same side of the room, about 12 feet away, and said, "That's Franchise Junior over there. The roles are reversed."

Johnson meant this as a joke. But to those who heard it, he seemed to be enjoying himself a bit much considering the seriousness of the occasion. Later, Johnson sent Westphal a conciliatory note.

"Nothing personal," Johnson insisted. "He made his choice."

Indeed, Westphal HAD made a choice. He put his eggs in Barkley's basket, and the superstar faded a bit too much, was more than a bit too reluctant to work out, and—try as he usually might—couldn't come through for him (nor did his slumping, injury-prone teammates) when his coach needed him most.

Johnson's observation implied other choices might have made a significant difference. This never would be known. But now they would at least be able to start finding clues about whether the reasons for their problems (other than the injuries) were rooted in coaching, or if there were even more intractable, perhaps terminal, factors at work.

Barkley played the soldierly role of defending Westphal (as did Kleine and Perry). He knew, as well as anyone, that he and Westphal were linked indelibly with the team, its successes and failures, its personality and general approach. Now, this approach had been judged off-course by Colangelo.

Under Westphal, Barkley's influence could scarcely have been greater. There could only be one direction that influence would go.

"I think it's a sad time anybody gets fired," Barkley said. "If the world was filled with people like Paul Westphal, it would be a better place.

"It's been a very difficult year. Everything that could go wrong, went wrong. And Paul's going to take the blame."

Though Barkley said Westphal got a "raw deal," he didn't want to take on Colangelo directly. So, he blasted the climate created by media members and fans, whom he thought had little understanding of the situation's complexities. Phoenix, he later said, was a "podunk" town spoiled by success, in effect saying the populace's enjoyment of the good times exceeded its knowledge of why those times were changing.

(To the extent the "podunk" label was true, it was also part of the reason Barkley had been treated so reverentially, with so few questions of anything he did. The public had never seen an international celebrity in their midst on the scale of Barkley; the collective reaction was what you might expect of Gomer Pyle taking his first trip down the Las Vegas Strip at midnight. "GOLL-LEE!")

Barkley had majority opinion, if not among the hard-core fans, then among the more casually interested general public, on his side. Certainly, on the national scale, the perception that the straight-arrow Westphal had taken the fall for the team's debilitating run of injuries caused the Suns' shiny image to take a hit.

Barkley had to concede one positive from the firing. At least the tension caused by the previous month's uncertainty had ended. Now they could concentrate on basketball.

THE FIRST GAME UNDER Fitzsimmons would be at home against the Orlando Magic, one of the NBA's three best teams.

The Suns came out full of fire and fury, enough to stay with the Magic for nearly a half. But they had no answer for the monstrous Shaquille O'Neal at center or for the smooth inside-outside game of Anfernee Hardaway. The Magic won in a rout. This was the last of the Suns' six straight games with eight players. They finished 1-5.

Afterward, media members eager to go along with management's "time for a change" theme, asked Barkley if the team didn't seem more energetic and enthusiastic.

"Yes," Barkley said. "We were very enthusiastic in getting our butts kicked.

"It's very simple. If we don't get our guys back, we're going to get our rumps rocked. No matter who your jockey is, you have to have the horse."

Afterward, Fitzsimmons called Westphal at home to see how he was doing. Westphal had called him after the firing to wish him well. Now, with the team about to leave on its longest road trip of the season, Fitzsimmons invited him to visit the team in hopes of making everyone feel better. But with some of the players, notably Johnson, seeming to enjoy the change, Westphal thought this would be a macabre get-together. He declined the invitation. The two would not speak again the rest of the season.

The result on the floor was the same at Portland, where Joe Kleine couldn't handle the Trail Blazers' Arvydas Sabonis, who put on a dazzling display of shooting and passing.

Sabonis, a Lithuanian, had been pursued by the Blazers for several years. Had he joined them when they were a dominant team in the early '90s, they might have gone on a title-winning dynasty. Now, he finally was in the NBA. He couldn't move well or play a full game because foot problems had taken a toll. Yet he understood the game's nuances so well that the normal adjustment period of a couple of years for a European player could be set aside. Immediately, he established himself as the game's best-passing big man. The only problem was that his ability to throw brisk, no-look passes sometimes exceeded his teammates' ability to catch them.

In this game, Sabonis took apart Kleine and the Suns with 15 points in just eight minutes of the second quarter alone.

Finally, in the Suns' "getaway" game, the one before they started the marathon road trip, they had their game come together. They shot well, they ran, they rebounded in a rout over the visiting Sacramento Kings. There was one noticeable difference: Johnson and Barkley were back in the lineup.

N·O·T·E·W·O·R·T·H·Y

DEC. 27, PHOENIX

Joe Kleine tells a visiting sportswriter, "Charles and I have no-trade clauses." How's that?

"His is written in. Mine? Well nobody wants to trade for me."

DEC. 30, PHOENIX

Kleine, who spent a great deal of time the past off-season dealing in labor matters, is reelected team player representative. He didn't have to wage an all-out campaign. "Nobody else wanted it," Hot Rod Williams says.

JAN. 4, PHOENIX

Westphal and assistant coach Paul Silas are watching TV in the coach's office before a home game with the Timberwolves. The team's satellite operation picks up the Knicks vs. the Nets. The discussion turns to Jayson Williams, a Nets forward who once was drafted then discarded by the Suns. He turned out to be a much better player than they'd ever imagined. He also had a Barkley-esque talent for talking. One memorable Williams-ism: "Fame is fleeting. One day, you're peacock. The next day, a feather-duster."

Then the conversation turns to more dour topics, such as players who seem insulted when they're "only" offered $3 million or $4 million a season, and others who are forever complaining or trying to out-coach the coach. Says Silas, "Why can't they just shut up and play?"

They talk about Kenny Anderson, the Nets' point guard.

He is one of the game's finest ballhandlers but worst shooters. Unfortunately for the Nets, he prefers to shoot as much as pass. He's also just turned down a reported $40 million contract offer, a figure many view as insanely high for such a limited player.

Westphal compares him to Perry, whom the Suns have signed for $12 million over six years. "I'm not sure I wouldn't want Elliot over Kenny Anderson," Westphal says. "Elliot brings it every night."

Replies Silas, who has coached Anderson in New Jersey, "I agree."

Says Westphal, "Forty million dollars doesn't go as far as it used to."

JAN. 18, PHOENIX

After being eaten alive by Shaquille O'Neal, Kleine says, "Man, I was sore afterward. I had a few beers before I went to bed. But even that didn't help."

6

On the road

EIGHT GAMES IN 14 DAYS. The Suns would start the longest road trip of the season hoping to come up with two or three wins, enough to avoid being hopelessly buried in the standings.

The itinerary included eight plane trips covering 10,000 miles, 13 wake-up calls, and a staggering 50 bus rides to and from airports, hotels, practice sites and games.

When the Suns arrived at their Indianapolis hotel, they were greeted by about a dozen autograph seekers. Generally, these are starstruck young-sters, but others are concerned only with the present and future values of autographed cards, balls and other paraphernalia.

They seem to know the schedules of teams—when they go to and from practices, when they arrive from and depart to airports—better than peo-ple who are affiliated with the teams. How they accomplish this is one of the eternal mysteries of the NBA, right alongside an interpretation of the league's complicated illegal defense rules.

Barkley is among the most willing and patient signers of autographs in sports. And he doesn't charge a dime. His only rules: He doesn't sign cards (thus minimizing his role in the lucrative and sometimes seedy busi-ness of autograph trafficking) and he gives just one autograph per person. When a woman approached Barkley in a Scottsdale bar in 1993 and insisted on more than one (becoming so indignant that she tore up the sole autograph Barkley signed), he responded by pouring a cold beer over her head. The incident became public, and such was Barkley's popularity that the public automatically and universally sided with him.

On this chilly night, Barkley sat at the hotel bar and handled the steady stream of admirers and autograph hounds with characteristic ease.

The bartender, impressed with his patience, asked, "Don't you get tired of people coming up to you all the time?"

"No," Barkley replied. Then, motioning toward a gentleman hovering near him, he said, "That's why I've got this guy. He's got a gun."

Inside the hotels, many of the better known players and coaches try to reduce the hassles of celebrity by checking into hotels under dual names: their real ones and—for the purpose of taking phone calls—an alias. This ruse has become more common in the wake of the explosion of local and national sports talk shows. Anyone with access to a live microphone from Sheboygan to "Truth or Consequences" can get the NBA directories that list the hotels that host each of the teams, then call at any hour. Many players and coaches also take the more traditional route of placing a hold on their calls.

Westphal had been checking into hotels under the names of characters in Bob Dylan songs. Barkley would change up, yet he usually thought big. A frequent name he used: Babe Ruth.

Whatever the drawbacks of traveling, there's no doubt conditions had improved dramatically over the years.

Though modern players complain of the rigors of back-to-back games, as late as 1983, the NBA had teams playing on as many as THREE nights in a row.

In the late 1980s, as the NBA was booming, teams started flying in chartered planes. Now they fly when it suits their convenience, not the airlines'. The practical effect: teams rarely travel on game days and arrive at the arenas reasonably fresh.

Still, there are no guarantees. This lesson was reinforced the previous season for the Miami Heat when their charter ventured into a tropical storm. The Heat avoided disaster, but only after 25 minutes of terror in the air.

"As the plane took off, you could tell something was wrong because the pressure was so great when we were leaving and it never eased up," said center Matt Geiger, who ended up in a hospital emergency room with a ruptured eardrum. Teammate Keith Askins was terrified. "I thought I was going to die. I thought my brain was going to explode."

The weaving, bouncing, careening landing was even scarier.

"I was terrified," Glen Rice said. "I forgot about the pressure when the plane starting tilting. It felt like the plane was going to land on one wing. It tilted over so far one time that I was trying to balance the airplane, knowing I couldn't do any such thing."

"My hands were shaking," said Harold Miner. "It's like all of a sudden you realize, 'I'm up here in a machine.'"

Just a few weeks before the Suns started their own marathon Eastern trip, the Orlando Magic had to deal with the elements in the East. The Magic's plane was headed for Philadelphia when it encountered the great Blizzard of '96, the one that impacted the entire East Coast, driving particularly hard into southeast Pennsylvania. The Philly airport had to shut down; the Magic could only get as far as Allentown, Pa.

They were stuck there for two days during the blizzard. The players moaned, but at least they had built-in entertainment. Also stranded at the same hotel was the cast from Sesame Street Live, along with the alternative punk band Marilyn Manson, and a wedding party.

Players ended up partying at the hotel bar with the remains of the wedding party, which was half wiped out by the storm. This eclectic group, NBA players, tattoo-laden rockers, Sesame Street actors, and blue-haired wedding guests played darts and drank together, with the players signing autographs and having their pictures taken.

Said the Magic's Jon Koncak, "It was like the scene in Star Wars, where you have all the animals from different planets in the bar. You couldn't find a more diverse group of people and stick them together if you tried. It was hilarious."

The players were fascinated by the band, which leaned toward dark, gloomy music and appearance. One member, who wore more tattoos than Dennis Rodman, was particularly frightening. Koncak called him the Grim Reaper, saying, "I couldn't look him in the eye. I figured if I made eye contact with him, I'd be dead."

By the end of the two days, local TV and radio stations had broadcast word of the Magic's situation, and fans braved two-foot-high snowdrifts to take a peek. After a radio station announced the Magic's presence, the hotel was besieged by hundreds of kids, plus senior citizens and rock bands.

The predicament inspired Shaquille O'Neal to write a rap ditty: "I woke up, there was 50 feet of snow, nowhere to go. All the stores were closed, frostbite on my toes."

Later, O'Neal was asked how he enjoyed Allentown.

"The people are nice," he said, "but I'm a tropical black man."

IN TAKING OVER AS COACH, Fitzsimmons preached to his players to take fewer perimeter shots (a goal Westphal sometimes lectured on without much success) and to put more emphasis on the fast break. Westphal desired this, too. But for most of the past season and a half, Johnson—

the spark plug for the racehorse attack—either was out of action or limited. The same went for the defense, which needed to come up with enough stops to start the attack. Johnson was the key to the perimeter defense. He was quick enough to stay with explosive scorers and—when assigned to more marginal types—could help double-team the opponent's big-time scorer. In addition, without their two best interior defenders, Williams and Manning, the Suns struggled to stop anyone. And defensive stops were needed to start fast breaks.

Because of the big win over the Kings just before the trip started, and since the pressure that came with the coaching uncertainty had been lifted, there was much talk of renewed energy.

They would start their trip against the Pacers, who had been only a half-notch below the NBA's top three or four teams the past few seasons. Indiana had excellent inside-out balance between towering center Rik Smits and sharpshooter Reggie Miller. They started the season slowly but now were starting to play to form. But Smits was unexpectedly out with an injury, so the Suns figured to have a decent shot at winning.

The Pacers generally were true to their name. They won with a deliberate attack, punctuated by Miller's jump-shooting plus solid team defense.

But in this game, the Pacers threw themselves into fifth gear and ripped holes in the Suns' defenses. The energy the Suns had talked about was nonexistent. Wesley Person was lit up every bit as brightly as downtown Tempe during this Super Bowl week by Miller, who pumped in 23 of the Pacers' first 43 points, and Indiana rolled to a 64-47 halftime lead.

It didn't get any better after the break. Miller finished with 40 points in a 117-102 Pacers' rout.

Said Person, "I was in his face, but he would rise up and shoot."

Person tried to bump Miller but was told by the refs to loosen up. By this time, "He already was in a zone. I was at his mercy."

To Fitzsimmons, this wasn't satisfactory: "If he wants to be a starting two guard, he'll be thrown up against great players. He'll have to get better."

What was worse was the overall lethargy, the sort of slow-footed awareness that characterized their last game against the Timberwolves, the one that started Westphal's final descent.

Fitzsimmons scolded his team, "Forget about Reggie making 40 points. He can do that, and we still can win. But you've got to give me the effort every night. I didn't see the fire, the energy, the intensity. Consequently, we got killed!"

IN MINNESOTA, THE PHOENIX attack was bogged down by poor shooting, particularly by Johnson. In the first half, he hit only 3-of-11 shots from the field (one of the misses was a wide open layup) and only 2-of-6 from the line. His teammates weren't much better. But the Timberwolves had enough ballhandling problems that they only managed a 51-46 halftime lead, so the Suns figured they had a good chance to nail down a win.

At long last, their two superstars finally lived up to their billing in the same game.

Johnson forced the action, racing the tempo, penetrating, and either scoring or dishing off for layups. Barkley controlled the inside game. The Suns took off for a 31-14 advantage in the third quarter and then coasted home.

With Barkley and Johnson playing their parts, Fitzsimmons got away with using only seven players. The youngest regulars, Finley and Person, played the entire 48 minutes and fared well. Barkley, now steadily improving, didn't even realize he played 40 minutes.

And in the continuing debate over "Who is Franchise Senior?" Barkley made his point with his usual clarity to Phil Taylor, a reporter who was in the process of chronicling the Suns' woes for *Sports Illustrated*.

"I AM THE PRODUCT!" Barkley roared in response to questions about a possible trade. He would control his eventual destination, he insisted. "I know how good I am."

As Barkley disappeared into the shower, Johnson walked up to Fitzsimmons, stuck out his hand, and said, "Thanks for sticking with me early. Man, I was struggling."

Replied Fitzsimmons, "Kevin, when have I abandoned you? Kevin, I'm not a dummy. I'm not going to abandon you. My wife would kick me out of the house."

IN MILWAUKEE, MICHAEL FINLEY got a hero's ovation. He had been a superstar at the University of Wisconsin. His success with the Suns was a huge embarrassment to the Bucks, who passed him by in the college draft. Instead, they made a draft-day trade and picked up another Big-10 stalwart, a shooting specialist named Shawn Respert who so far had been a big-time bust.

Finley would be guarding another former Big 10 great, Glenn "Big Dog" Robinson. Two years earlier, Robinson was the nation's best college player, a fluid 6-7 scoring machine who lifted Purdue to elite status in NCAA competition.

At this point, Robinson was a slightly more skilled player than Finley. But the greatest distinction between the two was their contracts.

Robinson was the No.-1 pick in the draft before the previous season, the last one in which no restrictions existed on the contracts of rookie players.

The high draft picks could demand any dollar amount imaginable and wait for the owners to respond. In Robinson's case, his agent sought the first-ever $100-million contract (prompting the Bucks' owner to say he'd be better off if he had the contract and Robinson took over the franchise).

Of course, owners didn't HAVE to pay Robinson or other rookies a dime. But if they didn't agree to a contract, they didn't offer much hope to fans. They would suffer major public relations problems and lost ticket sales.

And teams dealing with high draft picks already were in dire straits. That's why they had the top choices in the first place. The draft order is based on the inverse order of finish (i.e. the worst team pick first).

Inevitably, the owners would agree to the oversized contracts. In Robinson's case, though "Big Dog" eventually agreed to come down to a $68-million, multiyear deal, few thought the Bucks "won" the contract talks.

The end result was the highest-drafted rookies were the game's highest-paid players, even though they'd never proven a thing and many would turn out to be average pro players.

Finley had a chance to take advantage of this system. His best year at Wisconsin was his junior season. Had he declared himself eligible for the draft, he would have been a lottery pick and gotten a deal worth perhaps $20 million or more.

Instead, both he and his team were disappointments his senior season. He was forced to carry both the scoring and defensive loads, shot a poor percentage, and ended up with a label common to many college stars: "Great athlete, can't shoot."

He slipped all the way to No. 21, where the Suns grabbed him. By then, the players and owners had agreed to a system that set a maximum scale for rookies and limited the duration of their contracts to three years. Those who proved themselves could re-sign for a "big" contract after two years.

In Finley's case, this meant a guarantee of about $2 million over three years. The bottom line was that Robinson's guarantee was about 34 times, or $66 million, more than Finley's.

Finley's experience is evidence that those who say athletes should always stay in school as long as possible aren't necessarily giving the wisest advice. Often these self-styled advocates of "what's best for the player" really are merely advocating what's in the best interest of the college program.

Even more incredible, Robinson deals was much greater than that of Michael Jordan, the game's greatest player and attraction, who long ago locked himself into an 8-year, $25-million deal.

All the discrepancies in pay once prompted Westphal to propose his own system. He believed players should receive the same overall amount of money, roughly a 50-50 split of revenue with owners. But its distribution would be radically different.

Under his plan, each player would get a base salary of something like $500,000. The rest of the players' money would go into a pool, with a designated amount divvied up for every win—regular season and playoffs.

In round numbers, this might mean $150 million to be shared for everyone's base pay and more than $300 million to be split based on winning performances.

"So, if a team wins 60 games and the NBA title, that team might get $100 million. And if a team won only nine games, that team only might get an extra two million to divide."

That performance money would be divided up by the players themselves, who would debate the matter in private and vote the shares.

"If a guy carries a team, or lets the team down, who knows better than the other players? This way, players truly would be paid for their contributions," Westphal said.

Jordan, instead of earning $4 million, might get $25 million (probably close to his true market value). Even benchwarmers on a title team might get $3 million or $4 million. "There might be a lot of reasons it wouldn't work," Westphal conceded. Agents might not like it, nor would star players on bad teams. But just about everyone else could benefit. Everyone would be paid according to his contribution to winning. And winning would be the preeminent goal for everyone. "This almost would impose a good attitude on some players," he argued.

Because of the popularity of Finley and a snowstorm that limited the size of the crowd, Milwaukee's Bradley Center seemed nearly a neutral court at the game's start.

Another factor in the mix was the presence of Barkley, who may be more popular in Milwaukee than in any place except those in which he's played. This was where Barkley had his run-in with what was said to be a profane antagonist outside a bar on Water Street, the city's late-night party center. He was acquitted of battery by a local jury on the very day the Sixers traded him to the Suns. Popular sentiment was on his side (many thought the charges were completely misdirected). Barkley was cheered upon his introduction and throughout the game.

The Suns executed nearly flawlessly on offense in the first quarter but gave it back at the other end. They led, 37-33, heading into the second quarter. "Oh, if we could only cover!" sighed Fitzsimmons at the time.

But the Bucks had more problems than the Suns. They put on a Horror Show for the Ages in the second quarter. They threw the ball away eight times while making just 4-of-17 shots and scoring only 11 points. The Suns took advantage. With Johnson racing the ball up the floor, Phoenix pulled out to a 60-44 halftime lead.

All the while, Finley played Robinson to a practical standstill. The only Bucks player to really hurt the Suns was their other standout young inside player, the sturdy Vin Baker.

The Bucks did well to make a game of it, helped by poor Suns ball-handling. Milwaukee cut it to 98-94 in the final 2:00. Then Finley leaped to grab an offensive rebound and nailed two free throws. The Suns had the win. The next morning, they boarded a bus and made the 90-minute trip to Chicago.

THE FRANCHISE WHOSE BIRTH announcement Colangelo set up three decades earlier now was the sport's marquee attraction, thanks to Michael Jordan's decision to drop his experiment with playing baseball (which actually turned out better than some of his stodgy critics predicted) and return to basketball.

Barkley and Jordan had become fast friends. They first got to know each other when trying out for the '84 Olympic team. (Much to Barkley's misfortune, the team was run by the most serious basketball coach alive, Bobby Knight, who wanted no part of Barkley and sent him packing.)

They hit it off after the 1989-90 season when Jordan played in a celebrity golf tournament in Philadelphia, with Barkley acting as a caddy.

Barkley looked on Jordan as a brother. He considered him one of his closest friends, certainly far closer than anybody on the Suns.

More surprising was that Jordan, the NBA's greatest player, chief ambassador and reputed "good guy," would so eagerly associate with

Barkley, who relished the role of the naughty kid forever on his way back and forth from the principal's office.

Jordan once told the *Chicago Tribune*'s Sam Smith, "Charles says what's on his mind. I like him because it's like I'm the good brother and he's the bad brother. He says a lot of things the good brother wants to say, but doesn't. And I like that. I know I'm always laughing when we're together."

Jordan's return immediately changed the NBA's temperature. Before the season even started, there were whispers the Bulls could make a run at the NBA's long-impenetrable mark of 70 wins. Those whispers had boomed into a roar, what with the season half over and the Bulls having lost only three games.

The Bulls and Suns shared the remarkable similarity that each team had only two players left from their great Finals meeting three years earlier—superstars Jordan and Pippen for the Bulls and their Suns' counterparts, Barkley and Johnson.

But that's where the similarities ended. Since '93, the Suns had added big-name players whose production hadn't always matched their fame or the size of their paychecks. The Bulls had put together a completely different supporting cast from the one that helped Jordan and Pippen win championships in 1991, '92 and '93. Most of the new players were modestly to lightly regarded individually, but their roles were well defined (shooters, rebounders, defenders), and they were both smart and skilled enough to carry them out.

Their roster had been free enough of big, long-term contracts that the Bulls player personnel guru, Jerry Krause, could afford to pick up a specialist in mid-season.

Two days after the Suns played the Bulls, Chicago would visit Miami, where John Salley, a veteran big man, was seen roaming the bowels of the arena. He had just quit the expansion Toronto Raptors and was visiting old teammates with the Miami Heat. Salley was unemployed and available. The Bulls soon picked him up and squeezed him onto the roster with the idea he would be available against their chief Eastern rivals, the Orlando Magic, in the play-offs. He could be used to foul Shaquille O'Neal, a horrible free-throw shooter. As Salley would say of the Bulls' seemingly unending supply of role players, "We've got a lot of junk in the trunk."

That Krause, a gym rat who'd once served as a Suns scout for Colangelo, was responsible for much of the Bulls' success had become apparent. It hadn't always been that way, even when they were winning their three straight NBA titles. Krause didn't carry himself especially well in public. He was pear-shaped and rivaled the average newspaper reporter for his ability to wrinkle his wardrobe. He was considered high strung and he didn't answer questions from reporters well, shrouding the simplest topics in secrecy. He would be more likely to jump off his roof, flap his arms, and fly to Mars than to hold the title of a leading community mover and shaker. Some of the players, notably Jordan, were slow to accept the idea that he was a basketball mastermind. Yet the track record spoke for itself. Outside of Jordan, whose draft by the Bulls in 1984 predated Krause, this team was put together by him. To Bulls' fans, he more and more resembled Tom Cruise.

Krause had added one big-name player. In Dennis Rodman, the Bulls had a player whose brilliance at battling for rebounds was exceeded only by his flamboyant and erratic behavior.

He had become the self-created media phenomenon in all of sports. He had more tatoos etched into his body than could be found on an entire biker gang. He talked of how he identified with gays, "dated" pop icon Madonna, occasionally dressed in drag, and changed his hair color as often as others replaced their basketball shoes. He had his own TV show and appeared (provocatively) on the cover of every magazine whose publisher wanted an avant-garde appeal. All of this obscured that outside of rebounding, his skill level was generally pedestrian by NBA standards. Besides that, his arguments with officials and his pronouncements on how he wasn't treated with respect lacked Barkley's humorous edge. And unlike Barkley, Rodman had little to say on any subject but himself (or those conspiring against him). Then again, also unlike Barkley, he was known as a tireless worker. Often, he was stronger late in games (again unlike Barkley).

Before landing in Chicago, Rodman played in San Antonio, where he was wildly popular with fans but spent so much time arguing with coaches and management that he was traded for only modest return.

The Suns had a number of opportunities to trade for Rodman. Once, they laughed off the possibility of picking him up from the Detroit Pistons in exchange for a great young prospect, an acrobatic, high-scoring small forward who had a history of drug and alcohol problems. His name: Richard Dumas. Had the Suns made the deal for Rodman, they might well have enjoyed more than one celebratory parade down Central Avenue in Phoenix. Dumas had one good year, the '92-93 season when he ended by playing the great Pippen nearly even in the Finals. Then he succumbed to his personal demons.

During the '93-94 season, the Suns nearly pried Rodman away from Detroit for Cedric Ceballos and others. The Pistons backed away at the last minute. Instead, in one of the worst back-to-back moves in history, Detroit traded Rodman to the Spurs for rising young forward Sean Elliott, then traded Elliott right back to San Antonio for a lightly regarded prospect who never made it. The end result was they ended up with neither Rodman nor Elliott.

Before this season, when the Spurs were seeking takers for Rodman, Barkley believed the Suns should have gone after him. He understood the downside as well as anyone. When Barkley once discovered Rodman had the words "Bite the melon" shaved into his hair (an apparent suggestion to his critics to get lost), he shook his head and said, "Man, is that guy crazy!" Still he thought the Suns should have pursued him anyway. "But the holy rollers in the organization didn't want him," Barkley said. There were other considerations, as well. The Suns had big-money commitments to other forwards, including Manning, Green, Tisdale, and, of course, Barkley himself.

AGAINST THE BULLS, THE IDEA for the Suns was for Johnson to guard Jordan, and Finley to take Pippen. The Suns would try to use single coverage as much as they could get away with, figuring one or two players—even if they were the best in the game—couldn't beat them.

They didn't have to worry about defending a dominating center. Of course, the Bulls didn't, either. But at least Williams—now wearing a high-tech, low-weight knee brace—was back after missing 10 games. But Williams wasn't comfortable with the brace. He had the mobility of the majestic statue of Jordan outside the arena.

Colangelo seemed fated to miss the perfect marriage with a dominant center. Not only had he missed the chance to play with Chamberlain in college, he also lost out on the greatest center from the next generation.

After the Suns suffered a predictable last-place finish in their inaugural 1968-69 season, Colangelo participated in the most ballyhooed coin flip in sports history. The Suns would duel with their fellow expansion team, the Milwaukee Bucks, to decide the draft rights to Lew Alcindor (who soon changed his name to Kareem Abdul-Jabbar), the most publicized player since Chamberlain himself.

Colangelo requested that the Suns be allowed to make the call and that

NBA commissioner Walter Kennedy flip a Kennedy half dollar. Both requests were granted.

He then allowed fans to vote on whether the Suns should call heads or tails. They responded 51.2 percent in favor of heads.

Colangelo had talked himself into certain victory.

He listened to the three-way proceedings (the flip took place in New York) through a speakerphone. Kennedy flipped the coin, caught it and turned it over.

Colangelo heard a roar from the box. The noise was coming from Milwaukee. Stunned, he hopped into his Chevy and drove aimlessly around the Valley of the Sun for hours.

If only more fans had voted tails . . .

If only Kennedy had let the coin drop on the floor . . .

If only he'd used a two-headed coin . . .

Finally, Colangelo returned to the Suns' office, realizing he'd have to do things the hard way.

Over the years, Colangelo had grown to believe that except for the few superstar centers, everybody else was essentially a backup. Thus, he figured it didn't matter much who filled in at center.

In addition, Westphal—with his preference for agile, versatile players—preferred to use a small, centerless lineup whenever he could get away with it. Westphal's small units could score, but they usually had trouble stopping anybody.

At times, these theories seemed credible. The Suns had run up stunningly successful records by using overachieving marginal centers.

The previous season was a perfect example. Dan Schayes and Joe Kleine played better than anyone expected. They hit enough of their outside shots to draw the opposing centers out from under the hoop, creating more room for Barkley to operate down low.

Their success emboldened the Suns' view that the center spot wasn't crucial, and Schayes was jettisoned from the roster. But even if this most-unconventional theory was valid, they certainly couldn't afford to decline further from their perilous perch of mediocrity at the position.

Kleine was an old pro who did his best with available skills. The Sacramento Kings once made him a high first-round draft pick, based on his 7-foot stature and shooting ability. He wasn't quick enough to plug the lane or enough of a leaper to block shots. His court vision and ball-handling skills similarly were limited. He needed to hit his shots to be effective.

This season, those shots weren't falling. His task was made more difficult because he hadn't been able to squeeze into the regular rotation under either coach. His time came in spurts of four and five minutes. Unless he hit his shots, he got a quick hook. At 34, he seemed near the end of the NBA trail.

This made the Suns entirely dependent on Williams, the supposed key to the interior defense and the man who would cover for Barkley's well-known defensive deficiencies.

But because of Williams' leg problems, he didn't have the agility to defend like he had in the past. His modest offensive skills had faded, too. The Suns now had marginal centers playing to form.

Williams' struggles not only took the gas out of the Suns' tank for the present, but the trade for him—which called for the Suns to give up a first-round draft pick—clouded their future as well.

During a home game shortly after Fitzsimmons took over as coach, Williams and his teammates approached the Suns bench for a time-out. A certain leather-lunged fan whose New York-flavored voice is well known to those at courtside, screamed, "Take him out, Cotton! He's a BUST!"

This was the consensus view. NBA wise guys across the nation compared the Bulls' pickup of Rodman ("Brilliant!" they judged) to the Suns' acquisition of Williams ("a fleecing by the Cavs" they sneered).

Williams heard all the talk and said little in his defense. But he never wavered in his belief that he could still play.

Besides, what was the big deal about being called a bust? He'd been called far worse.

JOHN WILLIAMS WAS BORN into the sort of mind-numbing deprivation normally associated with life in the Third World. Then again, sociologists might call backwater Louisiana part of America's Third World.

Certainly, the life Williams leads now is a solar system removed from where he grew up, near the Mississippi River in a warm, dusty town named Sorrento, that sits about midway between New Orleans and Baton Rouge.

By the time he was a year old, he'd gone through more upheaval and intrigue than most people experience in a lifetime.

His mother died when he was eight months old. Shortly afterward, his father dropped him off with his maternal grandfather, Felton Williams, and said he'd return shortly. He never came back.

That left the care of the infant to an elderly blind man.

The baby spent much of those next few days on the front porch crying. Those cries pierced more than the ears of a next-door neighbor, a young divorced woman named Barbara Colar.

On her way home from work, Colar saw the baby crying. "I stepped across the yard and picked him up," Colar recalled. She couldn't bear to let go, and she took him home.

The elder Williams found out about this and the next day asked Colar how the boy was doing.

"Fine," she replied, "I've got a son now."

This was Williams' big break, if living with three other kids (Colar's children) in a 14-by-60 trailer could be called a break.

Colar worked two jobs. She was a school janitor from 6 a.m. to 3 p.m., then came home for an hour before taking off for her second job as a cook at a steak-and-seafood restaurant.

As he grew up, Williams often would wait up for his mom. She'd often bring home a meal for him at midnight.

Schoolwork was a struggle, though those who knew him say he gave an honest effort. He worked particularly hard at math. He befriended his high school algebra teacher, a white woman, and often played with her kids after school. She, in turn, tutored him.

A friend of the teacher came by her house once and wondered who was the black kid playing with her children. The man got to know Williams and liked him enough that he and the teacher helped guide him from that point.

(Williams' knowledge of math paid off. He's now an accomplished carpenter who can read engineering blueprints, a skill he used to build two churches in Louisiana.)

He always liked sports. He concentrated on his favorite sport, baseball, until a growth spurt between his sophomore and junior years in high school turned him into a premier basketball prospect. Soon, Williams developed into the best player on a powerhouse prep team.

Major schools came calling and nearby Tulane, in New Orleans, won the bidding for his services. Literally. Years later, Williams said he received $10,000 (neatly packaged in a shoe box) to attend this institution of higher learning.

His class list read like a textbook of how operators of college sports programs strive to keep athletes eligible: beginning racquetball, CPR, driver's ed. In coping with academic demands, Williams once was described as a "DeSoto among Mercedes." Though he had tutoring, he maintained he did the work himself and managed to come close to a C average.

"Nothing was ever fixed for me," Williams said years later.

Now there's an interesting choice of words.

WILLIAMS VIVIDLY RECALLS the day after he finished his senior season at Tulane when the police swarmed the family residence.

To his mom, it seemed like 30 or 40 cars from the law-enforcement world were on hand. She understood "Hot Rod" had been accused of bank-robbing.

Williams was elsewhere in town; his brother came and told him the police were looking for him. He returned home to wait for them.

When they finally connected, the police drove him to New Orleans while a frightened Williams wondered, "What the hell is going on?"

When they arrived, prosecutors had orchestrated a major media event. With TV cameras rolling, Williams recalls reporters shouting, "Did you take any money?" and "Did you sell drugs?"

Actually, he was being charged, along with other players, with point-shaving. In this case, it involved Tulane failing to cover the point spreads in games against Memphis State and Southern Mississippi.

The scheme was organized by a non-playing Tulane student who sold drugs to one of Williams' teammates. Six people (players and non-players) eventually either pleaded guilty to reduced charges or had no charges filed at all in return for testifying against Williams, the team's best player.

Williams was taken to a room where several police officers interviewed him. The scene, as Williams recalled it, could have been taken out of *In the Heat of the Night*. About the only detail missing was the cops spitting tobacco juice.

The police officers were all white, which Williams thought strange considering New Orleans was a heavily black city. The first words he recalled was one of them asking, "Why didn't you go to LSU, you (expletive)?" In Williams' mind, the process degenerated even further until he felt he was being intimidated into saying what the authorities wanted to hear. He didn't need to be a Philadelphia lawyer to come away with the view that his dignity had been violated.

He was asked whether he took money after games. He said, "Yes."

As Williams says today, "I took money after a lot of games. Sometimes it was left in envelopes in lockers, sometimes under my door."

He acknowledges that he didn't ponder the matter in moral terms.

"I thought people were taking care of me. I was glad they did it. I knew it was against the rules, but it wasn't against the law."

The weakness of the case was that Williams didn't go into the tank in either game. At one point, one of those supposedly involved complained to Williams that he was too "hot." Against Southern Miss, he hit his last six shots. Tulane, a 10-point favorite, won by one.

Against Memphis State, he scored 14 points in a 60-49 loss (Tulane was an eight-point underdog).

What's more, Williams invited his old high school coach and several of his players to the Memphis State game. All of them certainly figured to be watching him closely. The coach, Tommy Wall, visited Williams at length afterward and said he didn't seem at all ill at ease. Even more convincing for Wall, Williams looked his coach in the eyes when the charges surfaced and denied wrongdoing.

Wall once told the *Cleveland Plain Dealer* he was so convinced of Williams' innocence that, "I'll stake my reputation on it. I'll go to my grave believing that."

And so he did. Wall has since died of cancer.

The nickname didn't help.

Standing alone, "Hot Rod" paints a picture of a guy wearing gold chains and a Panama hat with a beeper attached to his belt. Add the name to a point-shaving case and it seems even more ominous.

What does "Hot Rod" really symbolize? Nothing except a toddler who used to make "Vroom, vroom" noises on his scooter. The nickname managed to stick.

Williams actually is about as flamboyant as a Yugo. His favorite pastime, besides carpentry, is fishing. Deep-sea fishing, Mississippi River fishing, bass fishing, catfish fishing. If there's a body of water with things with gills swimming in it, he's been there, done that.

Eventually, a judge threw out the point-shaving case, saying the prosecution withheld evidence that helped Williams. The prosecution appealed and the case went to another trial, though not before prosecutors approached Williams' lawyer, Michael Green, with a possible deal. Williams could plead guilty to a lesser charge, one that did not involve sports bribery, a deal that might clear the way for an NBA career for Williams. Green declined.

Green was a flamboyant Chicago attorney who was moved to accept the case when he met Williams and heard him say, "Mister, you've got to help me. I never did anything wrong." Green, like any criminal defense

Cotton Fitzsimmons talks things out with Barkley.

Joking with Bulls coach, Phil Jackson.

Westphal.

Kevin Johnson's game is defined by explosiveness.

A.C. Green wearing mask after attack by J.R. Reid.

Michael Finley dunks over Lakers' Vlade Divac.

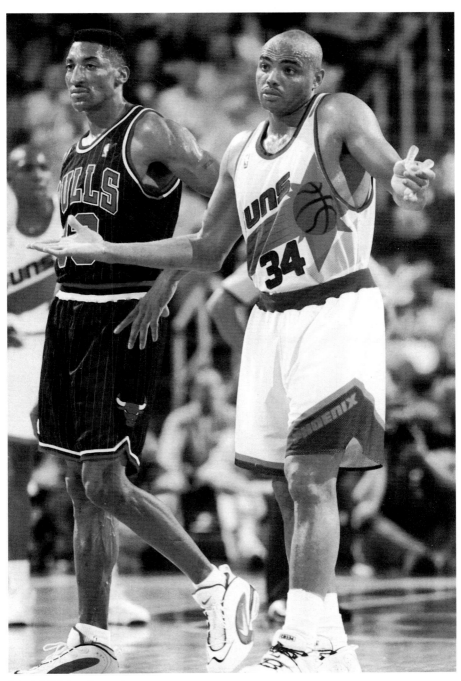

Seriously, I didn't do anything wrong!

Hot Rod Williams and Lakers' Cedric Ceballus scramble after loose ball.

Danny Manning vs. Tony Kukoc of the Bulls.

Suns vs. Rockets: Barkley blocks Chucky Brown.

Dan Majerle enjoyed Barkley as a teammate more than any other Suns' player.

Jerry Colangelo announces changing of guard from Cotton Fitzsimmons to Paul Westphal in 1992.

Kevin Johnson defending vs. Lakers.

Dan Majerle, at one time the most popular Sun of all.

Barkley with Danny Ainge.

Barkley accepts MVP trophy in June, 1993.

Barkley mania at its peak.

Barkley in happier times.

Barkley pleading his case.

Concentrating before a free-throw.

Barkley eventually wore out his welcome in Arizona. Trading him wasn't so difficult, yet the Suns knew they'd never see anyone quite like him again.

attorney, had represented a load of guilty clients. In this case, he was convinced Williams hadn't done anything to alter the outcome of a game, though he was less certain if Williams had taken money from the actors who initiated the scheme.

The trial's most dramatic moment took place when Colar was called to testify. She and Wall had met Williams after the Memphis State game. She was a poor, heavyset woman who worried before the court appearance that she didn't have the proper attire to appear in such a circumstance. She was wearing a simple housedress and slippers when her name was called.

The approach to the witness stand by this simple but dignified woman seemed to last as long as a journey from the backwoods to the big city. The only noise was the "Thh-wack!, Thh-wack!" of the slippers hitting the back of her heels. By the time she reached the stand, some of the jurors appeared near tears.

At this point, the prosecutors' chances were dead. To finish them off, Green attacked the credibility of the prosecution witnesses with devastating effect. The jury returned with an innocent verdict after deliberating for about two hours.

The ordeal left Williams with a mean streak. "I don't trust people like I used to," he said. "I don't want anybody giving me anything any more."

Next, the NBA looked into the allegations and cleared Williams to play for the Cleveland Cavaliers, who had risked a draft pick on him.

In Cleveland, Williams distinguished himself as the team's glue, the guy who did the dirty work of rebounding, defending, setting screens and blocking shots, on a star-studded team that included Brad Daugherty, Mark Price and Larry Nance. His coach, Lenny Wilkens, once was moved to say of Williams, "He knows how to fill up a box score."

Having established himself, Williams took a gamble in 1990 with the help of his lawyer and agent, Mark Bartelstein.

Because Williams was about to become a free agent, they turned down offers from the Cavs, first for $11.8 million, then $13.5 million over five years, believing Williams might attract an even greater offer.

As luck would have it, the Miami Heat had plenty of money to spend and wanted to attract attention in the crowded south Florida sports market. Because Williams was a restricted free agent, meaning the Cavs could match any offer and keep him, the Heat's proposal would have to discourage a match.

If the Heat hadn't put the offer in writing, nobody would have believed it: $26.5 million over seven years.

The deal, the biggest in NBA history at the time, shocked officials around the league. However, the Cavs thought enough of Williams to match the offer.

Thus Williams was the second-highest-paid athlete in team sports in America, trailing only baseball's Jose Canseco. At long last, he'd been in the right place at the right time.

Williams succeeded in larger areas. His family situation is a world away from his own traumatic start. He and his wife, Karen, were raising four children: John Jr., Johnfrancis, Johnpaul and Johnna.

This might seem like identity overkill. But Bartelstein, pointing to Williams' background, said, "He wanted to be sure his kids never forget who their father is."

AGAINST THE BULLS, THE SUNS played as well as they could have hoped. It helped that Person came out hitting his shots and that Finley—playing in his hometown—wasn't intimidated by his first game against the game's marquee team.

Phoenix played a nearly perfect first half, pulling out to a 52-47 lead. It didn't last.

The Bulls' defense was absolutely stifling after the break. They ran a second player, often Pippen, at Johnson, or they'd cut him off near the baseline. Rodman crashed the Bulls' offensive boards, not only giving Chicago second shots but also cutting off the Suns' fast break before it could even start.

At the other end, the Bulls got just enough offense from Jordan and Pippen. They won, 93-82.

The Suns scored just 30 points in the second half. At the same time, they'd shown they could play with the NBA's best team at less than full strength.

"We didn't play that well, and we still had a chance to win," Johnson said.

The game set off a mini-debate: Was this Bulls team as good as the ones that won three straight titles?

Barkley was skeptical. Their supporting cast wasn't as impressive. And few teams in the Eastern Conference, which comprised most of the Bulls' schedule, were strong enough to even give them a game. (Teams play rivals in their own conference four times, those in the opposite conference twice.) Perhaps the Bulls' record, now a stunning 38-3, was artificially inflated.

"They're a very good team," Barkley said. "But outside of Orlando and Indiana, they're really the only good team in the East."

Johnson was more complimentary. "I think they're a better defensive team now," he said. "They probably have to be without some of their old players like Horace Grant and B.J. Armstrong. Their defense is so steady and consistent. It was like a clinic out there. They knew what they were doing every single time."

IN MIAMI, THE SUNS FACED a Heat team that was reeling. Their high point came in nailing down the big win in Phoenix, a game Riley (who had won more than a few games in his career) called one of the biggest of his life. But this was the game in which Mourning was injured; the Heat immediately went into a steep slide. Like the Suns, they didn't have enough shooting or ball-handling.

Though both teams played the night before, the Suns knew the Heat would be especially vulnerable to a fast-paced game. The Heat had played the night before in New York, where they'd stayed with the Knicks before falling apart in the final three minutes.

So, the Suns raced the tempo and put on one of their best running and shooting displays of the season. Mourning was defended well by Williams and Kleine.

In the second half, Johnson continued to slice apart the Heat's defenses, and the Suns' lead reached 91-67 heading into the final quarter.

Barkley was at his best, controlling the boards, demanding double-teams, keeping his turnovers to a minimum.

Now, he had energy, enough to engage in the latest dance fad—the Macarena—after a time-out.

He shouted his own play-by-play at TV announcers. He leaped into the stands after a loose ball, tumbling virtually into the lap of Riley's wife. ("He's got good taste," he said later.) He waved to the crowd after hitting a slam dunk.

Said the Heat's Billy Owens, "The way he talks to the crowd and still does what he does, it really makes you hate him. He comes in like this is his home court. It makes the knife go in deeper."

The Suns grew careless in the fourth quarter, so much so that Fitzsimmons ripped them afterward. "If you play that way when you're ahead by 20, you can play that way when you're even," he said later. Still, their lead was safe enough to remove Barkley early in the final quarter.

Just as Fitzsimmons moved to replace him, Barkley saw that the Heat's

Dan Schayes was momentarily off-balance. So Barkley pushed him hard enough to send him sprawling.

"People shouldn't talk (expletive) about me in the papers," Barkley growled as he walked to the bench.

Early in the season, Schayes pointed out to a newspaper columnist that the Suns were run to accommodate Barkley's whims.

Schayes was an old pro who appreciated Barkley's humor as much as anybody. He was as adept as Barkley himself at tossing off one-liners. But like virtually all veterans, once the game started, he simply wanted to win.

Schayes landed with the Suns the previous season through blind luck. He and his wife always liked Arizona. So Schayes bought a house in Scottsdale, next door to his wife's brother. The plan was to live there part-time while continuing to play in the NBA for another year or two. Schayes closed on the house Sept. 1, just before the Suns' informal work-outs began. He read where the team might need help at center. So, he called the Suns and asked if he could work out with them. They said yes.

Schayes was 35 years old. He'd been a big-name player at Syracuse, with the emphasis on "name." His father, Dolph, was a high-scoring Hall of Famer.

Because of his background, Schayes had a sense of basketball history few players anywhere could match. He would ask a group of writers if anybody knew who held the record for most rebounds in a game. When he saw that nobody was quite sure, Schayes would answer his own question, "Bill Russell with 55." (Before Russell's arrival, Dolph Schayes frequently led the NBA in rebounding in the early 1950s.)

Schayes' father retired when Dan was five years old, so he didn't directly remember much about his playing days. But he'd read enough and seen enough films to know that Dolph was one of the game's first power forwards. He had a great outside set shot. And when defenders ran at him, he drove to the hoop, sometimes connecting on hooks with either hand.

After Dolph retired, he coached the Buffalo Braves (now the Los Angeles Clippers). He brought in his son to serve as the ball boy. Between Dan's work for the team and attending camps, he grew up with pro basketball. "I didn't have to imagine what it would be like," Schayes said. "I was always around it."

The greatest changes in the game he'd noticed had taken place since he entered the league as a high draft pick in 1981 out of Syracuse (where he earned a degree in organic chemistry).

"Everything is bigger. The players are bigger. The stadiums are bigger. The money is bigger. And so is the exposure."

Schayes had played for several teams. His best years came in the mid-to-late-1980s in Denver, where he played for a team with a racehorse style similar to the Suns.

But his career declined in three-plus seasons in Milwaukee, where the Bucks were more intent on developing young players than on winning games. Schayes was miserable, his career out of gas with a lousy team. He wanted to find a place that was fun again and leave the game on a high note. He and the Suns made for a good fit.

On the downside, he didn't have the grace of his father. And because he was surrounded by stars and superstars as teammates, he figured to be a guy who would seldom get a good call. Schayes was so slow that the Suns would joke that Kleine seemed like a sprinter in comparison. Yet he was adequate enough in all phases of the game. He could catch and pass the ball, a must for Westphal. He shot well enough from outside to allow Barkley to operate down low. He was crafty enough defensively even to stay with superstar centers for 15 minutes or so a game; indeed, his work on Olajuwon was a key to the Suns winning Game 4 at Houston to take a seemingly insurmountable 3-1 lead in the previous year's play-offs.

Entering this season, Westphal knew Schayes was his best option for interior defense. But the Suns already had too many players with guaranteed contracts, a problem that was exacerbated by their four-year, $2-million commitment to Rusconi. Perhaps the Suns would have to play games with the injury list, engaging in the somewhat common practice of exaggerating or outright faking injuries to prevent having to release someone from a crowded roster. (As it turned out, of course, they didn't have to worry about having too many players this season.)

Besides this, the holdovers all wanted more playing time as it was. Keeping Schayes would add to these problems, especially in light of Colangelo's personal interest in Rusconi.

Westphal didn't push to keep Schayes; his absence seemed to be minimized when the Suns worked out the trade for Williams. But when Williams turned up as damaged goods, the Suns' interior defense—already porous—resembled even more of a sieve. As the season played out, Westphal had misgivings about the decision-making process.

Schayes sat out the first quarter of the season, searching for an employer. He landed with the Heat at the prodding of Scotty Robertson, the ex-

Suns assistant coach who signed to help Riley with the Heat.

Now, Schayes was serving as Barkley's foil. He had been around the block enough to know that superstars were treated differently than others. But there was a brazenness about it all, both in the way Barkley claimed his Numero Uno status and in the way he was allowed to do so, that bothered Schayes.

The comments that set Barkley off pointed out how "Charles has his own set of rules and can do whatever he wants." But Schayes responded to Barkley's push by saying, "What I said probably was too close to the truth. That was the problem. But I'll take two free throws anytime."

If Schayes wanted to cite a concrete example of Barkley's approach, he didn't have to look far and wide. Barkley gave him one in this very game. Cameras picked him up shooting a free throw with his eyes closed.

IN ATLANTA, THE SUNS ENJOYED a sort of harmonic convergence.

Barkley and Johnson worked together splendidly, with Johnson penetrating and drawing the defenders. Barkley was the major option if the defenders successfully blocked Johnson's path. At the same time, Person—who was leaving his mark on games less and less frequently—found his shooting eye and grabbed 10 rebounds to boot. Even Tisdale played with great energy. He scored 19 points and—almost shockingly—grabbed nine rebounds in just 22 minutes. "You played hard," Fitzsimmons said in congratulating Tisdale. "That's what I like."

They also caught the Hawks, who had been about the NBA's hottest team outside Chicago, on a night when they had absolutely no gas in the tank. The Suns shot 68 percent against them in the first half. Their lead reached an eye-popping 38 points en route to a 120-84 win.

During the game, Fitzsimmons noticed a free throw by Barkley take an unusually high bounce before dropping through. He surmised, correctly, that Barkley once again shot with his eyes closed.

Barkley was demonstrating his independence. What could Fitzsimmons do? "Charles is Charles," he said. "He knows what we're trying to do. We don't have any problems."

THE ONCE-FAMILIAR FIGURE sat quietly at the far end of the visitor's locker room in Cleveland, wearing headphones hooked up to a tape player. His presence was the most welcome, the most awaited, the most celebrated event of the season.

Danny Manning was back in uniform. But how much of the real

Danny Manning would the Suns see now, by the end of the season, or ever again?

He'd come to the Suns in perhaps the most stunning contract signing since Big Money took over big-time sport. At the time he committed to the Suns, in the summer of 1994, the team's promise was unlimited.

By signing Ainge in '92 and Green in '93, the Suns had shown they could compete with any franchise in the NBA's free-agent marketplace. Increasingly, players were taking advantage of this contract option. And almost all of them viewed Arizona as a possible destination. The Suns ran a fast-paced attack. If an early opening was available, they took it rather than bothering to call a play. That's the style preferred by most players.

Then, too, the organization was solid. Westphal had been considered a players' coach, and the city wasn't as fast-paced or seemingly as dangerous as many other urban centers. The citizenry was unsophisticated but unvarnished. Ask a question and you'd likely get a straight, though not necessarily thoughtful, answer. (In this regard, Barkley, like Barry Goldwater, probably was the prototypical Arizonan as well as one of the state's most famous residents.)

Just as tempting, the desert climate coincided perfectly with the basketball season. From the opening of training camp in October until season's end, the only uncomfortably hot month is June. And living in Phoenix would be mandatory in June only if the team reached the NBA Finals. That would be tolerable indeed.

For these reasons, the Valley of the Sun came to rank at the top of many players' lists. Larry Bird once called Phoenix his favorite NBA stop. Barkley, of course, put Phoenix on his desired list of teams when he was campaigning for a trade. And players who joined the Suns tended to stay in town even after they retired or were traded.

The area even grew on Kevin Johnson, who, more well read than most, was familiar with the area's political embarrassments and social problems.

The long struggle to win approval for a full state holiday honoring Martin Luther King Jr. embarrassed Johnson, though it finally proved successful. A series of random acts of violence, always played up in TV news, shocked him, notably the slayings of nine people affiliated with a Buddhist temple. But even Johnson, satisfied with his contract extension, now listed Phoenix, not Sacramento, as his home. He declared he planned to live in Arizona "until my last breath."

Besides, Johnson's concerns were unusual. For most athletes, the availability of tee times ranked higher than social welfare concerns. Because of all this, the Suns had started to rise above the field in the free agent market. They snagged Ainge away from the Trail Blazers two years earlier, even though he grew up in Oregon. The next year they signed Green—1993's most coveted free agent—away from the arch-rival Lakers.

In this same vein, Manning had long toyed with the notion of playing with the Suns. He had no particular ties to Arizona, except that the state was home to some of his wife's relatives.

In addition to all the other reasons to consider the Suns, Manning was intrigued by the mania surrounding the team, both at home and even on the road, where Suns paraphernalia was extremely popular.

That wasn't the case during his five-plus seasons playing for the Los Angeles Clippers, a team that had trouble making the front pages of L.A. sports sections and whose games had the unimportant feel of an intra-squad scrimmage. The same went for the last half of the previous season when he played for the Hawks, who couldn't even sell out play-off games despite their surprising status as the No.-1 seed in the Eastern Conference.

Manning entered the NBA in 1988 as one of the most-heralded players ever. He stood nearly 7 feet tall, yet had the ball-handling skill of a guard. His resume included a legend's status in college at Kansas, where he led the Jayhawks to a shocking win in the 1988 NCAA championship game over heavily favored Oklahoma. But he hadn't attained first-rank superstar status in the NBA, a fact that critics held against him.

Armchair psychologists, and there are no shortage of them in sports, arrived at the tentative conclusion that Manning had the all-round skill of a superstar but lacked the necessary "give-me-the-ball" mentality. Instead, he supposedly thought like a complimentary player, a guy who tries to help guide, rather than lead, his team.

The analysis had a reasonable foundation. Manning learned the game at the feet of his father, Ed, who was the definition of a role player in nine seasons in the NBA and ABA. Manning also learned from his dad not to get overly sentimental about the business; during his father's pro career, the family jumped around from Baltimore to Chicago and Portland in the NBA and from Carolina to New York and Indiana in the ABA between 1967-76. Ed Manning was a behind-the-scenes, no-glory, set-the-screens, pass-the-ball complimentary player.

The younger Manning's career had gone well enough for him to attain all-star status in 1992 and '93. But the negative side of the reputation was all but set in cement after the previous season's trade when the Clippers dealt him to the Hawks for superstar Dominique Wilkins. Manning didn't give the Hawks much of a push. They barely survived a stunning first-round play-off series vs. the No.-8 seeded Heat, then were eliminated by the Pacers in the second round.

Even Westphal wasn't completely sure of Manning's level of play. He always considered him a terrific player but wondered whether he just happened to catch him on some of his better nights.

Manning, normally as mild-mannered as a librarian on his way to church, became animated when the subject of his approach to the game was raised. He didn't dispute the analysis so much as the suggestion that he should force his will on his team.

"I think it's bull," he said. "When I was in Los Angeles, I scored 23, 24 or 25 points a game and people said it wasn't enough. Then in Atlanta, I dropped to 20 points and people said it wasn't enough. You can't please everyone."

Critics failed to give him enough credit for versatility. He was a less spectacular version of Magic Johnson in that he could play all five positions in one form or another. He could battle the league's giants down low, while also possessing the grace and athleticism to be well-suited for an up-tempo, high-scoring team.

Manning had paid his dues. He was the NBA's marquee free agent. To reach this point, he turned down Donald Sterling, the Clippers' bumbling owner, who once actually offered Manning a blank check. He also rejected a seven-year, $35-million deal from the Hawks. But the Hawks made the offer grudgingly enough that it only reinforced his doubts that Atlanta, burdened by poor attendance, could ever contend for a title.

He pursued his options aggressively. He was interested in the Heat and the Lakers, both of whom had substantial salary slots open.

He also joined a lawsuit challenging the NBA's salary cap rules. It would be, his agent said, almost certainly Manning's only chance to join the Suns. That was because Colangelo only had a firm $500,000 salary slot to offer Manning. The Suns could make a couple of roster changes and clear slots of $850,000 and $1 million, but even those figures wouldn't be nearly competitive with the other suitors.

It helped the Suns that Manning's agent, Ron Grinker of Cincinnati, was great pals with Colangelo. The two cut their teeth together in the booming world of pro sports in the Midwest. They sometimes took vacations together. Grinker felt so close to Colangelo that he believed he could hand him a blank contract for one of his clients and trust the Suns president to fill in a number.

"And I would hope he would feel the same way about me," Grinker said. So, even after the lawsuit failed, the two talked on the phone.

"You know, I feel terrible," Colangelo said. "I just don't have a slot."

But knowing Manning's eternal interest, Grinker and Colangelo agreed to set up a meeting anyway. At the Suns' signing of A.C. Green to a contract extension in late July '94, Colangelo dropped the hint that landing Manning might not be an impossibility after all.

Two days later, Manning and Grinker arrived in Phoenix. They met Colangelo for lunch at the Phoenician, an elaborate hotel built by the now-imprisoned financier Charles Keating at the base of the area's best-known landmark: Camelback Mountain.

Then they drove downtown to the arena. Manning walked through the building that recently was voted overwhelmingly as the NBA's best and he began to form images of practicing here, of playing on a winning team in a packed, energized house. His mind was just about made up. He would play on non-contending teams no more.

They took the elevator up to Colangelo's office. Manning sat in an oversized leather chair five feet from the Suns president, who started to make his pitch.

By this time, there had been enough Manning sightings in town to prompt inquiries. Manning said he would meet with reporters informally; Colangelo figured he'd say he'd like to play for the Suns, but that financial considerations made the decision difficult.

So, Colangelo drew up an imaginary ledger, listing pluses and minuses. The Suns had the organization, the facilities, the coach, the style of play. On the downside, "The reason not to be here is money."

Manning had made up his mind.

"How do you feel?" Colangelo asked Manning.

"This is the place for me," Manning said. He directed Grinker to relay his decision to the Hawks and Lakers. "I don't want to go anywhere else."

Grinker told Stan Kasten, the Hawks' president, that Manning would play for the Suns. Kasten was unbelieving: The Suns didn't have the room under the NBA's salary guidelines to make a competitive offer!

The same question was raised moments later in the pressroom downstairs when Manning told stunned reporters he would play for the Suns, regardless of how much he could be paid for the upcoming season. Colangelo looked on, his eyes glistening like a kaleidoscope.

Eventually, Manning signed a one-year, $1-million contract. He would be a free agent again in a year and trusted Colangelo to reward him handsomely. To prevent a legal confrontation with the NBA, Manning didn't even ask for a multiyear deal with an escape clause after one season. That way, he at least would have the insurance of a contract guaranteed for about $9 million over seven years in case he suffered a career-ending injury. The NBA had been objecting to escape clauses after just one season.

This was a gamble unheard of in sports. And it came just as players and owners in baseball and hockey were about to shut down their sports for fear of losing a financial edge. "We'll have to see it to believe it," said an attorney for the NBA.

Manning had an insurance policy in force but didn't bother to increase it after he joined the Suns. Such policies usually could be collected only after a legal battle, Manning reasoned. Besides, he'd handled his money carefully.

"As long as I can eat and pay my bills from this day forward, I'm not worried," he said. If he indeed got hurt, he could coach, just like his dad did after his career. "I wouldn't be a bad coach, either.

"But when you play tentative, that's when you get hurt. I'm going to bust my butt to help us win games."

It seemed as though Colangelo had built a sports paradise so alluring that players now were signing up to play virtually for free (at least by current standards).

Manning's stunning commitment was followed a few weeks later by a visit by another sought-after free agent, Wayman Tisdale, a high-scoring forward who last played for the terminally mediocre Sacramento Kings. He was, like Manning, a devoted family man. He also was an accomplished jazz musician who soon would release an impressive album. In general, he was the sort of player any organization craves from a personal standpoint.

Colangelo went through the same sort of plus-minus ledger for him that he compiled for Manning. This time, there was a spicy addition. "Wayman, did you know that we'll be on national television 21 times this season?"

Tisdale was floored. In the five-and-a-half seasons he'd played in Sacramento, the Kings had been displayed on national TV maybe once! Tisdale didn't take long to sign up, too, just the way Manning had.

The Suns had reached the pinnacle. They absolutely dominated the free-agent market. No other franchise had remotely equaled their haul since the opening of the arena and the Barkley trade of '92. There was such a feeling of invincibility; some thought they had the greatest collection of talent since the '80s Lakers.

Under the NBA's complicated salary cap rules at the time, room had to be made for incoming players by casting out players already on the roster. To make room for Tisdale, the Suns jettisoned center Mark West. Tisdale actually took the salary space of another player, Jerrod Mustaf, in agreeing to an $850,000 salary and Manning took West's slightly more lucrative $1-million slot. But since Manning already had committed to joining the Suns, no matter how much they could offer him in the first year, the practical effect was that Tisdale replaced West.

This switch affected the team more profoundly than the front office and coaching staff considered.

West came to the Suns in 1988 as a throw-in to the Kevin Johnson-Larry Nance trade. Ever since, he'd been their one defensive constant inside. He had limited offensive skill, but he took only high-percentage shots. Sometimes, he led the entire NBA in field-goal percentage. Moreover, he seemed to care little if he never took a shot in a week. As Barkley said, "He only cares about playing defense and winning. I respect him as much as anybody on the team."

In Tisdale, they landed a proven low-post scorer. Westphal was enamored of his game because he could play forward and center and score. But he and the rest of the basketball staff failed to realize the extent of his defensive limitations. He didn't have a chance defending quality centers. His game mirrored Barkley's, though not of the Hall of Fame quality; playing them together seldom would be wise.

The character of the team had been changed markedly.

After Manning and Tisdale signed up, the Suns were so loaded with talent that the team's brain trust felt a move could be made for the longer run, even if it meant shipping out a major talent.

Out went Cedric Ceballos, who had been called by Pat Riley perhaps the game's best pure scorer. He was the Suns' only player who was both young and an established talent; he averaged 19 points while playing a mere 30 minutes a game. With both Manning and Ceballos on board, Westphal believed Ceballos might resist reduced playing time. His was a prominent voice in sending Ceballos to the Lakers for what figured to be a mid-first-round pick. Soon, there would be a sense the move had been a mistake, particularly when Ceballos helped lead the Lakers' resurgence.

They had traded one of their most marketable players and hadn't gotten a much-needed big man in return. But the Suns rebounded when the draft choice they landed in return for Ceballos turned out to be Finley.

Also sent packing was Oliver Miller, who'd signed a contract with the Detroit Pistons that the Suns declined to match, and all his personal baggage. But gone, too, was the only starting-level talent they'd had at center for a decade.

In dropping Miller and West, the Suns rid themselves simultaneously of their two leading centers. This gave future searches for a big man an even more desperate tone.

Colangelo made other moves after the Finals appearance in '93 that would affect them in the long run. Green, a few days short of his 30th birthday, was given a five-year contract, later extended another year. A four-year guarantee for Kleine also was generous, considering he was 31 years old at the time and a career backup.

The effect on the team's makeup wasn't fully understood when all the moves were made. Later, they would be debated individually and collectively. But the team clearly was different.

Now, they were loaded with big-name players with guaranteed contracts, but not with defensive-minded role players. Westphal didn't like confrontations over minutes. He tried to keep everyone reasonably happy by playing his biggest stars a lot, and everyone else whenever he could find the time for them. The result was that the Suns didn't have the well-defined roles of most championship teams.

THE SUNS' SHINY EMPIRE would be on display for the world to see at the 1995 All-Star Game. Six days—and two games—remained before the mid-season classic. Their record was 36-10; they'd been playing tag with the Orlando Magic for the status of the NBA's best team. Manning had just put together two 30-plus-point games against the Lakers and Bulls, performances that helped convince Johnson, among others, that Manning was becoming the team's best all-round player.

The Suns took the floor on their practice court. A bus waited in the arena basement to take them to the airport where they would fly to Dallas for a game the next night.

They were nearing the end of the practice session when they worked on their transition defense.

Manning ran a fast break and Kleine tried to slide over to stop him from driving to the hoop. The two collided and Manning crumpled to the floor and screamed. He knew immediately what had happened.

He told his teammates, "I blew out my knee. Just like the other one." He'd done the same thing to his right knee six years earlier when he was the heralded rookie who'd just led Kansas to an improbable NCAA title.

His teammates gasped. Schayes wiped away tears. They all knew instantly that Manning would be gone for the season. Surely, this couldn't be happening to the player who'd gone against the grain and given up more guaranteed money than anyone else—at least in the short run—to sign with the team of his choice. What's more, his team's title chances had been dramatically reduced.

Westphal immediately called Colangelo, who was having lunch at the arena's restaurant. Colangelo was unbelieving. It just couldn't be!

He entered the locker room just as Dr. Emerson was fingering Manning's knee like it was a bowl of jelly. Now, they all knew.

As always, Colangelo started thinking ahead. While trying to belie his own fears, he tried to cheer Manning: "Don't worry about a thing. Everything will work out fine. You'll be back next season. And you'll be rewarded for the sacrifices you've made."

And that was that.

"So be it," said a grim Colangelo.

In silence, the Suns boarded their bus to the airport.

For the next year, Manning performed various exercises, often using computerized weight-resistance machines, with the goal of becoming one of the first big-time athletes to return after having both knees surgically rebuilt.

The estimated time to return from anterior cruciate ligament surgery, using a one-incision method, was about nine to 11 months. But Manning's first injury was repaired in the old two-incision procedure that usually required a rehab process several weeks longer. But because the first operation went so well, "We decided, 'Why try to reinvent the wheel?'" said Grinker.

At training camp, Manning had agreed to a fully guaranteed, six-year, $40-million contract. The biggest deal in franchise history let every other NBA player and agent know they would be treated honorably if they ever made a deal with the Suns.

The contract also reaffirmed suspicions around the league that Colangelo, Grinker and Manning all along had an under-the-table agreement. Those suspicions were shouted almost everywhere, except in Suns-land, where they were merely whispered. But they were deflated among most fair-minded observers by the language of Grinker's denial: "I swear on the lives of my children we have no secret deal!"

Because of the severity of Manning's injury and the size of the contract, the road back would be traveled cautiously.

As the Suns began to sink in December and again in January, speculation intensified about the date of his return. The generally assumed date, one that Westphal figured to be as good a guess as any, was around New Year's. Manning, as he always did about most matters—and certainly about this one—kept to himself, saying only, "I'll be back when I'm ready."

He joined the Suns at the start of the road trip, exercising and working out with the team in hopes of getting into action by the time they returned home. Those close to him warned that "the real Danny Manning" wouldn't be visible until next season. Yet there were optimists, Fitzsimmons among them, who recognized that his game depended as much on smarts as talent. Perhaps his comeback would be quicker and more successful than generally thought.

Like Magic Johnson, whose much more ballyhooed comeback had taken place just days earlier, Manning had an understanding of the game's nuances matched by few players. Like Johnson, he made every teammate a better player. Along with Williams, he was the only Suns player who could cover defensive mistakes by stepping into the middle and blocking shots. At the offensive end, he could both shoot and pass. Maybe most importantly, he could make his decisions quickly, before the defense had time to adjust.

The game in Cleveland, No. 7 on the trip, would be Manning's comeback day.

The sight of him in uniform lifted everybody's spirits. In addition to his skill, he was a terrific teammate. For Manning, the camaraderie, the playful interaction of the team, was all important. Now he was one of them again.

He sat at the farthest end of the long narrow locker room. Barkley sat near the main entrance at the opposite end, instructing Aaron Nelson, the team's assistant trainer who doubles as Barkley's barber. As Nelson started to shave Barkley's head, Barkley told him to approach his work with extra care. "This is a national TV game. People in New Hampshire, Maine and North Dakota don't get to see me that often."

Hearing this, Manning walked toward Barkley and said, "They're not missing anything."

FITZSIMMONS DECIDED AGAINST starting Manning, reasoning that he didn't want to hurt the confidence of either Wesley Person or Michael Finley. One of them would have had to come off the bench.

Midway through the first quarter, Manning—accompanied by his personal trainer, Carl Horne—walked back into the Suns' locker room where Manning went through a warmup routine. The idea was to keep the process out of view and thus, better put a low-key spin on his much-awaited comeback.

With 1:24 left in the first quarter, he entered the game. The only sign of the yearlong process was a purple sleeve on the knee. It wasn't meant for support, just to keep the knee warm and comfortable after his warm-up.

Ten seconds later, Manning snagged a defensive rebound. Then he tried his first shot, a mid-range jumper. It missed, but Barkley hit the follow shot.

The next time down, Manning had the ball at the three-point line and whipped it to Finley in the lane. Finley hit a short hook to cut the Cavs' lead—12-2 at the game's start—to 29-25 heading into the second quarter.

That was the only time the game was close.

The Cavs put on a passing and shooting clinic, running up an 85-60 lead through three quarters before sitting on the ball in the fourth period. It was an even worse drubbing than the one that hastened Westphal's departure three weeks earlier.

Manning played 26 minutes, hit 4-of-10 shots, had three rebounds and blocked three shots. On the downside, he had five turnovers and four fouls.

"I had a lot of pent-up, nervous energy, and I rushed some shots," he said. "I settled for jumpers sooner than I'd like instead of exploring more. But I felt good to be back."

He also took a big-time charge (though no foul was called) from an old friend, the Cavs' Tyrone Hill. Manning bounced right up. His short and concise view: "The only thing positive about this game is that it's out of the way."

THE LAST STOP ON THE marathon trip was against the Washington Bullets. Barkley's doings in the nation's capital had a way of attracting attention. When he was there the previous year, he was the guest of conservative Supreme Court Justice Clarence Thomas, visiting the court and attending a birthday party for Sen. Strom Thurmond (who once ran for president as a proud segregationist).

In examining the Barkley-Thurmond visit, the *Village Voice* of New York quoted Barkley as lambasting the Democrats for not improving the lot of blacks in America: "I look at all my old friends back in the 'hood, and they're in the same place they've always been. On welfare, mostly. All the liberals have done is give the black man an inferiority complex. They gave us a little fish—instead of teaching us how to fish." Asked what the Republicans might do better, he acknowledged, "I don't know. Actually, to tell you the truth, I have no idea." Nevertheless, the usually sophisticated *Voice* went on to take Barkley's pronouncements—and potential political "career "—with such full seriousness as to denounce his ignorance of the history of the American civil rights' movement and how right-wingers had opposed such progress.

Barkley's meeting with Thomas was duly reported by the *Washington Post*, wherein a gossip column and the sports section of the paper dutifully mentioned Barkley's "plans" to run for governor of Alabama in sober, respectful tones.

All of this had raised the eyebrows of Westphal, who laughed and said, "Incredible!" He, like most everyone in the Suns' inner circle, knew full well Barkley's lack of seriousness about such matters.

The same Barkley who acknowledged never voting and admitted he didn't pay much attention to specific issues (and the same Barkley who deservedly won widespread praise in the media for cautioning that virtue and celebrity were not moral equivalents) was being taken seriously on politics by the celebrity-driven media.

THIS TIME, BARKLEY SPOKE at Georgetown University on the night before the Suns-Bullets game, drawing about 700 people on a Saturday night. He donated his fee for the speech, sponsored by the student association's lecture fund, to charity. This time, his appearance didn't generate publicity, except on campus.

Barkley stumbled on the subject of politics, saying Bill Clinton was from Georgia and rating presidential candidates on the basis of "charisma."

This prompted columnist Jamal Watson of the student newspaper *The Hoya* to bemoan the fact that Barkley outdrew more serious speakers, particularly distinguished black thinkers, to the campus:

"Americans in general are mesmerized by . . . an obsession with those select African-American sports heroes who can run fast, jump high and slam dunk. It's as if these guys represent the best of what the African-

American community has produced. They don't . . . Unfortunately, many individuals believe this is all black people can do . . . many only see black people as super-athletes or criminals.

"Certainly, the Lecture Fund could have picked a better speaker," Watson wrote.

But judging by the response to Watson in *The Hoya*, most of those attending seemed to appreciate Barkley, even if he came across as a less-than-skilled political pundit. His talk emphasized education, that more should be done to improve the schools in inner cities. His message also included, "The difference between success and failure is the ability to overcome adversity."

He closed by singing the jingle from the McDonald's commercial in which he starred.

IN PLAYING THE BULLETS, the Suns found the tables finally turned in their favor in terms of manpower. They were at full strength, while the Bullets were talent-challenged; they were missing Chris Webber, who was supposed to be the franchise's savior but hadn't proven resilient enough to play consistently, plus mainstays Mark Price and Robert Pack.

Fitzsimmons warned them against looking forward so much to returning home that they'd lose their concentration. Indeed, the end of the trip seemed reward enough. The weather had been cold, snowy and/or windy, throughout the trip except in Miami (even Atlanta had been chilly and windy). Now, an Arctic blast of air had blown in throughout the northern and eastern sections of the country. The days in Cleveland and Washington were bitterly cold. Residents of the D.C. area were experiencing their coldest weather in a couple of years; morning temperatures were dipping below zero, with wind chills dropping close to 20 below.

The prospect of wrapping up the series with a win against a shorthanded team should have been enough incentive to ward off any "pack-it-in" thinking. But the Suns came out shooting wildly; they hit only 8 of their first 32 shots as the Bullets pulled out to a healthy early lead.

Then Manning entered the game. His passes were sharp and, unlike in Cleveland, he found his shooting eye. The Suns managed to tie it by halftime, then gradually pulled ahead. Their lead reached a nearly safe 101-93 with 4:30 left.

Then Johnson began struggling in the half-court offense. Washington's Brent Price, Mark's younger brother, who had been developing into a decent NBA player, hit a couple of three-pointers.

The Suns had blown the lead.

The Bullets had a 108-106 lead with 10 seconds left. They had the ball, but the shot clock had only about five seconds left.

Price threw a short pass inside to Juwan Howard—now the team's franchise player—a bit lazily. Barkley saw it coming. He stepped in front of Howard, stole it, and—standing right in front of Fitzsimmons, who was starting to scream for a time-out—tossed it to Johnson and started to streak down the floor. Johnson whipped it back to Barkley, who caught it in stride and scored a tying layup with 6.3 seconds left.

The Bullets' Calbert Cheaney then missed a driving layup that would have won it.

In overtime, Barkley had a spectacular block on Price that set up a Johnson layup. That made it Suns 114, Bullets 111.

After the teams traded hoops, Cheaney missed two free throws, Johnson hit three of four free throws for a seemingly safe, 119-113 lead.

But the Bullets' Tim Legler hit two free throws, and Johnson threw it away with 35 seconds left to give Washington a chance.

Barkley raced down court, leaped and blocked Cheaney's layup, sending the Suns' bench into a celebratory frenzy.

"It was a great night for me to make plays," Barkley said.

The same was true for Manning. He scored 22 points in 25 minutes, managed to foul out Gheorge Muresan, the Bullets' giant center, at the end of regulation, then stole an inbound pass that helped the Suns run out the clock in overtime.

"It felt like I'd never left," Manning said.

This, of course, was just what the Suns wanted to hear.

THE SUNS FLEW BACK TO Arizona feeling renewed. They'd won five of the eight games and, more importantly, had their entire cast finally intact.

One member of their party, Donn Nelson, their 33-year-old assistant coach, fell ill and didn't make it back with them. Nelson had been an assistant coach under his dad, Don, at Golden State. Don was replaced, largely over the Chris Webber controversy, and later headed for New York to coach the Knicks. At this point, Donn decided to establish his own identity, so he signed to fill one of the Suns' vacancies.

Along the way, he had been something of a pioneer in integrating European basketball with the NBA. He spent much time in Lithuania, wooing the European star Sarunas Marciulionis to make the jump to the Warriors. At Marciulionis' prodding, Nelson ended up as the assistant coach for Lithuania's national team.

To support the team, the pride and joy of the nation that had just broken away from the Soviet Union, Nelson helped develop a novel approach.

George Shirk, a Bay Area newspaper reporter, wrote a story on the team's need for financial support, a report that was noticed by the legendary Jerry Garcia, along with other members of the rock group The Grateful Dead. The band members decided they stood for the same principles as the new country and its team, "new freedoms, freedom of expression," etc. So the band cut Nelson and the team a fat check and gave them some tie-dyed t-shirts to boot.

The t-shirts were a delightful contrast to everything dreary about the Soviet Union. The players wore them, slept in them, and put them on when they climbed the medal stand to accept third place in the '92 Olympics.

Upon returning to the United States, Nelson got the Warriors to start producing the shirts. They sold more than $1-million worth of merchandise in a few months, with portions of the proceeds going to support both basketball and charities in Lithuania. At Nelson's prodding, the Suns became the American outlet for Lithuanian basketball apparel.

Nelson had been bothered by what he assumed to be a head cold. With all the takeoffs and landings in the trip, he deteriorated. In Chicago, he got to the point where he needed medication from a doctor in the middle of the Suns-Bulls game. By the time he got to Miami, he couldn't make it to the team's practice, instead sitting in his hotel room's tub. Trainer Joe Proski had to come and pack his bags and, accompanied by the team doctor Richard Emerson, they got in a cab and told the driver to head to a hospital where they would meet the Heat's team doctors.

The cab driver, however, spoke little English and ended up taking them on an hour-long excursion to the wrong hospital, where the group had even more communications problems. By now, Nelson was starting to fade in and out of consciousness. Emerson demanded an ambulance take him to the correct hospital. The attendant shoved a mask over Nelson's face, actually making it harder for him to breathe. He tried to resist, but the attendant scolded him, "This is for my protection! You might have meningitis."

Nelson now thought the worst. He might be dying! Who would take care of his wife and two young children?

He made it to the hospital in a cold sweat. Tests showed all but one of his sinus cavities were impacted. If he'd taken one more plane trip, the infection could have spread to his eyes or brain, blinding or even killing him. He slept much of the next few days, losing 17 pounds.

When he finally came around, he started watching basketball. He took copious notes of the Bulls, who would visit the Suns in several days. He wouldn't be allowed to fly to Phoenix, and the Amtrak schedule wouldn't allow him to make it back in time.

He called his mother, Sharon, who said she could drive him across country. He pleaded with doctors to allow him to leave by Saturday; the Suns-Bulls rematch was on Tuesday. They agreed, but only if he took a class that would teach him how to administer I.V. drugs and—upon his arrival in Arizona—a promise for an immediate visit to a doctor.

They left on Saturday afternoon, sleeping little, testing the speed-enforcement methods of various state police agencies, with mom doing much of the driving while Nelson occasionally pulled out his I.V. kit. "I looked like a drug addict," he said.

They'd taken daylong trips together across the East and Midwest when he was a boy to see his dad play for the Celtics. (His parents had since divorced.) Over the previous hectic several years, they hadn't spoken as much as they liked. Now they had time to discuss every subject under the sun. She warned him not to follow the path of some NBA coaches and lower their family on their life's list of priorities. All in all, they had a wonderful time. And they made the Bulls game in time.

BARKLEY HAD WATCHED A promo for the Suns-Bulls rematch moments after the end of the game in Miami. At the time, the Bulls were in the process of winning 18 straight.

"Don't lose until then!" he cried at the image of the Bulls on TV.

Word of Barkley's eagerness for an upset try reached Pippen, who taunted a reply: "He was saying he was going to be the show until the All-Star Game. He's just trying to build TV ratings. Nobody wants to see the Phoenix Suns. You know he's going to try to show off in front of national TV. But when it's all said and done, you know he's going to hide in a corner."

Of course, Pippen knew as well as anybody that Barkley wasn't one to hide in a corner.

Besides, Barkley, more than most, considered the Bulls beatable.

"Most teams are scared of the Bulls," Barkley said later. "That's one of the reasons they're so successful."

The Suns seemed to play scared early. They were tentative, handled the ball carelessly, and the experienced Bulls converted the mistakes into enough easy hoops to take a 33-20 lead after one quarter.

Then, a defensive change from the game nine days earlier started to swing the game in the Suns' favor.

Instead of having Johnson guard Jordan, Fitzsimmons put him on Ron Harper, the Bulls' other starting guard. Harper was an erratic shooter, so Johnson dropped off to help Finley on Jordan or Person on Pippen. The points became more difficult for the Bulls. And when the Bulls' shooting specialist, Steve Kerr, came into game, Johnson stayed on Kerr and shut him down.

Then Johnson pulled up lame; his left hamstring had given out again. Up until the injury, Elliot Perry was sitting on the bench, minding his own business in a game in which he hadn't played.

Perry was a hustling, though undersized player, whom the Suns had picked up out of the CBA during a run of injuries two years earlier. Afterward, he thought about trying out elsewhere. The backup point guard spot was virtually ceded to a veteran journeyman who'd been guaranteed $250,000 just to try out. Perry had been guaranteed a miniscule $25,000.

But Perry's play in the exhibition game before the '94-95 season was so superior that he won the job anyway. He bailed out the Suns in the regular season when Johnson went down; the Suns were 38-13 in games he started. His success even started a debate, one mostly engaged in by fans and sports-talk show hosts who didn't follow the team religiously: Maybe Perry should actually start over Johnson. At least he was dependable.

Perry never joined in the talk. He knew Johnson was more explosive, more skilled at both ends of the floor. But he was an excellent backup, and he performed with the sort of zeal that gave the impression he wanted to play just a bit more than anybody else.

Suddenly, the most highly charged game of the season was in his hands.

As he stepped onto the floor, with the Suns hanging onto a narrow lead, "I thought, 'Lord, walk with me!'"

With the Suns leading, 96-93, with less than 3:00 left, Barkley missed a fadeaway 18-footer. As he returned to the bench, he seemed to anticipate questions and said, "I'll take that shot. If we lose, I'll take the blame."

Said Fitzsimmons, "Charles, we're not going to lose this game!"

Jordan took over the Bulls' offense and tied it at 96-96. Yet he also missed three straight free throws down the stretch.

Then Perry faked past Kerr, drew a foul, and hit both free throws.

The Bulls' Toni Kukoc responded by spotting up for an open three-pointer. This was the kind of shot that had been going in against Phoenix all season. Suns' opponents had the highest collective three-point percentage in the NBA. But this time, it spun out.

Perry pulled up at the top of the circle and buried a jumper to give the Suns a 100-96 lead.

Barkley recognized a pass coming from Kukoc to Rodman. He stepped in front, grabbed it, and headed down the floor for a slam. When the play was over, so was the game. Barkley celebrated by leaping up and down, pumping his arms.

Barkley had come through with his best game at the best time. He shot 14-for-19, scored 35 points, and out-rebounded Rodman, the NBA's top man on the boards, 16-14.

All of this earned a glowing tribute from Jordan:

"Charles came out and showed the character he has as a great player. He believes in himself and his team. That's why I love him so much.

"He showed everyone he still has a lot of heart and he still is one of the great players in this game. I have to bow my head to him."

For Barkley, who'd just read a review of the season's first half that questioned his desire, both his performance and Jordan's benediction served as vindication of his efforts.

"I think I've reached a point where I'm taken for granted," he said.

Earlier in the season, the Suns were hurt and relying on young players, he pointed out. The blame was assigned to Westphal and himself.

"That's why I just do my thing. If people like it, great. If they don't, (expletive) 'em."

N·O·T·E·W·O·R·T·H·Y

JAN. 22, INDIANAPOLIS

The first copies of the magazine *George* appear bearing Barkley's picture on the cover. The magazine, which covers politics in a sort of *People* magazine format, had just been started by John F. Kennedy Jr.

Barkley's head, topped with a Washington wig, forms the "O" in "George" on the cover. This is the magazine's third edition. The first-cover subjects, also adorned in Washington attire, were Cindy Crawford and Robert DeNiro.

In the magazine's centerpiece interview, non-voter Barkley convinces

Kennedy he's serious about running for governor of Alabama as a Republican. He indicates he wasn't fully serious at first but became more so when the idea "snowballed."

"When I'm in Alabama, I have at least 100 people a day come up and tell me they would love me to run." (Democrats perhaps?)

When the run-for-governor story heated up in the past, Barkley sometimes backed down, saying "I've got too many skeletons."

In the interview, Barkley declares himself in favor of abortion rights.

JAN. 28, CHICAGO

The Suns dress quickly after the game and hurry to the airport where they board their plane to Miami. They hope to arrive in time to catch the second half of the Super Bowl.

One of the reasons the Suns are on the road so long is that the Super Bowl is being played in Tempe, which borders Phoenix to the southeast. The Suns made money by renting their arena during pre-Super Bowl hoopla for a Rod Stewart concert.

Predicts Kevin Johnson, "I think Dallas will win. If they do, they have to be considered one of the best teams ever."

Jokes Barkley to a reporter, "I'm betting more money than you make on the Steelers."

Actually, Barkley says he isn't betting on the game, but says, "I think Pittsburgh will win."

Barkley has an unenviable record as a prognosticator. He regularly picked the Buffalo Bills to win the Super Bowl and, more recently, picked Florida over Nebraska in the Fiesta Bowl.

The Cowboys win, 27-17.

JAN. 28, TEMPE

Four Suns ball boys are in for the thrill of a lifetime: free Super Bowl tickets courtesy of Barkley. But when they show up at Sun Devil Stadium on game day, they're given the boot.

It seems the Arizona Cardinals sent the Suns eight tickets, four in the stands and four more in the stadium's luxury boxes. The envelope was addressed to a post office box in care of Bryan Colangelo, the Suns' general manager. When the United Parcel Service deliveryman checked his files for a street address, Barkley's name popped up. So, the envelope was mistakenly labeled with his name.

Barkley receives more mail than anyone connected with the Suns.

Sometimes, he gets gifts. So, he doesn't think to ask where this incredible freebie has originated. He gives his wife, Maureen, the luxury suite tickets and rewards the ball boys with the others.

Then the Suns notify the Cardinals they can't find the tickets they ordered. So, the Cards ask the NFL to void the originals and produce replacements. Somehow, the seats of both the original ticketholders and Maureen Barkley and her friends are juggled so that all can attend. Everyone but the ball boys.

Moral of the story: It's good to be a Barkley.

JAN. 30, MIAMI

A.C. Green plays only six minutes after hurting his back picking up a traveling bag in the Suns' hotel.

"A.C. got hurt because he's cheap," Fitzsimmons says. "I've been doing this for 26 years, and I never carry my own bags.

"A.C. makes millions and he won't give up five."

FEB. 2, CLEVELAND

In Cleveland, where sports fans seem to save their knowledge and enthusiasm for baseball and football, Hot Rod Williams makes his return. Though Williams was the glue that held a successful Cavs team together for a decade (he played 20,000 minutes, most in franchise history, often while injured), he receives a mostly seated ovation that lasts six seconds, less time than coaches Cotton Fitzsimmons and Mike Fratello spend shaking hands.

FEB. 4, LANDOVER, MD.

A panel of officials of the Washington Bullets and area celebrities, said to be stone sober, unveiled five possible new nicknames: the Sea Dogs, the Express, the Stallions, the Wizards, and the Dragons. The name "Bullets" is being dropped because of its connection with violence, a decision prodded in part by the assassination in Israel of Yitzhak Rabin, a friend of team owner Abe Pollin. The new suggestions are roundly booed by fans.

The Washington Post's Frank Ahrens has another idea: The Washington Justice, the idea being to tie the team to the Supreme Court. The uniforms would be black (like the jurists' robes), which would figure to score well in merchandising.

Also, the Bullets' new arena would be labeled The Supreme Court. Ahrens also pointed out, "NBA games now resemble rock 'n' roll concerts with the constant piped-in music, most of which is bad. The Justice, however, would play nothing but Supremes' tunes, all of which are great and all of which are perfect for the sort of sing-along, full-house frenzy owners drool over."

And how about these marketing slogans appearing below photos of unsmiling "Justices": "This Court Shows No Mercy" or "Justice is Served" or "You Can't Overrule This."

Alas, the Bullets settle on Wizards.

FEB. 6, PHOENIX

Before the big game with the Bulls, Barkley asks Finley if he has any extra tickets for the rematch. "I took care of you twice on the road," he reminds him in a slightly pleading tone.

Finley takes his tickets and—in a show of friendly defiance—pointedly puts them away for safe keeping.

Barkley shakes his head and says: "Young people not respecting their elders."

Said Finley, "Next time we play Alabama, you can have mine."

More and more, Finley's rookie status seems nominal.

FEB. 6, PHOENIX

Fitzsimmons starts to work the officials. "The Bulls are good, but they're not THAT good. You guys are enamored of them. Call the game the same way for both teams."

FEB. 8, PHOENIX

At the start of the Suns-Nets game, ref Ed Middleton approaches Fitzsimmons and says, "Just remember, you don't get every call."

7

The world's most famous
human . . . and friend

ALL-STAR WEEKEND IS A TIME to get away from the regular season grind and the overall pressure of big-time sport. Instead, the NBA game and its greatest stars are celebrated in an orgy of hype and hoopla fit for Hollywood.

This was the time for the game to present itself before the world. The result was that a successful and charasmatic player such as Barkley couldn't go unrecognized if he walked down a street anywhere from Australia to Zimbabwe.

The NBA's public relations machine (which now has both domestic and international divisions) long ago discovered the All-Star Game was the most profitable and efficient vehicle to market professional basketball.

The NBA Finals aren't suited for the task. The contestants and the sites aren't known until just days before the Finals begin. And sometimes the combatants don't pass the entertainment test, as in 1994's cold-shooting series between the Knicks and Rockets. Besides, hype and hoopla seem more appropriate, more harmless good fun at a glorified exhibition than at a championship event.

Certainly, there is no shortage of media types willing to join the party. In recent years, more than 1,000 media credentials were issued annually to people from around the word. Of course, some were there more to be seen than to enlighten. Once, a reporter with a cameraman following, went around asking players, "If you were a tree, what kind of tree would you be? If you were a sound, what kind of sound would you be?"

At the '96 game, 1,400 reporters, broadcasters and technicians joined staff members from all 29 teams, sponsors and team investors in descending on San Antonio.

Oh yes, the world's best players were there, too. But the game itself wasn't the most well-attended event. That distinction belonged to the Jam Session, a relatively new attraction that features all sorts of basketball exhibits and interactive games. In a city whose economy is fueled largely by low-paying service jobs, the Jam Session served as the only affordable link between the event and most of the citizenry. Over the course of the weekend, more than 100,000 people visited the Jam Session.

The choice of San Antonio was a guaranteed smash hit. The city had become one of the nation's premier convention towns, thanks to the spectacularly successful downtown area. In addition to the presence of The Alamo, the San Antonio River, which winds through the downtown area, also has been preserved and developed by local political and business leaders. Scores of restaurants, nightspots and walkways along a mile stretch of the river created one of the most energetic of all American city centers. This was truly a rare massive downtown redevelopment project that exceeded expectations.

On the night before the game, San Antonio old-timers believed the Riverwalk and surrounding downtown area may have attracted more people than on any other single evening. Hundreds of thousands of people jammed together, many of them trying to catch a glimpse of movie stars Arnold Schwarzenegger, Bruce Willis and Demi Moore, who were there for the grand opening of their Planet Hollywood nightclub.

The mid-season classic was once just a game and little else. The Suns first hosted the All-Star Game in 1975. Back then, there was no "weekend." The event was staged on Tuesday night. Sometimes, the spotlight on pro basketball's marquee event was further reduced when the NBA inexplicably scheduled it on the same night as the presidential State of the Union speech.

About the only accoutrement in '75 was a dinner the night before. The host: McLean Stevenson of "M.A.S.H." fame. And Paul Steingard, then the team doctor, hosted a reception for a couple of hundred people from the various NBA clubs in his backyard.

The Suns hosted their second All-Star Game 20 years later, in 1995. Then, the NBA rented an entire Western-themed amusement park to host a party for 5,000. On the day of the All-Star Game in 1975, one Phoenix newspaper had a single story about it on its front page. Another local newspaper had none. And in the sports pages, one writer railed against high player salaries which then started at around $20,000 and actually topped out in six figures.

By the 1990s, local papers' front pages were dominated by All-Star coverage; in addition, they produced entire special sections on the weekend's events. And few complained about salaries, which AVERAGED nearly $2 million and were much higher for players of All-Star caliber.

Most incredibly, the '75 game—at the time the highest profile event ever staged in Arizona—failed to sell out. About 300 to 400 tickets (priced from $8 to $15) went unsold at Arizona Veterans Memorial Coliseum.

By 1995, the NBA was selling tickets to see the All-Stars "practice." And those were gone a few hours after they went on sale. By now, the cost to see the game had risen to $130; tickets also were good for the slam-dunk and other contests. The trouble was that few tickets were available for average folks. Most were controlled by the NBA.

Most years, the weekend seemed to have a theme. In 1992, Magic Johnson—who had retired as a player after contracting the virus that causes AIDS—dominated the event; the game served as both a reappearance and an apparent final farewell. In '93, the idea was "the coming out party" for Shaquille O'Neal as both a superstar and—perhaps—as a marque spokesman for the game. In '94, sportswriters leaped on the subject of the reappearance of the dominant center.

At Phoenix in '95, much talk focused on the shortcomings of the whiny, selfish and inarticulate rising young stars of the game. Yet this "theme" had an obvious downside. Most of these players weren't at the All-Star weekend itself; they weren't popular enough to be voted in either by fans (who pick the starters) or coaches (who select the reserves).

So, because the game was being staged in Arizona, the theme in many people's minds came to be "Charles Barkley's Party." At one point, Barkley protested, "I'm not the unofficial host! I'm here to play golf, have margaritas, and lie in the sun." But he was the host, and he knew it. For the most part, he entertained reporters from around the world as deftly and charmingly as ever.

But not always.

In the weeks leading up to the game, more and more foreign reporters showed up in the Suns' locker room to interview Barkley. Hearing the accent of one, Barkley asked, "Where are you from?" "France," was the response.

Barkley shook his head and said, "First, they allow women in the locker rooms and now foreigners." Similar comments prompted another foreign journalist to tell an Arizona reporter, "You know, some of his comments would not be appreciated in my country."

"Well," the local reporter replied with an air of certainty he didn't fully possess, "you can't take what he says seriously." At about this time, Barkley tried the same routine on a Greek reporter. But this time, he let down his guard and said, "I'm just kidding." Then he went on to quiz the man about the preferred sexual practices of Greek women.

The "Charles' party" theme was in evidence at a $500-a-plate, black-tie roast of Barkley that kicked off the weekend's events. About 1,000 people attended, with proceeds going to charities sponsored by Barkley, Kevin Johnson and the Suns. Barkley dressed up in garish purple robes. Comedian Billy Crystal, the master of ceremonies, said, "It's perfect that he plays for the Suns. He thinks the world revolves around him." Said Cotton Fitzsimmons, referring to Barkley's occasional brushes with the law, "In Utah, they have the Mailman. Here, we have the Jailman."

Normally, Barkley brings his "A" material to All-Star games. In 1994, Johnson accompanied Barkley on the trip to Minnesota for the game. He was surprised to see Barkley studiously examining newspapers and magazines. Later, when Barkley began tying current events to his jokes, Johnson realized Barkley had been prepping himself! His most memorable line that weekend: Hearing that Tonya Harding was referring to herself as the Charles Barkley of ice-skating, Barkley said, "I was going to sue here for defamation of character. But then I realized I have no character."

This '96 All-Star Game in San Antonio was especially important to Barkley. In a downbeat year, with all the injuries and the coaching change, not only had fans voted him a starting forward, but they also made him the leading vote-getter in the entire Western Conference. Outside of the special thrill of his first All-Star selection, "This one meant the most," he said. Over and over, Barkley repeated his appreciation of the fans. "Even with all the distractions this season, people realized I've played well."

So, Barkley's first action at All-Star weekend was . . . to skip the major media session where those same fans could hear what he had to say. Instead, he stayed in Arizona to play golf with Jordan.

The NBA wisely encourages all its players to be available to reporters. The league's media-friendly image (in which the Lakers' Magic Johnson had been the standard-setter) was one of the reasons for the game's popularity boom over the past 15 years.

For the most part, players went along willingly. Basketball players had learned, more than those in other sports—particularly baseball—that openness with reporters can help endorsement potential. But Jordan, who already had more endorsement income than anybody in history, had long flouted the policy of being available for the media.

For Barkley, the downsides were obvious. He—and Jordan—would be fined $10,000 (a matter of more concern to Barkley than Jordan). Moreover, Barkley had more than once lectured to any who would listen that the game was bigger than any one player. His no-show was an obvious contradiction.

On the plus side, his golfing excursion reinforced the notion that he was a best buddy of the world's most famous human being.

When Barkley showed up the next day, he alternately joked and was defensive about the fine. "That's a lot of money," Barkley said. "But it's deductible."

More seriously, Barkley—who knew in advance how much his decision would cost him—complained the fine was too steep. "I DO think it's unfair," he said.

Asked if he thought the rule shouldn't apply to certain players, he replied, "No, I think the fine is too much. I don't understand why I should have to come and talk to y'all all day for two days in a row."

(Actually, the more formal session, which helps kick off the weekend on Friday, runs about an hour. The madcap Saturday session—which takes place on a practice court inside a convention hall packed with NBA Jam Session participants—takes about 30 minutes.)

The idea that superstars shouldn't have to assume the obligations of everyone else got an animated response from George Karl, coach of the Seattle SuperSonics. (Because the 'Sonics had the West's best record through late January, Karl served as the West's coach; his counterpart in the East was the Bulls' Phil Jackson.)

Then again, Karl usually seems animated about most everything. Much like Westphal, he believes what he says and says what he believes, only in a more frenzied fashion. Unlike Westphal, or any other coach, Karl doesn't really LOOK the part. Coaches usually are former athletes, often gray-haired but slender. Karl, though a fine player in college at North Carolina, is balding and stocky. By appearance, he looks like he should be one of the folks asking the questions, not the guy answering them.

"I think respect and responsibility in the game need to be redefined by everyone," he said. "We have a business that's growing and prospering. At times, it gets out of control. That's when you tighten it up and get it back under control. "You're talking about disrespect. It should be taken more seriously. Irresponsibility should be taken more seriously.

"My team knows I hate excuses. We have too many rationales and excuses. Our focus is too much on protecting failures than being our best."

Karl enjoyed the opportunity to talk. He saw the weekend as the chance to take the NBA's pulse, to see what's right and what's wrong.

Indeed, the most "serious" aspect of All-Star weekend is commissioner David Stern's address on the state of the league, followed by reporters' questions. Most every problem was discussed EXCEPT some of the serious institutionalized ones, such as ticket prices that increasingly are out of the range of average fans, and the anachronistic 82-game schedule that forces teams to play 20 or so back-to-back sets of games, guaranteeing players won't give their best performances. But any change in these methods of operation likely would involve cutting salaries and profits. There was little inclination by anybody to talk about these subjects.

Karl was one of the few to tread on serious ground. "It's a time to think," he said. And he thought he saw trends he didn't like, particularly the commercialization of the sport and the construction of basketball palaces that inevitably cater mostly to those with the deepest pockets.

"I love the old buildings, the dirty alleyways, the scoreboards that don't work. That's basketball.

"We're trying to put chandeliers in our places. But basketball shouldn't be played in pretty places. Basketball is about sweat. It's a street game. It's the gym.

"Too much of basketball now is MTV, Pepsi commercials, who has the best shoe commercials. Let's get back to basketball. Let's talk about who is doing clinics in the inner cities, who is giving back to their high schools.

"Basketball has gotten away from the sport itself. It's gotten to be entertainment. It's gotten to be for the rich. I don't like it."

One of the most-vivid examples of what he was talking about was taking place at that very moment in San Antonio. Three years earlier, the hometown Spurs moved out of the Hemisfair Arena, an old building that featured columns that obstructed the view from some seats. There was little debate that a new building was in order. But the Spurs made a major against-the-grain decision. Instead of moving into a new basketball arena with all the bells and whistles, they agreed to move into the city's new football-oriented Alamodome, a project built by civic leaders unaccustomed to dealing with major-league sports. The result was that their new digs were somewhat sterile, the feeling of intimacy was lost.

On the other hand, the Alamodome could seat 35,000 for basketball.

On many nights, the management opened the upper deck, making available thousands of low-priced seats. This helped a large fan base among the common folks in a city that lacked other major-league franchises.

Then the Spurs' ownership changed hands.

On the day the basketball world gathered for the All-Star Game, the San Antonio *News-Express* carried word that the team's new boss had decided the dome was a "mistake." The upshot was that even though the Spurs were in only their third season as the primary tenant of a $186-million facility, the team and the NBA were in the position of pushing for (another) new arena. The implicit threat was that if they didn't get their way, the franchise might be moved out of town.

Stern acknowledged that when the dome was finished in 1993, NBA officials "thought it was a good idea." Now he was reluctant to talk about the matter, saying, "Issues get raised about the Alamodome. . . . We're optimistic that things will take care of themselves."

Though Karl had been talking in a general sense, the bottom line in this case was just what he'd been addressing. Any new arena would be geared toward luxury boxes and other ways to tap the money spigot of the rich. Lower-priced tickets would be few and far between. It was the way of the world in major-league sports in general and the NBA in particular.

Karl also didn't like the increasing pressure on coaches to produce both instantly and all the time. He pointed to the man who preceded him as the West's All-Star coach two of the preceding three years: "The Paul Westphal scenario scares the hell out of me. Before, success gave you an opportunity to be more successful. But now, the pedestal of coaching is shrinking and becoming more and more wobbly."

Karl pointed to his own situation, indicating his dissatisfaction about not landing a new contract even though he's had the NBA's highest winning percentage over the past two seasons.

"They don't even want to talk to me about a new contract," he said. Because the SuperSonics were bounced from the play-offs in the first round the previous two years, Karl indicated management believes "there still are things to prove." "Winning 70 percent of your games is not enough? I resent people saying it's not enough. The truth of the matter is that it IS enough."

IF THERE WAS A THEME in San Antonio, it was Jordan's prominence. Because of his season-and-a-half hiatus, he last played in the All-Star Game in '93. His first appearance of this weekend came at the East's practice Saturday morning. When the players finished, the OK was given for reporters to interview the players.

So, at once, hundreds of reporters and cameramen moved quickly toward Jordan. For just an instant, there was a trace of fear in His Airness' eyes. After all, he was merely trusting them to stop short enough to spare his life. He looked a little like the proud Mufasa in *The Lion King* suddenly made vulnerable in the stampede of wildebeests.

"Well," he said, after the assembled throng started to settle, "it's good to be back here. But I don't miss this."

The next greatest object of interest was Barkley, who always could be counted on to give the most entertaining of interviews.

Q: Charles, what about the trade rumors? (The latest talk involved Barkley and the Houston Rockets. The other part of the deal supposedly would be Robert Horry, the young 6-10 forward and other considerations.)

A: Obviously, it would be a great honor to play with Clyde and Hakeem. I know there have been discussions. But I have no control over that.

Q: How do you feel about being here?

A: It's a great weekend. You never know when you'll make another All-Star team. (A few days earlier in Phoenix, he said, "The weekend is a grind. There are too many autograph seekers. You can't go out in public. It's no fun. The only fun time is the game.")

Barkley turned to a reporter from Korea and said, "Y'all are taller than I thought . . . (comic pause). . . . Just kidding." The previous year in Phoenix, Barkley got into trouble along these always-sensitive lines. One reporter (perhaps the same one asking "If you were a tree . . .") tossed out a question that almost no player would answer seriously, one that dealt with groupies. Barkley turned to a reporter with whom he is friendly and said, "That's why I hate white people."

A national cable network picked up the comment, and its anchormen went wild with the story, playing it with stone-cold seriousness. Barkley reasonably could be accused of his share of negatives, but a hater? A racist? He was, after all, married to a white woman and had lived in fairly integrated surroundings most of his life. His closest friends in the mostly black basketball world were more likely to be white than black. It was an absurd spin on a poor choice of words, one that embarrassed the regular NBA reporter for the network. For several weeks, Barkley wouldn't speak with the organization.

Oddly enough, the same fellow who was the recipient of Barkley's "hate white people" comments (who, incidentally, is white) was standing next to him when Barkley joked about Koreans. But nothing came of it this time. The questioning continued, and—depending on the topic—Barkley shifted from serious to whimsical. It was left to those on hand to separate the wheat from the chaff.

Q: How was your golf game with Jordan?

A: We played golf all day. It was a great day for me. But I've got a long way to go before I can beat him.

Q: What about the Bulls?

A: They might win 70 because the rest of the league is so bad. But they won't be handed the championship. Orlando and Indiana can both beat them. Out West, some teams can beat them. But in the regular season, they'll win a lot because the talent is spread so thin because of expansion.

Q: What do you think about expansion?

A: A bad idea. This season has proven it. Stealing would be a better way of raising money.

Q: Would you prefer to be traded to more of a contender, so you can cash in?

A: I'm cashing in now. I get paid a lot of money twice a month.

Q: But what about a championship?

A: A championship is not that important to me. I keep hearing how important it is to me. If we win it, great. If we don't, I'll be all right. I'm not going to kill myself over it.

Q: What's been the differences in your coaches?

A: One is old. The other was young.

Q: What about philosophy?

A: Paul Westphal got screwed. He shouldn't have been fired. If we get healthy, we'll be good. But I like playing for Cotton Fitzsimmons.

Q: Why did he get fired? Because his players weren't healthy?

A: I don't know why.

Q: What about the game?

A: I just hope everyone plays hard, nobody gets hurt, and it's a fun game. I hope the fans enjoy themselves.

Q: Do you think defense will be the difference?

A: I try not to play defense if I can help it.

Q: Why didn't you show up yesterday?

A: We lost some money not coming. But it was good to get away from you guys. You don't ask any significant questions anyway.

Q: What do you think of the Bosnian situation?

A: Blow 'em all up. If they're not Americans, just kill them all. (Mercifully, no network played this comment seriously. In fact, everyone ignored it.) Barkley met Kurt Rambis, his teammate briefly after he came to the Suns in 1992, and noticed Rambis was carrying a microphone.

"OH, NO! Don't tell me you're one of those dogs in the media!"

Rambis: "They're just people!"

Barkley: "No, the media's only purpose is to make people's lives miserable."

As consolation, Barkley told Rambis he shouldn't have left the Suns early in the season they made their run to the Finals. "Jerry Colangelo, you ruined us by letting Rambis go and keeping Jerrod Mustaf. You (Rambis) could have saved us in the Finals."

FINLEY HAD A FEW moments in the sun that night. He passed for nine assists in a highly competitive rookie game (won by the East only when the West's Joe Smith hit a three-pointer at the game's end that barely failed to beat the buzzer).

Afterward, league officials hustled away Finley to join other contestants in preparing for the night's grand finale: the slam-dunk contest. Had he decided which dunks to try?

"Not yet," he said with a smile. Finley hadn't been much of a dunker growing up. As a high school sophomore, a couple of his teammates, players who later went on to the NBA, teased him about it. He barely dunked for the first time before his junior year, then decided he could go higher. He did, winning every dunking competition he ever entered.

Finley relied on a series of windmill slams to get into a three-way final with the Celtics' Greg Minor and the Clippers' Brent Barry. On his final try, Finley bounced it high, then grabbed the ball near the peak of his jump and slammed it home. That was enough for a tentative lead.

Then Barry got the crowd roaring by waving to fans as he retreated to the far end of the court. He raced down the floor and took off from the free throw line. He made the shot, a feat performed previously in live competition only by the likes of Julius Erving and Jordan. There was no debate about the winner. Barry scored 49.5 out of 50 possible points from a panel of basketball celebrity judges.

Said an admiring Finley, "I've never tried that, but I think I can do it. I just didn't want to risk missing." Finley examined his $10,000 second-place check approvingly and said, "I think I'll give it to my mother." Finley already was thinking ahead to the next time he got a chance to participate. "Next time, I might practice," he said.

The night's competition was a huge hit, the best in years. In addition to Barry's gravity-challenging slam, Legler, the player Finley shut down only with great difficulty several weeks earlier, won the three-point shooting contest. He proudly displayed his $20,000 winner's check. It was more than he'd made in an entire season in the minor leagues.

THE PLAYERS CARE LITTLE about which team wins the All-Star Game, though the side that has been beaten most recently generally is a bit more motivated. This clearly was the case in San Antonio; the East had lost three of the previous four games, including a lopsided defeat in Phoenix.

Nobody stays up all night plotting strategy. The plays are basic, the defensive setups even more so. Before leaving home the previous year to coach the Western All-Stars, Westphal made an announcement to his family: "I've got 15 minutes to figure out what to do in front of 90 million people." And so he retired to the place where one often can think the most clearly. He went into the bathroom and closed the door. The West won easily, moving Westphal's All-Star coaching record to 2-0.

Fans don't place much emphasis on who wins the game either. Most root for the "home team" but with little passion. This is due in part to the game's commercialized nature.

The regular (and enthusiastic) fans generally are relegated to the upper-level seats at All-Star games, the better to make way for sponsors and other VIPs in the choice seats. Each team is allotted a few dozen tickets, but because of the desire to please sponsors, even coaches, team officials and their families often have to sit in the nosebleed seats. As the Charlotte Hornets' staff climbed toward their seats near the top of the arena the previous year, assistant coach Bill Hanzlik yelled, "Have you seen Bob ("I must be in the front row") Uecker? Replied club executive Dave Twardzik, "Yeah, he's three rows in front of us."

Before the game in San Antonio, Barkley was the center of attention in the West's locker room. He was battling a chest cold, and his voice wasn't much more than a gravelly whisper. But that didn't stop him from talking.

A reporter with whom Barkley is friendly, the same one who was the recipient of his poor joke the previous year about "hating white people," got together with Sir Charles again before Sunday's game.

"What can we start this year?" wondered the reporter. The reporter answered his own question, asking Barkley, "What do you think about the first white slam-dunk champion (Brent Barry)?"

Replied Barkley, "Most white people can't even play. Don't take it personal."

Later, Barkley joked, "The NBA is in disarray. We have a white slam-dunk champion. We need another Million Man March."

Barkley next was approached by a French reporter, a young woman who sat MUCH closer to him than your average Joe with a microphone or pen.

"Do you have any girlfriends?" she asked.

"Several," Barkley said. "Well, no, I'm married."

"How many children do you have?"

"One that I know of."

Then he took a microphone and said, "This is Olivia from Paris. I was in Paris once. But I was drunk. I don't remember much."

BOTH LINEUPS WERE FULL of future Hall of Famers, but the East's glittered most. In the backcourt, Jordan, probably the greatest player ever, teamed with Anfernee Hardaway, probably the NBA's most valuable player in the season's first half. At forward were Scottie Pippen, Jordan's near-equal on the Bulls, and Grant Hill, the smooth small forward whose good-guy image had worn so well he received more fan votes than anybody else.

And at center, the East had the massive Shaquille O'Neal, who figured to be the game's dominant big man well into the next century. Throughout the early '90s, the NBA and corporate sponsors marketed him as the heir to Jordan as the game's dominant force. And thanks to a series of clever commercials, he was one of the rare Goliaths to come off as kid-friendly.

Jackson, the East coach, marveled at all this. To have four outstanding ball handlers plus a dominant center in the game "is every coach's dream," he said.

As expected, both teams poured in points without much resistance. But as the game wore on, the West started to look vaguely like the Suns—older and slower than their opponent.

The game was still close at halftime. Then Jordan started hitting from all over the court. (In addition to his other skills, he had developed from a good to a great shooter, something few players ever are able to do.)

For his part, Barkley hit four early hoops, then faded completely. This gave his teammates a chance to turn the tables on Barkley, who usually is forever in search for humorous targets. "We lost because of

Charles," joked the hometown hero, David Robinson.

During the game, Barkley got some unsolicited advice from Jason Kidd, the Dallas Mavericks' playmaker whom Barkley had continually praised as the player most worth watching over the next several years. "Charles runs with his head down," Kidd said. "So, I very nicely asked him, 'Just make sure you're looking for the ball.' I didn't want to hit him in the head with the ball and make him mad."

Barkley's reply, "I hear you."

Said Kidd, "I'm glad he didn't say, 'Just be quiet and play.'"

Barkley seemed surprised a young player would give him a suggestion, but he later nodded in appreciation, saying, "I take advice well."

The East's only anxious moment came when some of the West's younger players helped cut the margin to nine in the fourth quarter. Jackson put on his diplomat's hat and asked Jordan and Pippen which one wanted to reenter the game. The three of them looked at each other, then Jordan made the call. He told Pippen, "I'm a couple of years older than you. You go back in."

Jordan was the key figure when the East pulled away, while O'Neal dominated the game's ending. He supplied the exclamation mark with a rim-rocking dunk that may have shaken the earth from Austin to Laredo. Logically, the vote on the game's most valuable player could have gone to either Jordan or O'Neal. The vote was taken with about three minutes left, before O'Neal had done his most spectacular damage. Not surprisingly, Jordan won on a 4-3 vote by writers selected to participate by the NBA. The local fans were pulling for O'Neal. He had gone to high school in the area. As the product of a military family, this could be called his hometown as much as anyplace. (Lost in this debate was the outstanding play of Hardaway, who directed this all-world cast nearly flawlessly.)

All of this led to the strangest sight and sounds of the weekend: Jordan, the most popular athlete in history, accepting the MVP trophy at midcourt as a chorus of boos resonated in the cavernous Alamodome.

O'Neal, clearly perturbed by the vote, stared into the distance. He had little to say afterward, though he talked up the age-old athletic lament later in the season of how he didn't get the respect due him. Jordan wisely stayed above the fray, saying, "I appreciate the votes. But I think Shaq probably should have won. He can have the trophy if it's going to make him mad the second half of the season. He can take it."

O'Neal had a good case. But as injustices in basketball go, this was fairly mundane stuff. In the world at large, it wasn't even worth mentioning. All in all, there seemed little chance that Barkley would have to give way in the twilight of his career to O'Neal as the game's marquee personality.

While O'Neal sulked, Barkley faced a media throng full of unfamiliar faces. Barkley was told that one TV crew was from Costa Rica. So he turned toward that camera and said, "Hello, Costa Rica! I don't know where you're at, but you sound like fun. Am I big in Costa Rica?"

The reporter with the cameraman replied tersely (and in full seriousness), "No."

Barkley rolled his eyes and said, "Well, that's why I don't know where it is."

N·O·T·E·W·O·R·T·H·Y

FEB. 9, SAN ANTONIO

This exchange occurred between Alonzo Mourning and a reporter— one of the 277 from 38 foreign countries at the All-Star Game:

Reporter: Do you think the Heat is really a rude team?

Mourning (puzzled): I haven't heard that, to tell you the truth. A rude team? Where do you come from, man?

Reporter: Germany.

Mourning: You heard we were a rude team over there?

Turns out the reporter's more precise understanding was that the Heat was a "hard-nosed" team.

8

In search of the holy turning point

AFTER THE SUNS PULLED OUT their big win over the Bulls, Johnson—who hurt his chronically sensitive left hamstring in that game—got a message at home.

"We had a great win. Hope you're feeling better."

The greeting came from one Charles Wade Barkley.

Three weeks later in Utah, the Jazz' Karl Malone nudged Johnson when he was down on the floor. Barkley momentarily went ballistic. Though both he and Malone both knew Barkley would no more fight him than he would pass up a wide-open slam dunk—they had been Dream Team members and were reasonably good friends—he got up in the face of the massive Mailman, warning him to watch himself.

Said Barkley later, "He messed with Kevin. He can't mess with my players, especially Kevin. We need him."

In a "down" season, this was the "up" story: Barkley and Johnson—the superstar antagonists—had made amends. The needling about who is "Franchise Senior" had been put away.

The injury-dominated season, swinging wildly from mediocrity to disaster and back, had nudged them along. They needed to put out their own personal fires or else they and everything around them would burn.

There was no profound meeting of the minds, just a few casual talks. Barkley, whose "Go talk to Kevin" outburst in Oakland the previous spring sent the relationship spiraling downward, tried to sew up the wounds by inviting Johnson to dinner a couple of times. He was quick to praise him in any public comments.

And when he did take a jab at Johnson, he made sure Johnson understood no harm was intended. When it became clear Magic Johnson would return to the NBA, Barkley told his teammate, "If you ever guard him, he'll take your little ass into the paint and score." Then, he added a rejoinder—one that might have been left out in the past—"Of course, he can't guard you either." (In fact, Barkley would end up guarding Johnson, who rejoined the Lakers playing mostly at forward.)

Johnson reciprocated. When Barkley spoke to students at Georgetown, Johnson slipped into the audience to listen. "He was great," Johnson judged. "He was in his element."

"I have no problem with Kevin," Barkley said. "The only problem is his attitude toward me. At times, I don't think he likes me. I don't know why. I just have to deal with it." Barkley said he wanted Johnson to understand that, "I'm not competing with him. Sometimes I think he listens to other people instead of me. But as for me, I really like him."

Said Johnson, "We're a lot closer now. We put things behind us, and we're trying to win ball games." He recognized that their past blowups took place in the midst of the team's struggles, down times that now seemed quaint in comparison to this season.

"When things don't go well, we pull together," Johnson said.

In part, he credited Fitzsimmons, who stressed a family atmosphere in his dealings with players (different from Westphal's approach that tended to emphasize each individual was responsible for his own welfare).

When a player asked to fly to a game separate from the team's charter, even for a charity event, Fitzsimmons vetoed the idea. They were a team, so they traveled as a team.

Fitzsimmons told his war stories in hotel lobbies. He'd slap the players on the rear ends in the locker room after games. Sometimes, he'd even change clothes with them instead of doing so in the coach's office.

Fitzsimmons tried to get Barkley to join team huddles (with success that was only fleeting). He had a bit more luck getting Barkley to cut down on his three-point shooting, which contributed to a surge in his overall game. So did the addition of Manning.

With Manning on board, finding holes in opposing defenses and filling gaps in the Suns' interior defense, opponents had to risk more by concentrating on Barkley. As soon as Manning rejoined the team (playing all three inside spots and even the point guard—or in his case, the "point forward"), Barkley began scoring more and making fewer turnovers. He put up an amazing string of 19 straight games in which he had double figures in both scoring and rebounding. These were the kind of performances that had made Barkley a legend in the first place. For this, he was named the NBA's player of the month for February. Along the way, the

Suns won 11 of the first 16 games after Manning's return (though most came against losing teams).

At times, Barkley even showed life on *defense,* which is a little like Shaquille O'Neal expressing eagerness to shoot free throws with the game on the line. Barkley always felt he had enough energy to score and rebound, while only picking his spots on defense. In an earlier time, he said, "I get paid $3 million to score and rebound. If they want me to play defense, they'll have to pay me a million more."

This was a joke, but one with a point. He knew as well as anybody that as much as NBA executives and coaches preached the timeless value of defense, they paid for the more tangible statistics that could be tallied on offense. Though even during this great stretch his defense wasn't consistent, he did manage to sneak into the top 10 in the entire league in steals.

Barkley made the case that his resurgence wasn't all that dramatic. "I've felt good all year. What's happened is that guys are starting to get healthy, and that takes a lot of pressure off me.

"Early in the season, I was getting double-teamed really hard and other guys were missing shots. When Danny came back, it made my game better. The better players I play with, the better I'm going to be. I don't have to score all the time. It gives me more energy to rebound or fast break."

Barkley did all this while Fitzsimmons was trying to limit him to about 32 minutes. Hearing this, Barkley said, "That's what they've been telling me for three years. Somebody always gets hurt."

WHEN FITZSIMMONS WAS A broadcaster, he used to joke to Barkley that, "I'd rather die than coach you." Barkley would poke fun in return, saying, "I'd rather retire than play for you." They could afford to joke then. Now, they had to work together.

For Fitzsimmons, the greatest challenge was to try to keep Barkley's emotions under control and his attention on the game.

At times, this was like swimming upstream in the rapids of the upper Colorado River. During the time it took the 24-second clock to run down, Barkley would talk with the referees, the fans, the opponents.

In a game against the SuperSonics, Barkley ran past George Karl after the coach was whistled for a technical for arguing a call. He deadpanned, "Y'all are so emotional." Later, when the Sonics were whistled for another technical, this time for an illegal defense call, he turned to Bob Weiss, an assistant coach, and said, "Y'all are playing good defense. I like killing people who play good defense."

All of this could be wonderfully entertaining for folks with courtside seats, everyone except whoever might be coaching him.

"But when he stays focused, he plays this game as well as anybody," Fitzsimmons said.

The two tested and challenged each other. Even when Barkley played his best, Fitzsimmons kept pushing him. He was positively manic in his arm-waving, shouting courtside demeanor, probably more so than any other NBA coach.

"I've never seen anybody who talks as much as him," Barkley would say. Fitzsimmons, of course, could easily say the same about Barkley.

After Barkley finished a game against the Celtics with 27 points and 16 rebounds, Fitzsimmons said, "Charles might be the greatest player off all time if he didn't mess around.

"How can any coach argue with his (stat) line? But I can, because he messes around."

When he learned of Fitzsimmons' "could-be-the-greatest-ever" theory, Barkley replied, "I think that way anyway. But he doesn't have to worry. I'm definitely going to fool around. I'm here to have fun."

FITZSIMMONS CERTAINLY HAD the credentials to oversee Barkley. During his 20 seasons of leading NBA teams, he'd coached the likes of Pete Maravich and Walt Bellamy, players who made Barkley seem as rational as your average calculus professor. Maravich, the gunning sharpshooter, told Fitzsimmons how he painted circles and saucers on his roof. The purpose: "Whenever the aliens came, he wanted them to know he was their friend," Fitzsimmons said.

Bellamy was a high-scoring big man who liked to talk to refs in the third person: "Walter said this," or, "Mr. Bellamy said he wasn't in the lane for three seconds."

Then there was the even more erratic Marvin Barnes, a superstar-in-the-making in the 1970s. Fitzsimmons would call him up to three times a morning to try to get him to practice without having to fine him (which led to negative press for the team). Still, Barnes operated on his own timetable, sometimes chartering his own plane to take him to games.

Now, Fitzsimmons was dealing with another player who liked to test the limits. And under Fitzsimmons, much like under Westphal, those limits could be stretched far beyond the norm. Barkley still arrived for games an hour or so before tip-off, at least a half hour later than everyone else. Barkley toyed with his new coach. When Fitzsimmons took him out for a rest, he exclaimed—in mock seriousness—"You're killing me!"

At times, he turned genuinely nasty.

He glared at Fitzsimmons when the coach removed him during the second half of the Suns' big win over the Bulls. Fitzsimmons wasn't sure if this was part of the show or if he was serious. (The latter view was bolstered by Barkley's choice of words: He was silent.)

In Utah, Fitzsimmons took him out late with the Jazz leading comfortably. At that point, Barkley threw down a cup of water, splashing those around him. Fitzsimmons explained that if the Suns got within 10, he could reenter the game. Barkley then calmed down.

Because Barkley and Johnson were the team's leaders, Fitzsimmons was most critical of them. In this endeavor, Barkley actually was the easier player to coach. If Fitzsimmons threw out advice or criticism, Barkley would—at best—reply with a joke. At worst, he'd ignore him.

But Johnson often would take on Fitzsimmons. Both were headstrong and reluctant to admit mistakes, at least not until they had time to reflect. In a game at Dallas, with the Suns milking a lead in the waning moments, Fitzsimmons shouted at Johnson to work the clock. Instead, Johnson spotted an open man under the hoop and delivered the ball. But the Suns failed to score, so Fitzsimmons continued to yell at him, with Johnson shouting back, neither much listening to the other.

"I have a hard time correcting Kevin," Fitzsimmons would say. "We're a lot alike." Because they'd always been close, these disagreements would pass quickly. Neither felt threatened.

THOSE WHO KNOW FITZSIMMONS say he was "born to coach," thought this wasn't quite literally true. Lowell Fitzsimmons was born in the Mississippi river town of Hannibal, Missouri, a generation after the death of that town's famous native, the great writer Mark Twain. His birth, to a family headed by a dry-goods deliverer, took place at the depth of the Great Depression.

When Fitzsimmons was a youngster, his family moved to another small town, Bowling Green. There, his fourth-grade classmates, who had trouble remembering his odd first name, came up with another one, based on his fluffy white hair: Cotton. It stuck.

The next year, his father died, leaving his mother to raise him and his brother and two sisters. Fitzsimmons was adrift, in search of male guidance. It was about this time when he started playing basketball. And this, in turn, led him to the town's basketball coach, a man named James A.

Wilson, who was in charge of coaching all the boys from seventh grade through high school.

Wilson was born in the century's first decade. He was a straight arrow, who—when excited—shouted such rural colloquialisms as "By doggies!" Or "Thunderation!" He took an interest in the young Fitzsimmons, teaching him the difference between rules, which could be bent, and principles, which would be unwavering. Fitzsimmons decided he wanted to grow up to be just like Wilson, a coach. (Wilson lived to be 86. Fitzsimmons was a pallbearer at his funeral.)

But first, he played the game, and quite well for someone who barely made it to 5-foot-7. He helped his high school team in Bowling Green run up a 65-7 record during his last two years. Fitzsimmons was a 5-foot-3 forward and still managed to be the team's second-leading scorer.

Instead of going to college right away, Fitzsimmons worked in a brick factory for a couple of years to help support his family and also played for an independent team. Eventually, he played at a junior college in Hannibal, then was off to a four-year school in Wichita Falls, Texas, the geographically incorrect Midwestern State.

According to a Midwestern State clipping, "The towheaded brash youngster from Bowling Green set the nets afire with his sensational shooting from every position on the court." According to the same clipping, "After college, Cotton hopes to enter the coaching field." He did just that, advancing from Moberly Junior College where he had a stunningly successful record from the late 1950s through the late '60s. Then he landed the assistant's job at Kansas State, and when the head coach Tex Winter moved on to another job in 1968, he took the heading coaching job.

As much as he loved his job, he found the risks of college coaching sobering. He always considered himself responsible for his players. And though the potential negative influences weren't as all-encompassing as they are today, he continually worried that he had to deliver his young men safely back to their parents at the end of the school year.

His chief concern was that somebody didn't drink too much beer and get in a car accident. He'd suffered through one tragedy, when one of his players was stabbed to death at a party in St. Louis during summer break.

He stood over the casket next to the slain young man's mother. As she was crying "He was such a good boy!" Fitzsimmons was thinking that as terrible as he felt, "It would have been ever worse had it happened on campus." His favorite day was the last day of the school year. He always tried to make sure his players completed their academic requirements in the regular school year so he wouldn't have to be responsible for them when they went to summer classes. "I felt the weight of the world was off my shoulders."

At least on his watch, he could look back and say, "I never lost a kid."

In 1970, Colangelo was looking for a coach to lead the Suns. He surveyed the field and considered K.C. Jones, who had a strong defensive background as a player, Winter, and a young coach at Army named Bobby Knight. But he best liked the young coach at Kansas State. In interviewing Fitzsimmons, "I sensed immediately a guy who was very flexible about the game," Colangelo would say later. "I felt he would change with the times. In retrospect, I think I read him right."

At the time Fitzsimmons entered the NBA, pro basketball had a much lower profile. He realized the game needed to be promoted. In this sense, he was perfectly suited for the NBA. He had the knack for salesmanship that would have made him at home in the center of a three-ring circus; during his career, he'd had offers to sell insurance or get into the car business.

"LAY-DEEZ AND GENTLEMEN! Step right up and see 48 minutes of FANTASTIC ACTION!"

In the most practical sense, he knew how to turn on the charm in front of the cameras. He did so without trying to overshadow his players. Not that this was ever too much of a problem. Until this job with Barkley, he'd never really coached a player whose presence so dominated the landscape. Most of all, he knew the game was as much entertainment as anything else. Only one team could win the title each year. Those who coached the other teams better be competitive and fun to watch in order to survive.

All this fit well in what would come to be known as a "players' league" in which the coach—unlike in college—is less important (in both tangible and in marketing terms) than the marquee players. With the Suns, Fitzsimmons enjoyed two solid winning seasons, making them one of the NBA's five winningest teams even though the franchise wasn't even five years old.

Even now, his office displays the photos of his five starters from that first Suns team in 1970-71: forwards Connie Hawkins and Paul Silas (now his lead assistant), center Neal Walk, with Dick Van Arsdale and Clem Haskins at guard (the first four all worked for the Suns, and Haskins was head coach at the University of Minnesota).

"They were solid people, they were willing to work, and they wanted to win," Fitzsimmons said. "I give them credit for me remaining in the NBA for 26 years."

But Fitzsimmons had the feeling that Colangelo was watching a little too closely over his shoulder. Colangelo had finished the '69-70 season as the team's coach. He'd fared extremely well, taking a second-year franchise—led by Hawkins, its new star—and making the play-offs on the season's final night, then taking a preposterous 3-1 series lead over the Lakers. Though the Lakers came back to win en route to an NBA Finals appearance, the Suns' run gave the franchise credibility.

Though Colangelo tried to convince Fitzsimmons that he'd gotten the coaching bug out of his system, Fitzsimmons didn't fully believe it. So, he took off on a coaching tour of the NBA, to Atlanta, to Buffalo, to Kansas City, to San Antonio, and back to Phoenix, with a couple of front-office stops stuffed somewhere in between. Generally, he patched together competitive teams with mediocre talent.

In Atlanta, they had to be magnificent to win.

"If Pete Maravich and Lou Hudson hit every last-second shot, we could go 46-36, which we did. But if they started to miss, we'd win 35."

His lowest moment came in San Antonio. He earned the wrath of fans for pushing the trade of superstar George Gervin, the greatest attraction ever in the city. He knew this was a public-relations fiasco, so he suggested to his bosses that they fire him. They took his advice.

All the while, Fitzsimmons knew something the fans didn't. Gervin had drug problems. But he didn't complain about his treatment. He knew that those who complained were less likely to be handed another opportunity. Besides, he figured coaches were hired to be fired. "As long as the checks keep coming on the first and fifteenth," he would say. "If not, then you've got a gripe."

Along the way, he won more than 800 games, putting him among the top 10 coaches in history. And though he never won a title, he had a couple of significant highlights. In 1981, his injury-battered Kansas City Kings shocked the Suns, who at 57-25 were then coming off their best year. Then, in 1990, back with the Suns, he led Phoenix to a 4-1 play-off exorcism of those old demons, the Lakers. In that series, they posted two straight routs at home. "We played as well as we could play," Fitzsimmons said. "Twice in 24 hours. And it was on national TV."

Now, he was back, working on his handshake agreement with Colangelo.

His wife, JoAnn, hadn't much looked forward to this change. They met back in the 1970s in New York, where she worked as a buyer in the garment district. At the time, NBA players often worked part-time in the summer to supplement their less-than-staggering incomes. The garment industry found them useful in selling clothes. So, there was a connection between people in the two fields.

One day, Fitzsimmons took Pete Maravich to the district to buy a coat for the player's wife. They met a salesman with whom Fitzsimmons was acquainted. The three, along with JoAnn, went to lunch. A few years later, Cotton and JoAnn were married. She was along for the NBA journey.

Shortly after Fitzsimmons stepped down from coaching the last time, he underwent surgery to clear an artery blockage. His health now was excellent; his blood pressure was along the lines of a marathon runner. They'd comfortably put the coaching life behind them.

She watched him carefully during that first game back against the Magic as he jumped up and down, bantered with officials, drew up plays. She then realized once again how naturally he fit in the game, how much he loved coaching. She thought to herself, "How can this be bad for him?"

ALL AT ONCE, THE SUNS' luck changed.

Every other team they'd been competing with for a play-off spot collapsed almost simultaneously. Down went the Clippers, as usual. Some poor off-season moves by the Nuggets caught up with them. The Mavericks, who'd lost the high-scoring Jamal Mashburn—and later rebounding specialist Popeye Jones—quickly faded from view.

The Trail Blazers had started their own descent. They'd fallen to the Suns' level, on the fringe of the play-off picture, when the Suns dispatched them in a solid win at Portland. A week later, Rod Strickland, their temperamental point guard, quit the team for several games when the Blazers didn't work out a deal to trade him. Their fall accelerated.

Most spectacularly of all, the Sacramento Kings, a team that played on an emotional edge, fell apart. Early, they boasted one of the NBA's best records. Now they were in free fall.

The Warriors had hung tougher than the others, though their prospects were damaged by a season-ending injury to their established star, Chris Mullin, and a questionable trade with Pat Riley's new Miami Heat. The upshot was that simply by winning the games expected of them, the Suns found themselves in position to make the play-offs, perhaps even comfortably. As they got into late February, they were No. 6 in the West out of 13 teams. Eight would qualify for the play-offs.

The schedule now was favorable. They needed to get past the expansion Grizzlies and Raptors, sandwiched around the lowly Celtics, to get back to the .500 level.

Their practice that Sunday afternoon, the day before they hosted the Grizzlies, was as lively as any they'd enjoyed all season. For only the fourth game in the entire season, all their major players—Barkley, Johnson, Manning, Finley, Williams, Green, Person, Perry, Tisdale and Kleine—were ready to play. At long last, they were ready to make a move.

But the explosion never came. The Grizzlies, owners of the NBA's worst record, were sharper than expected. The Suns, with their typically erratic shooting, struggled to stay ahead. When they went to their once-vaunted bench, they gained no advantage because Tisdale and Person were cold.

The Suns led, 45-41, at the half. Surely, they would wear down the Grizzlies, a collections of castoffs, most of whom had been buried deep on the benches of other NBA teams until the expansion draft.

But the Grizzlies stayed sharp. The Suns never managed to take control. The Grizzlies took a two-point lead with little more than 2:00 left. And when Johnson missed on a drive to the basket and Green fumbled away the rebound, they started to sense this was their game.

But then, as expansion teams often do, the Grizzlies started to misfire. Manning scored on a reverse, and both he and Johnson hit one of two free throws. The Suns led by two in the closing seconds.

The Grizzlies had to make a big decision: Go for two and try to send it into overtime, or go for the kill with a three-pointer. The longer the game went, the greater the chance the Suns' superior firepower would prevail. Yet the Grizzlies threw the ball down low to Bryant Reeves, their massive rookie center. He hit a 10-footer at the buzzer to tie.

The Suns were reduced to trying to avoid their season's most embarrassing loss by outscoring the NBA's poorest team in a five-minute overtime. Finley got them going by scoring down low, then stealing a Reeves' pass. It was enough to give them control and, after a couple of free throws by Barkley, the win. On a night when the Big Three of Barkley, Johnson and Manning (together on a rare occasion) all had so-so games, Finley had 26 points and eight rebounds. With a mere 50 games' experience, he was clearly among their five best players and their chief hope to avoid a lottery era whenever Barkley chose to depart.

WITH PERSON STRUGGLING both to shoot and to play defensively with the aggressiveness required in the NBA, Fitzsimmons thought of trying out Chris Carr. He was a gifted athlete and streak shooter but had rudimentary knowledge of the NBA game. Yet, if Fitzsimmons sat Person down at a time he was struggling, Person might lose confidence. And as their best perimeter shooter, he was a player they couldn't afford to lose in the rotation. So, Fitzsimmons took him aside and told him, "I've still got confidence in you." Said Person, "Those were big words."

More tangibly, Fitzsimmons put him back in the starting lineup. Person responded with a near-perfect game against the Celtics. He hit all six of his three-point shots. The Suns figured they would win any game when Person or Tisdale, their other shooting specialist, got hot. Yet Person's performance gave them only tentative control through most of the game that ended with a 13-point Suns' win.

Person came back to play well against the Raptors, a game in which the Suns did the minimum necessary to win.

They had established a pattern. They were beating up on the NBA's weaker teams (though not as convincingly as a title contender would do) and losing to the solid-to-excellent teams.

WINTERS IN THE ARIZONA desert (winters being roughly defined as when early-morning temperatures dip into the 30s) come and go quickly. Take a holiday vacation and you may miss it entirely. By late February, the feel of spring was prevailing. On a mild Sunday afternoon, the Suns would host the Knicks, a nemesis with whom they had a stormy history.

Under Don Nelson, the Knicks maintained a winning record, good enough to be a solid fourth wheel in the East.

But like the Suns, the Knicks' best days clearly seemed behind them. With the trade deadline having just passed, management already had cleared a couple of players with hefty contracts to leave room under the salary cap to attract free agents for next season. On the floor, there were a few signs of friction. The team's aging leadership seemed to have decided that for all their gripes about grueling practice sessions under their previous coach, Pat Riley, that all the hard work was responsible for what had been an overachieving stature the previous few years.

Nelson, in an effort to keep them together, took a less demanding approach. But the team's veterans were deciding they liked many of the old ways better.

Before the game, Nelson sent greetings to Fitzsimmons, an old comrade in the coaching wars, through a Suns staffer who shuttled starting lineups between the coaches. The messenger told Fitzsimmons, "Nellie said, 'You go first.'" This is the way it always went anyway: The home team names its starters first, leaving the visitor with the option of responding.

Then Fitzsimmons bantered with journalists. A columnist asked him if he considered himself a "players' coach." He replied, "I think that's something that's invented. If you win, you're a players' coach."

Nobody needed to say what happened if you lost. For some reason, he pointed out, pro coaches are fired, college coaches are allowed to resign.

Then Bill Frieder, the disheveled Arizona State coach, poked his head in Fitzsimmons' office. The Suns' coach wished Frieder well, telling him he hoped the Sun Devils could battle their way to a winning season and a spot in the post-season NIT. (They didn't.) Frieder started to continue the conversation, but he found Fitzsimmons conversing with assistant Donn Nelson (the son of the Knicks' coach) about the Knicks' personnel.

(Within two weeks, the senior Nelson would be gone, fired by Knicks management, and Frieder's program would be in severe turmoil because of alleged misbehavior by his three most prized recruits. In the coaching world, one never has to look far to find examples of the profession's perils. But here were two of them anyway, up close and personal.)

Fitzsimmons sent Nelson his lineup: Johnson and Person at guard, Finley and Barkley at forward and Williams at center.

The Knicks were crippled by the loss of superstar center Patrick Ewing and rebounding forward Charles Oakley because of injuries. Oakley was thought to be out for an extended period, a potentially ruinous injury because he was the team's glue, the player who did the dirty work that freed Ewing to score and rebound.

In this game, the Knicks' injuries meant the Suns didn't automatically have to double-team anyone, which lessened the Knicks' ability to break free for open shots. The Knicks went with Derek Harper and John Starks at guard, J.R. Reid (a journeyman big forward who had just been acquired in a trade) at center and their only two solid young players, Hubert Davis and Anthony Mason, at forward. They had little depth.

For the Knicks to have a chance, they almost certainly had to have a good game from Mason, who had the brawn of a power forward with the ball-handling skills of a guard. It was Mason who was a key to the Suns' win in Madison Square Garden for getting himself thrown out for arguing with the referees.

He went right back at it in this game. After Barkley drew a foul on him, Mason glared at Joey Crawford, one of the NBA's most experienced and well-regarded refs.

"Talk to me, don't stare at me!" Crawford instructed.

"You've got a lot of balls," Mason retorted.

"We'll see how tough you are," Crawford said.

Soon enough, Mason had two fouls and a seat on the Knicks bench. He never was a big factor in the game.

The Suns gradually wore down the Knicks. As Phoenix began to pull away in the fourth quarter, Green and Reid started to get in position for a potential rebound. This was the sort of mundane battle that takes place hundreds of times in a game, one that is required for frontline players, with one player leaning on another, trying to gain a leverage advantage while—at the same time—trying to gauge the flight of the ball. But before they could even get that far, Reid threw a hard forearm at Green's head. He caught Green square in the mouth with his elbow.

It was a vicious blow, one that made even the most seasoned observers of pro sports squirm when they took a good look at the replay. Reid caused extensive damage to Green's mouth, breaking tooth plates and completely knocking out two of Green's lower teeth.

Green's reaction struck many as remarkable. He didn't fight back. Instead, he simply reached down, as if he'd just spotted a quarter on the floor, picked up his teeth, and walked off the floor. (The teeth were re-attached by a dentist that night).

Green's response seemed to mark a classic case of a spiritual man guided in crisis by his faith. And it was true enough that Green wasn't a brawler, no matter what his reputation for stretching the rules (literally, in the example of his shirt-pulling tactics). But even if he'd been so inclined, he wasn't in position to duke it out. He'd just been devastated, physically and emotionally. He knew the damage might be serious. He certainly wasn't weighing the options of retaliation: a possible suspension and the end of his consecutive-game playing streak, now the third-longest in NBA history.

Because Reid's attack took place away from the ball, few people saw it. The Suns' players didn't realize anything was wrong until Green started to leave the floor. Their anger grew afterward when they saw replays and word circulated that Reid may have been threatening to take a cheap shot beforehand.

Barkley, as might be expected considering no two players on the team were as distant as he and Green, gave him a left-handed show of support.

Barkley said Reid actually hit him first. "He knocked me out of bounds. But I'm from the old school. You hit me, and I'm going to hit you back." And so Barkley did. "And he didn't bother me the rest of the game."

As for Green, maybe he really is a "dirty player," Barkley said. "But a cheap shot is not right. This deserves strong punishment." After the media horde left, Kleine told Barkley he heard Reid tell one of the refs shortly before he hit Green, "Get him off me or else I will!" Kleine wasn't positive Reid was referring to Green. As it turned out, he apparently was referring to Williams. But this was no time to give the benefit of any doubts.

Even Barkley was taken back by this. "That's the kind of (expletive) that makes you want to fight."

Replied Kleine, "I agree. I didn't know it was that bad."

Yet if Reid hadn't actually threatened Green beforehand, he seemed to be pleased with himself afterward. Tisdale, like the other Suns, hadn't seen what happened. But shortly after Green left the floor, he heard Reid say, "Tell A.C. I got him." After Tisdale saw the replay, he got the message: Reid was boasting.

The next day, NBA officials levied a penalty of a two-game suspension without pay, plus a $10,000 fine, amidst much ballyhoo about how they'd just assessed the stiffest penalty ever for throwing an elbow.

But was this really justice? Green's consecutive-game streak, something he spent 10 years building, was in jeopardy. The streak approached 800 games. It was central to his athletic identity and the key to raising funds for his charitable foundation that was geared to helping young people. Less damaging incidents take place on city streets every day and sometimes end up in arrests. But commissioners and operators of franchises, not wanting to give the impression they can't keep their houses in order, are reluctant to rely on law enforcement to cut down on sports violence. Arrests in such cases have been extremely rare. Yet it's safe to say if sports officials don't do more to meet the problem, instigators of these matters may be on increasingly risky legal ground, especially when their attacks take place on opponents' home turf.

The Suns were split on the matter. Johnson and Tisdale, who formed (with Green and Perry) the team's "preachers" (the Christians), deemed the penalty not to be harsh enough. Barkley and Manning figured the message to Reid got across.

The external reaction was much more incensed. The combination of the ruthlessness of the attack, the good-guy reputation of the victim, and

Green's turn-the-other cheek response resulted in nationwide public outrage. Fans vilified the NBA for a tepid response. Particularly ripe for criticism was the $10,000 fine, the exact same amount assessed to Barkley and Jordan for missing the media session two weeks earlier in San Antonio. NBA officials seriously misjudged the public's lack of tolerance for violence.

Reid later apologized, saying the incident happened in the heat of the moment. But this "sentiment" could only be found in a public statement, not in communication with Green. And David Stern, the NBA commissioner, later acknowledged the penalty was too light.

As the Suns began a two-game swing to Utah and Minnesota, Green rested in Phoenix as long as possible, then made the 90-minute flight to Salt Lake City on the afternoon of the game. The Suns were curiously awaiting his arrival when he walked into the locker room an hour before tip-off. They stared at him like he was some exotic zoo animal, waiting to see if he could talk. He could, but because of his discomfort, he opted against it.

What followed was a strange question-and-answer session, with Green nodding or shaking his head, shrugging his shoulders, or else speaking through his "interpreter" Danny Manning.

Manning referred to a seldom-used Bulls player who sometimes acts as a liaison between Dennis Rodman and more normal types.

"I'm the Jack Haley of this locker room!" Manning shouted.

No, Green hadn't decided whether Reid's penalty was severe enough, Manning said. This was a matter Green continued to keep at arm's length, even when he spoke for himself.

Q: Did you do anything to provoke the attack?

A: "No, he was just playing hard," Manning said.

Q: Did you see it coming?

A: "No, he would have ducked if he did!"

The Suns broke up laughing. Green pounded fists with Manning to show his appreciation.

That's all they really could do anyway, just keep things as light as possible. Tisdale offered to help Green with sign language. Manning donned a tiny face mask brought for Green's use (he declined to wear it) and pretended he was a catcher waiting for a fastball.

The jokes couldn't hide the fact that the damage was more severe than first thought. A more substantial mask had to be built; Green wore it for the next several games. Bryan Colangelo, the general manager, sent the

NBA office a memo detailing the broken tooth sockets and the root canals Green had to undergo. The Suns even talked vaguely about filing legal action or assisting Green with a suit of his own (neither of which ultimately happened).

Green began making token appearances. He stepped into the Utah game long enough to launch a three-pointer, then headed back to the Suns' hotel. A debate began on whether the streak now was bogus, cheapened by this and several more brief stints.

Barkley took his chance to take a jab at Green.

"I think the criticism is fair," Barkley said. "There's some justification for it."

To buy into this argument, one had to believe that Green should lose his legacy because of Reid's impulsive, rash act. That didn't sell.

Fitzsimmons never thought twice about keeping the streak alive. The debate might have been livelier had Green been trying to play through a normal injury, a muscle pull or the like.

"Because of the way his injury was inflicted, I don't feel bad about it at all," Fitzsimmons said. Besides, he coached the holder of the record, Randy Smith, who played in 906 straight games for Buffalo. Smith struggled through the final several games of a season with a hamstring injury, "But I kept playing him," Fitzsimmons said.

The debate over the streak's legitimacy buried a subterranean issue, one infinitely more sensitive. Green had always come through to play his best when the Suns were in dire straits. When they had their full assortment of weapons up and running, he tended to fade into the scenery.

Green hadn't been producing much in the games leading up to Reid's assault. It was increasingly difficult for him to guard younger, quicker forwards. Injury or not, he'd continually have to prove himself to earn playing time. It wasn't that the Suns didn't want to give him minutes. He was under contract for another three seasons at $5 million per. But when healthy, their great assortment of forwards gave them a choice. It would become tougher to find minutes for him. Yet he needed to play to keep his streak alive.

THE WIN OVER THE KNICKS, which pushed their record to 27-26, was serviceable enough. Yet at relatively full strength, the Suns had merely managed a series of perfunctory wins against weaker teams. Fitzsimmons began to recognize that this team was not the juggernaut of years past.

"It's going to be a struggle," he said. "I'm convinced of that now."

Nothing happened to change this view when the Suns failed to live up to even their own modest standards early in a game at Minnesota.

The Timberwolves were coming off a spirited challenge of the Bulls the previous evening, while the Suns had enjoyed a night off. Nevertheless, the team that appeared that night was the Sun City Suns, more suited to a round of nine holes and a game of checkers. They managed to pull down just two rebounds in the first nine minutes. The Timberwolves out-rebounded them 22-12 for the half, though the 'Wolves didn't have the firepower to open a big lead.

This was the Suns at their worst, and there no longer was a "laid-back" coach whose personality could be labeled the root of the problem.

Fitzsimmons launched a tirade in the locker room.

"We usually play to the level of these losing teams! We can't do that. We can't just win off our talent!

"I won't let you give up. I'm going to push you and push you."

Said Tisdale, "I thought we were at a campfire meeting."

Only one player didn't seem to soak much of it in. "I didn't really listen that much," said Barkley. "I was thinking about what I'm trying to accomplish."

The Suns came out and blitzed them 45-15 to start the second half. They won easily, continuing their unbeaten history in Minnesota. They got a great game from Barkley (21 points, 11 rebounds, nine assists, three steals and just one turnover).

They faced a much more probing test at home against the Pacers, a team that had one of the most imposing front lines in basketball: Rik Smits, a 7-foot-4 center with a knack for scoring, Dale Davis, a physical 6-10 forward, and Derrick McKey, a versatile 6-9 player who could fill either forward spot effectively.

McKey was a smart player who concentrated on defense but could produce points when the Pacers needed them. So, at first glance, it seemed fairly loony to have somebody who'd never played an NBA minute go against him. Mario Bennett displayed scoring instincts in college but had been even better as a shot-blocker. He could run, and he had enough size and quickness to be able to guard a variety of players. He was exactly the sort of player the Suns could use.

Bennett was friendly to a fault, but his maturity was a question. He'd had a couple of minor scrapes with the law—nothing serious enough to think he was destined to wash out, but enough to make the Suns think long and hard about drafting him.

They knew all about him. He played at Arizona State, about 10 miles from downtown Phoenix. He had a history of serious knee problems but battled back to lead the Sun Devils to the Sweet 16 of the NCAA tournament. He was thought to be a mid-first-round draft pick. Then, when concerns about him began to surface, he slipped on draft day all the way to the Suns at No. 27. Before the season, he underwent minor knee surgery to clean out some rough spots. He was just now practicing himself back into playing form.

At one point, when Fitzsimmons didn't think Bennett was working hard enough, the Suns' coach virtually wrote him off for the season, saying he should try to improve in the summer leagues and report to fall training camp ready to go. But Fitzsimmons figured Finley could switch from small forward to off-guard to cover Reggie Miller, who embarrassed Wesley Person en route to 40 points against them in Indianapolis. That opened a spot at forward, where the Suns needed someone tall enough to guard McKey, who towered over Finley and could score with a turn-around jumper.

McKey was the type of player Green matched up well against. But with Green still limited by his injury, Fitzsimmons put Bennett on the active list. Bennett figured this merely meant he would sit and learn from a bit better vantage point: the end of the bench. But Fitzsimmons figured that starting a rookie often was the best thing to do. That way, he didn't have time to sit on the bench and battle his nerves while waiting to play. Perhaps, he thought, "Mario can bother McKey a little early."

Bennett was stunned by the move.

"I didn't think I'd play this year. I thought I'd learn and wait until next year." Bennett played decently enough in the exhibition season. He'd even been their leading rebounder. On the downside, he had a maddening tendency to miss free throws. The odds were nearly 50-50 that he'd throw up an air ball.

Fitzsimmons figured Bennett would play for a few minutes, then Manning would come in to guard McKey.

This all seemed a prescription for three quick fouls by Bennett and a trip to the bench. But he scored the game's first hoop, a layup off a feed from Kevin Johnson 55 seconds into the game. He was in the game as the Suns streaked to an 18-6 lead. He even swished his first two free throws!

Bennett did so well, he played the entire first quarter. He finished with eight points, three rebounds and a steal in 19 minutes. "And he made people change some shots," Fitzsimmons said. "I'm delighted he did well." Said Barkley, "He's got a bright future."

(Fitzsimmons would continue to start Bennett; if he played well, which he often did, he got to stay in for 15 or 20 minutes a game. If he started making mistakes, he'd take a quick seat on the bench.) The Suns defended well enough; at the other end, they were at their running and shooting best. Barkley, Johnson and Manning, together at last, were in sync. They won easily. For the first time all season, they were actually two games over .500. The popular theme now was: "The Suns are back!"

Then they went to Denver to visit the Nuggets, one of the NBA's biggest flops (the teams were competing on this point). There, the Nuggets beleaguered coach, Bernie Bickerstaff, put 7-foot-center Dikembe Mutombo on Barkley. Mutombo was quick enough to prevent Barkley from blowing by him easily and rangy enough to block his shots down low.

The Nuggets packed their defense around the paint, hoped the refs wouldn't call an illegal zone too often, and prayed the Suns would shoot outside.

It worked. The Suns had enough to stay with them for three quarters, but they sagged in the final quarter. It was their first loss to a losing team since Fitzsimmons took over.

THEY FLEW HOME AFTERWARD to prepare for the next night's game against their oldest rivals. And the Los Angeles Lakers once again featured Earvin "Magic" Johnson, now back after his nearly five-year exile after contracting the virus that causes AIDS.

As long as the Suns and Lakers had battled each other (194 meetings in the regular season and play-offs over 28 seasons), they'd seldom done so on equal footing. The Lakers usually held the upper hand, of course, but the pattern was reversed by the early '90s. As in any long-standing rivalry, the feelings of those on the bottom at any particular time were spiked with the greater dose of venom.

This was particularly true after Johnson tried, then gave up, his comeback attempt in the fall of 1992. At the time, Colangelo's had been one of the leading voices to oppose Johnson's return. In the face of such criticism, Johnson—after playing in a few exhibition games—re-retired. Colangelo said he'd spoken up on behalf of three of his players who voiced concern about sharing the court with somebody who carried the AIDS virus. (Publicly, all Suns quoted on the matter supported Johnson, some enthusiastically.)

In Johnson's view, Colangelo acted out of self-interest.

Johnson said, "He wants to win. And he's done everything but win a championship. If I'm playing, that minimizes their chances of doing that. We've been a thorn in their side."

But was this Colangelo's primary motivation?

"Of course," Johnson said. "He's not protecting his players. Their players said they had no problem with me playing." In Johnson's view, Colangelo's opinion ruled, in part because he "probably is the most powerful man in the game next to the commissioner. He knows people will listen to what he says."

Despite all this, Johnson said, "Life goes on. I don't hate him. He's a model owner. I respect him from a business standpoint. I'd like to be where he is one day. That's the highest compliment I can give a person."

In truth, there didn't seem much evidence to support Johnson's view of a Colangelo-led conspiracy to protect the Suns' title chances. At the time Johnson opted to re-retire, the Lakers were fading. The Suns already had acquired Barkley. They were starting to look more at the Jazz, Trail Blazers, SuperSonics and Rockets as their most dangerous opponents. There was a belief among those who followed Johnson's career closely that his decision to drop his comeback in 1992 was influenced more by criticism from his fellow players (notably the Jazz' Karl Malone) than by Colangelo. But the Suns' president was a more convenient target; the less-than-unanimous support by players (whose paychecks had increased exponentially in the 1980s, thanks much to the exploits of Johnson and Larry Bird) was an awfully sensitive issue.

Then again, there seemed to be even less evidence to support Colangelo's argument. That some players feared stepping onto the court with Johnson no doubt was true. That he actually posed a danger had not been demonstrated. An entire decade had passed from the emergence of AIDS in America until even the most minimal rules were put in place for treating bleeding wounds immediately or for removing a bleeding athlete from competition. No case of HIV transmission had been demonstrated in this unknowingly carefree era, let alone after safety guidelines were put in place.

By hounding Johnson into retirement, his critics not only jump-started the idea that HIV-positive people were some sort of lepers, they also may have set back the cause of safety itself (to the extent that concerns were warranted). With Johnson's case as a backdrop, would any HIV-positive athlete now let his condition be known publicly if he or she possibly could avoid it? Wouldn't athletes prefer to know who carried HIV?

Colangelo was silent on these aspects of the dilemma. Later, he seemed to sense this wasn't his noblest move. After his first initiative, he resisted talking about the subject.

As for Johnson, his return was a double-edged sword. He played much more effectively than anyone (including himself) expected. The Lakers' record improved immediately upon his return; the energy level for home games at The Forum jumped dramatically. The view that he was heroically showing that HIV-infected people could perform admirably, even in a physically demanding setting, seemed to be prevailing. Yet many young people saw his accomplishments as evidence that AIDS wasn't the scourge the medical establishment, and their parents, warned them about.

In Boston, Robert Johnson, an HIV counselor at the Whittier Street Neighborhood Health Center, spoke to young people about abstinence and safer sex. Their reaction: The entire HIV issue is a waste of time. One told him, "You older folks have just been trying to freak us out. Your information is whacked."

Said Robert Johnson, "They see a guy running up and down the court and think if they get (HIV), they can still play basketball and chase girls."

A male high school senior said, "I have friends who say, "(Expletive), if Magic looks that good, I don't care if I have AIDS. No girl will ever know." Added a female student, "When (Magic) first got it, I was sad. I thought he was going to die in a couple of months. Magic's living a nice life. I don't think it's that bad."

Tom McNaught, spokesman for the AIDS Action Committee, said, "For some kids, being shot is more real than dying of AIDS."

Reading this, Magic Johnson said, "This is hard."

"I understand what (the counselor) is saying, but if he really wants the kids to see what's going on, all he has to do is take them right there to that hospice in Boston. I visited there when I was on the (federal) commission. You take the kids there and they'll really learn something."

But, Magic was asked, how can a guy from a neighborhood health center make himself heard when a famous athlete with HIV is starring on national television? To whom will high school students listen?

"That's a big part of the problem," Johnson said. "I think me being back is a positive thing for a lot of people. But when kids see me, they see me out there playing and performing.

"What they have to understand is that today looks fine, but there are still the questions about tomorrow with me. There's still the questions about what's going to happen.

"Everything's going well now, but I have HIV and something's going to happen."

JOHNSON WAS ON THE MARK in his basketball side of the analysis. The Lakers weren't just a thorn in the Suns' side; they were more like a supercharged vine that choked off any chance of their growth in the 1970s and '80s. During the first half of the 1990s, the Suns spent the most enjoyable years in franchise history returning these favors.

But after the Suns traded Cedric Ceballos to the Lakers before the '94-95 season, the power began to shift to the coast once again. By the middle of this season, bolstered by Johnson's return, the Lakers were starting to resemble a possible title contender.

Barkley, sounding as if he'd been a part of the rivalry for a couple of decades, refused to concede anything. In his view, the Lakers were more "spoilers" than contenders, a remark that received much notoriety in Southern California.

Their early March game in Phoenix had all the makings of the renewal of one of the NBA's best rivalries, a game not to be missed.

As it turned out, it was a game best not arrived at late.

Moments after tip-off, Ceballos nailed a three-pointer. Then Elden Campbell, the 6-foot-11 forward who sometimes went through the motions against other teams but usually played well when matched against Barkley, dropped in a hook and drew a foul for a three-point play. Williams was active enough to keep the Suns within 12-10. But then Eddie Jones, the Lakers young off-guard, slashed to the hoop and finished with a spectacular slam. It was the sort of athletic display much more common for the younger, successfully rebuilt Lakers than for the Suns.

Then Nick Van Exel, their playmaker, fired in a three-pointer, and Ceballos scored on a drive. The Lakers suddenly had a 19-10 lead.

By the time Johnson entered the game, the Lakers were up by 13.

Johnson had entirely remade himself. He was heavyset, the oldest, slowest player on the floor. Instead of terrorizing opponents on the fast break, as he'd done throughout the 1980s, he picked them apart in the halfcourt offense, sometimes from his old spot up top, other times in his new role as a low-post forward. He took only high-percentage shots, the kind that made him one of the smartest and most effective offensive players in history. To be sure, he wasn't a superstar any longer, but he was a superb complimentary player.

The rivalry still had spark. There was some jawing and even pushing and shoving as competitors new to this old routine got in on the act; the Suns' Williams with the Lakers' Campbell, Magic with Manning. Said Ceballos, "It's always going to be a rivalry, owner to owner, player to player."

But for this game, the Suns never even challenged. The Lakers won in a rout, 119-97.

In a colloquialism that would have made his high school coach proud, Fitzsimmons said, "Sometimes you get the bear, and sometimes the bear gets you."

The Lakers' strategy had mirrored the Nuggets'. Try to force Barkley and everyone else to shoot from outside, even if this meant giving up mid-range jumpers.

"That creates a real problem," Fitzsimmons said.

Fitzsimmons also started to recognize what he was up against in more intangible matters. Often, his team reflected the plus-30 nature of most of its key players. Younger teams might have bad games, but they could be counted on to bounce back with energy, if not effectiveness. The Suns weren't like that.

"I worry about this team," he said.

With age comes experience and game smarts. But the Suns also had lost much here, too. In giving up Ainge, Majerle and Schayes, they'd lost three players who could shoot and handle the ball and also knew the game.

Of the five rookies that had been brought in, only Chris Carr possessed shooting skill. But he was still learning the game's nuances. If a shooter didn't know how to get a shot, his ability was neutralized.

Yet young players could hardly be blamed for their problems. After the debacle against the Lakers, Fitzsimmons turned to his veteran players and implored them, "We need more leadership."

But who could he really count on, other than Barkley and Johnson?

Fitzsimmons had just about given up on Williams when his leg improved to the point where he could at least give them 20 journeyman-caliber minutes in the middle. But everyone doubted he could return to the starting form he'd usually displayed with the Cavaliers.

Then there was Tisdale, a key to reducing the pressure on Barkley. He was one of their best mid-range shooters, and he'd had a few big games. When he did, it could push the Suns to a win.

Tisdale had a huge body but a finesse game. In the NBA, this was a prescription for earning the label "soft." At times, it amounted to unfair stereotyping, with racial implications as well. Around the league, the biggest players, particularly the biggest black players, were supposed to be "power" players. This view overlooked the fact that finesse players, even those standing 6-foot-9 and weighing 270 pounds, could be just as valuable.

Yet the questions about Tisdale ran deeper. He'd never learned to play defense with consistent effect. Moreover, his very availability often was in question. He sat out several games with injuries whose severity was questioned by those in the team's inner circle.

After he got a finger in an eye, he missed a game. Would A.C. Green EVER sit out in such a circumstance? Now Tisdale was out because an arthritic condition in his right (non-shooting) shoulder was bothering him. Tisdale used his right shoulder for leverage in making his scoring moves down low, so the injury limited him. At the same time, he was reluctant to take a cortisone shot that would allow him to play.

The idea of players being shot with a needle to perform effectively is one of the least appealing aspects of big-time sport. Yet the shoulder is one of the safest areas of the body for taking such a shot, unlike a knee or foot where masking the warning signs of pain could cause serious long-term problems. And he was, after all, being paid $3.5 million dollars.

Tisdale said he took a couple of shots earlier in the season and deemed the effects to be only temporary. He didn't want to do it again. The upshot was that he found himself crawling further into the Suns' doghouse (a familiar residence for him). Eventually, he agreed to take another shot; he managed to finish the season, then had surgery on the shoulder.

Then there was Person, one of their few young, healthy players. At first, Fitzsimmons talked of how Person was playing better under pressure since he took over, that Person now recognized he had to drive to the basket instead of passively waiting for three-point attempts. But as the games went on, he became just as inconsistent as he was under Westphal. Fitzsimmons also found it increasingly difficult to find opponents Person was capable of guarding. Fitzsimmons prided himself at knowing how to praise as well as criticize. This was a key to building a player's confidence. Yet Person seemed to have lost his.

All in all, these worries were familiar. They were the same concerns

Westphal had pondered. "I'm frustrated," Fitzsimmons said, "just like my predecessor was frustrated."

At times in the weeks after he took the job, he'd taken gentle jabs at Westphal for the Suns' lack of defensive consistency and for what he thought was an overreliance on Barkley at the offensive end. But these remarks were becoming increasingly rare. At one point, he reminded reporters, "I didn't blame Westy. They've been inconsistent because they haven't played much together. It's hard."

And it wasn't much fun either. Yet he couldn't fully share his doubts with his players, lest they lose heart. They were proud men. The veterans had been used to kicking opponents for years. But now, if they lost their confidence, they had no chance because they no longer could win on skill alone. For them, he had to try to talk up their high points. If they hustled on defense, if they hit their shots, this was proof they were still capable. And if they ever could get their whole team together for a prolonged period, who was he to rule out their chances?

WHEREVER MAJOR SPORTS teams travel, there are bug-eyed kids waiting to greet them and, if they're lucky, obtain their autographs.

Take, for instance, the teenage girl who visited the Suns' locker room after their game in Orlando.

The Suns had played reasonably well, hanging with the Magic for three quarters before Orlando came on strong late to record an NBA-record 39th straight home win. Barkley had a decent game but never was an emotional force. He started slowly, had two turnovers in the first minute, then gradually started making his presence felt.

After the game, he was subdued. The Suns used to be able to compete with the Magic for four quarters, not three.

Long after most everyone had left, Barkley lingered. So did the Orlando Sentinel's Larry Guest, who heard of a request for Barkley to meet with a special fan, the teenage girl. After some initial reluctance, Barkley agreed. The girl was cancer-stricken. Her father, fighting back tears, told Guest, "This was her dying wish, to meet Charles Barkley."

Barkley turned upbeat, posing for photos, signing the girl's No. 34 jersey. He gave her the basketball shoes he'd just worn. Barkley shook hands all round, hugged the girl, then she and her family were gone. And so was Barkley, off to the team bus. And no longer as grumpy.

THIS WAS A STRANGE TRIP indeed. The Suns had to get away from Florida, where it was cold, windy and rainy (even snowing a couple hours' drive from Orlando), to enjoy crisp but clear and comfortable late-winter weather in New Jersey. The game against the Nets did nothing to change the unpredictable nature of this five-game road trip.

They needed a win as badly as ever. They'd lost three straight, once again dropping under .500 at 30-31. But the sense of urgency was missing, particularly by Barkley, who seemed disinterested. He shot 7-for-19 and had six turnovers. "Charlie wasn't Charlie," said Jayson Williams, a former Barkley teammate in Philadelphia (and the player Barkley gave a map in his mock challenge for a locker-room fight during the exhibition season). "He was cruising. They weren't up for us."

The Suns couldn't get the ball off their hands, let alone in the hoop. They had 17 shots blocked (four short of an NBA record), 10 by 7-foot-6 center Shawn Bradley. They shot an embarrassing 31 percent in trailing, 41-36, at the half.

Moments before the half ended, Manning ran tentatively into the lane on a fast break, then stumbled and fell in sections on his left leg. He had the sort of deer-in-the-headlights look of somebody who feared the worst. Perhaps he injured the left knee for which he'd just labored so mightily for the past year. Perhaps this moment was game, set and match for Manning's career and the Suns as now structured. The player who seemed to be emerging as the team's leader until the injury a year earlier, in those giddy days of boasting the NBA's best record, motioned for help from courtside, not sure what to think.

He got up and . . . the exhales could have blown up enough balloons to supply birthday parties for 100 5-year-olds. He had merely suffered a mild ankle sprain. With trainer Joe Proski's help, he limped to the locker room. He would miss the final three games on the trip.

Then the Suns started to adjust to Bradley, throwing enough fakes and hitting enough mid-range shots to pull even. Person hit a couple of three-pointers. He'd nearly been replaced in the Suns' rotation by the rookie Carr. But just when things looked worst for him, he scuffled briefly with Carr in a practice in Orlando, just before the Suns headed for New Jersey. This seemed to energize him; he enjoyed a great practice and got another chance.

The Suns led, 78-76, when Williams hit two free throws. Then Finley got the ball in the left corner and—with assistant coach Donn Nelson pleading with the basketball gods, "JUST ONE, BABY!"—nailed a three-pointer. Barkley made two free throws. Then Williams took over, blocking a shot, making a steal, hitting a jumper, then a slam. The Suns had their most desperately needed win since Fitzsimmons took over.

THE NEXT NIGHT IN SUBURBAN Detroit, they shot as well as they ever had or ever would from the perimeter, hitting an astounding 10-for-20 from three-point range. Barkley converted an amazing 6-for-9 (briefly raising his three-point percentage out of the 20s) en route to a season-high 45 points. With all this, the Suns moved to an 87-80 lead early in the final quarter.

Then Otis Thorpe, an old Suns-killer from his days with the Rockets, softened the Suns' underbelly by shooting hooks over Williams. At the same time, the Pistons' perimeter shooters began to roam free outside. Barkley was forced to play the perimeter on defense, an unfamiliar spot for him. He would drop down to double-team a low-post player, then neither he nor anybody else recovered in time to defend the outside. Joe Dumars, the last great veteran from the Pistons' title teams of several years before, and Allan Houston each hit two three-pointers, fueling a 23-6 Pistons' charge. This was the sort of devastating inside-outside attack the Suns possessed in Barkley's first two-and-a-half seasons in Phoenix. On this night, it was enough for Detroit to beat the hot-shooting Suns.

"There are NO moral victories," Fitzsimmons emphasized. Yet they really played better than in their win at New Jersey, probably better than in any back-to-back set since they won in Miami and Atlanta in late January.

IN PHILADELPHIA, THE SUNS visited the NBA's netherworld.

The once-proud 76ers had been reduced to a laughingstock. They were competing with the expansion teams to avoid the NBA's worst record, although there was none of the forgiving enthusiasm enjoyed by the shiny new franchises. The team's owner, Harold Katz, who had made his fortune in the dieting business, had displayed both impatience and off-key judgment in personnel matters over the years. The result was a string of coaches and front-office executives who took the franchise through a bottoming-out process that seemed never to end. Now, he was in the process of selling the team to a giant communications firm.

Katz' latest decision was to trade Bradley, the center who'd swatted away all those Suns shots in New Jersey, for Derrick Coleman, a talented but moody player who had problems with his health and in controlling his weight.

Barkley never understood the Sixers under Katz, why he'd never even gotten a thank-you for his efforts in carrying the team in its post-Julius Erving years. They might have remained a frontline contender through Barkley's prime had they not, in the span of 24 hours in 1986, traded both Moses Malone, their Hall of Fame center, AND the rights to a player who could have ably replaced him, Brad Daugherty, in exchange for little.

Barkley had made a peace of sorts with Katz by getting together with him in the previous off-season. So, he toned down his acrimonious comments about the Sixers as the Suns' date in Philadelphia approached.

Much had changed since that Barkley trade that Katz now acknowledged was a mistake. (Indeed, the Sixers turned the deal into more than a mere mistake. They compounded matters by jettisoning the three players they got in return, Jeff Hornacek, Andrew Lang and Tim Perry. Hornacek and Lang were still NBA mainstays.)

When Barkley made his first return to his old stomping grounds in the spring of 1993, the subject was discussed for several days beforehand. Upon arrival, he staged a private party for all his old buddies, acting as a gracious, low-key host.

He even talked up Philadelphia, saying what a great city it was, thereby reversing some of what he'd said in his autobiography in which he pointed to racist tendencies in the supposed City of Brotherly Love. The Suns also set up a press conference at which "Sir Charles" was treated as a visiting dignitary.

This time around, he said almost nothing about his old team or about the place he still called his summer home. Media interest was perfunctory. A couple of Philadelphia writers visited him when the Suns were in New Jersey, but that was about it. From both perspectives, Barkley/Philadelphia was out of sight and just about out of mind—but not so much that Barkley couldn't get something off his chest.

When the Philly media gathered near Barkley's locker before the game, he spoke in calm, measured tones. But his words were stinging enough that a few of the reporters took the bait.

Speaking of Philadelphia sports figures, he said, "A lot of black guys with strong personalities were overly criticized." As examples, he pointed to Randall Cunningham, Seth Joyner and Reggie White of the Eagles and Andrew Toney of the 76ers.

"Y'all are rednecks," he said. "Not all of you. Some of you. You're racist. You're overly critical. You don't appreciate what you have."

Speaking of the 76ers' current plight, he said, "Y'all deserve what you're getting."

Not everything can be explained in racial terms, of course, he pointed out. The Phillies' great third baseman, Mike Schmidt, also was a punching bag, he noted. "Mike Schmidt is a hero. He should be revered."

Of the criticism of himself, "It wasn't always a racial thing. But it's a racially divided city." The reporters gathered were virtually all white. Some started getting uncomfortable.

A couple of reporters wanted Barkley to identify these racists. How many are there? Are they still working?

"A couple still are," he said. "They're bad guys."

The Suns who happened to be in the locker room at the time took in the show with keen interest. Manning, positioning himself just outside the media swarm, seemed to be enjoying the repartee the most. As a couple of reporters started to move toward the door, he playfully noted the deadline for their departure still was several minutes away. "You still have time!"

Next, Barkley was asked: Are there black racists?

"No question," he replied. "But they don't control anything."

Then Barkley added, "Don't be so sensitive. If I struck a nerve, well, you know what they say. A struck dog will holler."

By the time the discussion was winding down, a black reporter and a white one began debating the meaning of racism vigorously as they left the locker room.

The room was tense enough that Manning was moved to ease it, joking, "Where is the love in this room?" Hot Rod Williams, who was flat on his belly getting a rubdown from trainer Proski, said, "Like Rodney King said, 'Can't we all get along?'"

The game itself was a bit more tranquil. Barkley started slowly, then got a halftime tongue-lashing from Fitzsimmons. "He was on vacation in the first half, and I let him know it," Fitzsimmons said. Then Barkley told Fitzsimmons, "I'll take care of it, little fella." He did, shooting 8-for-9 in the second half.

Barkley acknowledged in a sign of how much space he's put between himself and Philadelphia, "It was a hard game to get motivated."

The game was most notable for the emergence of Williams, who gave the Suns the sort of dominant performance at center their followers were used to seeing, say, once every five or 10 years. He looked like the real deal, plugging the lane on opponents' drives, rotating to cover open men, blocking five shots, grabbing 11 rebounds, scoring 18 points.

It might have been dismissed as a gauge of the opposition (only the expansion Grizzlies had a worse record than the Sixers), yet this was his third straight fine game. He finally seemed to have found the right balance, not too much rehab work, not too little. Same for his practice routine. His right leg still was sore, particularly when he had to play two nights in a row, but the problem seemed manageable. The moral of the story: "It's hard to play when you're hurt," he said.

Perhaps with Williams starting to play to his form and—if the Big Three ever could do likewise simultaneously—there was hope. Said Fitzsimmons, "Hot Rod is the anchor to our whole defense if we're going anywhere in the play-offs."

FOR THE FOURTH WEEK in a row, the Suns were featured as one of NBC-TV's Sunday games, this time at Charlotte. This wasn't all that unusual. For years, the Suns had been at or near the maximum number of national TV appearances allowed by the NBA. They were, after all, a natural TV team. In addition to their high-profile status (they were among the NBA leaders in merchandise sold bearing their logo), they had a marquee player in Barkley, their games usually were high-scoring, entertaining, and often wildly unpredictable with cliff-hanger finishes.

This game was to start at 10 a.m. Arizona time, meaning the players would start rising around 7 a.m. This was not a tried-and-true method of getting their best performances, particularly from Barkley. He was known as someone more likely to get to sleep at sunrise rather than to awaken at its call.

It was all fodder for a theory: that if roosters could be heard when the team bus prepared to pick them up for the game, the Suns would be swimming upstream that day. Perhaps they could slip the NBA schedule-maker a nice gift come play-off time—like a small paper bag containing a few large bills and the message: "Please be kind. No morning games!"

Sure enough, the Suns appeared to be looking for the nearest pot of hot coffee when the game started. They offered no defensive resistance and didn't rebound at all. Barkley was particularly stiff. He didn't get his first rebound until the final seconds of the first quarter. He got one more the rest of the way. Two rebounds in 38 minutes! This might have been a career low. "I don't like morning games, but I just had a bad game," he said testily afterward.

The Hornets were ready to play from the start. They jumped to a 27-

12 lead, then had a blowout in hand when they extended it to 52-31 late in the first half.

This was not the Hornets team of the past couple of years that had been thought to have a chance to join the NBA's elite. They had traded their center, Alonzo Mourning, one of the game's best young big men, after a nasty contract dispute. Mourning demanded $13 million a season, a staggering sum (even by modern standards), especially for someone who'd never led his team even to the third round of the play-offs, much less an NBA title. Yet the Hornets played in the same ballpark, offering $11 million a season. The difference couldn't be settled, so the Hornets shipped Mourning to Pat Riley's Miami Heat. (This prompted one veteran NBA official to lament to a Hornets counterpart, "When I came into the league, there were 10 teams and five great centers. Today, there are 29 teams and five great centers. You had one. How could you let him get away?")

Now, the Hornets were battling for the East's final play-off berth, which would mean a first-round elimination by the Chicago Bulls.

In this game, Fitzsimmons started fearing the worst. Might the Suns be blown out by 40 on national TV? All of a sudden, Johnson put on a head-spinning display of jump-shooting and penetration. He'd finally gotten completely healthy. And as long as referees enforced the no-hand-checking rules, he could dominate a game. By halftime, the Suns had cut the lead to 56-49.

Slowly, they caught up. And when Finley spotted Williams underneath for a slam with 3:20 left in the game, the Suns led, 95-92. It looked like their rarest of accomplishments: a comeback from a huge deficit and a win.

Then, an obscure point guard named Anthony Goldwire, a refugee from the minor-league CBA, got the ball up top.

Goldwire was drafted and released by the Suns in '94 when he was beaten out for the backup point guard spot by Perry. He got a chance in Charlotte because of an injury to Mugsy Bogues and another to Kenny Anderson. (Anderson had just been acquired in a trade with New Jersey, where he had done little except turn down a reported $6 million a year contract.) Anderson played on a gimpy ankle in this one. The Hornets realized they were better off going with Goldwire.

With the shot clock running down, Goldwire launched a three-pointer. He buried it, both tying the game and waking a sleepy crowd. In the same situation again, he lofted a prayer, a running shot from the free throw line. It accidentally banked in. The Suns couldn't answer. They headed into the final seconds trailing by two.

Barkley had a 15-footer on the left baseline to tie it, but he missed. NBC had gotten a typical game from the Suns, who flew home after a 2-3 road trip.

EVEN WITH IMPROVED HEALTH, the Suns had settled into the role of a .500 team. Barkley knew this as well as anyone. For the Suns to win the title, "We'll have to get every conceivable break," he said.

In the long run, he wondered aloud whether he'd even want to give it another try with them next season. It seemed clear enough that some of the Suns' moves had not worked out. The roster was loaded with players who were best suited to his own power forward spot. The price of this unlimited depth at Barkley's position (six of the team's 12 active players could ably fill the spot) was that they had stripped themselves of shooters.

Barkley said he wanted to carefully scrutinize the Suns' off-season moves before committing to another season.

"I don't want to go through another year like this one," he said. "I don't need that. I'll have to take a serious look at what I want to do.

"I'm planning on playing. But I don't want to play unless we can be a serious contender. I want to see what the team is going to do."

Their record stood at 32-33. They were running No. 6 in the West. There were 17 games left. The first five were against losing teams, but eight of the final 12 were against the West's top five; the Suns had a collective record of 1-11 against them. It was imperative they win at least four of the five against the weaker teams, both to obtain the highest play-off spot possible and to have a chance at a winning season.

Fitzsimmons gathered his team on the practice court and implored them, the way thousands of coaches have done to their teams in the past and would do so in the future: "We've got to dig in defensively and hit the boards." On offense, "We've got to move the ball." Otherwise, "It's one round and out in the play-offs."

The first two games were against the Warriors, whose personnel gaffes made the Suns' decisions seem like small stuff. They had made a succession of moves that all steered the franchise downward. Just three years earlier, they drafted Anfernee Hardaway, now the game's premier point guard. And after the Webber-Nelson blowup and a series of trades, they wound up with a lean forward named Donyell Marshall, who hadn't shown enough consistency to earn regular playing time, even on a losing team.

They'd also just traded two of their better players, point guard Tim Hardaway and forward/center Chris Gatling. The Warriors feared losing both to free agency and wanted to get something for them. But they didn't get equal value in return.

Any loss of talent in an already mediocre setting often leads to disaster, so it wasn't surprising that the Warriors—who'd gamely hung in at No. 8 in the play-off watch for much of the season—were starting to fade. Add injuries to Chris Mullin, the team's fading superstar, and center Rony Seikaly, and the Warriors simply had nowhere near the Suns' horsepower.

In Phoenix, the Suns blitzed them by a staggering 51-15 margin at one point to close the first half with a 26-point lead.

Then, almost on cue, the Suns seemed to be bent on proving the cliche that no lead is safe in the NBA. In truth, many leads are safe, but not so much on a team whose turn-it-on-and-off personality is led by Charles Barkley. He turned to his comic role, bantering with fans and opponents. Twice, he allowed entry passes into the paint to be slapped away, resulting in steals. Even the mild-mannered Elliot Perry was taken aback; he got in Barkley's ear, reminding him that the team still needed him. Said Perry, "He has nights he doesn't play as hard as he should. That hurts us because we're going to continue to go to him."

The Suns hung on—barely. They won by eight. But the Warriors almost came up with a steal in the closing minute that could have cut the lead to two.

Said an exasperated Fitzsimmons of Barkley, "I maintain that if he really worked at it, he could get the same stats in 24 minutes that he gets in 40. But you're not going to change him at this stage."

In between the two Warriors games, Fitzsimmons reminded his team, "We can't float in and out. The NBA has had millions of games where teams had 20-point leads and then lost."

The next game didn't qualify as one of them, but only because the Suns' second-half lead reached a mere 15. Then, all their worst tendencies surfaced.

Barkley, who was pounding the Warriors inside with great success early, began drifting outside—as he often did when he appeared tired—with little effect.

Johnson, who'd always been more intellectual than instinctive, then began hesitating. He wasn't eager to throw it to Barkley, but he didn't find other options quickly enough. He dribbled the shot clock down, then began forcing passes and shots.

The Suns' offense shut down completely. They scored at a pace that would be expected of NBA players wearing blindfolds: 15 points over a 16-minute span.

At the other end, Marshall, the Warriors' disappointing prospect, connected on four three-pointers. The Warriors won going away.

Now, the cutoff for merely making the play-offs seemed to be approaching from behind as inevitably as sunrise on a cloudless desert morning.

The Suns responded by dispatching the Clippers, avoiding an unconscionable season sweep by a team that—though improving—had come to be identified with chronic losing more than perhaps any other in sports.

To win, they had to shoot well enough to cover for awful ball-handling. This, at least, was one problem that had been bedeviling them less frequently, thanks to the return to health of Johnson.

The season's first half had been maddening for him.

His body once again had failed him. He hated the constant questions about his health. At one point, he began ducking reporters until it was pointed out that NBA guidelines said all players were supposed to be available for 15 minutes or so after practices and games. More importantly, he worried he was becoming a distraction to his teammates.

If he were one of them, he'd want himself healthy and ready to go once and for all, rather than popping in and out of the lineup with no warning, just so everyone would know what to expect. Otherwise, even he believed they were better off with Perry.

Now, Johnson was at his best and that gave the Suns both style and substance. With him leading fast breaks and exploding to the hoop in the halfcourt offense, their games were far more entertaining for fans and the players. Defenses had to be so wary of slowing him down that other players were more able to free themselves for shots.

Fitzsimmons would shout frequently during games, "Get the ball to Kevin!"

Said Fitzsimmons, "The worst thing we can do is to throw the ball to Charles, then stand and watch him decide what to do. Kevin breaks the defense down and gets more people involved."

At a time when Barkley's passion and performance had dropped from his world-beating February, Johnson began to carry them. In March, he averaged 20 points and 10 assists per game, shooting well over 50 percent. He now was among the league leaders in assists, free throw and field-goal percentage. The game was fun again, and Johnson was buoyant. He'd always played his best down the stretch and in the play-offs; this year was heading in the same direction. "I'm a spring chicken," he joked.

Even with Johnson's reemergence, any sign that the Suns truly were righting themselves, or even were capable of fully doing so, had yet to surface.

A home game against the Kings was a microcosm of their entire season. They got off to a horrific start, hitting three of their first 15 shots, then spent the rest of the night struggling to overcome their early failures. In the end, playing against a short-handed, sub-.500 team, they eked out a 4-point win.

The Suns closed the last soft stretch in their schedule against the Milwaukee Bucks, a team in disarray after losing 13 straight. Their coach, Mike Dunleavy, once guided Magic Johnson's Lakers to their last NBA Finals run. He'd given up the bright lights of Los Angeles for the security of a long-term deal as both the coach and general manager in a low-key NBA outpost. He'd come up with a stellar forward in Vin Baker and a sometimes productive one in "Big Dog" Robinson, but his moves elsewhere hadn't panned out. The players were unhappy, and it showed increasingly in their uninspired play.

In this game, Bennett and Finley badly outplayed Robinson, whose selection to the Olympic Dream Team now seemed like a poor choice. The Suns displayed some of their old blowout power, taking control from the opening minutes and not letting up. They'd done what they needed. They were 36-34 heading into that last miserable stretch.

THAT THE SEASON'S FINAL portion began in San Antonio was appropriate. Fitzsimmons would make his first return as coach to the place where he'd been the most villainous figure in the city's limited sports history. During Fitzsimmons' second stint with the Suns, his wife, JoAnn, accompanied the team for a game in San Antonio. She sat next to a fan, who—not knowing her identity—casually remarked, "That Cotton Fitzsimmons sure is doing a good job with the Suns. But boy, was he lousy when he was here!"

In contrast with his previous coaching stint, Fitzsimmons was at peace with himself. Back then, particularly in his final season of '92-93, he had been contentious. He put much pressure on himself to make the NBA Finals at least once, and—thanks in part to the remarkably rapid decline of high-scoring Tom Chambers (like Barkley, a reluctant off-season worker), it was becoming increasingly clear that he wasn't going to make it. He ended the season in a public argument with Chambers over his defensive effort, and he was turning even inoffensive questions from reporters into a game of one-upmanship.

It all seemed to be lost in a late-season game against the Lakers at the Forum in Inglewood (where Fitzsimmons once went about 20 years without winning). The Suns had just blown a big lead and lost. Instead of his usual sunny, "We'll-be-fine" optimism, he sat alone on a trainer's table, staring at the post-game stat sheet, detached from everyone around him.

Shortly afterward, he announced he was turning the reins over to Westphal.

This time around, at age 64, surely figured to be the final stop on his coaching tour. He seemed more determined to enjoy himself.

To be sure, coaching was much more all-consuming than had been his broadcasting work with Al McCoy. Sometimes, Fitzsimmons' wife would say something to him and he'd be lost in such matters as interior defense, a fast tempo, and how to work for high-percentage shots. When he was a broadcaster, he pointed out, "I didn't have Al McCoy on my mind."

THE SUNS WOULD PLAY the Spurs twice in a row, first on a balmy Sunday night in San Antonio, then back in Phoenix two nights later.

Fitzsimmons awaited the game in San Antonio as anxiously as any the entire season. The Spurs were the NBA's hottest team, having won a remarkable 16 straight games. Yet the Suns had cause for optimism. The day before the game, for the first time since taking over more than two months earlier, Fitzsimmons finally staged his first practice with all of his main players—Barkley, Johnson, Manning, Williams, Finley, Person, Green, Perry, Tisdale and Kleine—healthy and available to work.

Whereas the "soft" Westphal had started the requirement that everyone expected to start had to practice first (a rule meant for Barkley and Johnson), the "tough" Fitzsimmons backed off on this. Forcing his older players to practice did more harm than good, he concluded. The games used them up. Trying to squeeze in many practices around an 82-game schedule was too much for them.

Their work just before boarding the plane for San Antonio was a pleasant exception. They all were ready to go, now that Tisdale finally was available. They competed hard; they looked like a group worthy of their individual and collective fame.

Now, all they needed to do was play this way in the games. If they did, perhaps they might have one last shot at it, the final realistic crack Fitzsimmons would have at a title.

Williams was playing at a level where—at long last—the Suns had a dependable interior defender. He knew when to stay at home on the opposing big man, when to help his teammates. And he had the lateral movement to accomplish both. More than that, he competed with a defensive zeal unmatched by his teammates.

Because he could guard opposing centers one-on-one, Williams allowed the Suns' other defenders to better stay with opposing perimeter shooters instead of helping out down low. Their three-point defense, once the NBA's worst, was improving. Their overall defense no longer was a sieve.

The "bust" had come through.

Gushed Fitzsimmons, "It's unfair to say our defense is better because I took over as coach. That's not the case at all. Our defense is better now because Hot Rod Williams is playing. He's the center of it."

Then came the biggest compliment of all: "He's the best player I've coached at playing defense inside."

This gave the Suns the sort of balance between offense and defense that his Suns' teams (and Westphal's) had lacked. When the Suns put their five best players on the floor—Johnson and Finley in the backcourt, Williams at center, with Barkley and Manning at forward—they sometimes had more of a defensive presence than an offensive one.

About an hour before tip-off, Fitzsimmons sat at courtside thinking about the team's upside as the Alamodome started to fill. More than 30,000 people, one of the biggest crowds of the entire NBA season, would be on hand.

"I believe in this team," he said. But with all those close losses, with all those fragile stars, with the erratic shooting, did they believe in themselves? Now was the time to find out.

"What put us in this fix was injuries," Fitzsimmons said. "But you can use that excuse for only so long. I think everybody is ready to play. And you'd have to say we're playing the hottest team in basketball.

"I'm interested in how we play. Can we come in and play well for 48 minutes?"

He didn't have to wait long to get an answer.

Instead of showing they were ready for prime time, another time slot seemed to be in order. Like at 2 a.m., opposite a public-service program on which a beancounter discusses the merits of various city governments' bond ratings.

They started a pratfall immediately.

Barkley appeared spent, almost from the tip-off. He drifted outside, got the ball on the left side, backed up even farther, and took a three-pointer. He missed, as he did on a couple of early 20-footers.

By the time the first quarter was over, Barkley was 1-for-9, including 0-for-3 on three-pointers. By contrast, the Spurs worked for good shots and converted. They also got a few fast breaks on the long bounces from Barkley's prayerful perimeter shots.

They raced to a 25-10 lead, and the Suns never challenged.

Barkley shot 4-for-18, including 0-for-6 on three-pointers. He finished with eight points and nine rebounds. And, in a telling measurement of effort, for one of the few times ever, Barkley failed to get to the free-throw line.

At times, Fitzsimmons had challenged Barkley's shot selection in front of other players, if not in hopes of having an effect on Barkley, then at least to preserve his own credibility with the rest of the team. This time, however, he chose to use "we," both in talking to the team and with reporters.

"I was disappointed with our shot selection early," he said. "We needed to take the ball to the basket." Noting the Spurs, like many Suns' opponents, preferred to sag in and tempt the Suns to shoot outside, he said, "You have to have pretty good shooters on the court against them. "The way they play defense, everybody has to be able to score. So you pass the ball to the open man for the shot. But it better not be a 25-footer, or else you play into their hands."

Barkley would admit no mistakes, saying, "If I'm open, I'm going to shoot it."

But his teammates weren't buying it. Manning, asked about Barkley's choice of shots, sounded uncharacteristically angry. "All I'm going to say is we got our asses beat."

Williams pointed out the obvious. "Three-point shooting can be tempting when you're open. But that's not our game. They stuck with their game plan, and we didn't."

The Suns flew back to Arizona, with Fitzsimmons lamenting they still were searching for an identity. Increasingly, though, others had one for them.

Fitzsimmons had overheard another NBA coach describe his team as "old, tired, beat-up" and heading for a fall. The evidence was tangible enough. The NBA's winningest team the previous three seasons was a mere one game over .500—even though they'd added maybe the best group of rookies in the NBA, even though they finally boasted an inside defensive presence in Williams, even though they'd returned to reasonable health.

One game was enough to bring back the realist in Fitzsimmons.

"You're looking at us," he said the day between the two Spurs' games. "We're 36 and 35. The record is staring us right in the face, and we can't run and hide from it. That's who we are. If the players don't want to hear, then I can't help them.

"If anybody expects me to wave my magic wand in the play-offs, they're sadly mistaken. I tried to walk on water once, and I went under. I can't do that."

He'd just watched a game on TV in which a young Orlando Magic team had taken apart the elderly Knicks. "That's what life is about. I could see us there. We're an old team. I'm not down on us. That's just the way it is.

"I think the old days are gone forever. I don't think we'll ever see again what we saw in the past. You would be just hoping against hope. But what we are hoping for is one last run. That's what we're going to try to do."

Their most tangible problem hadn't gone away. They no longer could shoot their way out of trouble. Johnson always had great perimeter threats around him, players who demanded attention, thereby helping open the lane for him to drive to the hoop, players such as Tom Chambers, Eddie Johnson, Majerle and Ainge. Now there were none. Against the Spurs, the Suns took 13 three-pointers. They missed them all.

They had one genuine threat outside in Person, and his season-long fade had continued with only the most infrequent interruptions.

Chuck Person, the Spurs' sharpshooter, had noticed younger brother Wesley heaving the ball up in a hope-for-the-best manner.

These two did not take their relationship casually. The first time Wesley stepped on the floor against the Spurs the previous season was one of his most extraordinary moments. Gazing at his brother from an opposing NBA bench, Person fairly choked with emotion. This had been their lifelong dream. Chuck had been a skilled perimeter shooter, one of the game's best, for years. At the same time, he carried the reputational baggage of being a loud trash-talker.

"Our mom always told him to stop it," Wesley said. "It doesn't look good and it embarrassed us." Eventually, Chuck followed mom's advice.

On the day between the two Suns-Spurs games, Chuck drove to Wesley's house after the Spurs arrived in Phoenix. He counseled him on mechanics, suggesting he push "up rather than out" and gave him a tip on holding the ball. The next night, Wesley would get another chance to start because of an illness suffered by Bennett, with Finley shifting to forward.

In San Antonio, Williams and Kleine had done an effective enough job that David Robinson didn't have a monstrous game. Neither had Sean Elliott, covered by Finley and Manning. But they had enough three-point shooting, enough of an inside-outside attack, that they'd kept the Suns off balance.

In Phoenix, Elliott got away from Finley. Robinson played volleyball under his own basket, knocking in the Spurs' missed shots. The Spurs moved to an early lead. This looked like a win by a two-headed monster instead of by a balanced attack.

Then Robinson picked up his second foul and headed for the bench. The tone of the game changed.

Barkley began scoring inside. Johnson and Finley attacked the basket with less resistance.

Then Person stole the ball, pulled up and hit a three-pointer. Perry made another steal and Barkley followed it with a layup. The crowd roared with the sort of passion that had been missing the entire season.

The Suns—for years the only major sports franchise in Phoenix—had enjoyed both a loyal and boisterous following. This was particularly the case at the old Arizona Veterans Memorial Coliseum, so much so that the building was called "The Madhouse on McDowell." The Suns' fans were a source of their strength. With the creation of their new building and with the acquisition of Barkley in 1992, the mania reached unprecedented levels. In response, Colangelo jacked up ticket prices to where they were among the NBA's highest.

Fans also came to expect thrilling games and Suns wins. The team had never been worse than 32-9 at home since 1988.

The result was not only a country club mind-set, but a spoiled one. The ambience sometimes resembled a cemetery at dawn. Westphal once addressed the issue, even using the word "spoiled," which elicited a mild lecture by Colangelo. But not in this game. The fans put away their pitching wedges and immersed themselves in a game that would be played on even terms throughout.

Barkley was whistled for an offensive foul after colliding with Robinson. As Barkley began to argue, Fitzsimmons instructed Green, who was about to enter the game, "Tell him not to get a technical. It's too tight a game!"

Too late. Barkley already had drawn the "T" for throwing the ball (gently, actually) on the prone Robinson. The Spurs carried a 53-51 lead into the second half, one that became a wondrous shooting battle featuring none other than Chuck and Wesley Person.

Wesley didn't hesitate. He went up strong and confident, his shot a bit higher, his release smoother. Even when he missed, his shot seemed to have a chance from the start. He nailed a three-pointer to put the Suns up, 68-65. The Spurs' Vinnie Del Negro hit one of his own to tie it.

Chuck buried another three-pointer to put the Spurs up, 75-72. Wesley promptly tied it with a three-pointer. Chuck answered with yet ANOTHER shot from beyond the arc to give the Spurs a 78-75 lead.

The Spurs, like most contenders, didn't have to rely on one perimeter shooter. With Del Negro, Person and Elliott, they had more weapons outside. And then there was Robinson inside. With Williams resting, Robinson started scoring against Manning, then Barkley. The Spurs seemed to have a little too much for the Suns.

As the teams battled on, Wesley Person turned the ball over. So Fitzsimmons screamed "GET THE BALL TO KEVIN!" when the Suns got it back. He was sticking with the pronouncement he'd made when he took over. He wanted Johnson to be responsible on the floor, and Johnson would answer to him.

This would be a good move. In an intangible sense, Johnson's seriousness of purpose was the perfect antidote for Barkley's comedy routines and wandering attention. Of course, it helped even more that Johnson, in top form, was truly a great player.

The Spurs led, 90-87, as the game headed into the final four minutes. Then Johnson and Barkley managed to tie it at 91. Next, Wesley Person buried his sixth three-pointer of the game. It seemed the Suns actually had a chance to win a big game.

The defining moment came with the Suns holding a 94-93 lead. Finley had the ball up top. He eyed Robinson patrolling the paint, then sprinted toward the hoop, leaped and . . . swooped past Robinson for a spectacular tomahawk slam. ("Whew!" said an appreciative Robinson later.)

The fans now roared like they used to at the Coliseum when the din was so loud that a member of the Portland Trail Blazers named Danny Ainge actually put his hands over his ears so he could hear himself think. Finley leaped, clapped his hands, and yelled, "LET'S GO!"

For this, referee Bill Oakes—an experienced official who must have been surprised by the extent of emotion in a mere regular-season game—slapped Finley with a technical, interpreting his celebration as taunting Robinson. (The NBA, unlike the NFL that penalizes enthusiastic reactions to scores, had not become so sterile as to outlaw celebrations.)

The crowd was disbelieving. They had endured the most downbeat of seasons, and now, at long last with something to shout about, they were being penalized. So, all 19,000 fans remained standing. They began to boo. They continued, louder and louder, throughout a full timeout and beyond. Even the most seasoned observers never had seen anything like it. For two full minutes, while Oakes stiffly folded his arms across his chest, all that could be heard was "BOOOOOOO!"

This went on whenever the Spurs touched the ball on their final possessions and even as the refs left the court AFTER the Suns had their huge win (thanks to a big shot by Barkley to seal it).

The Suns were joyous. The Spurs took the loss in stride. Their 17-game winning streak had to end, sooner or later, and it took a great performance to beat them.

For Oakes, the boos must have been ringing in his ears the rest of the season.

THE SUNS HAD TO PLAY the next night against the Jazz, the team that—more than any other—was their mirror image. The Jazz were starting their own fade. If the Suns could grab the sixth play-off spot in the West, they would almost certainly face the Jazz in the first round. This seed might be a fortuitous turn in a season where all their luck had been bad.

Twice this season, the Suns had followed big wins (the early season miracle over the Lakers when they survived Barkley's Vegas sojourn) and the rout at home over the Knicks (in which Green lost his teeth) by playing the Jazz. Both times, they'd lost, with the Jazz in control throughout. If this happened again, the sense of possibilities created by their win over the Spurs would be deflated.

Fitzsimmons wanted to scrimmage the day before the Jazz game, but when he saw the knee-wraps on Manning and Williams, when he saw Johnson's left leg hooked up to a muscle-stimulating device, when he saw Barkley being treated for a sore ankle, he decided against it. No, this wasn't a season to spend time and energy on practice.

From the start, Johnson attacked. The Jazz' defense didn't hold.

Barkley, struggling with his ankle, had enough energy to get inside and draw fouls. Once, Johnson threw a wraparound, behind-the-back pass to Barkley, who—in an instant—drew a foul, fell backward and flipped the ball toward the hoop. He watched from his back as the ball hit the rim and somehow dropped through.

It was that kind of game.

The Jazz made one rally, cutting the Suns' lead to two with 2:40 left. Then Williams hit two free throws.

Malone got the ball on the left baseline for the game's biggest possession. He threw up a 15-footer that missed. Barkley leaped high for the rebound. At the other end, Finley connected on a short hook.

Then the Jazz' Antoine Carr, a reserve big man, stumbled while reaching for a wide pass from Stockton. The ball sailed out of bounds.

Johnson got the ball up top, spotted an opening, squeezed through it, and put the ball in the basket. The Suns had the win.

Johnson had been at his best, pouring in 31 points and passing for 10 assists. Finley filled in wherever the Suns needed him, even guarding Stockton at times. Person played his season's best game, hauling down 11 rebounds and playing surprisingly sound defense. He also did what the Suns counted on him for so much. He kept the Jazz off balance with 22 points.

"When Wesley is shooting well from the perimeter, we become a great team," Johnson said. "Without perimeter shooting, it's such a struggle."

This time, it was the opposition that was being scrutinized as a tired, old team. Perhaps, it was suggested, Malone (who looked uncharacteristically groggy) and Stockton should get more rest with the upcoming play-offs in mind, even if that cost them in the won-loss column.

Their coach, Jerry Sloan, didn't accept this. In his day with the Bulls in the 1960s and '70s, he was as hard-nosed as anybody who'd played the game. "They're not supposed to be tired," Sloan said. "I don't want to hear it. These guys are paid big money. I have a problem with people saying 'Rest them for the play-offs' when people are paying them big money to play now."

Though the words didn't sound like Barkley's, the directness of their angle was vintage Sir Charles.

Immediately afterward, the Suns boarded the bus to the airport. They flew to Seattle to play the SuperSonics, the West's top team virtually the entire season. Probably more than any other team, the Sonics had the talent, depth and experience needed to challenge the Bulls for the title. They'd won eight straight games. The Suns had won five of their last six.

Yet when they played back-to-back games, they were a dismal 5-10 on the second night.

This, as Barkley well knew, was the prescription for a rout by the Sonics. So, before leaving, he threw down a challenge: "We'll see what we're made of in Seattle. That's where we'll judge ourselves.

"There's been a gradual decline the past three years in that we've been getting blown out by good teams on the road. Are we a force? Or do we just win games at home?"

If so, they would exit the season in the first round for they would have no home-court advantage, regardless of who they played.

Fitzsimmons decided to throw a couple of curveballs. He had Finley, his best small forward, start out covering the Sonics' point guard, Gary Payton, one of the game's best. Payton was big and strong for his position and liked to work inside against smaller opponents. Fitzsimmons figured his move could neutralize this tactic.

Johnson would take Hersey Hawkins, the Sonics' shooting guard. Fitzsimmons figured Williams was quick enough to take Detlef Schrempf, the Sonics' versatile small forward. Barkley would guard Shawn Kemp, one of the game's great forwards and the Sonics' dominant inside force. "I wanted to give Charles a challenge," Fitzsimmons said.

That left the strangest matchup of all, Person, the shooting guard, taking the Sonics' center, the strong but inexperienced Ervin Johnson.

This seemed like a formula for Person to get into foul trouble. Instead, Ervin Johnson committed silly, early fouls and headed for the bench. That, in turn, allowed Williams and Barkley to pound away down low.

The Sonics got early inside baskets from Kemp. Otherwise, they attacked from the perimeter, much like the Suns had done when the two teams—along with the Rockets—had battled for supremacy in the West.

Johnson once again controlled the floor. For once, he had weapons all around him: Finley and Manning out on the wings, Person up high, Barkley and Williams down low. Even Tisdale, out for the past month, got extended time and played well. The Suns took a 62-54 lead into the second half.

The Sonics started to double-team Barkley, who had 17 points in the first half. Not only did he stop scoring, but he started turning the ball over and arguing with the referees. The Sonics put on a sizzling shooting display and took an 82-78 lead. The Suns stayed in striking distance. They managed to tie it on a three-pointer by Person with 2:00 left.

The game turned into the season's classic, the kind that had helped popularize the pro game: great players in a wide-open style matching pressure shot after pressure shot.

Barkley wasn't fully a part of it, failing to score in the second half until he hit one of two free throws in the final minute. Then, with the Suns trailing by one, he hit a mid-range jumper with 25 seconds left. The Suns led, 103-102.

Schrempf drove to the basket, found himself in traffic, and put up a short jumper. He missed, and the Suns scrambled for the rebound. The most improbable win was about to happen.

The Sonics put down the obligatory foul, and Finley stepped to the line. He needed to make both shots to give the Suns a three-point lead, then the Suns merely would have to foul as soon as the Sonics' inbounded the ball so they couldn't get off a three-point shot to tie it.

But Finley missed one of the shots. The Sonics, down 104-102, inbounded the ball at midcourt with 2.6 seconds left. Schrempf got the ball to the right of the lane, and he found himself guarded by Barkley.

Having Barkley in this spot, in the open court, against a rangy, quick scorer, would not be the way to go in a Theory of Basketball seminar. And sure enough, instead of letting Schrempf go and hoping his teammates could cover the middle or that Schrempf would rush his shot, Barkley reached across his opponent, trying for a game-winning steal. Instead, he was called for a foul with 1.5 seconds left.

Schrempf stepped to the line, the game on his shoulders, and made them both.

On they went into overtime, the teams matching baskets until it was tied, 116-116, with the Suns having the last chance. Johnson dribbled the clock down, and with five seconds left, made his move. He dashed toward the right of the basket and threw up a driving layup. The ball hit the back of the rim and bounced away, forcing a second overtime. Barkley had fouled out, and by the 55-minute mark, the Suns finally went cold. The Sonics pulled away.

Afterward, all the clutch shots and near misses seemed a blur. "How many overtimes did it go?" asked Johnson.

The Suns' genuinely were pleased with their play. "Outside Arizona, we just look like a team two games over .500," Johnson said. "But we're headed in the right direction. Quietly, we're taking a big step forward."

At the same time, they knew they'd missed a huge opportunity for their season's biggest win yet.

"I blew it," Barkley said.

But the coaches knew they had blown it. Barkley certainly shouldn't have been guarding Schrempf in the final three seconds. He probably shouldn't have been in the game at all.

The Suns rebounded on Sunday afternoon in Vancouver. Johnson ran circles around Greg Anthony, his old nemesis from the Knicks' brawl three years earlier. Along the way, Anthony took a couple of hard shots at him. Barkley saw an opportunity to return the favor, and he didn't hesitate to take it.

As Anthony ran down the floor near him, Barkley caught him off guard. He stepped in front of him and leaned into him, knocking him hard to the floor. "He was bothering Kevin," Barkley said. "That made my day," Johnson said approvingly.

The two superstars who could barely speak to each other a full year ago, now had adopted the most incongruous of roles. They were more than merely coexisting. With Johnson reestablishing himself as the team's most effective player for the third straight year down the stretch, Barkley was fully acting as Johnson's protector and enforcer.

The Suns won in a rout. This was the first week of the entire season when they truly looked like a contender again. They headed for the ocean-side airport on a sunny, nearly tropical day. They might as well have been enjoying beach weather in San Diego, nearly 2,000 miles to the south. It was the start of spring. It was Easter Sunday. The symbolism was all there.

THE FEELING DIDN'T LAST. Williams, on his way up and back down on one simple blocked shot in the home win against the Jazz, banged his right hand against both a teammate and an opponent. A knot formed. It was getting worse instead of better.

Even more troubling was Manning's condition. He'd known his knee would be sore after games, perhaps for up to a year or so. But the problem now had reached the point where he couldn't finish shots and he struggled to defend quicker forwards. At the offensive end, he was hesitating, trying to find his niche in the Suns' jumbled mix of players. Frequently, he'd make his move an instant before dribbling; the refs would call traveling. Now, he had to take a few games off.

On top of this, it seemed like every opponent was carrying the latest title of the league's "hottest team."

This time, it was the Trail Blazers, who'd finally found the right combination of players after struggling through more than half the season. They'd won 13 of their past 15.

The teams both carried 39-36 records. The winner of the game not only would move one game ahead in the play-off race, but also would win the tiebreaker—and the No.-6 play-off seed—if they finished with the same record. And the No.-6 seed would get to face the fading Jazz, while No. 7 would have to play the Spurs. Plus, if both the Suns and Trail Blazers won their first-round series, the No.-6 seed would have the home-court advantage in Round 2.

The Blazers knew well the reason for the Suns' takeoff. Teams now monitored upcoming opponents not only through the traditional in-person scouting, but also with sophisticated satellite TV operations. Coaches could watch their upcoming opponents' recent games and learn their nuances. The Blazers knew they had to cover Person carefully.

The Suns set up so that Barkley and Person were on the same side of the floor, Barkley down low. The idea was to get the Blazers to pick their poison; cover Barkley one-on-one or double him and leave Person alone. The Blazers chose to stay on Person.

Barkley started well enough. But the rest of them didn't come through. The Blazers' Harvey Grant, a decent mid-range shooter, got loose repeatedly from Finley. Grant poured in 16 first-quarter points as the Blazers took a 27-22 lead.

Johnson struggled early to get through the Blazers' huge front line and get to the hoop. Finally, he found some holes and broke down the defense with a mix of drives and jump shots. "He's definitely my toughest matchup," said Rod Strickland, the Blazers' point guard and key player.

But by this time, Barkley was struggling again. For him to take advantage of his one-on-one situations, he needed to make his move quickly, before defensive help arrived. "There's no reason for Charles to stand and hold the ball," Fitzsimmons said. But too often he did. Compounding the problem, his energy level was fading consistently as games wore on.

He shot 2-for-8 and had two turnovers down the stretch.

Johnson and Williams carried the Suns. Johnson poured in 21 second-half points, and Williams—playing with his hand swollen and fingers bent to the point he had trouble holding the ball—blocked five shots and grabbed 13 rebounds.

And when Williams hit a layup with 1:30 left to give them an 87-85 lead, they were in good shape.

Then the Blazers got the ball down low to Arvydas Sabonis. They had figured out they needed him as a starter rather than as a sixth man. He had taken less than one season in America to develop into one of the game's better centers.

Sabonis scored down low, drew a foul, and converted the three-point play.

At the other end, Barkley didn't draw iron; his shot sailed out of bounds to the Suns, but without enough time for them to get off a good shot.

Johnson then committed an ill-timed foul on Strickland, who converted both shots. The Blazers had the win.

This was a game nearly everyone expected the Suns to win. This was to be their first chance to get four games over .500. This was supposed to be the turning point! The Blazers were playing their fourth game in five nights, yet it was the Suns who were lethargic.

Perhaps they were emotionally drained. They felt they passed a huge test in their big week. Maybe they'd spent themselves in doing so. Then again, maybe they just lost another battle against permanent mediocrity. Maybe there was no turning point.

They flew to Salt Lake City immediately afterward. After the late morning shoot-around, Fitzsimmons scorched them, saying, "Chuck and KJ can't carry us all the time. When they don't, other people need to do the job. But it's over. Let's move on."

It was clear they would lean most heavily on Johnson from here on out. But the flip side of Fitzsimmons' supreme confidence in Johnson was the lack of same in Perry.

Whereas Westphal saw in Perry a gritty player whose hustle often sparked the Suns, Fitzsimmons looked at his downside in greater detail. Perry, at times, hesitated in his defensive assignments, and his size would always be a factor in deciding whether he could cover a bigger point guard.

This often was the way it was with coaches. The superstars' weaknesses usually were overlooked or at least minimized in the coach's mind. The backups' flaws were magnified. The reserve had more pressure to play at peak efficiency.

Perry knew the score. Though at 28 he wasn't as experienced as fellow reserves Green and Kleine, he was as thoroughly professional. "I'll hang in there," he said. "There are worse situations."

The players and coaches knew Perry was in a lamentable, looking-over-his-shoulder posture whenever he stepped on the floor. They were pulling for him. They hoped he could take his shots whenever he was open. He was a good shooter from 15-to-20 feet, one of the best among guards in the entire NBA the previous season. If he played with confidence, he would make enough shots to stay in the game longer.

But Perry resisted the suggestions to shoot as soon as he had the chance. One of the keys to his success the previous year, when he was the runner-up for the NBA's most-improved player award, was his knack of picking his spots. He wanted to shoot only when he felt completely sure he had a great look at the basket. He could do this much more naturally playing seven or eight minutes at a stretch, rather than three or four. This was the consummate dilemma faced by reserves.

Predictably, Perry's play became inconsistent. His stat line read: 0-for-2, 1-for-3. His minutes declined. The result was that the Suns were truly playing with fire. Johnson's fragile upper left leg wasn't built for playing 40 minutes a night. If he went down, this team was finished—now and perhaps, as presently constituted, forever.

In the long run, there was the even larger problem of how to divide the minutes between all those big forwards. For this one game, the night after the Blazers' loss when they visited the Jazz, carving up the minutes wouldn't be such a problem. Williams' hand hurt so badly that he stayed in Phoenix to undergo tests. Manning, hoping to rest his sore knee sufficiently for the play-offs, was out for the third straight game. Both Tisdale and Green would get time. But most of all, the Suns needed Barkley to play well to give their depleted front line a presence.

The Jazz knew Stockton couldn't guard Johnson alone, so they ran the player guarding either Person or Finley at Johnson to cut him off. But neither Person nor Finley responded well enough to the scoring opportunities this opened for them. This was the age-old problem within the team, the one Fitzsimmons addressed that very morning. The complimentary players needed to be able to have an impact. Finley, in particular, was sluggish for the second straight night. That he'd led the team in minutes played, that he'd helped carry them through the times when they were lucky to field half a team, now was telling.

Then there was Barkley. He played with all the enthusiasm of a dental patient en route to a root canal. He would set up down low, wait for the ball, catch it, hesitate.

In one embarrassing sequence, Barkley took too many steps, threw a bad pass for a turnover, missed a layup, committed an offensive foul, then was called for traveling again. By this time, the Jazz were in control.

A couple of veteran scouts at courtside were aghast at Barkley's play.

"He doesn't move!" said one. "He's mailing it in." Said the other, "He'd rather be out on the golf course."

Given Barkley's reputation, those were arguments difficult to counter. In fairness, he had been kicked in the right calf, the first real injury he'd suffered since the toe problem in January. Yet it was clear his problems reflected larger forces at work. This was the second night in a row the Suns played, and Barkley had been erratic in these situations for the past three seasons.

Every player has a defined, though unknown, number of quality performances inside him. A statement once attributed to a baseball pitcher attempting a comeback seems appropriate: "I can still do the things I used to do in my prime. The trouble is I can only do them two-ninths of the time."

If Barkley's career as a superstar wasn't finished, it was edging toward the horizon.

By now, he seemed to see the vague image of Father Time. At long last, he was becoming more willing to put in the time needed to stay in shape. He seemed finally to be taking to heart the advice given him before the season's start by—among others—Emerson, the team doctor, who told him, "Charles, you're gifted, physically and athletically. But it's not an automatic deal for you anymore."

He was lifting weights regularly and soothing his body in swimming pool workouts and by sitting in an oxygen chamber that was supposed to speed the healing of bumps and bruises. He also underwent acupuncture treatments. Most surprising, he even went on a beer fast.

By the end of the Jazz game, Barkley had more problems. In leaping for a rebound, he collided with Kleine and crashed to the floor, landing so hard that his body went limp, then started shaking forcefully. It was a frightening moment, yet Barkley gamely got up and played a few more minutes before retiring for the evening with a sore shoulder and a hip bruise.

The Suns lost by 24, their biggest blowout of the season, worse than their 23-point loss the last time they visited Utah. The theory that the Jazz would be easy pickings if only the Suns could meet them in the play-offs now could be put to rest.

They now had four days until their next game, the last extended break until the play-offs. Yet Fitzsimmons couldn't use the time to fine-tune the team in scrimmage, not with Manning resting his knee and Williams tending to his hand injury and Barkley to all his ailments.

They had five games left: on Sunday afternoon at the Lakers; at home two days later against the Rockets; on the road the next night vs. the Kings; then at home two nights later against the woeful Mavericks; they'd close the season at Houston the following Sunday afternoon.

They needed to win at least two of the five to break even for the season and, more importantly, to guard against slipping to the eighth and final play-off spot. That would put them against George Karl's Seattle SuperSonics, the West's most powerful team. Nobody expected the Super-Sonics to be eliminated in the first round for the third straight year.

ONE WEEK BEFORE THE SEASON ended, on a perfect spring afternoon, the Suns visited the Lakers at the Forum where they'd enjoy some attention. Because of their star power and their rivalry with the Lakers, the Suns usually played before a fair number of Hollywood types. Today, Charlie Sheen and (as almost always) Jack Nicholson were sitting in the front row. Arsenio Hall, who used to schedule members of the Suns on his old late-night talk show, was there, too.

The Suns went through the usual pre-game routine against the Lakers, checking out of their Marina Del Rey hotel, then taking the 20-minute bus ride to the Forum in Inglewood. The game would start shortly after noon, early enough to generate the usual curiosity about how Barkley would respond.

It was another national TV game. Johnson was featured as NBC's pre-game guest. Reporter Peter Vecsey noted that after the Suns' elimination by the Rockets the previous season, Johnson immediately visited sick kids (a fact that probably wouldn't have come to light had the visit not been publicized by a relative of a dying child). Johnson also indicated he was sticking to a long-standing plan to play one more season; he wanted both to leave when he still was playing well and to show that he didn't want his life defined by basketball.

There also was a slider thrown among Vecsey's rountine questions. How come Johnson returned to practice immediately after the Westphal firing? Did Johnson hold out as long as possible before rejoining the team? Johnson answered with a dense analogy. Anything can seem ironic, he said. "It's ironic that the wind blows on Easter." Besides, he pointed out he missed Fitzsimmons' first two games, both losses, as well.

The Suns didn't see the interview. Other than Green and Perry, who (as usual) arrived earliest to practice on a nearly empty court (this day joined by the Lakers' Magic Johnson), the Suns got to the Forum moments after the tape concluded.

NBC's Bill Walton, one of the great centers in history before foot ailments cut short his career, stopped briefly to thank Johnson and wish him well. The Suns took the floor and stood in a line parallel to the free-throw stripe, facing the American flag at the building's north end.

At center court, trumpet player Jesse McGuire started his usual stirring rendition of "The Star Spangled Banner" when suddenly the biggest player in front of him fell backward, his head hitting the floor with a frightening thump. Joe Kleine had collapsed, his body crashing to the floor in an unconscious heap.

At various times during the season, the Suns had been down, divided, distraught and dejected.

Now, they were scared.

Person, in particular, was in a panic state. As he saw Kleine's eyes roll back and his body shake, he thought of the time nearly two years earlier, before the start of a rookie league game in Utah, when his college coach at Auburn, Tommy Joe Eagles, came to visit him. Person was standing right next to Eagles when he collapsed and died of a heart attack. Something this terrible couldn't possibly be happening again!

Kleine had fainted just a couple of weeks earlier after working out on a treadmill-like device. Tests were run and nothing unusual was detected.

The Lakers' doctor, Steven Lombardo and their trainer, Gary Vitti, immediately rushed to Kleine's aid. Within a minute, he regained consciousness, not remembering a thing. He made a halfhearted attempt to walk off the floor on his own ("a male thing," Lombardo said later), only to hear the doctor bark, "You're not leaving until you get on this stretcher!" Kleine was wheeled off for a ride to a local hospital. There, and later in Phoenix, more tests were run with equally benign results.

McGuire restarted the anthem, with the Suns wondering what would happen next.

THE SUNS WOULD PLAY without Manning, still resting his sore knee, and Williams, out with his badly swollen right hand. Barkley was still trying to shake the effects of his fall in Utah plus a sore calf that had worsened during the intervening days.

The Lakers were missing their young point guard, Nick Van Exel, for reasons altogether different. Van Exel had just drawn a seven-game suspension for knocking over a referee with a forearm shiver. His departure followed an even stranger incident involving the Lakers' leading scorer, Cedric Ceballos, who—apparently angry over a reduction in playing time—had taken a vacation from the NBA grind on a houseboat in Lake Havasu, Ariz., without telling a soul!

The operators of big-time sport continually are on the defensive about justifying the huge salaries of modern-day athletes to the general public. With incidents like these, plus Dennis Rodman head-butting a referee, plus the Trail Blazers' Rod Strickland taking an unannounced vacation because he didn't get along with his coach, plus a short-lived protest against standing for the national anthem by the Nuggets' Mahmoud Abul-Rauf, the task could be impossible.

Said commissioner David Stern, "I think this is the post-All-Star, pre-play-off, dog days where the moon is full for us for about 40 days. We all have those members of the family that we know about but don't talk about." Prominent figures around the league pointed out that players from the "old school" never would do such things, the implication being that young players—products of an environment influenced heavily by the country's social pathologies—were tarnishing the game.

It was true enough that the players with the most disagreeable reputations, Derrick Coleman, Christian Laettner, Latrell Sprewell among them, were generation Xers who were ripe targets. The same went for players who taunted opponents, particularly through the form of expression known as trash talking, verbal assaults that often were the stuff of junior-high boys' bathroom conversation.

Said Fitzsimmons, "I'm seeing things from young players I never used to see. These guys who never have made an imprint on the NBA make one good play then celebrate. Does it come from high school? Does it come from college? I guess so."

Around the league, players such as Kareem Abdul-Jabbar, Michael Jordan, Larry Bird and Magic Johnson were held up as models to be emulated, a view that conveniently excluded from memory these superstars' foibles. Bird, in particular, was known as an accomplished trash-talker.

Said Fitzsimmons, "Those are the great players who have made this league. Not the show-off guys. They haven't made anything."

Magic Johnson himself was particularly outspoken. At the time of Van Exel's eruption, the Lakers were coming together nicely and were threatening to move up in play-off seedings. That their young point guard lost his composure particularly galled Johnson.

"First of all, it's not very smart," Johnson said. "You can't do that, no matter how frustrated you are or what foul has happened. Not at any time in the course of the season, but especially not now. It's going to set us back.

"I've been through more in one year than I have in 11 or 12 years with my other squads," said Johnson. "It's just . . . arghhh!

"I should have stayed retired, I guess."

All of this came to be of even more interest near the end of the first half of the Suns-Lakers game. Johnson, whose performance had sagged in recent weeks after his comebacks's surprisingly fast start, drove to the hoop and missed badly. Then he called for a foul. He didn't get one, and—if the replay was to be believed—none was easily apparent.

Johnson always had been a fairly argumentative player with referees, so it wasn't shocking that he continued to carry his beef to the point of charging from the basket, down the baseline toward the right corner in pursuit of a young referee named Scott Foster.

"That was good enough for a technical," Foster said later.

Now, Johnson lost control, persisting to the point of actually bumping Foster, who blew his whistle, and—coolly but firmly—whipped an arm similar to the way a baseball outfielder makes a long throw. Johnson, the senior statesman on the NBA's spring madness, had been ejected for making contact with an official.

The fans booed wildly, making the case (shared by few outside the arena) that Johnson somehow was above the rules. Several minutes later, Johnson still hadn't come to grips with the hypocrisy of it all; he maintained that Foster actually initiated contact. Finally, after looking at a tape of the incident, he backed down and—unlike Ceballos and Van Exel—made a thorough and humble apology after the game. It wasn't good enough to avoid the humiliation of a three-game suspension.

Through all of these problems, Barkley's own misdeeds (he led the NBA in technical fouls) struck many as nearly harmless. Indeed, compared to these vacation-taking, referee-pummeling, trash-talking punks, Barkley seemed to some to be a model of civility and rational thought. In fact, just before the Suns left for Los Angeles, the New York-based panel in charge of picking the U.S. Olympic basketball team selected Barkley and the Sacramento Kings' Mitch Richmond for the two final spots on the latest Dream Team.

The choice of Barkley struck many as astounding. It followed a lofty debate on how the Olympic panel was looking for the best personal representatives for the country. The Sonics' Shawn Kemp was left off the team, in part because of concern over his behavior. He missed a series of plane flights (one after that epic double-overtime battle with the Suns) at the time the committee was about to make its decision. This seemed to confirm doubts about Kemp, who caused a stir by grabbing his crotch during his appearance with the U.S. team at the World Championships in Toronto (the same team for which the Suns' Johnson played.)

Rod Thorn, the NBA official who chaired the panel, told the *Washington Post*, "You're representing your country first. That's different than just playing on some regular team. You want the best of what your country is about. Does that mean the standards are higher? They probably are."

So, how could they pick Barkley, whose wicked elbowing of a frail-looking Angolan player during the '92 Olympics at Barcelona caused fans and non-fans alike to wince? Some of his teammates even warned him that this type of behavior was a mistake, that it risked losing the team's overwhelming popular support. Then Barkley and Jordan pushed their loyalty to their athletic equipment company (Nike paid them millions to use their names) to the point where they wouldn't display clothing produced by a rival company on the medal stands. To many, it seemed they deified their commercial arrangements.

The negative response to these antics ranged from a thunderous denunciation of the team by the *New York Times* to many fans who wished that less talented, but infinitely more humble college stars could get the chance to play in the Olympics again. (The original pressure to include NBA stars in the Olympics came not from the United States—where the amateur officials in charge were reluctant to see their power reduced—but from the international basketball community that wanted to measure its progress against the world's best.)

Barkley himself panned the idea of returning to the Olympics. He reiterated the point several days before the announcement when he recounted his high-minded response to the committee's interest in him when it picked the first 10 players in 1995.

"They approached me with it, and I thought about it for a split second. It would be a wonderful experience. But I don't think they should use any guys who played the first time. It's something that everybody should get to experience once."

The whole experience had been loads of fun. Chuck Daly, the coach of the first Dream Team, described it as like traveling with 12 rock stars. The Fab Four times three. A dozen Elvis Presleys.

To Barkley, it was even more. "Words can't do it justice," he said. Just getting to the basketball venue was an adventure. Thousands of people camped at the team hotel to watch the players get on the bus. Security people, armed with machine guns, were everywhere.

"People would be lined up on the highway the whole way to the arena just waving at us," Barkley said. "We had three cars in front, three cars in back, motorcycle cops on the sides and a helicopter over us. It was unbelievable!"

Of course, passing up this sort of attention, with the accompanying endorsement potential, wasn't in Barkley's nature (or in human nature for that matter). The Olympic panel asked him again and got the desired response. This was a flip-flop that was easy to read.

Barkley was defensive at first, saying, "I changed my mind. You don't have to have a reason. You're allowed to do that." Then he allowed, "I look at it selfishly." The Olympics were to take place in Atlanta, a couple hours' drive from his hometown of Leeds, Ala., and the experience should prevent him from wandering too far from game shape in the offseason. "Obviously, I don't like working out in the summer. So there are positives in it for me."

That the basketball moguls who picked the Dream Team opted for Barkley was much less predictable. Having Thorn, who acted as the NBA's disciplinarian, as the selection panel's chairman was the ultimate irony. He was intimately aware of Barkley's flagrant fouls, fines and suspensions over the years. Indeed, he was the one who dished them out!

Thorn's committee was looking beyond a common barroom debate over who actually were the best players and past the principled concerns about who would "best represent the country." The NBA had nearly reached a saturation point in North America. The game now was being promoted worldwide, and Barkley had one of the few universally recognized names. Jordan wouldn't be there (he actually followed through on his desire to take the summer off). Magic Johnson, who really hadn't been considered, also opted out of the debate. The team could use a marquee personality, so Barkley's deviate tendencies would be overlooked for the moment.

The selection was a victory for his often agreeable form of self-promotion. Said Jordan, admitting surprise at the selection, "Barkley is a well-marketed player."

PLAYING THE LAKERS WITHOUT Williams, without Manning, without Kleine meant the Suns were without an interior defense.

Barkley moved so sluggishly that they had to double-team anyone he was guarding, usually the 6-foot-11 Elden Campbell. That left somebody open on the perimeter. But they'd already seen the alternative was worse: Campbell dropped in a few easy hooks over Barkley with all the difficulty of somebody practicing alone on a nine-foot hoop. Barkley was nearly useless. He asked Fitzsimmons if he could stay in the game and concentrate on rebounds (which really was what he always should concentrate on), but Fitzsimmons declined because of Barkley's weakened condition.

The Lakers scored at will. The Suns tried valiantly to respond. Johnson whirled around the floor, shooting and setting up Tisdale and Person for open shots.

In the final minutes, Finley hit a three-pointer, Green scored underneath, then Tisdale buried a mid-range jumper to close it to 115-114. And when the Lakers' Sedale Threatt missed a long jumper and Green grabbed the rebound with 30 seconds left, the Suns were in business.

For about five seconds.

Green, seeing he was surrounded by two Lakers under the hoop, figured there must be teammates open down the floor for a possible fast break. If only he could get the ball to Johnson.

He threw wide to the right, before Johnson had time to react. The ball sailed out of bounds. "I shouldn't have thrown it," he said. Twenty-five seconds remained, so the Lakers could just about run out the clock unless the Suns fouled. They were slow to do so and, as Fitzsimmons screamed at them to foul, they left Campbell open for a dunk.

They'd lost another close one to an elite team.

Afterward, celebrities Sheen and Hall visited the locker room. Hall pointed at Barkley and—in a joking reference to an old rumored Barkley dalliance—said, "He's running away from Madonna." Barkley had other concerns. His knees had huge elastic wraps around them, nearly as big as the one around his right calf.

"My legs are gone," he said.

THE SUNS FACED THE PROSPECT of falling to No. 8 in the play-off race. If they lost at home two days later against the Rockets, they would be under pressure the next night in Sacramento against the Kings. A second loss there would put the Kings within a game of the Suns and—if the teams finished with the same record—the Kings would win the tiebreaker. That would send the Suns to No. 8 and a first-round date with the Sonics.

Barkley would miss the game (as well as the other three remaining regular-season games), but so would the Rockets' Hakeem Olajuwon. Beating the Rockets always was a monumental task for the Suns, and this game followed that pattern early.

Fitzsimmons rolled the dice in Los Angeles, playing Johnson 48 minutes, and got away with it. He knew he couldn't try this again. So Johnson rested extensively in the first half. When he reentered the game, he was stiff. He missed a layup, prompting Fitzsimmons to shout, "We need some scoring!" Replied Johnson, "I've just been in a minute!"

The Suns fell back, 43-35. Then Johnson got his legs under him. He scored on a reverse layup, on a drive to the hoop, on a mid-range jumper, then on another drive. They cut it to 46-45 at halftime.

Johnson took complete control in the second half, scoring, setting up teammates, and defending the Rockets' Sam Cassell effectively. Finley and Person had solid games, and Wayman Tisdale shocked everyone with a season-high 11 rebounds. The Suns won going away, leaving everyone to marvel at Johnson's dominance.

It was just that time of year, he explained, using the same sort of reference Barkley tried earlier in the season. "I'm resurrected in the spring," Johnson said. With him, the comparison fit better than with Barkley. No matter what exercises he tried in the off-season, his early performance was either sluggish or limited by muscle injuries. Now, he'd returned to form, right on schedule.

The game at Sacramento now was less important, a development that turned out to be fortunate for them. The Suns ran up an 18-point lead in the third quarter, blew it entirely, then built back up a five-point edge in the final three minutes.

It is an axiom in these situations not to foul, which both stops the clock and gives a team an easy opportunity to score from the free-throw line. This was part of the Suns' game anyway. They were a smart, experienced group. Drawing more fouls than their opponents was part of their game. They could do so with Johnson's penetration and by Barkley working inside. At the other end, they tried to avoid fouls, sometimes giving up layups so they at least wouldn't allow a basket AND a free throw. Statistically, it worked. They led the league in free throws, and they were among the best at shooting them.

But now, with no rhyme or reason, their brains deserted them.

Finley was whistled for a most unusual foul—for making contact with Richmond AFTER a shot. Johnson then gave away two points by bumping Richmond. Johnson also had a turnover, setting up two points by the Kings, and he hit just two of four three throws.

Richmond drove the lane again, drew no contact, but fell down anyway, hoping to hear a whistle. As a superstar just named to the Olympic team, this was a good idea. The referees obliged. Finley, standing closest to him, was called for a foul and Richmond hit the free throws. The Suns managed to stay in the game on a hook by Tisdale and a three-pointer by Finley.

In the final 15 seconds, the Suns trailed by one. Johnson lost the ball in traffic; the Kings should have had the win. But somehow the ball rolled to Tisdale on the right side and, defying his reputation, he hit the clutch shot.

The Kings trailed by one, but they had no time-outs left. Their point guard, Ty Edney, raced to the middle, but the Suns cut him off. He got the ball to Richmond on the left baseline, but he wasn't positioned to shoot. He was facing the fans at the end of the court, instead of the basket. Any shot would be a prayer. But he threw a fake at Johnson, who defied every coach's admonition to "never leave your feet" until the opponent did first. Once Johnson jumped, so did Richmond. He drew the foul and hit the free throws with two seconds left.

The Kings had the game. The Suns' chance at a winning season was just about shot.

It was left for two nights later, in a game against the Dallas Mavericks, for the Suns to clinch the No.-7 play-off spot. The Mavericks had little defensive presence. Johnson, with help from Finley, Person and Tisdale, led them to one of their old-fashioned, run-and-gun wins.

FOR ONE OF THE FEW TIMES all season, the Suns could relax. They headed into the season-ending game at Houston with nothing at stake. They were 41-40. If they won, they'd have a winning season. But Fitzsimmons waved this off. For him, it was more important to avoid the stigma of a losing season. What was the difference between 42-40 and 41-41?

He held out Johnson, who was facetiously designated to have—like Barkley—a "strained calf muscle." Kleine was still out until all the tests on his fainting spells were complete. (No abnormalities were found.) Williams would make only a token appearance, as would Manning. That left Fitzsimmons rolling the dice with two key figures for the play-offs: Finley and Person. They needed to get out in one piece. Tisdale, now back in the team's good graces, would get significant time, as would Green, Bennett and Carr. Perry would go the distance at the point.

It was another Chamber of Commerce afternoon, a nationally televised game.

Barkley traveled with the team (how could he miss visiting one of his favorite cities?) and talked easily before the game. The subject of the day was the passing of Jimmy "The Greek" Snyder, the oddsmaker who brought gambling to the mainstream of network television.

Snyder became just about as well known for the way his CBS career ended, with off-the-cuff remarks on his beliefs that blacks were superior athletes because of "breeding" (the physically strongest survived slavery, etc. He also angered many by saying if blacks started moving into management, there wouldn't be enough jobs for whites).

Barkley joked about Snyder's ideas on breeding, "Hey, he spoke the truth!" Then he turned more serious, saying, "What he said didn't bother me." He contrasted Snyder's theorizing with that of Al Campanis, the former Dodgers executive who paid with his job for stating his belief that blacks neither had the brains nor the desire to become baseball managers and executives. "What Al Campanis said, I took personally," Barkley said.

THE ROCKETS PLAYED NEARLY as many deep bench players as the Suns, with Clyde Drexler, Robert Horry and Sam Cassell sitting out. Hakeem Olajuwon appeared only long enough to set the NBA career record for blocked shots by swatting a shot by Green. ("It's an honor," said Green. Manning teased him, saying, "I'd have thrown it out of bounds rather than be the answer to a trivia question.")

Perry had a great game, matching his career high with 35 points. This delighted everyone who felt he'd been put on trial unnecessarily.

For the Rockets, a young shooting guard named Sam Mack led the way. Mack, like Perry, was a veteran of the last-chance Continental Basketball Association where players might earn $20,000 and the hope of filling in during an emergency on an NBA team, then somehow hanging on. Perry did so two years earlier when the Suns suffered a series of injuries among their point guards. Mack did the same when Houston offguards Drexler and Mario Elie were hurt.

Playing in the CBA, however briefly, gave a player the reputation of having marginal talent. That usually followed him for life, much like "murder suspect," a veteran of the league once said.

For Mack, the CBA really had been a last opportunity. He carried a bullet slug in him, the result of his presence in the armed robbery of a fast-food outlet during which police fired on the suspects. Mack was acquitted in a trial, though. He moved from Iowa State to Arizona State, where he got in more trouble, then to the University of Houston. The Rockets signed him out of the CBA in mid-season, and he'd performed remarkably well, taking advantage of Olajuwon's presence inside to free himself for open perimeter shots.

Mack hit six three-pointers against the Suns. The Rockets seemed to grow three-point shooters as if they were mesquite on a south Texas plain. For the game, they hit a stunning 16 three-point shots, just two short of the NBA record. The final two wrapped up the game.

Otherwise, this one should have been quickly forgotten. But it wasn't.

With 4:30 left in the final quarter. Finley went up for a routine mid-range jumper. He was the team's most durable player, appearing in every game, even leading the team by averaging 39 minutes per game. Fitzsimmons' competitive instincts were such that—with this one up for grabs—he might have Finley finish the game. He came down near the feet of a journeyman named Pete Chilcutt and, in an instant, lost his footing, crashing awkwardly to the floor. Finley didn't get up, instead rolling on the floor, his hands covering his face.

The Suns were stone-faced, unbelieving. They merely needed to get out of the game without any more injuries, and they couldn't do that! What's more, they'd seen this all before with Manning on the practice court more than a year before. Nelson, the young assistant coach, grimaced the way someone might who'd just eaten a pile of rocks for lunch and muttered a few obscenities softly. Barkley and Johnson were glassy-eyed as they walked toward Finley. Maybe he'd blown out a knee. Maybe he, like Manning would be out for all of NEXT season.

Instead, the injury was to Finley's left ankle. It was only a sprain, but it was a bad one. "I'll be all right," Finley said in the locker room, adding he'd "never" seriously been hurt and vowing to be ready for the play-off opener in San Antonio in five days.

Then, he hopped to the team bus, looking like a man practicing for a one-legged race.

N·O·T·E·W·O·R·T·H·Y

FEB. 19, PHOENIX

The Suns start a homestand against weak teams. In the opener, they barely beat the expansion Grizzlies. Says Barkley, "People say, 'You're playing Vancouver. You should blow them out.' That's the stupidest thing I've ever heard."

The previous day he'd said, "If we play well, we should blow every team out this week."

FEB. 19, PHOENIX

Kevin Johnson, back after a four-game injury absence, drives to the hoop with 4:00 gone in the game. His shot misses, but Barkley crashes in from behind and grabs the rebound. This is his 10,000th career rebound, making him only the 10th player in NBA history to record 20,000 points (he did that 10 days earlier) AND 10,000 boards.

As the crowd rises to start a prolonged roar, Sir Charles' follow shot spins around and out. So, up Barkley goes again, this time bringing down No. 10,001. This time, his shot finds the mark, and the game is stopped briefly to record the moment.

Says Barkley afterward, "Just because you're short, just because you're from the ghetto, just because you're from a small town, doesn't mean you can't be successful."

That's the same message he gives when he talks to kids at school.

"Height is overrated," says Barkley, who stands just short of 6-foot-5. "I've played with a lot of tall guys who couldn't play. (Comic pause) Joe Kleine comes to mind." Sis-boom!

The next day, Kleine—Barkley's closest friend on the team—noting these comments went out nationally, stuffs Barkley head first in his locker, spanks him, and says, "Don't ever say anything bad about me on national TV again!"

FEB. 20, PHOENIX

Barkley turns 33 years old.

"I have no special plans. My life has been perfect. I couldn't have dreamed it any better."

FEB. 24, PHOENIX

Asked about the Suns nearly blowing a late lead (when he was on the floor) to the expansion Raptors, Barkley has a ready response: "I didn't kill the Lindbergh baby, I didn't have anything to do with the JFK assassination, and every time we blow a lead, it's not my fault." So, were you driving the Ford Bronco?

"No," replies Barkley, "everything that's wrong isn't my fault."

FEB. 25, PHOENIX

Barkley says he likes presidential candidate Steve Forbes' ideas, but he's more vociferous about who he doesn't like in Arizona's Republican presidential primary.

"I hope the people in Arizona won't make the same mistake the people in New Hampshire did and vote for that knucklehead (Pat) Buchanan . . . I may even become a Democrat."

Barkley seems to like politicians who favor lower taxes, but don't make an issue of sex and related matters. He most enthusiastically backed Colin Powell, who didn't run. His next choice was Phil Gramm, but he'd already dropped out of the race.

Forbes wins Arizona, Bob Dole comes in second, and Buchanan finishes third, a disappointing showing that leads to his fade from the front-runners' scene.

"I'm glad the neo-Nazi didn't win," Barkley says.

FEB. 26, SALT LAKE CITY

Speaking with John Stockton's four-year-old son after the Suns lose to the Jazz, Barkley says, "Are you going to go to school at Gonzaga? You should go to Auburn. It's a good school and they pay well."

FEB. 27, KANSAS CITY

Clayton Lonetree, the first U.S. Marine ever convicted of espionage, is released from a military prison in Fort Leavenworth, Kan. He is wearing a Suns hat, emblazoned with Barkley's No. 34.

Learning this, Barkley says, "I represent people like him . . . the underclass, people who don't have a voice. Glad he likes me."

MARCH 3, DALLAS

After the Suns escape with a narrow win over the lowly Mavericks, Barkley rips the referees, saying, "The officiating was terrible. They kept the game close because it was on TV, like they always do."

For this, the NBA fines Barkley $7,500.

MARCH 7, DENVER

Fans on talk radio question why the Nuggets' Mahmoud Abdul-Rauf won't stand for the national anthem. It turns out that for months, as a form of antinationalistic protest, he's been either waiting in the locker room during the anthem or even sitting and stretching on the floor.

Abdul-Rauf misses this game with an injury, but the issue hits the national fan five days later.

The player at first says he'll "never waver" in his decision, but then drops his protest immediately after the NBA suspends him.

MARCH 17, CHARLOTTE

A reporter for NBC-TV examines the mask worn by A.C. Green to protect his injured mouth. When he's finished, he's not sure where to return the mask, since the visitor's dressing areas don't have the players' names marked.

Barkley solves the problem by pointing to Green's locker and saying, "Over there, in the condom-free zone."

MARCH 17, CHARLOTTE

Dennis Rodman, who has just been ejected from a game and is about to be suspended for six more for head-butting a referee, complains of what he calls a double-standard in the NBA.

Says Rodman, "Charles Barkley cusses out referees from the time he gets out of bed until he goes home to make love to his wife, and they won't say anything. I just look at a referee and they think I'm trying to cuss him out."

Replies Barkley, "I'm leading the league in technicals. How can I be getting away with anything?" Adds Barkley, "It's better to be silent and a fool than to open your mouth and remove all doubt."

MARCH 22, PHOENIX

Wayman Tisdale is positively ecstatic over his selection as the Big Eight's greatest player of all time. In a media vote conducted by a Salina, Kansas, newspaper, Tisdale edged Danny Manning, 7-5.

The former Oklahoma great shows the newspaper clip to anybody who cares to see it. And even to those who don't.

"Best player ever! EVER!" Tisdale cries. "That's a long time. That's 37 seasons, baby."

Replies Manning, the former Kansas superstar, "I'm happy. I got a national championship (in 1988)."

As Tisdale continues (he even starts an acceptance speech), he receives a few lighthearted barbs.

"Those sportswriters must have been drinking," says Hot Rod Williams.

Says Joe Kleine, "These glory years are being brought back by the *Salina Journal*."

Says Manning, "That's not a real paper. Bring in the *New York Times.* There's only one reporter in Salina. How do they get a 7-5 vote?"

Adds Manning, "You got more shots up in three years than I did in four. Besides, you're missing a piece of jewelry."

Responds Tisdale, feigning a wound, "Oh! You had to hit me because you had no place else to go."

MARCH 23, SAN FRANCISCO

The Suns' bus, nearing the team's hotel while returning from a practice at the University of San Francisco, is stopped by a traffic jam. Barkley begins bantering out the window with a few police officers, then steps outside to continue the conversation.

Suddenly, the traffic clears. The bus driver asks Fitzsimmons for instructions. Should they wait for Barkley to get back on the bus? The coach directs the driver to get going. Barkley gets a ride the rest of the way on the back of a police motorcycle.

MARCH 28, PHOENIX

Barkley leaves these instructions on the blackboard in the coach's office outside the locker room: "Cotton's things to do!

1) Leave Chuck alone.
2) Leave Chuck alone.
3) Another day off.
4) Buy team dinner.
5) Leave Chuck alone."

APRIL 7, VANCOUVER, B.C.

At game's end on the court, in front of Canadian national TV, Barkley says, "Thanks for the hospitality. Welcome to the NBA. You've got a great country."

Moments later in the locker room, as the Suns dressed to catch their plane to Arizona, Barkley says, "Let's go back to where we have culture. We can't survive without light beer and ESPN."

APRIL 23, PHOENIX

Joe Kleine on health tests finding no serious problems in connection to his fainting spells: "I feel good. They found out I have a brain and a heart. My wife made them double check."

9

A chance at redemption.
Is there a savior in the house?

IN BARKLEY'S VIEW, THE REGULAR season was a "bust." Fitzsimmons labeled it a "disaster." There were few arguments with either assessment. The Suns' 18-game drop, from 59 to 41 wins, was the deepest in the league. Only an extended play-off run would allow them to avoid the belief, inwardly and publicly, that they'd failed.

For Barkley and Johnson, this would be their fourth go-round together in the play-offs. In the past, anything less than a championship meant they'd come up short, yet there was always the hope of next year.

But failure now would have the ring of finality. This was an old team, viewed increasingly as a group whose best moments could be found in scrapbooks. Of their regular players, Barkley, Johnson, Williams, Green, Kleine and Tisdale had passed 30 and Manning would hit the milestone at season's end. Perhaps they couldn't possibly be more prone to injuries the next season, but they certainly wouldn't be younger and faster. Besides, Barkley had twice made noises over the previous month that he didn't want to play for the Suns again if they were non-contenders.

They had to do something now, else the aura that followed the team, the unprecedented unity they brought to their community and state, might be lost for good.

This time, the public had a more restrained enthusiasm for the play-offs, not wanting to be set up for a fall. Even so, Johnson noticed the purple signs popping up around Phoenix. He heard people talking nervously about their chances and saw them wearing Suns garb.

"This is the time of year you dream about," he said. "There's nothing like it. The air is different. You can feel it."

Certainly Johnson felt it. For the past two years, he was the Suns' most consistent play-off performer. In the Suns-Rockets series of '95, he was outranked in effectiveness only by Hakeem Olajuwon, the game's dominant player that spring.

At play-off time, Johnson always sat down and went over in his mind the past post-season struggles, the high and low points, what he'd learned, how he could do better. He recalled how the Suns shocked the Magic Johnson-led Los Angeles Lakers in 1990. Then, the Suns dominant players were himself and veteran all-star Tom Chambers. The supporting cast consisted of a couple of rising young players, Dan Majerle and Jeff Hornacek, and the journeyman center, Mark West.

In Johnson's mind, this year's Suns had more ability.

Even so, they would be swimming against the historical trend. Only three No.-7 seeds had ever beaten the No.-2 seed. Twenty-one times, the No.-2 seed had prevailed. The first two games would be played in San Antonio. If they only could win one of those games. "Then everything changes," Johnson said.

There was reason for optimism. The Suns had experienced more success in the play-offs over the years than the Spurs. The previous season seemed to be the Spurs' best chance to win the title. They'd run up an NBA-best 62 wins in the regular season, only to lose 4-2 in the Western Conference Finals to the Rockets (who had just dispatched the Suns in the most harrowing play-off series of all).

In the Spurs-Rockets series, Olajuwon—going against Robinson—played at a higher level than perhaps anyone else in NBA history in a single series. He poured in 40 points three times and scored 39 in a fourth game! For this, Robinson's reputation was damaged. Not as many people remembered that the series may have been lost in the very first game at home when Sean Elliott cost them the game by missing two free throws. Or that shooters Vinnie Del Negro and Chuck Person performed poorly. Or that Dennis Rodman, after a series of disputes with management and coaching staff, hadn't given the series his best effort.

The Spurs relied more on finesse than physical prowess. They were so-so rebounders. For these reasons, they were labeled "soft" or lacking in aggressiveness, with Robinson taking most of the heat.

That Robinson was as straitlaced as he was well-spoken didn't help him in this regard; athletes considered wild and crazy seldom were tagged as "soft." He, along with the Suns' Green, promoted abstinence and a spiritual approach to life as much as anyone in big-time sport.

Considering this, it was a bit surprising that he struck up a solid friend-ship with Barkley. The two shared a fondness for golf and a good joke. Asked if his socialization with Sir Charles ended at sundown, Robinson laughed and said, "You might say that!"

On the basketball floor, there'd been more truth to Robinson's "soft" image years earlier. Then, he struggled in the play-offs against second-line players. He didn't really have many inside moves, instead preferring to shoot jumpers. But now, he could do it all—drive to the hoop from the baseline, where he'd score on reverse layups, or connect on short hooks around the basket. He was just as adept defensively. Like Olajuwon, he was quick enough to guard a center standing outside the paint, then slide over to plug the middle and block shots.

As the Suns' luck would have it, the Spurs "soft" label became fodder for sports talk shows and publications throughout the country in the days leading up to the series. The Spurs replied, correctly but to little avail, that most of the great title teams—the Celtics, Lakers and Bulls—relied on finesse and overall basketball skills rather than brute strength and that the Pistons of the late '80s were the only really successful exception.

The Suns, not seeking to add to bulletin-board material, wanted no part of any of this. Given an opportunity, they labeled the Spurs' image a myth, a meaningless product of media hype.

Making matters worse for the Spurs, Rodman was taking shots at them from afar. He blamed Robinson for their loss to the Rockets, though some viewed this as revisionism: Rodman went AWOL during the season over a contract dispute, and the matter never was resolved. He continued to show displeasure with the situation during the play-offs, arriving late and taking off his shoes on the floor after being removed from games. The fans, instead of pressuring him into getting with the pro-gram, cheered him wildly throughout all this. He was the biggest celebri-ty ever to hit town. The Spurs decided he was too big for San Antonio and dealt him to the Bulls for Will Perdue, an able but unspectacular career reserve.

Now, the Bulls had won an NBA-record 70 games. Rodman took a few bows for this, simultaneously throwing bricks at his old team.

"In San Antonio, I wouldn't respect the guys because they wouldn't go out there and give it 110 percent every night," he said. "In San Antonio, no one had that desire to kick it up a notch when we needed it. Not one, not even David." Then, in the middle of the series, Rodman released a book taking even more shots at his old teammates and employers. The

Spurs were wildly motivated to show they were just as good without the tattooed media creation and that they weren't "soft."

The intangibles all favored the Spurs.

THE WORD ON FINLEY WAS that his availability would be a "game-time decision," Fitzsimmons said. The Spurs doubted this, figuring that surely the Suns were trying to confuse their preparation. "The Suns are playing tricks," said coach Bob Hill. "Finley will play."

To be sure, they were playing tricks, but in the opposite way Hill imagined. Finley was out, almost certainly, for the first two games. But there was no point in making matters worse by telling the Spurs in advance. Of course, even if they had sworn Finley wouldn't play, the Spurs still would have had their doubts.

Finley was one of the players the Suns could least afford to lose. He was the only player both quick and strong enough to stay with the athletic Elliott at small forward. His absence exaggerated the team's imbalances. The group that would challenge the Spurs included Barkley, Green and Tisdale, all best-suited to play the big forward spot. Manning, before his knee surgery, was most effective at the "three" spot or small forward, because he was too tall (and too skilled) for most any opponent to match up with him. But now, struggling to overcome the soreness in his left knee, he was the one who suffered the mismatch in trying to cover someone as quick as Elliott. He, too, was best-suited for the power forward position. In an ideal world, so was Williams. At 245 pounds, he didn't have the massive frame of most of the superstar centers. He CERTAINLY didn't have the superstar reputation. Battling the game's greatest centers, he seldom would get the benefit of the doubt on any close foul calls. But he would have to do.

Kleine wasn't quick enough to stay with Robinson. He didn't figure to play much.

At point guard, Perry would play in spots.

Rookies Bennett and Carr would get a fine view of the game, better than most spectators, from the Suns' bench. (Reserve Tony Smith, whose game was viewed in a less-positive light by Fitzsimmons than by Westphal, followed Rusconi's path; he had been jettisoned from the roster.)

The upshot was that the Suns' roster was constructed so that of their top eight players, four played Barkley's spot, one could handle the center's role, two were guards, and other was hurt.

Johnson and Person would go virtually the entire 48 minutes in every game in the backcourt. Manning and Green would split time at the "three" spot. Williams would get as much time at center as his foul situation would allow. When he was out, Manning was the only player with the defensive instincts to guard Robinson. But he didn't have the size or, with his knee problem lingering, the quickness. Barkley was too short; besides, his energy was saved for offense. Green was neither quick enough nor big enough to stay with Robinson. Kleine wasn't mobile enough. Tisdale didn't have the instincts, the inside warrior's mentality. His exhibition season comment, "I'd rather spend more time at forward than center, if that helps you," still held.

Their plan was to have Green start against Elliott, even though Elliott sped around him like a dirt bike past a Saguaro cactus during the teams' final meeting three weeks earlier in Phoenix. The idea was to give him help every time Elliott went one-on-one against him. Most often, Johnson would drop off the Spurs' point guard, Avery Johnson, or else Barkley, would leave the Spurs' big forward, Charles Smith.

Williams would be left to fend for himself against Robinson. Person would try to cover Del Negro, the Spurs' off-guard who used to be considered a journeyman but now was enjoying his career year.

THE SERIES WOULD START Friday night, April 26, at San Antonio. In devising his preparation schedule, Fitzsimmons raised some eyebrows by scheduling two practices each on Tuesday and Wednesday before tapering off to one on Thursday in San Antonio. Even though the early practice didn't involve a great deal of physical activity, just emphasis on watching videotape, the Suns—as Fitzsimmons himself admitted—were "a beat-up old team that has a hard time practicing. Two-a-days are not their style."

One of the tapes they watched was of the motivational variety. The producer was Garrick Barr, who was hired by Westphal to be the team's "video coach." This was the person who not only put together tapes of the team's own highlights and lowlights, but scouted other teams, too. Barr would hone in on opponents through satellite TV and assemble tapes showing their tendencies. The advancement of this technology was thought by some to be a partial reason for the increasing effectiveness of defensive preparation and the subsequent drop in scoring throughout the NBA over the past several years.

The highlight of the Suns' video fare was a tape showing a series of their greatest plays, sometimes followed by celebrations. It was all done in slow motion, with music to boot, an uplifting number called "Whatever We Imagine."

This was slick stuff, a mind-cure worthy of a TV infomercial. All the negatives were out of sight. No way would they see Williams going down in Dallas or Finley in Houston!

Otherwise, the tapes were routine material. (Not like the time two years earlier when Westphal had Barr splice in a scene from the movie "Animal House." At the time, the Suns had blown a two-game lead to the Rockets. So, Westphal had them watch the leader of the wayward fraternity give his "We're-not-going-to-take-it anymore!" speech before the frat boys stormed the campus and disrupted a parade. The Suns responded by winning the next game, if not the series.)

Everyone on every team pretty much knew every opponent's plays anyway. With this in mind, Fitzsimmons designed a few new plays. One was a segment of the Bulls' triple post (where whoever has the ball has three teammates surrounding him looking for openings.) Another was set up for Barkley, Johnson and Manning to work on the left side.

On defense, assistant coach Paul Silas devised the basic strategy.

Silas was one of the most experienced figures in the game, having been involved as a player, union leader and coach for more than half the NBA's half century of existence. Along the way, he earned a rare level of respect, both for his work in the trenches—where he was one of the fiercest rebounders ever to play the game—and for having the guts to deliver unpleasant messages.

A conversation with Silas has a way of opening doors to understanding multiple levels of the game's past and present. He grew up in Oakland, Calif., where he went to the same high school as such sports legends as basketball's Bill Russell and baseball's Frank Robinson, Curt Flood and Willie Stargell. He was highly rated enough to earn a scholarship to Creighton in Nebraska (a deal that also included a scholarship for his older brother). The school was strictly run by Jesuits, and Silas found he could no longer skate by as he'd become accustomed in high school. He was deeply embarrassed when he flunked an accounting class as a freshman. He decided he would put forth whatever effort was necessary to rebound. He graduated with academic all-America honors.

The St. Louis Hawks drafted Silas in the second round. At the time Silas entered the NBA, the league had only 90 spots for players—nine teams with 10 players each. The players had no rights; they were bound to the teams that drafted them.

Silas' college coach solicited advice from the great Dolph Schayes on the salary Silas should request. The number came back at $10,000. In his "negotiating" session with the Hawks' Marty Blake, Silas made his pitch. Blake said he could get $9,000. "You've got a night to sleep on it," Blake advised him. "If you don't sign tomorrow, you can go play the Harlem Globetrotters." So Silas signed for $9,000. "But I asked him for a $500 bonus. He gave it to me."

All in all, Silas was pleased. He'd never had anywhere near this kind of money.

The Hawks, as was usually the case in those days, were a small-potatoes operation owned by a man named Ben Kerner. "His only business was basketball," Silas said. "And every dime he saved went right into his pocket." Silas recalled a bargaining session similar to his own between Kerner and Lenny Wilkens. They, too, were a mere $1,000 apart.

Said Kerner, "You mean $1,000 means that much to you?"

Replied Wilkens, "Hell, no. Does it mean that much to you?"

"Yes it does. So sign the contract."

One of Silas' first memories of the NBA was walking into the Hawks' locker room for an exhibition game and seeing Bob Pettit and Wilkens taping their sore ankles. Pettit was at the end of his career; Wilkens was a rising star. Both would be Hall of Famers. No matter, everyone taped themselves. The notion of trainers was an idea whose time had yet to arrive.

The Hawks weren't poor when it came to talent. Silas was part of a wonderful starting five during the 1967-68 season. He teamed with such NBA greats as Zelmo Beatty and Bill Bridges along the front line, with Wilkens and Joe Caldwell in the backcourt. They got off to a 17-1 start and won 56 games, only to be bounced from the play-offs by a Warriors team led by future Hall of Famers Nate Thurmond and Rick Barry.

There was one perceived "problem" with this team. All five starters were black. The NBA was changing from an informal "quota" system that was in place when Silas entered the league, one in which teams were supposed to have a majority of white players. For conservative St. Louis, the quota was a more comfortable fit than the change. The Hawks, despite their winning ways, drew poorly.

So, the Hawks moved to Atlanta and—after another contract battle with Wilkens—traded the great playmaker. They began to fade. In 1969, the Hawks traded Silas to the Suns. By this time, his annual salary was starting to break into the forties.

To help insure the progress continued, Silas and other players fought a proposed merger between the NBA and the upstart American Basketball Association. Silas traveled to Washington and lobbied a Senate leader named Sam Ervin, whose syrupy drawl led Silas to believe he was dealing with a country bumpkin.

"We thought he understood nothing," Silas said. "But he understood everything." Ervin was, in fact, a lawyer with the sophistication of a Wall Street money mogul. The players pointed out that two leagues had spread the game to more cities than before. Congress was pleased enough with this that the merger died. (Ervin went on to become a congressional superstar for the firm, but amiable manner in which he handled the Watergate scandal.)

A few years later, about the time Silas took over as the Players Association president, the NBA absorbed the ABA's strongest franchises; the players went along in return for a limited form of free agency.

Eventually, the players won much larger freedoms. Today's players average about $2 million per season in salary.

The Suns traded Silas to Boston for the high-scoring but less team-oriented Charlie Scott, a deal they came to regret.

Upon arriving at the Celtics' training camp on Cape Cod, he first met a young, though extremely haggard player who had just been through a meat-grinder of a practice run by coach Tom Heinsohn.

"He was so sore," Silas recalled with a broad grin. "He said, 'You will never see anything like this in your life!'" The player's name: Paul Westphal.

That team went on to a wondrous season, winning 68 games but losing a title (eventually won by the Knicks) when their superstar scorer, John Havlicek, went down with an injury. But the next season, Silas and Westphal contributed to an NBA title-winning team.

Through all his 16 years as an NBA player, Silas' best-remembered quote probably came as he was helping lead the Seattle SuperSonics to the title in 1979. His career was winding down, and the Sonics featured rising star Dennis Johnson, a clutch player but one who continually challenged and squabbled with the coach. The coach happened to be Lenny Wilkens, the great playmaker on Silas' old Hawks teams (and who would go on to be the winningest coach in NBA history). When Johnson hit a big shot to defeat the Celtics, Silas muttered, "Too bad an asshole had to make it."

After joining the Suns in the summer of '95, Silas came to respect

Westphal as an excellent tactician and bench coach. But he also noted the contrast with the teams run by Pat Riley (the title-winning coach for the Lakers whom Silas served under for the Knicks) and Chuck Daly (the title-winning coach for the Pistons whom Silas assisted for the Nets). These were two of the most successful coaches in history. Both ran their practices in more of a down-to-the-minute, prepare-for-any-eventuality fashion than Silas saw with the Suns.

This wasn't such a problem with talented, experienced players, he figured. But this team had added several young players. And as the season progressed, it became obvious the talent was more evident in the players' resumes than in their performance. Silas began to wonder whether Westphal was cracking the whip hard enough.

One factor in the team's method of operation stood out: Barkley didn't practice much or do much work, in general. "That shocked me most of all," Silas said.

In New Jersey, even the moody Derrick Coleman, who was fond of challenging a coach's authority, practiced with a reasonable effort. A better model was Patrick Ewing in New York. "He was a superstar, and yet you could talk to him, criticize him, and he would accept it and keep working. As a result, everyone fell into line."

With the Suns, "That was a problem," Silas said. "When your main guy can't practice or won't practice, it has a big effect on the whole team.

"It's hard to measure shortcomings when you're winning 60 games a season, but it's human nature when one guy is getting away with things that it will have an effect on others. You may not say anything, but it eats away at you."

In Silas' view, there could be no winners in these situations. "If you challenge a guy, it will be ongoing, every day. Your life will be miserable. If you don't, you compromise your principles, the guy gets away with bloody murder, and you don't feel good about yourself.

"If you fight for what you believe, you can at least look yourself in the mirror."

As you are escorted out the door to the unemployment line?

"Absolutely. You can't win."

FOR THIS SERIES, THE PLAN of Silas and Fitzsimmons was to have Williams play Robinson "straight up" (one-on-one) unless "The Admiral" backed him down too close to the hoop, whereupon he would get help. Double-teaming him made more sense if the Spurs were using a "big lineup" with the 6-11 Smith in the game, than if they had all their best shooters (Elliot, Del Negro and Chuck Person) in at once. In the latter case, Robinson could more easily pass out of the double-team to an open three-point shooter.

The Spurs hurt the Suns in the regular season by using a pick-and-roll play run by Avery Johnson. The ball often would go to Robinson, then to Johnson, who'd run the play quickly, before the Suns recognized it and reacted. This time, they would come at him automatically when he got the ball—usually with the off-guard or small forward—and try to force the play to the baseline.

The player who would need the most help, of course, would be Green in covering Elliott.

As much as possible, the Suns wanted to shut down the players who could not create shots for themselves, such as Del Negro, Smith and Avery Johnson.

The pre-game routine was the norm. Perry and Green, as almost always, arrived on their own, ahead of the team bus, to practice shooting in the empty Alamodome.

The bus arrived 90 minutes before tip-off. In this most unusual venue, built with the pipe dream of attracting the NFL, the bus actually drove into the building, driving on the cement floor to what would be about the 50-yard line, stopping just behind what must be the world's largest drapes, 30-foot-tall blue covers that served to wall off half the stadium for basketball.

Finley walked off the bus first, "walked" being a notable word. He used crutches the previous night, tossed one of them aside by the morning shoot-around, and now wasn't using them at all. Maybe he'd be available for the second game on Sunday, after all.

Jerry Colangelo was aboard as well. He'd been deeply involved in finalizing plans for his Major League Baseball team, the Diamondbacks, and in attracting the National Hockey League to Arizona. But he almost always accompanied the team in the play-offs.

Inside the locker room, Nelson wrote on the blackboard in the visitor's locker room the Spurs' starters and reserves, and he diagrammed their basic plays. Johnson studied the Spurs' plays in a booklet, then scanned their statistics. He looked up at a reporter and said, "We're going to be around longer than people expect."

Manning had his left knee wrapped by the training staff. Trainer Joe Proski put a foam pad on Williams' right wrist and upper hand, covered it with hard plastic and wrapped it with so much tape that it appeared his hand and wrist would break apart from each other without it. His hand swelled after he banged it against someone. Sometimes it puffed up at night while he slept. But at least he could use it.

Barkley was on edge. Noticing a reporter in the team's midst, he shouted, "I want the media out 15 minutes earlier than usual! I don't care what David Stern says. He can go ahead and fine us." Reporters were allowed in locker rooms until 45 minutes before tip-off. The NBA, eager to preserve its media and public-friendly image, had warned and fined teams—notably the Bulls and Heat—for ducking reporters.

By the time Barkley's deadline arrived, the few reporters who showed up early had already left; the Suns weren't as high profile as in the recent past.

The Suns filed out for the final warmups about 15 minutes before tip-off, with the coaches following several minutes later. Fitzsimmons noticed that Finley, dressed in street clothes, remained behind longer than anyone else. Finley sat in front of his locker, lowered his head into his hands and cried. He sobbed so heavily that his body fairly shook. When Fitzsimmons realized the depth of his distress, he recognized more than ever—more than when Finley lit up the home crowd with a spectacular windmill slam—that he was looking at the future of the franchise.

The Suns took the floor in front of a shockingly small crowd, about 16,000, or barely half the average that came to see the teams play twice in the regular season. In San Antonio, there always had been the feeling that NBA ticket prices were a bit of a stretch for a working-class town. Play-off tickets were even more expensive, and not everyone budgets for an extended season.

Yet this was the city's only major pro sports team. They'd been a powerhouse, and their two best players, Robinson and Elliott, were the sort of intelligent, thoughtful, solid citizen/athletes who were increasingly in greater demand than supply.

The novelty of all this appeared to be wearing off. Attendance had dropped by more than 10 percent from the previous season. The news had broken that the team's owners were borrowing money to pay the bills through the end of the season. The word was that they might have to go all the way to the Finals just to make a profit. And this for a team whose average attendance wasn't so bad, nearly 20,000, fifth in the NBA! The team's operators were opening their books to city officials to show their desire for a new arena, with income-generating luxury boxes, was more of a necessity than an extravagance.

SILAS' DEFENSIVE STRATEGY started on the money. The Suns began with Green on Elliott, so the Spurs got the ball to their all-star forward to exploit the obvious mismatch. Johnson came over to help Green and knocked it away for a steal. No team can survive double-teaming two players, so Williams stayed with Robinson alone. The results were solid.

Johnson hit a jumper and two free throws, Green scored on a slam dunk, a relatively rarity for him given his pedestrian jumping skills. The Suns were off to a 15-10 lead. The only danger sign was Person missing a three-pointer by a good two feet.

Barkley missed inside, then leaped up twice more to grab the rebound. There appeared to be contact made by the Spurs on each of his three tries. The foul was called on his final shot, but Barkley was not appeased. He leaped up and down, raving at referee Nolan Fine, who promptly whistled a "T."

Fitzsimmons worried before the game that Barkley would try to do "too much," meaning that he would fear his teammates couldn't score and would respond by taking low-percentage perimeter shots. If he did, Fitzsimmons would have to yank him from the game.

Except for a nice mid-range jumper from the left side, Barkley had lost his outside touch. His insistence on throwing up three-pointers had failed again. He'd backed off them for a while after Fitzsimmons first took over. Then he gradually felt emboldened to start trying more of them. For the season, he was in a virtual deadlock with his old pal Cedric Ceballos for the distinction of being the worst three-point shooter in the entire NBA among players who took them so often.

Fitzsimmons needn't have worried. After this initial engagement with the officials, Barkley was sluggish, perhaps tired from all the practice. He took only seven shots in the first half and hit only two.

The Suns had a 20-18 lead when Robinson got the ball and leaned into Williams. The Suns' center put his hands straight up and held his ground, playing what seemed like textbook defense. The whistle blew . . . the foul was on Williams, his second, with nine minutes gone in the game.

This was the sort of call for which the NBA was famous, the kind that Barkley had enjoyed for years. The superstars almost always got the benefit of the doubt.

Williams came out and immediately the Suns began to run uphill. They would have to double-team Robinson while somehow keeping the lid on all the Spurs' other weapons.

For a few minutes, they survived, staying within 38-36 early in the second quarter.

Fitzsimmons gambled the Suns could continue to stay in range using reserves. He reached ever deeper into his bench, pulling out Kleine to try to help guard Robinson. At the same time, he momentarily kept Green on Elliott.

The Suns were trying to cover up too many deficiencies. The result: The Spurs found openings everywhere.

Once, Tisdale rushed to cover Robinson at the free-throw line, leaving Perdue, the veteran backup who played for the Bulls' title teams, open near the basket. He was a savvy, if limited, big man, the definition of a journeyman.

But he could hit a layup. In this game, he often circled toward the hoop away from the ball. Later, Perdue said the Spurs noticed in watching old game tape that the Suns didn't rotate properly to protect the basket. He was correct. He ended up scoring on several uncontested shots as the Suns' big men (everyone outside of Williams) left the basket unguarded.

For nearly five minutes, Barkley, Johnson and Williams all rested together. Williams didn't play at all in the first half after those first nine minutes. The suspicion arose on the bench that Fitzsimmons lost track of the fouls, that he thought Williams actually had three.

Fitzsimmons adamantly insisted he knew exactly what he was doing, that he wanted Williams to have just two fouls at the half so he could play the second half aggressively. "Other people have to step up and do the job when they come in the game," he argued.

At the other end, the Spurs had made two basic defensive decisions. They were going to pay more attention to Johnson than Barkley, running a second player (usually a forward) alongside Avery Johnson to guard him. The other tactic: Barkley would be double-teamed only late in possessions, when he had just a few seconds to shoot.

They watched Johnson wherever he went, trying to get him to stop his dribble and pass. They'd used the same approach in the late-season Spurs-Suns game in Phoenix. Then, Johnson still managed to force the attack in leading the Suns to one of their most impressive wins. This time, he shrank back and passed.

A commonly held view was that Johnson was at his best when he did precisely that, when he assumed the traditional pass-first, score-later point guard's role.

But inside the Suns, the criticism often ran the other way over the years. According to this view, Johnson was better off looking to score MORE, that he was often too unselfish, that even with his best efforts to get the team's complimentary players going, they frequently didn't respond at crunch time.

To be sure, Johnson now got everyone involved. But as had happened so often in the past, the Suns' complimentary players didn't produce. Tisdale entered the game after Williams' second foul and threw up an air ball. He would finish with a brutal 1-for-9 shooting game and just one rebound. The early miss by Person had been a signal. He would be off course throughout.

This was a case when Fitzsimmons deemed Johnson needed to fight through the defensive pressure. Said Fitzsimmons, "Kevin wants to get everybody involved, and we're down by 14. We don't need that."

The Spurs' plan was all the more effective, given Barkley's sluggishness. The Suns sometimes passed up good shots and ended up with worse ones—or no shot at all. Once, Barkley backed Spurs forward Charles Smith down low. Instead of turning for a short jumper, he threw a pass in traffic that was picked off to start a Spurs' fast break.

By halftime, San Antonio had a 56-44 lead.

The Spurs then displayed a weapon the Suns really couldn't call on. They started raining shots from all over the floor, no matter what the Suns tried defensively. They hit their first nine shots of the second half to take a 77-55 lead.

Barkley tried to respond, but the Suns no longer were explosive enough to make up such a huge deficit. With the score 86-67, Barkley missed a layup. He was so distraught that he approached the scorer's table on the verge of tears, kicking it with stunning force. At this point, he knew the outcome as well as anybody.

A few minutes later, out of the game for the final time, he sat—alone—at the far end of the bench, despondent, staring off into the netherworld that was the Suns' season. The game had gotten away from them too quickly and they never challenged. The final was 120-98 and it wasn't even THAT close.

The old warriors retreated to the locker room and bowed their heads. They knew they weren't this bad. Yet they'd never turned the corner all season. And in the season's biggest game yet, they'd been humiliated.

"Get your heads up!" Fitzsimmons barked at them. "This is a marathon not a sprint." The pressure was on the Spurs to win the first two at home, he reminded them, then it would revert to them in Arizona, whether they won or lost here. "But right now, it's on them."

Fitzsimmons himself was fitted for the goat's horns by the Arizona media. There were questions about whether he had overpracticed his team. And his decision to "save" Williams had backfired. The player they'd acquired for just these situations, to battle a superstar center in the play-offs, was on the floor for just 17 minutes (two fewer than the staggering Tisdale), even though Williams finished with just three fouls.

Internally, the Suns wondered why they'd added those new plays and gotten away from two that had worked in their lone win over the Spurs: One run by Johnson and Williams up high, the other a screen for Barkley down low.

All in all, the night was a complete bust. The word now was most familiar.

THE DAY BEFORE GAME 2 of any play-off series often is called Adjustment Day. But one didn't have to be Red Auerbach or John Wooden to figure out which team needed more adjustments. The Spurs had played almost perfectly. It seemed all they had to worry about was inflating the basketballs to proper pressure.

The Suns, by contrast, not only had to tinker with their plan, but also had to convince themselves they had a chance. They had not coped well with the loss of Finley, who had averaged 18 points vs. the Spurs. Nobody had taken up the slack. And Johnson and Barkley both had so-so games (even though Barkley scored 26 points, mostly after the game was decided).

This time, Johnson was determined to try to score as well as set up his teammates. They would use more of their most familiar plays.

Once again, the game was close early. Because of the desperate situation, the Suns argued close calls intensely, hoping for an edge.

With the Spurs leading, 8-7, Wesley Person launched a three-pointer with the shot clock ticking down near zero. The ball hit the bottom of the rim, which should have restarted the shot clock. But the timer thought the shot missed everything and allowed the buzzer to sound, just as Barkley was grabbing the rebound and scoring.

Referee Don Vaden, who saw the ball hit the rim, decided the Suns' basket should count. But he was overruled by ref Hue Hollins. The end result was a sort of compromise. The basket was disallowed, but the Suns got the ball again. This didn't help them when they failed to score.

Barkley approached Hollins from behind at the scorer's table and screamed "F—k you." No technical was assessed. An official's moral authority is at its lowest after a poor call.

This time, Barkley's passion lasted. He bounded around the court, grabbing not only every rebound within reach but—when fans near the Suns' bench gave him a bad time—his crotch as well. He shouted more obscenities. (What would the Olympic selection panel think of this?)

The game was wonderfully and intensely played throughout. Johnson overcame the defensive pressure, both scoring and setting up his team-mates. Barkley struggled to guard anyone, and once again his outside shot was erratic. His game had evolved into that of a rebounding specialist with scoring instincts. He played to his strengths with great effort and effect, finishing with 30 points and 20 rebounds.

The Spurs countered with their superior inside-outside balance, Robinson down low and Chuck Person hitting from the perimeter.

To win, the Suns needed Williams to stay in the game to guard Robinson, and they needed somebody other than Barkley and Johnson to produce points.

They seemed like they might have one of the holes plugged when Wesley Person hit a three-pointer to give them an 87-85 lead moments into the fourth quarter.

At the time, Williams rested on the bench with four fouls. Fitzsimmons hoped to squeeze out a few more minutes without him, so he could battle Robinson aggressively at game's end.

Robinson found himself being guarded by Green, who had to foul. Robinson hit two free throws. Then the Spurs' Avery Johnson stole the ball from the Suns' Johnson for a layup. Then Robinson and Perdue raced past Barkley for scores with little more resistance than in a layup drill. Perdue hit two free throws, then Barkley missed a short jumper.

By now, Williams was off the bench, waiting to enter the game. Before he did, Robinson hit another layup. The Spurs led, 97-88. Once again, it appeared Fitzsimmons had waited too long to make his move.

But as soon as Williams came back, the game changed markedly. Williams cut Robinson off, wrestled with him, made him shoot jumpers. The Suns started to recover, narrowing the lead to 97-95. Barkley was moved to walk up to Fitzsimmons and kiss him on the forehead. And when Elliott was called for traveling, Barkley came over to the press table, slapped some baby powder on his hands and shouted, "This is so much (expletive) fun!"

But Johnson and Manning misfired. Elliott took Person down low and scored. The Spurs knew very well that Wesley was the Suns' only effective outside shooter, so they tried to wear him out on defense by taking him into the paint. Brother Chuck now tried this tactic. He missed, but Robinson got the tip-in.

Williams countered by hitting two free throws, then forced Robinson to take a tough fadeaway jumper. The Admiral nailed it.

Wesley Person missed on a three-pointer; the hoped-for explosion by one of the Suns' complimentary players never happened.

Then Robinson drove, and Williams couldn't quite get his position in time. He'd fouled out. So, when Robinson missed both free throws and the Suns' Johnson hit a jumper, Fitzsimmons' judgment in holding Williams out so long seemed on the mark. The Suns trailed, 104-103, in the final minute. This was their chance.

But now there was nobody to guard Robinson, who faced no resistance from Barkley en route to the basket for an easy score. Johnson managed to hit two free throws to keep the Suns within a point.

Fewer than 20 seconds remained. The Suns were forced to foul Elliott, who hit both shots to give the Spurs a 108-105 lead. Johnson wanted to try to penetrate for a quick two points or else set up a three-pointer. He started to drive, then decided he didn't have an opening. He realized he'd passed the three-point line, stopped, stumbled, then tossed the ball to Green, hoping to get it right back.

But Green tossed up a prayerful 25-footer. It fell well short of the basket.

At the Spurs' end of the floor, Colangelo, occupying a front-row seat near the baseline, buried his head in his hands. It was over. They'd given it everything they had. It just wasn't enough.

This time, the mood was more one of resignation. As was usually the case when they'd played well, Fitzsimmons said little. "I'm disappointed we couldn't finish. But we know we can beat this team. We're right there." Had they hit more than a modest 21-for-30 from the free-throw line, they probably would have won, he told them.

Teams rarely came back from 0-2 deficits. The Suns had been one of the few to accomplish such a comeback three years earlier against the Lakers en route to their dramatic run to the Finals. With this in mind, Johnson repackaged the pledge made by Westphal at the depth of that debacle: "We're going back to Phoenix and we're going to win Game 3. Then we're going to win Game 4. Then we're going to come back here to San Antonio and win Game 5. Then everybody will say what a great series it was."

The circumstances had been far different then: The Suns were a No.-1 seed, the Lakers No. 8. For a top-seeded team to drop down 0-2 required a collapse. Westphal's pledge was made nervously.

Now the roles were nearly reversed. A No.-2 seed gets off to a 2-0 lead for the obvious reason: It's the better team. Johnson's pledge had the ring of somebody whistling past the graveyard.

The Suns lingered far longer than usual in the locker room. Barkley still had enough energy to be full of bluster: "That (expletive) soft team! How can we lose to them twice?" More seriously, he repeated his musings about bailing out for next season.

"I feel good physically. I feel like I'm going to play next season. But I want to be in the right environment. If a trade situation comes up, I'll go where I want to.

"We have an old team. We need to see how far we can progress, then take a hard look at ourselves. I'll make my decision after the season."

As Barkley finished dressing, Fitzsimmons slapped him on the back. Manning sat in front of his locker talking quietly to an older man, who now put his arm around him. It was his dad, Ed, a Spurs scout.

Donn Nelson sat fully inside a locker space, staring blankly at the final stat sheet as if waiting for the 110-105 final score to somehow reverse itself. Johnson did the same on a chair in front of his locker; Williams walked by, then stopped to peak over Johnson's shoulder. Finley walked out to the bus, hoping somehow he could play again this season.

THERE WAS LITTLE SENSE OF desperation evident in the Suns' locker room before Game 3 in Phoenix, not judging by the way Barkley kept to his routine, arriving at 6:30 p.m. (The chalkboard instructions read: "6 p.m. Be here.") The game would start at 7:30, a half-hour later than usual, to accommodate national cable TV. The chalkboard assumed a win, as was customary in these situations, listing a schedule of activities through Game 4.

To push them to get that far, Johnson decided to make a personal appeal to every player.

The team's leadership had long been in question. Barkley effectively assumed the mantle with his breakthrough MVP season three years earlier. His voice remained the loudest, his influence the greatest. But if he wasn't quite the antithesis of a leader, he certainly didn't fit its traditional definition. Players who set up their own routines, who sit at the end of the bench, outside the earshot of that most traditional team function—

the huddle—can hardly be looked to consistently for leadership. Barkley was an individualist, but basketball is a team effort.

Johnson wasn't ideally suited for the leadership role either, not with his own loner nature and his jack-in-the-box status in the lineup due to all his injuries. In Westphal's view, Johnson hadn't maintained his leadership role when injuries forced him out of the lineup. Johnson never had resigned as the team's captain, but he wasn't officially listed as the captain either. The matter was left deliberately ambiguous.

Yet Johnson's seriousness was a solid counterweight to Barkley's comedy routines. He had the virtues of talent and intellect, backed by his history of terrific clutch performances. Fitzsimmons' return as coach had helped him. So now he would assume the role.

He approached his teammates, one by one, imploring them to do whatever they could to get this one win.

To Person: "Be aggressive offensively. Defensively, you've got to be tougher."

To Kleine: "If you're in there, we need you to rebound and take some hard fouls on David."

To Carr: "If you get in the game, keep your head. Play under control."

Cautiously, he approached Barkley, saying, "I feel good about this one."

"Yeah, me too," Barkley said.

"We really need your emotion and enthusiasm. We need to feed off that."

He tried to cheer up Finley, whose hoped-for return hadn't been realized. He spent several hours a day undergoing treatments on his ankle that was wired to machines for which he did not know the names. But this would be no miracle of modern medicine. Ankle sprains generally heal when they heal.

Johnson knew as well as anyone the loneliness of an injured player. "Just be ready for the second series," he told Finley.

"I'll be ready," he answered.

THE SPURS FINALLY EXPLOITED their mismatch in waiting, getting the ball to Elliott, who tried to make his move before the Suns' player guarding him (usually Green or Johnson) could get help. But in doing so, they got away from Robinson, their bread-and-butter scorer.

Barkley came out a step slow, picked up a couple of fouls and headed for the bench. But Johnson and Person played well enough to keep the Suns close.

Then Barkley came back, stayed inside, grabbed follow shots and drew fouls in exploding for 17 second-quarter points. The Spurs maintained a narrow edge, thanks largely to their superior outside shooting. This was the way the Suns wanted it: Barkley working inside, the Spurs taking their chances outside. The problem was they still trailed, 54-52, at the half, even though Robinson hadn't been much of a factor.

Williams knew he had a huge battle on his hands, but he managed to avoid fouls. He won the tedious, strenuous battle of leaning, pushing, shifting weight under the basket, and he beat Robinson to rebounds time and again. And when Robinson tried futilely for a rebound by crashing over Williams' back, he had to sit down with his fourth foul.

Barkley spun down low, at his favored spot on the left baseline. Bob Hill, the Spurs coach, screamed "TRAVELING!" Early in the season, the replacement refs would have called it. But not now. Barkley converted a three-point play. And when Person hit a three-pointer, the Suns assumed a narrow lead, 74-70. Then Fitzsimmons decided to rest Barkley and Johnson simultaneously, and the Spurs quickly caught up. The game came down the stretch with the season hanging in the balance.

Johnson noticed Manning set up on the left side, tilting his head, peering at him, his eyes calling for the ball. Manning was playing on instincts, certainly not on his aching left knee. Had it not been the play-offs, he wouldn't have even been in uniform. He was having trouble finishing plays, struggling to shoot, finding it difficult to guard quick players he once had little problem matching up against. But he still knew *how* to play as well as anyone.

Johnson started down the right side where Barkley was set up. When his eyes connected with Manning's, he shifted left and got the ball to him. Manning now worked himself free, and the shots that had missed badly early in the game started dropping. By the time he put in a follow shot of a Barkley miss, Manning had scored 12 points in the fourth quarter. The Suns led, 92-89.

Then the Spurs' Person scooted past Barkley for a layup. Manning misfired, but Williams grabbed the rebound and the ball went to Johnson. He spotted an opening, charged toward the hoop before the Spurs could react, and scored.

As the Spurs hurried the ball up the floor, Nelson instantly recognized their play and screamed "POST UP!" Indeed, the Spurs did just that, getting the ball to Robinson. Working against Williams, he nearly drove too far past the basket, but he leaned back and managed to bank the shot against the glass and in. The Suns led, 94-93.

Barkley set up for a three-pointer, which the Spurs gratefully gave him. He missed. Then Elliott and Johnson traded misses. Thirty seconds remained.

Robinson and Williams wrestled for position near the Spurs' basket. Robinson slipped and fell. Williams, recognizing his opportunity, "accidentally" fell on top of him, their bodies flailing about in a scene out of a second-rate pro wrestling match. Finally, Robinson managed to get up and catch the ball down low. He started to go up, Williams reached for the ball, the whistle blew. . . .

A clean block and a jump ball. Could Williams' reputation be solidifying with the officials? Now 13 seconds were left.

The tip went back toward midcourt, where Elliott grabbed it and called time.

The Spurs again got the ball to Robinson, who started to drive to the basket and this time got the call. Williams had used his fifth foul. But this was a non-shooting foul; the Suns hadn't fouled enough in the quarter to give the Spurs two shots. So once again, the Spurs inbounded the ball, this time with nine seconds left.

Avery Johnson drove along the baseline from one side of the hoop to the other, spotted Del Negro open on the left side, and whipped the ball to him.

Del Negro squared up to shoot just inside the three-point line at almost precisely the same spot that the Bulls' John Paxson had shot the Suns down to win the NBA Finals three years earlier. The thought flashed through Johnson's mind, then he banished it. No, that was then, this was now, he swore. But Barkley's reaction was the more common one . . . an obscenity. The crowd gasped.

The ball seemed to take several seconds to float toward the goal. The shot hit the front of the rim and bounced back to the middle. Barkley tried to bat it as far as he could toward midcourt, but he could only get it to the top of the lane, where Elliott picked it up. With a second remaining, he took one last running shot from 16 feet away. It missed to the right.

They had lived to play another day. For once, they could celebrate.

"Sit down and relax," Fitzsimmons told them in the locker room. "Enjoy the moment."

THE SUNS' SPACIOUS LOCKER room was mostly empty an hour before tip-off on Game 4 as several players were attending the pre-game chapel service.

The game would start at 6 p.m. on a Friday night on the third day of May.

Spring had left the desert in every meaningful way. The days were starting to boil, and the heat didn't fully escape after sundown. The "snowbirds" had left town, leaving the year-round populace to fend for themselves over the summer.

Barkley made his usual grand, and belated, entrance. It was time to laugh in the face of danger. He'd done so three years earlier, when the Suns were facing one of the most humiliating eliminations in NBA history. Down 0-2 to the Los Angeles Lakers, they were on the verge of becoming the first No.-1 seed ever to lose to a No.-8 seed.

Then, the visiting locker room at The Forum was filled both with nervous teammates and much of the national basketball press who'd gathered to shovel dirt on the Suns' grave. Barkley then launched into a 40-minute comedy monologue, one that helped loosen up his teammates and himself. (His early-series slump helped put them in their fix.)

Barkley noted that his old Sixers team had won nine fewer games without him. "Let's see, they got three starters and a lottery pick for this season, and we still won more games with me. Man, am I (expletive) good!"

Then he pointed out that some of the writers predicted the Suns would accomplish the improbable: come back and win the series.

"For once, I hope you guys are right. Even a blind acorn finds a nut once in a while."

The subdued atmosphere was punctured, however unintentionally. Everyone broke up.

"That's a blind squirrel!" Ainge shouted.

This was vintage Barkley. He'd given his teammates just what they needed.

Now, a reporter mentioned to Barkley that Rodman's book, a rambling collection of ravings, had been released. Barkley was told that the Bulls' Steve Kerr, hearing about the book, said, "I'll wait for the movie."

That started Barkley on an improvised stand-up routine.

"I thought they already made the Dennis Rodman story. It was called *Psycho*!

"If Dennis Rodman kills Madonna, we'll have 'Psycho, the Sequel.' But they better give that role to a white guy. We don't want a 'brother' with that role. That's what promotes racism. People who live in Nebraska and Montana, who don't get out all that much, think all black people are like that. All they see is Dennis Rodman."

While Barkley finished his monologue, others finished their prayers, and Person took several dozen shots out on the floor. With Nelson whipping him the ball time after time, he shot from the baselines, from out front, right up until the last minute he had to head back to the locker room. He'd shot well, even played solid defense against Elliot in the previous game. They would need another good game from him.

The Suns knew what the Spurs knew, that the Spurs had failed to work the ball enough to Robinson in the previous game until it was too late. They knew that the superstar would pound away inside from the start of this game, and that Williams—who had mostly gotten away with guarding him alone—would need some help.

Fitzsimmons tried to fire up the Suns by pointing out statements by the Spurs that the Suns hadn't so much won Game 3 as the Spurs had lost it.

Perhaps if he concentrated on such intangible matters, the Suns might not think so much about their concrete problems. Johnson, who had been as healthy—and effective—as ever the final two months of the season, now was struggling. His left knee slammed to the floor in the previous game. Even worse, his left thigh muscles were failing to cooperate. His left leg had enough wrapping on it to suggest he'd been the victim of an industrial accident.

There were danger signs early. Barkley hoisted two three-pointers and Johnson was a step slow and picked up two quick fouls. Perry entered the game and—as usual—held his own. But this time, Williams had a hard time, even with help, trying to stay with Robinson, who tipped in shots and took feeds from Del Negro and Avery Johnson. Person was off the mark, too.

But Barkley responded. He stayed near the basket, got his own follow shots and drew fouls. The Suns got a stunning lift when Fitzsimmons, trying desperately to inject life into his offense, resorted to the rookie Carr. He didn't nearly have Finley's knowledge of the game or defensive presence, but he had shooting and rebounding skill and was Finley's equal in running the floor and leaping. He hit two three-pointers and poured in 13 points in 12 minutes. Somehow, they managed to be down just 52-51 at the half.

As the second half started, Barkley backed away from the Spurs' Charles Smith, whose knees were ailing and who had been dormant through the series, to help on Robinson.

Smith buried two jumpers.

"CHARLES SMITH?" wondered Fitzsimmons.

A minute later, Barkley whacked Smith on the back with a forearm.

Smith pushed back halfheartedly, then was stunned to discover they BOTH had been hit with technicals. This was Barkley's last act of bravado. As had been the case often the last several weeks, the passion was gone. It was as if he knew he was fighting forces beyond his power to vanquish. He became distant, withdrawn, not calling or even looking for the ball.

Johnson dribbled an inordinate amount of time, looking for holes that didn't appear. He drove to the hoop and missed, then pounded the top of his head, protesting the silence of the officials' whistles.

He shot and missed and started fast breaks his teammates failed to convert with layups. At one point, Fitzsimmons shouted at him, "Find someone who can finish!"

But this was one of their dilemmas.

In tracking the team's offense, Fitzsimmons had discovered they didn't score on a high-percentage of fast breaks. Outside of Johnson, they didn't handle the ball well at a breakneck pace. So, Fitzsimmons had subtly pulled the reins in a bit late in the season, looking less for fast breaks and a bit more toward a half-court offense (not much different than the way Westphal operated).

On the other hand, they couldn't play a straight half-court game either. This worked into the Spurs' hands, because Robinson could both plug the lane and block shots; their strategy was to try to funnel Johnson toward the middle, where The Admiral was waiting to sink him. And of course, the Suns didn't have the shooters to make the Spurs pay consistently for playing this way.

Wesley Person finally connected on a three-pointer to cut the lead to 67-61, but the Spurs' Smith scored down low in response. Barkley launched a three-pointer. He missed, and the long rebound started a Spurs fast-break that ended in a three-point play by Robinson. The Spurs now led, 72-61.

Robinson departed, giving Fitzsimmons a chance to rest Williams. In came the offensive-minded Tisdale. A few moments later, Elliott also went out for a breather. This would be the chance to close the lead. In theory, they wouldn't have to double-team much, thus leaving fewer chances for the Spurs to pass to an open shooter.

Instead, they continued to double-team, and—true to their worst instincts—left the most dangerous shooter open. Del Negro buried two three-pointers within 33 seconds at the end of the third quarter.

This was it. The Final Act. Finis. The fat lady had cleared her throat and was starting her final aria.

Fitzsimmons rested Barkley for 1:30 early in the fourth quarter. Barkley returned to a few muted cries of "C'mon, Charles!" But he had nothing to offer. In 19 minutes in the second half, he shot 0-for-3 and grabbed two rebounds.

As the clock ticked down, Barkley sat at the end of the bench, a towel draped over his head. The fans rose to give a respectful, mournful ovation, the kind that's sometimes heard when the passing of a sports legend is announced at an arena or stadium. They all sensed the passing of a magical era, one that spanned not only Barkley's four years, but also the previous four seasons when the mania around the team was just about as unrelenting.

The past two years, the post-game emotions were of anger and frustration after blowing the two-game leads to the Rockets. Johnson had spoken of how it all "burned in my belly."

Now, there seemed more a tired sense of resignation. Only Fitzsimmons spoke, telling them, "Don't hang your heads. They played better. Give them credit."

Johnson took the wraps off his leg, Manning did the same with his knee. Williams unfurled the tape from his right hand, around and around and around until his bare hand appeared. It seemed there were enough wrappings to stage a burial ceremony in an ancient ruler's tomb.

As the reporters filed in, the talk immediately turned to Barkley's possible departure.

He was their most marketable player. And if they were now sentenced to rebuilding, he likely wouldn't be satisfied, nor would management be satisfied with idly watching his market value decline.

At first, he had the quiet sense of finality, saying, "It's been a lot of fun." But when the bright lights of TV clicked on, he turned defiant. "I will let everybody know when the Charles Barkley era is over.

"I wish everybody would just leave everything alone and let the Suns make their decision and let me make my decision." He wanted to stay in Phoenix, he said, praising the fans and management. "But I do realize that I'm one of the few tradable options the Suns have."

The one difference from the past: He said nothing about retirement. Even the people who tended to take everything he said at face value might have their doubts if he repeated this routine for the third straight year.

It was left for a weary Johnson, slouched in a chair in front of his locker, his left leg badly bruised, to put the carnage in perspective.

"The only way we could have redeemed our season would have been to get out of the first round. We couldn't even do that. This series epito-mized the whole season."

He knew there would be change. That was Colangelo's style. He'd seen the departures of Tom Chambers, of Jeff Hornacek, of Dan Majerle. "I don't know what qualifies as an era, but if Charles left, that certainly qualifies."

In any case, hardly any team ever returned intact. Some of these play-ers never again would be his teammates. "Your mind starts racing," John-son said.

There was a sense of closure now. Their descent had been stunning.

THERE CAN BE DIGNITY IN DEFEAT.

Barkley's rapprochement with Johnson demonstrated class.

Manning had continued to play, finding a way to get the Suns over the hump in their single play-off win, even when his aching knee told him to hang it up for the season.

Williams had suffered in silence at the mocking judgment that he was a bust. Instead, he quietly worked out for hours a day until he returned to form.

Green, in refusing to retaliate in the vicious attack by J.R. Reid, had accomplished something memorable: He had practiced what he'd preached.

Johnson, for all his fragility, had carried the team on his back in the final several weeks, ensuring they at least made the play-offs and avoided a losing season.

He thought back to his training camp prediction of a "defining moment." In the end, what defined them most was the period, starting in early March, when they got virtually their entire arsenal together. They were three games over .500 and ready to explode.

In the end, they didn't. They were a .500 team. When they had all their weapons, they were somewhat better; when they didn't, they were somewhat worse. But the overall record was staring at them: 41-41.

Less than 48 hours after their season ended, Johnson found himself in church, listening to the minister lament the number of people who had no destination in life, no plan.

As far as the summer was concerned, he joked, "That's me. I have no plan." He'd figured the Suns would be playing basketball much longer.

Johnson did have a longer-range schedule. Even though he was only 30 years old, he planned to play one more season, then retire when he was at the top of his game. He didn't like discussing the subject much, lest it become a distraction. Nor did he want to be seen as wavering, lest he look like just another athlete who couldn't stand the thought of no longer hearing those cheering crowds.

As his career wound down, he could look back at the Barkley years with magnanimity, even appreciation. The two now were at peace. "He's got that rock-star persona," Johnson said. "Wherever he goes, he creates a frenzy." Indeed, the ride often had been exhilirating.

COLANGELO'S MAJOR LEAGUE Baseball team boomed long before it even played. The stadium, the one funded by the hated sales-tax increase, practically sold out for the opening season—two years before the ceremonial first pitch.

The prospects for the National Hockey League franchise were less certain, but the initial response was favorable.

The NHL team had come to Arizona in much the same way the Suns had. The decision had nothing to do with Phoenix meeting sophisticated tests of interest level or a campaign that played to a civic inferiority complex ("We must have an NHL franchise or we won't be a major-league city!") The NHL was coming to Arizona simply because the move suited the convenience of the team's new owners, who wanted to ship the team out of Winnipeg, and the NHL, whose commissioner, Gary Bettman, knew Colangelo well when Bettman worked in the NBA.

But the immediate prospects for the cornerstone to all Colangelo's operations, the Suns, were a bit clouded.

They were so ingrained as a local institution that they would continue to sell tickets. But their window of opportunity to dominate as a team had all but closed in the near term. They had thrived, in part, because of loopholes in the salary cap rules. Now, those rules had changed. Teams with players whose salaries were under the cap could still offer huge multiyear contracts to free agents. The NBA proved it still was a cash cow when several young stars took advantage by signing mammoth deals; a couple actually topped $100 million.

But the rules had been tightened for teams such as the Suns, who had exceeded the cap. They were committed to huge contracts negotiated under the old guidelines, which provided for more escape routes to add new players. Until some of those contracts with their older players expired, they were limited in what they could do.

The league's new rules would be called an "equalization mechanism." The Suns had been at the top; now they were being equalized. Colangelo's major decision at hand was whether to try one last run at a title with Barkley or to fold the tent on the show, trade him while he still had value, and rebuild. Action or caution?

WESTPHAL FOUND HIMSELF with a lot of unplanned time on his hands. So, he devoted himself to his family while keeping his ears tuned for job openings. He also killed time by taking a drive to Amarillo, Texas, and back along parts of old Route 66, accompanied by a friend, the folk-rock singer John Stewart. Stewart has Southern California music roots that date to playing the guitar with a teenaged buddy named Frank Zappa. He played with the Kingston Trio and recorded a few recognizable songs, including "July, You're a Woman" and "Gold." His most-noted tune was "Daydream Believer," which had been turned into a megahit in 1967 by the Monkees.

Stewart was in the process of writing a book and recording an album on the old cross-country highway.

"It was a lot of fun," Westphal said. "The funny thing was, we should have been driving a '59 Cadillac with tail fins and the top down. Instead, we were driving my Infiniti, and the romantic poet of the neon highway (Stewart) was on his cellular phone half the time. It was the '50s meeting the '90s."

Westphal had few regrets on anything he'd done. Maybe, he allowed, he needed an image consultant. He never could get rid of the "laid-back" label, internally or with the public.

"The only thing I would have done differently is build a different perception of myself," he said.

"Regrettably, a lot of this business has become trying to convince people you're something they want you to be. Some people are good at trying to be all things to all people. It's hard for me to sell myself as something other than what I am."

In the end, he probably wouldn't actually have tried to make himself over. All the same, "It probably would be a good skill to acquire."

He hadn't changed his view of coaching. He recalled laughing when his team's national title chances at Grand Canyon were being decided by Rodney Johns' free throws, because he knew he'd be considered a genius . . . only if the player hit the shots. Veteran college and pro coach Larry Brown found out about this and chided him mildly, telling him—in effect—that coaches must not shrink from taking credit when things go well because they surely will be blamed when things go wrong.

He respected Brown and understood his message that the mystique of the coaching profession should be preserved as much as possible. But he couldn't quite agree. Grand Canyon won a series of overtime games to win the title. Had they come up short, they still would have had a great season. Sometimes, he believed, the coach's fate often really does come down to whether a shot goes in or not. In 1988, Rodney Johnson ensured he was a genius. In 1993, John Paxson ensured he would come up short.

His expertise and earning power now were in the pro game. But he couldn't help but think fondly of those fulfilling times as a small-college coach. At the start of this ill-fated Suns' season, he attended a reunion at Southwestern Bible College, where they celebrated a terrific season played 10 years earlier.

Back then, Westphal had about seven pretty decent players, seven or eight more who basically practiced with the team but seldom played with the game on the line. One of those who fell into the latter category was a young man named Tim Fultz.

His father was stunned when he told him he was going out for basketball. "But you can't play," his dad said.

"They need me," he assured him.

Indeed they did. The school didn't have a gym, so the team practiced several miles from campus. Fultz was one of the few players who had a car. He could give a third of the team a lift. He practiced faithfully, actually improving a little as a player along the way.

The season went well, so well that Southwestern had its first chance to make it to the National Little College Tournament in Bristol, Tenn., big doings indeed for this team. But first they had to beat Arizona College of the Bible ("our hated crosstown rival," Westphal said).

Southwestern was in fairly good shape, up by seven or eight points with several minutes to go. Then one of their main seven players fouled out. No problem. Westphal still had six real players left. Then another player fouled out with about three minutes left and they were down to five experienced players.

Moments later, yet another player fouled out.

Westphal asked the refs if he could use four players. No, he was told. If there were players on the bench, somebody had to enter the game.

Well, Westphal figured, Fultz had been a loyal team member and he probably was the best free-throw shooter of the bunch he had left. So, in he went, with instructions to stay away from the action.

The opponents knew what to do. They chased him all over the floor, fouling him and sending him to the line. Fultz missed eight straight 1-and-1 free-throw opportunities and Arizona Bible pulled back into the game.

As the game came down to the final seconds, Southwestern led by a single point. Once again, Fultz found himself on the line. This time, he hit both shots. Southwestern won the game and the big trip. Hundreds of fans descended on the court, carrying him on their shoulders, shouting, "Tim, Tim!"

Fultz' goal in life had been to become a missionary. That he accomplished. A couple of years later, he had just married and was helping to build a church in Zaire when he fell from the roof and hit his head. He died almost instantly.

Afterward, they finally found the means to build a gym at Southwestern. It bears the name of Tim Fultz.

Westphal had been a member of the Celtics' '74 title team and probably would have won a championship as a coach except for that darned three-pointer by Paxson. But seeing Tim Fultz at the center of a frenzied celebration after hitting those free throws was as great a highlight as anything he'd ever experienced in big-time sport.

AS THE TEAM MET FOR the final time before breaking for the summer, Barkley was asked to describe his fondest memories and his greatest regrets in four years in Arizona. In response, he unloaded on the front office. The harsh tone suggested what he'd hinted during the lowest part of the season, that he wanted to bail out of a sinking ship. Yet his analysis seemed as heart-felt as it was detailed.

Noting that he and Johnson were the only players left from the '93 Finals team, he said, "The thing that disappoints me the most is how quickly they broke up our team. "To win 60 games a year and then get rid of everybody. . . . It's terrible, a disgrace." Changes should have been subtle, not wholesale, he said. In particular, getting rid of both Ainge and Majerle simultaneously was "a mistake, no question. Our two best shooters: one is on TNT, the other is in Cleveland."

The criticism of dumping Ainge, in particular, had never stopped. Colangelo moved to rectify this by trying to persuade Ainge to give up his high-paying, low-pressure job as a broadcaster and rejoin the team as a coach.

Ainge had attended several Suns' games as both a broadcaster and spectator. Often, he would pass through the locker room and wish Barkley, with whom he had a strong relationship, and others good luck. Once, Barkley greeted him by shouting, "There's Danny Ainge, the future head coach of the Phoenix Suns!" Barkley turned out to be a prophet. Now, Ainge would join them as an assistant coach to be groomed to take over from Fitzsimmons. The immediate effect was to steer attention to the future and away from their fade from the elite. Ainge, the pale anti-hero, also would provide them not only with a sharp basketball mind but with a media star in any post-Barkley era.

In Barkley's view, "Management underestimated the chemistry factor and the role-player mentality. I knew where Ainge and Majerle would be at any time. It takes a long time to build that." Pointing to the Bulls and Rockets, he said, "If you look at the great teams, sometimes 'less' is 'more.' We have so much talent that we all want the ball."

If he were in charge, "I'd put us all in a room and blow us up." More seriously, "I would have kept Kevin and me and kept more defensive role players." Only Williams fit that description on this team, he pointed out. Barkley said he knew from the start the Suns would struggle because if either Johnson or he got hurt, the team neither shot the ball nor defended well.

"I can honestly say this season was terrible," he said.

In the end, Johnson missed 26 games and Barkley missed 11. The nine most regular players, those who played every game they were available, missed 126 games combined.

Maybe he could stay. Maybe management could make a few adjustments, maybe the players could stay healthy, then they could make a run. "But will we ever be healthy?" he asked. "We're an older team."

"If they want to trade me to a team that has a chance, I'll go. If they want to trade me just anywhere, I'll sit at home, play golf, and see if NBC will use me. I'm frustrated. I know Mr. Colangelo is frustrated. He obviously has to give me some help or he's got to start rebuilding. And that probably means trading me."

As that process of talking trade got under way, Barkley once again denounced Colangelo's personnel moves during a nationally televised interview in which he complained about being treated like a "piece of meat." Colangelo bit his tongue, but Ainge reminded people that every NBA player is in the same meat market, only Barkley was much more highly paid than most of his fellow sides of beef.

There were a number of people who knew Barkley well who believed he had a calculated reason for all this. Behind all the bluster, they believed, Barkley deeply wanted to be told he was a beloved and invaluable member of the franchise who could play out his years with the Suns if he so chose. In this scenario, he could retire as a grand old man of the game, much like Julius Erving had early in Barkley's Philadelphia days. The question, as far as the team's inner circle was concerned, was whether Barkley had consistently acted in such a manner to merit such treatment.

His star had fallen in the team's brain trust in the past year after his collapse against the Rockets and his slowness to work out in the off-season following knee surgery. Besides, Fitzsimmons was known to be a proponent of the Branch Rickey theory that, "Better to trade 'em too soon than too late."

Yes, it was a meat market. Barkley recognized this, said those who knew him, and he wanted to be perceived as forcing a move. "Charles is in charge" was his persona, after all. Barkley's mastery of the media, such a plus for management in happier times (when it insured a high profile for the franchise) now was cutting in a much different direction. He was demanding an "apology" from Colangelo for being the subject of trade talks. This was fairly outlandish, considering most every player is brought up in such talks, but some in the media and public deemed Barkley's request an item for serious discussion.

Certainly, he could still play. Though he no longer was as consistently explosive, he averaged 23 points and nearly 12 rebounds for the season. He was still an amazing rebounder, finishing fourth in the NBA. He was named third-team all-NBA. This was the only time other than his rookie season that he wasn't named to the first or second teams, reflecting a league-wide view that other, younger players were stepping to the forefront.

Beyond this, he faded at the end, averaging 19 points and nine rebounds in the final month. His defense sagged as well, meaning that he often played to only average effect down the stretch.

The Colangelos would spend the summer taking calls from other teams interested in Barkley's services. He still had enough ability and marquee appeal that they could at least get a functional player or two for him. Knowing this, Barkley yelled to Kleine on the day the Suns broke for the summer, "Take my (locker) nameplate, Joe!"

If the Suns traded him, they knew they'd never see another like him. His combination of humor, candor and charisma were unmatched. His bluster and bravado made for such a great act that his on-court performances had little chance to match them. In the end, they didn't. During his four years in Arizona, his teams qualified for nine rounds of the play-offs, precisely the same amount of play-off action they enjoyed in the four years before he arrived.

There always would be the lament that he succeeded mainly through talent rather than work. Silas, the assistant coach who had been in the game longer than anybody in the organization, noticed Barkley started what Silas deemed an unusually intense workout regimen after he was named to the Olympic team. To Silas, this was a clear signal that Barkley was working diligently to make sure he made a good account of himself in front of the world. To the extent that he hadn't been doing so all along, Silas told Barkley that he was full of it.

Few people, anywhere, have the intestinal fortitude to say such a thing.

The other regret was that Barkley didn't more clearly distinguish his theatrical and playing roles. "There are times you need to be serious and focus," Silas said. "But he can't separate the two. He's on stage all the time."

Then again, if only Paxson had missed that shot. If only that phantom Game 7 had arrived and Barkley had led the Suns to victory in the '93 Finals. Then in most people's minds, any blemishes would have vanished.

The most enduring recollections of Barkley still were that dramatic Finals run and that raucous parade.

There were others that were more instructive. Away from basketball, there were those Christmas Eve trips with the homeless kids to the toy store. Indeed, his most appealing (and perhaps least known) trait was his genuine empathy for life's underdogs.

On the floor, there was a game at New York's Madison Square Garden in January of '93. Barkley's shooting arm appeared to have been slapped as he let go of a jumper in the closing seconds. The whistles were silent as the ball fell several feet short of the target, a non-call that assured a win for the Knicks.

Barkley went ballistic, leaping over the press table (perhaps setting a record for the standing broad jump), then chasing a hapless official down the runway to the refs' locker room, continuing his protest all the way.

It was the Good Charles (who cared passionately about winning) and the Bad Charles (volatile, out of control) merging at once.

Then, in June of '93 in the Western Conference Finals, Barkley and the crowd at the Seattle Coliseum (one of the NBA's noisiest arenas) were taunting each other. At one point, the boos directed at Barkley became earsplitting. In response, Barkley raised his arms high, his palms turned upward, as if to say, "Can't you do any better than that?"

At this point, a writer from Seattle shook his head in awe, pounded his first, and shouted, "What a performer! What a showman!" Alas, the show would never reach such a crescendo in Arizona again.

Colangelo knew this. So when the Houston Rockets finally, after months of negotiations, met Colangelo's asking price for the Rockets' mainstays Sam Cassell, Robert Horry and Mark Bryant, the Suns president jumped on it. All three, as well as a fourth player thrown into the deal, Chucky Brown, would be free agents after one season. The Suns could evaluate the results of the trade for a year, then have the option of trying to re-sign these players or look elsewhere to rebuild the team.

From the Rockets' perpsective, the spin of the trade was that they'd gained a superstar necessary for one or two more serious runs at the title. But it seemed at least equally true that the Rockets' owner Les Alexander met the Suns' demands for another reason. Barkley's persona guaranteed the Rockets the high visibility that would create a favorable climate for the Rockets' top long-term goal: a new arena.

As for the Suns, the trade gave them a good chance to rebuild without hitting bottom.

SEVERAL OF BARKLEY'S teammates either had surgery or otherwise tended to their various physical maladies. Among them was Williams, who needed rehab work on his hand and tests on his leg.

Within a few days after the season's end, Williams made his first visit back home to Louisiana. There, his mom still lives in the same neighborhood, though not in the trailer. Hot Rod had bought her a five-bedroom house.

Barbara Colar was 57 and disabled; one of her daughters lived with her and helped out. Together, with Williams' support, they were raising a 13-year-old girl, a relative who came from a background not terribly different from his own. Williams positively beams when talking about "my little cousin. I love her like she's my own." Seems as though Williams could understand when a kid needs a break.

Williams would spend a good deal of the summer with his family in Louisiana. But finding him would not be easy. Much of the time, he would be aboard one of the thousands of boats that dot the Gulf of Mexico and the Mississippi River. He'd gone fishing.

Acknowledgments

THIS BOOK WILL GIVE YOU an inside look at the workings of one of the most colorful big-time sports teams ever assembled at a pivotal point in its existence—one that culminated in the most significant trade of the '96 season.

To put it together, I needed the help of enough people to fill a small city, too many to name here. But before the thank-yous, a few apologies.

To my wife Kathy and sons Andy and Matt, I'm sorry about all the time spent on all those trips, plus all the time in town spent on this project.

I apologize to anybody I've cut short (an exception being telephone solicitors; and don't call back!).

In putting together this project, I want to thank everyone at the *Tribune Newspapers* of Arizona, particularly one of the nation's finest sports staffs. This includes the folks who catch my mistakes: Lee Rasizer, Mark Hvidsten, Brad Sheets, Kevin Stone, Randy Weisberg, Dan Zeiger and Dan Miller.

Appreciation also to fellow reporters Jerry Brown, Lynn DeBruin, Les Willsey and Darren Urban. Special thanks to Bob Moran for sharing his decades of wisdom.

Special thanks to sports editor Dave Lumia, the guy who somehow makes it all work so well.

Thanks to the extraordinary writer/reporter Doug MacEachern and to the incomparable Mark Harris, who virtually invented the baseball novel (*Bang the Drum Slowly, The Southpaw,* plus many fine books on non-baseball topics). Their suggestions were most helpful.

Special thanks to photographer Dave Cruz, the human dynamo whose work is displayed in this book, and a fine photo staff headed by Rick Wiley.

Thanks also to Will Brownfield, the computer guru who bailed out the computer-ignoramus author numerous times. Thanks also to office staff members Cathie Johnson, Sandra Alteri and Lynn Brooks.

Special thanks also to the management team of publisher Sandy Schwartz, managing editor Jim Ripley and executive editor Jeff Bruce. Jeff's insights and advice have been keen and valuable.

Appreciation to travel agents Carol Griesel, Suzanne Melching and Shirley Smith and typist Betty Risley.

Thanks to some old colleagues for their help along the way, including Tom Fitzpatrick and Dave Walker (who has a fine book on rock 'n' roll history, *American Rock 'N Roll Tour*).

Acknowledgements to all of the members of my NBA writers group, including Sam Smith of the *Chicago Tribune*, Steve Bulpett of the *Boston Herald*, Mark Heisler of the *Los Angeles Times*, David Moore of the *Dallas Morning News*, Amy Shipley and Bob Rubin of the *Miami Herald*, Kerry Eggers of the *Oregonian,* Richard Justice of the *Washington Post*, Theresa Smith of the *News Tribune of Tacoma*, John Romano of the *St. Petersburg Times*, Shaun Powell of *Newsday,* Eddie Sefko of the *Houston Chronicle*, Corky Meinecke of the *Detroit Free Press*, Mike Monroe of the *Denver Post*, Richard Walker and Mike Smith of the *Gaston Gazette*, Jeffrey Denberg of the *Atlanta Journal-Constitution*, Raad Cawthon of the *Philadelphia Inquirer*, Craig Daniels of the *Toronto Sun*, Chuck Barney and Matt Steinmetz of the *Contra Costa Times* and technical coordinators Frank and John Cooney.

Thanks also to other NBA writers who have helped me along the way, particularly Jesse Barkin, Glenn Rogers of the San Antonio *Express-News*, Peter May of the Boston *Globe*, Bill Fay of the Tampa *Tribune*, Phil Taylor of *Sports Illustrated*, Greg Bouek of *USA Today* and Ric Bucher of the San Jose *Mercury News*. Along the same lines, thanks to fellow Suns beat writers Jack Magruder, Bob Young and John Davis. Thanks also to Jamal Watson of *The Hoya* at Georgetown University.

Thanks to loads of people in the Suns organization, including president Jerry Colangelo, assistant Ruth Dryjanski, general manager Bryan Colangelo, player personnel chief Dick Van Arsdale, scouting director Dick Percudani, Garrick Barr and Seth Sulka of basketball staff, and Rob Harris and Connie Hawkins of community relations. Thanks also to JoAnn Fitzsimmons and Cindy Westphal.

Thanks to all members of the Suns' media relations staff, past and present.

Thanks also to broadcasters Al McCoy, Greg Schulte, Gary Bender and Keith Erickson.

Thanks to all Suns' players past and present. Of the former players, special thanks to Mark West, Dan Majerle and Danny Ainge, Dan Schayes and Jeff Hornacek. They were gracious, regardless of the outcome of a particular game.

Of the players on the '95-96 team, special thanks to Elliot Perry and Hot Rod Williams. Thanks also to Charles Barkley for all that candor and all that humor. Figuring out which was which was one of the challenges of this book. And special thanks to Kevin Johnson, the only player who's been around all the years I've covered the team and who has been helpful all the way.

Thanks to the medical and training staff, who are part of the news much more than they desire, especially Richard Emerson, Craig Phelps, Joe Proski and Aaron Nelson.

Thanks to all coaches, past and present, including Cotton Fitzsimmons, Paul Silas and Donn Nelson. Special thanks to Paul Westphal, whose grace under pressure is one of the most enduring memories of the making of this book.

And now, for the people who have helped more than anybody.

Thanks to Chuck Perry of Longstreet Press for his support. Also of great assistance at Longstreet was Shannon Maggio. Thanks also to Gary Caruso for his editing.

Thanks to my most regular companions in both home and road coverage: Scott Bordow, the *Tribune*'s assistant sports editor, and columnist Mark Emmons (who has since moved to the *Detroit Free Press*). If anything slipped by me, it didn't get past them. Nobody has ever had finer co-workers.

Thanks to Rauna and Angelo Tulumello and Lisa Collinsworth for helping with the family and with the car. Also helping at key moments were my wife's parents, Jim and Joann Brady of Ballwin, Missouri.

Thanks to my late father, who took me to all those games as a kid and who taught me by example about how hard one needs to work in this life. Thanks to my mom, Nina Tulumello of Tempe, Ariz., for all the help with the kids. (Mom, you are, without a doubt, the world's most reliable person.) This book couldn't even have been attempted without her help.

And thanks to Kathy for all her help, patience and understanding.